A COMPARATIVE
GERMANIC GRAMMAR

OTHER BOOKS FROM TIGER XENOPHON

An Anglo-Saxon Reader
HENRY SWEET
ISBN 978-1-904799-28-3

An Anglo-Saxon Primer
HENRY SWEET
ISBN 978-1-904799-25-2

A Middle High German Primer
JOSEPH WRIGHT
ISBN 978-1-904799-26-9

Grammar of the Gothic Language
JOSEPH WRIGHT
ISBN 978-1-904799-22-1

From Latin to Italian
CHARLES H. GRANDGENT
ISBN 978-1-904799-23-8

A Greek Grammar
WILLIAM GOODWIN
Hbk ISBN 978-1-904799-21-4
Pbk ISBN 978-1-904799-24-5

ALSO FROM TIGER OF THE STRIPE

The Student's Dictionary of Anglo-Saxon
HENRY SWEET
ISBN 978-1-904799-09-2

An Introduction to
Greek and Latin Palaeography
EDWARD MAUNDE THOMPSON
ISBN 978-1-904799-30-6

A COMPARATIVE GERMANIC GRAMMAR

BY

EDUARD PROKOSCH

*Former professor of Germanic Languages
at Yale University*

TIGER XENOPHON
2009

This edition first published in 2009 by
TIGER XENOPHON
50 Albert Road
Richmond
Surrey TW10 6DP
United Kingdom

Originally published in 1939 by
The Linguistic Society of America

ISBN 978-1-904799-42-9

Tiger Xenophon is an imprint of
Tiger of the Stripe

Printed and bound in the US and UK by
Lightning Source

PREFACE

The whole book was in type when the author died in an accident August 11, 1938. Galley proof of the book had been read and the galleys of the word lists and other appendices were already in the hands of the author. Dr. Bernard Bloch has helped me read the page proof and Mrs. Margaret Chase George the galleys.

Prokosch had doubtless intended to make full acknowledgement of stimulation and help received from his colleagues at Yale University, from the editor of the publications of the Linguistic Society, George Melville Bolling of Ohio State University, and from the secretary of the Society, Roland G. Kent of the University of Pennsylvania. Franklin Edgerton of Yale University and Hans Sperber of Ohio State read the entire manuscript before it went to the printer and the author was grateful for their comments and suggestions. If one were to go through the author's correspondence, the names of others who made contributions would certainly come to light. To all these persons grateful acknowledgment is made herewith.

The publication of the book has been made possible by a grant of Yale University through the Committee on Research in Language and Literature.

The writer of this note considers Prokosch's treatment of the strong verb a masterpiece. It is probably his greatest contribution to our understanding of the history of the Germanic languages.

The book will be welcomed by all scholars in Germanics, especially by the large number of younger scholars in this country who received their training from Prokosch or came under the influence of his magnetic personality in some other way. They will find here a comprehensive and consistent account of the phonology and the morphology of the Germanic languages by a great scholar with strong well-considered personal views. To some the book will doubtless prove a challenge. If its publication should lead to a vigorous discussion of moot questions, all who knew Prokosch would be gratified, knowing as they do that he was ever hospitable to the ideas of other scholars and enjoyed nothing more than a clear-headed vigorous discussion of such problems.

HANS KURATH

BROWN UNIVERSITY

TABLE OF CONTENTS

Table of Abbreviations

7

THE GERMANIC CONSONANTS

A. The Consonant Shift

The Germanic Shift

The Intermediate Shift

The High German Shift

B. Other Consonant Changes

C. The Semi-Vowels

VOCALISM

ACCENT AND ITS EFFECTS

Gradation

Unstressed Syllables

PART THREE: INFLECTIONS

THE VERB

THE STEMS

The Present

The Preterit

The Strong Preterit

The Classes

The Weak Preterit

INFINITIVE AND PARTICIPLES

THE PERSONAL ENDINGS

ABBREVIATIONS

I. Languages and Dialects

Al.	=	Alemannic
Alb.	=	Albanian
Am.	=	American
Angl.	=	Anglian
Arab.	=	Arabic
Armen.	=	Armenian
Av.	=	Avestan
Bav.	=	Bavarian
Celt.	=	Celtic
Crim. Go.	=	Crimean Gothic
Dor.	=	Doric
E.	=	English
EFr.	=	East Franconian
Finn.	=	Finnic
Fr.	=	French
Franc.	=	Franconian
Gall.	=	Gallic
Ger.	=	German
Gk.	=	Greek
Gmc.	=	Germanic
Go.	=	Gothic
HG	=	High German
Hitt.	=	Hittite
Hom.	=	Homeric
Icel.	=	Icelandic
IE	=	Indo-European
Ion.-Att.	=	Ionic-Attic
Ital.	=	Italian
L.	=	Latin
Lesb.	=	Lesbian
Lett.	=	Lettic
Lith.	=	Lithuanian
LG	=	Low German

15

ME = Middle English
MFr. = Middle Franconian
MHG = Middle High German
MLG = Middle Low German
NE = New English
NHG = New High German
Norw. = Norwegian
NWGmc. = North West Germanic
OCymr. = Old Cymric
OE = Old English
OFris. = Old Frisian
OHG = Old High German
OIr. = Old Irish
ON = Old Norse
OS = Old Saxon
Osc. = Oscan
OSl. = Old Slavic
OSw. = Old Swedish
Pruss. = Prussian
RFr. = Rhenish Franconian
Run. = Runic
Russ. = Russian
Sk. = Sanskrit
Sl. = Slavic
Span. = Spanish
Sw. = Swedish
UG = Upper German
Umbr. = Umbrian
Ved. = Vedic
WGmc. = West Germanic
WS = West Saxon

II. GRAMMATICAL TERMS, ETC.

abl. = ablative
acc. = accusative
adj. = adjective
adv. = adverb
Anm. = Anmerkung
aor. = aorist
dat. = dative

diphth.	=	diphthong
du.	=	dual
fem.	=	feminine
gen.	=	genitive
Gramm.	=	Grammatik, Grammar
imper.	=	imperative
ind.	=	indicative
infin.	=	infinitive
instr.	=	instrumental
intr.	=	intransitive
loc.	=	locative
masc.	=	masculine
monophth.	=	monophthong
neut.	=	neuter
nom.	=	nominative
O	=	Otfrid
opt.	=	optative
part.	=	participle
pass.	=	passive
perf.	=	perfect
pers.	=	person
pl.	=	plural
prep.	=	preposition
pres.	=	present
pret.	=	preterit
pret. pres.	=	preterit present
prim.	=	primitive
S	=	strong
sg.	=	singular
trans.	=	transitive
V.L.	=	Verner's Law
voc.	=	vocative
W	=	weak
>	=	becomes, becoming
<	=	comes from, coming from
/	=	alternating with

III. Books and Periodicals

Ad. Gr. = Altdeutsche Grammatik by A. Holtzmann

Ae. Etym. Wb. = Etymologisches Wörterbuch der englischen Sprache
by F. Holthausen

Ahd. Gramm. = Althochdeutsche Grammatik by W. Braune

Aisl. Elb. = Altisländisches Elementarbuch by A. Heusler

Aisl. Gramm. = Altisländische und altnorwegische Grammatik by A. Noreen

AJPh = American Journal of Philology

Akad. d. Wiss. = Akademie der Wissenschaften

Altg. Dial. = Laut- und Formenlehre der altgermanischen Dialekte, ed. by F. Dieter

Am. J. Psych. = American Journal of Psychology

Angels. Gramm. = Angelsächsische Grammatik by E. Sievers

Anz. z. Anglia = Anzeigen zur Anglia

Ar. Forsch. = Arische Forschungen

As. Elb. = Altsächsisches Elementarbuch by F. Holthausen

Asw. Gr. = Altschwedische Grammatik by A. Noreen

BB = Bezzenbergers Beiträge zur Kunde der indogermanischen Sprachen

Ber. d. kgl. sächs. Ges. d. Wissensch. Phil.-hist. Klasse = Berichte der königlich-sächsischen Gesellschaft der Wissenschaften Philologisch-historische Klasse

Btr. = Beiträge zur Geschichte der deutschen Sprache und Literatur

Compendium d. vgl. Gramm. = Compendium der vergleichenden Grammatik by A. Schleicher

Dem.-Pr. = Die Demonstrativpronomina der indogermanischen Sprachen by K. Brugmann

G.G.L. = Grammar of the Gothic Language by J. Wright

GddS = Geschichte der deutschen Sprache by O. Behaghel

GE = Gotisches Elementarbuch by W. Streitberg

Germ. = Germania. Vierteljahrsschrift für deutsche Altertumskunde

Germ. Dem. Pr. = Germanische Demonstrativpronomen by E. Prokosch

Germ. Gutt. = Die germanischen Gutturale by J. Zupitza

Germ. Phil. = Germanische Philologie. Festschrift für O. Behaghel

Gesch. d. idg. Sprwsch. = Geschichte der indogermanischen Sprachwissenschaft

GEW = Etymologisches Wörterbuch der gotischen Sprache by S. Feist

Grdr. = Grundriss der vergleichenden Grammatik der indogermanischen Sprachen by K. Brugmann and B. Delbrück

GS = Germanische Sprachwissenschaft by R. Loewe

Hdb. Sk. = Handbuch des Sanskrit by A. Thumb

HGG = Handbuch der vergleichenden gotischen Grammatik by E. Kieckers

Hitt. Gramm. = A Comparative Grammar of the Hittite Language by
    E. H. Sturtevant
HU = Handbuch des Urgermanischen by H. Hirt
Idg. Gr. = Indogermanische Grammatik by H. Hirt
IF = Indogermanische Forschungen
IF Anz. = Anzeiger für indogermanische Sprach- und Altertumskunde
JEGPh = The Journal of English and Germanic Philology
J. Exp. Psych. = Journal of Experimental Psychology
KG = Kurze vergleichende Grammatik der indogermanischen Sprachen
    by K. Brugmann
Krit. Erl. = Kritische Erläuterungen zur Lateinischen Laut- und For-
    menlehre by F. Sommer
KZ = Kuhns Zeitschrift für vergleichende Sprachforschung auf dem
    Gebiet der indogermanischen Sprachen
Lang. = Language, Journal of the Linguistic Society of America
Lit. H. = Handbuch der litauischen Sprache by O. Wiedemann
LLFL = Handbuch der lateinischen Laut- und Formenlehre by F.
    Sommer
Mitt. d. Anthrop. Ges. = Mitteilungen der Anthropologischen Gesell-
    schaft in Wien
MLN = Modern Language Notes
Mod. Phil. = Modern Philology
MSL = Mémoires de la Société de Linguistique de Paris
MU = Morphologische Untersuchungen auf dem Gebiete der indo-
    germanischen Sprachen by H. Osthoff
Neophil. = Neophilologus. Zeitschrift zur wissenschaftlichen Pflege
    lebender Fremdsprachen und ihrer Literaturen
N. F. = Neue Folge
NTS = Norsk Tidscrift for Sprogvidenskap
OE Gramm. = Old English Grammar by J. Wright
Oerg. Hb. = Oergermaansch Handboek by R. C. Boer
OH = Oudnoorsch Handboek by R. C. Boer
PG = Grundriss der germanischen Philologie, ed. by H. Paul
PMLA = Publications of the Modern Language Association of America
QF = Quellen und Forschungen
Sch. Prät. = Das schwache Präteritum und seine Vorgeschichte by H.
    Collitz
UG = Urgermanische Grammatik by W. Streitberg
UL = Urgermanische Lautlehre by A. Noreen
Urg. = Urgermanisch by F. Kluge

Vgl. Synt. = Vergleichende Syntax der indogermanischen Sprachen by
    B. Delbrück
WP = Walde-Pokorny. A. Walde, Vergleichendes Wörterbuch der
    Indogermanischen Sprachen, ed. by J. Pokorny
W.S. = Wörter und Sachen. Kulturhistorische Zeitschrift für Sprach-
    und Sachforschung
Z. f. allg. Sprw. = Internationale Zeitschrift für allgemeine Sprach-
    wissenschaft
ZfdA = Zeitschrift für deutsches Altertum
ZfdU = Zeitschrift für deutschen Unterricht
Z. f. d. Wortf. = Zeitschrift für deutsche Wortforschung

PART ONE

THE EXTERNAL HISTORY OF THE GERMANIC LANGUAGES

1. Indo-European Origins. The linguistic relations between the Germanic group and the other Indo-European branches are a corollary to their geographical location and spread. The actual starting-point of the Indo-Europeans, their original home ('Urheimat'), is not known. At present, the greater weight of arguments seems to point to Northern or Central Europe,[1] but the views favoring South-Eastern Europe[2] or the steppes of Western Asia[3] are not to be underrated. The conflicting views can in a measure be reconciled by assuming that the ethnic and linguistic conformity of the Indo-European group developed in a wide zone of migration,[4] which extended 'from the 35th parallel N.L., from South-East to North-West, towards the Polar Circle',[5] or 'on a long belt of land, reaching from France through all of Europe and the Kirghiz Steppe, as far as Iran'.[6] a

The concept of an Indo-European family is based upon linguistic facts, but does not imply any anthropological coherence. We have no right whatever to speak of an Indo-European ('Aryan') race. Linguistic archeology (Hirt, Schrader, Much, Feist, and others) has drawn from linguistic material important conclusions as to common elements of an Indo-European culture, and many of these conclusions are doubtless correct. A varying proportion of identical vocabulary in the several Indo-European languages indicates certain facts of social and economic conditions common to all or most Indo-European linguistic groups. But to what extent this postulates the assumption of an 'Urvolk' is still problematic. Even the process through which separate Indo-European languages developed is not entirely clear. August Schleicher[7] conceived the Indo-European primitive language as the trunk of a linguistic 'Stammbaum'. This branches out into a northern and southern group (Slavo-German and Aryo-Graeco-Italo-Celtic), and these main branches are subdivided in the form of the diagram (adapted) shown at the top of the following page. b

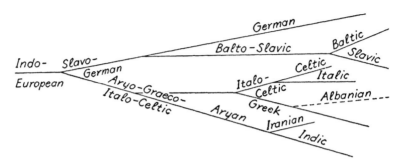

More conservatively, Johannes Schmidt[8] represented the relationship of the Indo-European languages in the form of intersecting circles, indicating that any two neighboring groups possess certain common characteristics (the diagram is slightly modified; Schmidt could not include Tocharian and Hittite):

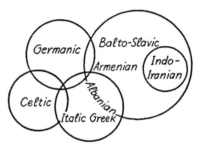

A. Meillet[9] uses the following diagram as an adaptation of Schmidt's 'wave theory':

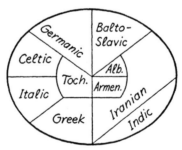

Schleicher's theory is demonstrably incorrect. The systems of Schmidt and Meillet are not theories, but graphic representations of undeniable geographical facts. As such, they are obviously correct, but they do not attempt to explain the facts.

LINGUISTIC SUBSTRATA.[10] Both racially and linguistically the Indo-European c
group constitutes a complicated blend in which the proportions of the common
elements vary greatly from branch to branch.   In addition to the common stock,
every one of them had absorbed a great deal from the languages that had formed
in the course of earlier migration all along the Indo-European belt.   In many
instances we have archeological, or even historical, evidence of aboriginal elements; thus the Celts largely represent an Indo-European expansion over Iberian
(Basque) territory; the Slavs expanded over wide stretches of Finnish soil; the
Hindus overwhelmed and partly absorbed Tibeto-Burmese, Dravidian, and
Austro-Asiatic populations.   The assumed aboriginal stock in a language is
commonly termed the 'linguistic substratum'.   The existence of such elements
has been established with some probability in many instances, but the task is
very elusive, and little certainty has as yet been attained.   As to the Germanic
languages, it has frequently been assumed that in the Baltic basin Indo-European
speech was super-imposed over a pre-historic population of northern Europe, of
whose speech, race, or culture nothing whatever is known.   So far, all attempts
to define it or to identify it with any known stock, for instance the Finns, have
failed.   Nevertheless, the existence of some 'Pre-Germanic Substratum' is probable, although for geographical and other reasons the common Indo-European
element seems to predominate more definitely in the Germanic group than anywhere else.   Some authorities, indeed, attach great importance to the hypothetical substratum.   Their weightiest argument rests on the assumption that a
very large proportion (one third or more) of the Germanic vocabulary has no
cognates in other Indo-European languages, a claim based chiefly on the con-
cluding table in Bruno Liebich's Wortfamilien der deutschen Sprache ([1]1899,
[2]1905), which lists 504 Germanic, 211 West-Germanic, and 159 German 'roots'
against 611 roots of Indo-European, or at least 'European', origin.   But this
table merely sums up the ultra-conservative etymologies in Heyne's Deutsches
Wörterbuch.   Since then, further etymological analysis has reduced the sup-
posedly non-Indo-European element to a negligible quantity.

2. Indo-European Expansions. The assumption of an Indo-Euro- a
pean zone of migration presupposes very early expansions, but we cannot define the center of radiation.   By the second millennium B.C. the
natural limits of the 'Eurasian Tract' had doubtless been extended,
and the more or less homogeneous ethnic and linguistic stock had disintegrated into numerous smaller units.   In the course of time, many of
them re-integrated, being absorbed by leading groups, and these new,
larger units in turn again split up into sub-divisions—a process which
is illustrated most clearly by the Romance group: The Italic group
was absorbed by one of its members, namely Latin.   This formed a
number of dialects, in France, in Italy, in Spain, in Rumania.   The
rise of the dialect of the Isle de France as 'Standard French' super-
imposed a new standard upon the numerous sub-languages of French—
and the process still continues.

The earlier phases of the expansion that led to the formation of the Indo-European languages seem to have been these:

b
I. The PRAIRIE GROUP of Southern Russia spread partly towards the southeast, forming various Indo-European languages in western Asia (Phrygian, Armenian) and eventually branching out into the important *Indo-Iranian* group; to this belong the Hindu languages, of which Sanskrit is an early representative, and the languages of the plateau of Iran (Avestan, Persian), Ossetic, Scythian, and others. Another part of the Prairie Group expanded to the north and west, forming the *Balto-Slavic* branch (Baltic = Lithuanian, Lettish, Old Prussian; Slavic = Russian, Polish, Czech, Sorbian, Slovenian, Serbo-Croatian, Bulgarian). A third branch spread to the south-east, into Asia Minor (*Phrygians*), and later a part of them migrated to the Balkan Peninsula, where they appear under the name of *Thracians*. The *Illyrians*, who occupied the northwestern part of the peninsula, may also have belonged to this branch. We know very little of their language. The *Albanians*, who at present inhabit the southern section of the former Illyrian territory, may be Illyrians, or they may be Thracians who had to abandon their more eastern home in consequence of the Turkish invasion.

The spread of the Prairie Group over Asia Minor had been preceded by that of a people that spoke a sister language of Indo-European, the *Hittites*.[1] In eastern Turkestan linguistic vestiges of a later Indo-European immigration have been found, the *Tocharian*.[2]

c
II. The PARK LAND GROUP inhabited the forest and meadow districts of central Europe; a more accurate demarcation of its home is hardly possible. Apparently it separated during the second millennium before our era into an eastern and a western branch. The former migrated south and south-east, forming several Balkan languages, notably *Hellenic* (Greek), possibly also Illyric. The remainder of this group probably lived in the territory between the middle Danube and the Hercynian Mountains, that is, chiefly in present Austria, Bohemia, Moravia, and perhaps parts of southern Germany. They expanded to the north as far as geographical and climatic conditions made the land inhabitable after the ice cap of the last glacial epoch had receded—a process that occupied thousands of years.

One branch of this group either skirted or traversed the eastern Alps and drifted into Italy from the northeast. These formed the *Italic* languages, of which Latin became the most important. Another branch spread over southern and western Germany and later over

France, the British Isles, and parts of Spain and northern Italy: these were the *Celts*.[3]

The northern expansion gradually extended over northern Germany between the Elbe and Oder or Vistula, and southern Scandinavia. This is the *Germanic* group of the Indo-Europeans.

The distinction between the eastern and western spheres of expansion **d** (the 'Prairie' and 'Park Land' groups) is not merely geographical, but linguistic as well. In sounds, vocabulary, and certain features of declension and conjugation, the languages of either group are closer to one another than to those of the other group. Thus Greek has probably more features in common with Italic than with any of the Eastern languages, although there is no foundation for the frequent assumption of an especially close connection between the two 'classical' languages; in fact, Latin is more closely related to Celtic and Germanic than to Greek. It has become customary to designate the eastern group as *satem* languages, the western group as *kentum* languages ('100' = L. *centum*, Av. *satəm*; cf. **11**). While this distinction in itself is of minor importance, it offers a convenient nomenclature for the two branches.

Even at present a part of Europe remains non-Indo-European. The **e** Lapps and Finns (of many tribes) in northern Scandinavia, Finland, Russia, together with the Hungarians, belong to the *Finno-Ugrian* branch of the Ural-Altaic family of languages, which covers the larger part of northern and a good deal of central Asia. The *Turks*, who now occupy but a very small part of Europe, also belong to this family. In the western Pyrenees there still lives a remnant of the *Basques* who formerly must have occupied a very large part of France, since the Vosges Mountains still bear their name (L. *Silva Vasconum*, MHG *Wasgenwalt*). Many other languages of early Europe are extinct. Of these, perhaps the most important was *Etruscan*, which, like Basque, is of unknown origin. The meaning of very few Etruscan words is definitely known, although it was still a living language in late Roman times.

It is a moot question whether the Indo-European languages are related to other groups. Arguments for relationship between Indo-European and Finno-Ugrian, or Semitic, or some languages of the Caucasus, have frequently been offered, but no proof has as yet been furnished.

3. The Germanic Languages represent, on the whole, that branch of **a** the Indo-European group that remained longest in or near the original home of the Indo-Europeans. Aside from their gradual expansion towards the uninhabitated or sparsely settled north, they remained there during the pre-Christian era. The land between the Elbe and the Oder, north of the Hercynian Mountains and extending into southern Scandinavia, was the 'Urheimat' of the Germanic group in the sense that it was there that they developed those linguistic, cultural, and physical characteristics that made them a separate branch of the Indo-European family. Apparently, this is not in agreement with numerous reports of historians, from the Goth Jordanes (550) to the Frank Frechulf (about 830), according to whom at least the Goths, or even all Germanic tribes, came from Scandinavia—'ex Scandza insula' (Scatinavia, Scadanau, ON Skāney, Sw. Skåne, OE Scedenige). The tradition as such is probably well founded, but the scope of the geographical term is hardly identical with its present meaning. (The spelling Scandinavia has come down to us from Pliny's Historia Naturalis, where also the correct form Scadinavia occurs.) The name is a compound from Gmc. *skaþō(n)-, ON skaþe, OHG scado 'harm, damage', OE sceaþe 'fiend' and Gmc. *awī 'island, land by the water' (Latinized to -avia, as in Bat-avia), Go. *awi, gen. aujōs, ON ey, OE ēg, īg, ēglond, īglond (NE island), OHG ouwa, NHG Au; it must have meant something like 'Perilous Shores', Schadenau. Karsten (Die Germanen 72 ff.) has made it extremely probable that Scadinavia denoted the lands around the southern Baltic—at least, southern Sweden, the Danish Isles, and Jutland, but probably also northern Germany around the Elbe (according to the Historia Langobardorum, the Langobards came from Scatenauge on the lower Elbe). It is possible that the name merely referred to the dangers of navigation in the southern Baltic, with its sudden squalls and rocky cliffs, or it may have been due to the inundation of parts of that territory during the last millennium B.C., through which Scandinavia and the Danish Isles became separated from the European main land.

b   In this territory of scanty natural resources, overpopulation was a chronically recurrent condition, leading to frequent emigrations and expansions. Shortly before the beginning of our era, the Germanic group appears to have been a fairly homogeneous linguistic and cultural unit. This is the period that is termed Urgermanisch, Primitive Germanic. For that period we may speak of an incipient division into a North Germanic, Central Germanic, and South Germanic branch. The first of these occupied most of southern Sweden and a fringe of Norway; the second originally extended over the southernmost part of Sweden, Jutland, the Danish Isles, and the zone of inundation that gradually became Kattegat, Belt, Sund (and Limfjord, in northern Jutland): the third belonged to northern Germany, between the Elbe and the Oder. When the larger part of the central group had emigrated to the southeast and east (see below) and its remainder had been absorbed by the converging expansion of the other two groups, we find a new grouping—approximately since the beginning of the Christian era—, which we term *North Germanic, East Germanic,* and, in contrast to the latter, *West Germanic.* The eastern group, as is to be expected, shows linguistic contacts with both groups, due to its former location between them.

NOTE: 'Urgermanisch' and 'Gemeingermanisch' are different linguistic concepts, although for the purpose of this book the distinction is of little importance. The former refers to the Germanic language in that pre-historic period when the division into dialects was not yet clearly apparent; the latter is applied to linguistic developments that took place in all Germanic languages, but independently of each other. Thus, the first consonant shift is termed 'Primitive Germanic' 'Urgermanisch', for which this book uses the term 'Germanic'; the development of the definite article is termed 'General Germanic', 'Gemeingermanisch'.

4. North Germanic (Norse) is the language 'of the Scandinavian North, including Iceland, Greenland, and the Fär-öer' (Noreen, Aisl. Gramm 1). To what extent the Danish Isles had been Norse in prehistoric times, is unknown. Jutland became North Germanic (Danish) after a large part of its Anglian (West Germanic) population had emigrated to England, during the fifth and sixth centuries. The Norse occupation of Iceland began in 875; later, Icelandic-Norwegian settlements were founded in Greenland, the Fär-öer, the Orkn-öer, the Shetland Islands, and northern Ireland. The Norse settlements in Greenland disappeared during the sixteenth century, those in the British Isles about two centuries later; in the Fär-öer (Danish), Norse is still spoken.

'Primitive Norse' ('Urnordisch') covers the period from the earliest (Runic) inscriptions (end of the third century A.D.) to the beginning of the Viking Age (about 800). These inscriptions, of which we have more than a hundred, show hardly a trace of dialect variations, but during the Viking Age the division into Norwegian, Swedish (including Gutnic), and Danish became more and more marked. Norwegian and its offspring, Icelandic (and the closely related dialect of the Fär-öer) are generally termed West Norse, Swedish and Danish, East Norse. 'Danish' (*dǫnsk tunga*) was the general name for the Norse languages during the Viking Age (800–1050), and even later. Swedish, Danish, and Icelandic developed independent literary languages, but Norwegian had since the end of the Middle Ages been greatly influenced by Swedish and later still more by Danish, and finally Danish became the literary and city language of the country. This was partly due to the political union of the three countries (1397: Union of Calmar; 1597: Norway became a part of the Danish kingdom), and partly to the Reformation, through which the Danish Bible and other religious writings in Danish were introduced into Norway. During the nineteenth century, however, the Danish standard language in Norway was more and more influenced by the home dialects; writers such as Ibsen and Björnsen developed a new, classical Dano-Norwegian standard, but the success of efforts to create a purely Norwegian literary language on the basis of local dialects and Old Norse—the *landsmål*—is still in doubt, although they were sponsored by important scholars such as Ivar Åsen and writers such as Arne Garborg.

a   **5. East Germanic** is the language of those tribes that settled on the south-east shores of the Baltic, east of the Oder, during the last two or three centuries of the pre-Christian Era. Inundations were a primary cause of their emigration from Jutland and its surroundings, and over-population probably contributed. Historians report that the Cimbrians, who invaded the Roman territory together with the Teutons and Ambrons, were driven from their home in the Chersonnesus Cimbricus by storm floods. The Cimbrians certainly came from northern Jutland, still called *Himmerland*, and the other two tribes probably had been their neighbors (Teutons from *Thyland*, west of *Himmerland*, *Ambrons* from the isle of *Amrum*, west of Sleswig?); '*Toutoni*' (acc.-os) are named on a boundary stone near Miltenberg on the Main;[2] but they may have been Celts who joined them later on their migration, somewhere in the South. Of their languages we know nothing. The only reason for grouping them with East Germanic is the fact that the latter is a subsequent development among tribes that came, more or less, from the same territory.

b   The *Goths* were the most important part of this expansion. The earliest known form of their name is Lith. *Gudai*, with unshifted *d* for *t*.[1] It is identical with the first element of OSw. *Gutland*, Sw. *Gotland* (island in the Baltic Sea), *Götaland* (*Götland*, district in southern Sweden), and with Sw. *Götar*, ON *Gautar* < *ʒautōz*, OE *Gēatas*. It is very probable, in spite of phonological difficulties, that the name is also contained in *Jutland*. In that case, ON *Iǫtar* would have to be interpreted as an archaic retention of the spirantic pronunciation of Gmc.

ʒ- (**24**) by the later Norse ('Danish') immigrants, in whose language it had become *g*. Bede's *Juti*, OE *Ytas*, *Ytan* (designations of the Anglo-Frisian Jutes who emigrated to England) are hardly more than spelling variations of the form Gmc. *$\check{z}ut\bar{o}z$, *$\check{z}utanaz$, ablaut variation of *$\check{z}aut$-.

The Goths appear to have had their name from their country. (Cf. Karsten, l. c. 85, where literature is given.) They came from a general district called *Gutland*, from Gmc. *$\check{z}eut$-, *$\check{z}aut$-, *$\check{z}ut$- (Go. *giutan*, *gaut*, *gutans*). The Old Swedish *Guta-Saga* relates in legendary style, but probably with a background of facts, that Gutaland was 'bewitched' so that it was under water by day and above by night. But after the grandfather of *Guti* had settled there it sank no more: *Gutland hitti fyrsti maþr þann sum þieluar het. þa war Gutland so eluist, at þet dagum sanc oc natum war uppi. Enn þann maþr quam fyrsti eldi a land, oc siþan sanc þet aldri. þissi þieluar hafþi ann sun, sum hit Hafþi; en Hafþa cuna hit Huitstierna. þaun tu bygþi fyrsti a Gutlandi* ... (Their sons divide Gutland:), *so at Graipr, þann elzti, laut norþasta þriþiung, oc Guti miþalþriþiung, en Gunnfiaur, þann yngsti, laut sunnarsta*.[3] This seems to indicate that Gutaland was inundated ('poured-over') land, similar to the Halligen and Watten in the North Sea.[4] While old Gutaland, like legendary Vineta (Vandal home?), sank below the surface, some of the people of the submerged land migrated to Sweden, transferring the name there; since they came from 'Gutland', they were themselves called *Gutar*, *Gautar*, and in turn called the new homes *Gutaland*, *Gotland*. But the bulk, according to Jordanes, the historian of the Goths, went from 'Scandinavia', the perilous shore, to the continent, landing near the mouth of the Vistula, at *Gothiscandza* (*$Gothi$-$Scandza$* = Gothic Scandinavia, or *$Gutisk$-$andia$* = Gothic Shore; = Danzig?, Pol. *Gdansk*). There they had been preceded by the *Ulmerugi*, settlers in the island (ON *holmr*) of Rügen, and the *Vandals*, who came from the district of *Vændæl* 'Fair Valley', surrounding the Limfjord in northern Jutland; they were followed by the *Burgundians*, from the island of Bornholm (*Borgundarholmr*).

About 200 A.D., forced by overpopulation, the Goths migrated southeast, through the Rokitno Swamps (Jordanes' *Oium*), and settled in the plains north of the Black Sea. There they separated into two branches, the *Ostrogothae* east of the Dniepr, and the *Visigothae* west of it. *Ostro-* is related to L. *aurora*, Sk. *uṣās*, Gk. ἔως, Lith. *auśrà* 'morning light', *Visi-* (*Visu-*) either to L. *ves(per)*, Gk. ἕσπερος 'evening' or, less probably, to Gk. εὖ < *$wesu$*, Sk. *vasu-* 'well'. It is more likely that the names referred to the eastern and western location of the two groups, than that they meant 'the brilliant Goths' and 'the good Goths'. The most important Gothic document, the Gospel translation of their bishop Wulfila (about 350), is Visi-Gothic, but contains some traces of Ostro-Gothic influence, due to a later Ostro-Gothic scribe. The Gothic kingdoms were destroyed by the Huns, and later the Goths disappeared in the Roman Empire. But some Gothic settlements in the Crimea survived the Hunnish invasion and existed as late as the sixteenth century.

d   It is generally assumed that Gothic was more closely related to Norse than to West Germanic. The principal arguments for this view are 'Holtzmann's Law' (*uw* > *ggw*, *ij* > *ddj*, *ggj*, cf. **33**) and the ending *-t* of the 2 sg. pret. of strong verbs (cf. **73**; also see Hirt, HU 22). But these are hardly more important than the parallels between Gothic and West Germanic on the one hand, and Norse and West Germanic on the other. Among the former, the most conspicuous are the use of Go. *is*, OHG *er* as anaphoric pronoun as against ON *hann*; the development of a prepositive article from the *to*-demonstrative in Gothic and West Germanic as against a post-positive article from the *n*-pronoun in Norse (**93**); the different treatment of the reflexive (**70**); the prevailing use of Go. *haban*, WGmc. (OHG) *habēn* as against Norse *eiga*. Norse-WGmc. parallels are chiefly the rhotacism (**28**), the loss of the reduplicated preterit (**62**), the umlaut (**41**), and the loss of the mediopassive (**74**). But none of these three groups of parallels is important enough to have any influence on the classification of the Germanic languages, and it seems best to consider the three groups independent branches. It is true, of course, that in the sense of section **7** Gothic and Norse are in many respects more archaic than West Germanic, especially Old High German.—Cf. H. Arntz, Germ. Phil. 41 ff.

a   **6. West Germanic** comprises the expansion of the continental stock between the Elbe and the Oder to the west and south-west. Tacitus divides this group into *Ingaevones*, *Istaevones*, and *Herminones*, but this division is of relatively little importance for the later tribal formations, although the three branches roughly correspond to the *Anglo-Frisian*, the *Franconian*, and the *Upper German* groups respectively. The overpopulation that had caused the northern and eastern expansions continued and led to a gradual spread over the Celtic territory west of the Elbe and south of the Hercynian Mountains. The former Celtic character of this territory is to this day indicated by a number of features, such as the specifically Celtic type of village planning and a considerable

number of Celtic geographical names. Of the latter, the masculine
river names are especially noteworthy: *der Rhein, Main, Neckar, Inn,
Lech, Regen, der* or *die Eisack* belong to formerly Celtic land, while *die
Elbe, Oder, Weichsel* flow through ancient Germanic territory.

This expansion proceeded essentially in a form that might be compared to the opening of a fan, the country around the lower Elbe being
considered as pivot, and led to the formation of these dialect groups:

I. ANGLO-FRISIAN. After the Cimbrian and East Germanic migra b
tions the Ingaevones spread from Schleswig-Holstein over all or most
of Jutland and later appear under the name of *Anglians*. Probably
they had even before that time occupied the coast region between the
Elbe and the Rhine, where they absorbed the Celtic population. This
earliest part of the West Germanic expansion represents the later
Frisians. The tribes south of them, in present Hannover, Oldenburg,
Westphalia, towards the end of the 'Germanic Migration' formed the
Saxon Tribal Alliance ('Stammesverband'). This whole series of expansions is often called the *Anglo-Frisian* group. During the fifth
century the northern section of the Anglian group emigrated to northern
England, and their territory in Jutland was occupied by Danes. Frisians and Saxons had founded settlements on the northern coast of
France, which was therefore called *Litus Saxonicum*, and during the
fifth century, at first from this coast, but soon also from the main land
of the Saxons, England south of the river Humber was occupied;
'Northumbria' was settled by Anglians, probably slightly later. Most
of the land between Thames and Humber (Mercia, East Anglia, Essex,
Middlesex) can be called literally 'Anglo-Saxon', since it was settled
jointly by the two branches. The name is first used by Paulus Diaconus
(*Angli-Saxones*; eighth century). The first occupation, that of Wight,
Hampshire, and Kent, is ascribed to 'Jutes', but these did not come from
Jutland direct, but were probably remote descendants of earlier emigrants from Jutland, who had settled in northwestern Germany. Since
the Saxons became the political leaders, their name was applied to the
Germanic settlers of southern England, although linguistically these
dialects are more Frisian than Saxon. *West Saxon*, the language of
King Alfred, might be termed the standard dialect of the Old English
period (about 500 to 1066). However, some important works were
originally written in Anglian, for instance *Beowulf*, which we possess in a
later West Saxon rendering.

Anglian and Saxo-Frisian coalesced into the *English* language, which
in the course of centuries absorbed a multitude of Scandinavian, Nor

man French, and cosmopolitan words, but the fundamental material of the language is almost exclusively West Germanic.—Cf. E. Wadstein, On the origin of the English, Uppsala 1927.

On the continent, *Frisian* originally occupied the coast region of the North Sea from southern Jutland to the Zuyder Sea, but it was gradually absorbed by German and Dutch; it is still spoken in northwestern Holland and on some of the coast islands.

c The language of the *Langobards* ('Lombards'), who originally lived in southern Holstein and eastern Hanover, is usually classed with the Anglo-Frisian. But since it shows the High German consonant shift in its Upper German form, it should really be considered as closely related to Alemannian and Bavarian.

d II. GERMAN and DUTCH. The West Germanic expansion had started two or three centuries B.C. and continued approximately until 500 A.D. The Saxon group, its oldest layer, had more or less coalesced with those Anglians that had stayed on the continent. Although dialect differences exist, the two branches have so much in common that in most respects they may be considered one group. But the fact should not be lost sight of that the 'Anglians' of Schleswig-Holstein and the surrounding country inhabit the only part of Germany that, in historical times, has always been Germanic. The West was Celtic before our era; the East became Slavic about 450 A.D. and remained so for centuries.

Numerous Germanic tribes occupied Central Germany during the two or three centuries before and after the beginning of our era. The Romans safeguarded their dominion by the chain of fortifications called *limes*, extending from Mainz to Regensburg, which delayed further spread for a considerable time. The tribes of the central group gradually consolidated into the *Franconian* Tribal League, which occupies a wide zone in Central Germany, north and south of the Main, but also extends into southern Holland and northern Belgium.

The most important tribal group in the old territory were the *Suevians*. In 73 B.C. a group of them under their leader Ariovistus apparently occupied Bohemia, migrated southwest and finally reached Gaul, where they were defeated by Caesar. The Suevian expansion was thereby delayed, but not stopped. In 213 A.D., Suevians under the name of *Alemanni* reached the *limes*, and after several unsuccessful attempts to break it, gradually occupied southwestern Germany, where they have been firmly established since 409. The Suevians in Bohemia, under the name of *Marcomanni*, retained their connection with the home land as long as it remained Germanic. But by the middle of the fifth century most of the Germanic population had migrated to the west and southwest, and their land was occupied by Slavs as far west as the Elbe and Saale rivers, and in some places even beyond. Around that time the Romans withdrew their garrisons from the province of Vindelicia and, possibly under the pressure of the Slavic immigration, the larger part of the Marcomanni left *Boiohaemum* (= Bohemia, 'the land of the Boians') and settled as *Baiuvarii* in Vindelicia, which then became 'Bavaria'.

Continental West Germanic (aside from Frisian) developed two (or three) standard languages in consequence of political separation. During the sixteenth and seventeenth centuries the Netherlands secured their independence from the German Empire. Subsequently the *Dutch* language developed there as a standardized combination of the three dialects of that territory. Low Franconian predominates, but there are considerable Frisian and some Saxon elements. *Flemish*, essentially identical with Dutch, is standardized Low Franconian in present Belgium.

The other continental West Germanic dialects formed the *German* language. Its present dialect grouping is virtually the same as in Old High German times (about 750-1100). However, since the ninth century, there has been a constant Eastern expansion beyond the Elbe and Saale, over the territory that had been occupied by Slavs.

We distinguish the following dialect groups:

1. *Low German* (*Niederdeutsch, Plattdeutsch*), north of a line that **e** extends from Aachen and Düsseldorf to Frankfort-on-the-Oder ('Benrather Linie'). It comprises *Low Franconian, Low Saxon,* and *East Low German* (east of the Elbe).

2. *High German* (*Hochdeutsch*), consisting of:

a. *Middle German* = *Middle Franconian, Rhine Franconian, East Franconian, Thuringian,* and *East Middle German* (*New Saxon, Sudetian German,* and *Silesian*).

b. *Upper German* = *Alemannian* (*Alsatian, Swabian, Alemannian* in the narrower sense, and *Swiss*) and *Bavarian* with its eastern expansion, *Austrian.*—For Langobardian, see above, I.

NOTE: The original meaning of most of the tribal names is uncertain. Cf. M. Schönfeld, Wörterbuch der altgermanischen Personen- und Völkernamen.

7. Chronology and Drift. The successive waves of expansion de- **a** scribed above had led to the formation of the Germanic tribal groups.

Since we have detailed historical evidence for the most recent period only, we must broadly assume a general Norse expansion and a general East Germanic spread, but we can clearly recognize the series of West Germanic expansions. This process of tribal growth is reflected in certain features of the development of the Germanic languages.

They had become a distinct linguistic unit among the Indo-European languages through a number of far-reaching changes in sounds and forms. Virtually all of these changes exhibit a significantly homogeneous character; they follow the same 'drift' (cf. Sapir, Language 160 ff.), revealing uniform characteristics of the several Germanic languages. The following is not a hypothesis, but a mere statement of facts, for which no explanation is attempted at present: Every Germanic language followed the general, more or less uniform, trend of development as long as it was in close contact with the main body of the nation. After the separation, this fundamental trend came to a standstill, but in certain cases a new trend developed. Thus, Norse and Gothic represent the oldest layers within the Germanic tribes: In these languages the results of the Germanic drift are restricted to those changes that took place in pre-Christian and very early Christian times. But certain characteristics of these languages point to the rise of new trends.

b In the West Germanic dialects, which were formed essentially as the result of the Germanic Migration ('Völkerwanderung'), the symptoms of this process are highly significant. In the course of the fanlike spread described above, the Germanic drift came to a virtual standstill in a relatively short time—perhaps sometimes in a generation—after the settlement of each tribe in the new home and the consequent separation from the main group. As far as the effect of the Germanic drift is concerned, the north-western group—Frisian, Anglian, Saxon, and Low Franconian—, together with its insular 'Anglo-Saxon' expansion represents the general West Germanic condition of the period when Norse and Gothic had become independent groups, while central and southern Germany were still Celtic. These dialects, from the point of view of the drift, are younger than Gothic and Norse, but older than the High German dialects. In exact keeping with the chronology of the West Germanic spread, Middle and Upper Franconian show very consistent gradations of the drift: Middle Franconian is slightly farther advanced than Low Franconian, and Rhine and East Franconian present still more recent features. The two Upper German dialects, especially in the older period, show the greatest number of features that are the result of the Germanic drift and are in that sense as well as historically the youngest among the Germanic dialects.

PART TWO
GERMANIC PHONOLOGY

8. Reconstruction. The established method of Indo-European comparative grammar has in a tentative way 'reconstructed' the most essential phonological features of prehistoric Indo-European. If in a given word all, or most, Indo-European languages show the same sound, we assume that this represents the original condition of Indo-European. For instance, the root consonants in the Greek words πατήρ, μήτηρ, δῶ(ρον), δόμος, are identical with those of many other Indo-European languages, for instance, L. *māter, pater, dō(num), domus,* OSl. *matь, da(nъ),* Sk. *mātā́, pitā́, dá̇(nam), dámas,* and we assume that they also occurred in the corresponding Indo-European words. But in the case of differences between the Indo-European languages, we take it for granted that variations of sounds are due to phonetic changes in some or all of them. Thus, the stem vowel of an important type of present tense forms is *e*, and the ending of the first person singular is *ō* in the earliest accessible forms of many Indo-European languages. The Indo-Iranian languages, however, have *a, ā*: Gk. φέρω, L. *ferō*: Sk. *bhárā(mi)*. It was formerly assumed that Indo-Iranian in this respect represented the original condition of Indo-European. But since 1878 (**34 a**) it has been quite generally admitted that *a, ā* in these languages is a development from earlier *e, ō*. Accordingly, from these verb forms is now reconstructed an IE **bhérō*; the sign * implies that the form is not found in any document, but represents a reconstruction on a comparative basis. In principle, such reconstructions are merely tentative formulae stating, for instance, that 'IE *bh*' is the sound that appears under ordinary conditions as *bh* in Indic, as φ in Greek, as *f* or *b* in Latin, and as *b* or *ƀ* in the other Indo-European languages; or that 'IE *e*' represents Indo-Iranian *a*, but Greek, Latin, Celtic, Germanic *e*. Nevertheless, in most cases the reconstruction implies the phonetic character of Indo-European sounds with a considerable degree of probability. This is not even altered by the assumption that phonetic variations in different parts of the Indo-European territory may have existed at all times. It is, for instance, quite possible that in the extreme East, Indo-European *ŏ*, which became *ă* in Indo-Iranian, had a more open

35

quality than in the rest of the territory.   The sound that we represent
by 'IE *bh*' may have varied since earliest times.   Perhaps it was pronounced as a fortis in some districts, and as a lenis in others.   The
former articulation may have led to L. *f*, Gk. *φ*, the latter to Gmc.,
Celt. *b ƀ*, Sl. *b*.   Even as mere formulae, these reconstructions are of
the highest systematic value and have greatly contributed to the development of Indo-European comparative grammar into an exact
science.   But we should of course attempt, in selecting symbols for
reconstructed sounds, to reach the closest possible approach to their
actual phonetic character.

   9. Phonetic Drift and Phonetic Law.   The habitual ways of pro-
ducing and combining speech sounds constitute a group of habits for
every language, which is generally called its basis of articulation, or its
organic or phonetic basis.   It is felt as the dominant note of a language,
impressing upon it its peculiar stamp: the clean-cut preciseness of
French, the contrasting ruggedness of North German, the self-con-
strained calmness of English, the 'insinuating grace' of Russian (Jespersen, Growth and Structure of the English Language 3).   This can
only be understood when it is realized that the individual habits of
sound production and combination harmonize with one another in their
typical characteristics to such an extent that they represent an acoustic
unit—one chord composed of many single elements.   Within certain
limits, this acoustic dominant of a language is a rather permanent
quality pervading long periods of its life and governing its historical
changes.   The sum of these habits of articulation may be called the
Phonetic Tendency or Phonetic Drift[1] of the language.   The Phonetic
Basis is the static, descriptive aspect of the acoustic character of a
language, the Phonetic Drift its dynamic, historical aspect.

   Continuing through generations and centuries, the phonetic drift
exerts either a stabilizing, or a modifying influence upon individual
sounds.   Thus, contrasting, strong accentuation tends to weaken the
articulation of unaccented syllables; a general trend towards energetic
articulation may increase the muscular tension and force of expiration
in the production of certain sounds, changing, for instance, 'lenes' to
'fortes', pure stops to aspirates or spirants; in languages of relatively
gentle articulation neighboring sounds are apt to be assimilated, while
in those of harsher articulation they may tend to retain their original
character.   The isolated types of such sound changes are termed Phonetic Laws, and since 1876 (A. Leskien, Die Deklination im Slavisch-
Litauischen und Germanischen) it must be considered one of the chief

tenets of linguistic science, that in principle phonetic laws do not admit of exceptions. They are consequences of the phonetic drift of a given language at a given time, and like causes lead to like effects. In that sense phonetic laws are truly 'ausnahmslos'. But the very concept of phonetic drift implies various articulations of the same type of speech sound—the same 'phoneme'—under various conditions. For instance, in languages of the Germanic group, the phoneme *t* may be fortis or lenis, aspirated or unaspirated, and this may lead to *apparent* exceptions to phonetic laws, since the sound may develop differently under different conditions: In Middle Franconian, *t*, as a rule, develops into an affricate or a spirant (*ts* or *ss*), but in habitually unstressed words, such as *et, dat,* it remains unchanged (**17 d**). But such variations do not diminish the methodical value of the formulation and application of phonetic laws.

The drift of living languages can be ascertained by actual observation. The drift of dead or reconstructed languages can only be deduced by combining and comparing their phonetic laws as isolated consequences of the drift. But it must always be kept in mind that the drift is the primary factor, and that the phonetic laws are merely its component parts.

H. Schuchardt, Ueber die Lautgesetze 36: 'Welchen Sinn haben alle die Tausende von Lautgesetzen, solange sie isoliert bleiben, solange sie nicht in höhere Ordnungen aufgelöst werden? ... Im Einzelnen müssen wir das Allgemeine finden lernen, und demnach ist auch die Erkenntnis einer Tatsache, welche das ganze Sprachleben beherrscht, von grösserer Wichtigkeit als die Erkenntnis irgendwelcher Erscheinungsformen.'

J. Vendryes, Mélanges linguistiques 116: 'Une loi phonétique ne peut être reconnue valable que si elle est d'accord avec les principes qui régissent le système articulatoire de la langue au moment où elle agit. ... Tout changement phonétique peut être considéré comme du a l'action de forces intimes et sécrètes, auxquelles convient assez bien le nom de tendances. Ce sont ces tendances qui modifient sans cesse la structure de la langue, et l'évolution de chaque idiome résulte en dernière analyse d'un jeu perpetuel de tendances. ... La notion de tendance phonétique est plus exacte theorétiquement, et practiquement plus féconde que celle de loi phonétique. Elle seule permet de déterminer avec précision la cause des changements phonétiques et d'interpreter scientifiquement ceux mêmes qui paraissent les plus rebelles à toute discipline scientifique.'

CONSONANTISM

THE INDO-EUROPEAN CONSONANTS

10. Modes of Articulation. According to present standards of reconstruction, Indo-European had very few genuine spirants. Only *s* and its assimilated form *z* are generally recognized (**12**). Brugmann assumed a spirant of undefined phonetic character, for which he used the signs *þ ð*. Probably this was really a palatal spirant (*ç j* or *š ž*), voiceless or voiced according to surroundings; cf. Brugmann, KG 301; Hirt, Idg. Gr. 1. 231.

Among the numerous stops, the following modes of articulation are assumed:

b (1) The Pure Voiceless Stops, **p t k** pronounced without aspiration, as in modern Romance and Slavic languages:

IE *pǝtḗr* 'father', Sk. *pitá*, Gk. πατήρ, L. *pater*
IE *ped-/pod-* 'foot', Sk. *pād-*, Gk. ποδ-, L. *ped-*
IE *swep-/sup-* 'sleep', Sk. *svápiti*, Gk. ὕπνος, L. *sopor*
IE *ten-* 'stretch', Sk. *tanóti*, Gk. τείνω, L. *tendō*
IE *trejes* 'three', Sk. *tráyas*, Gk. τρεῖς, L. *trēs*
IE *tod* 'that', Sk. *tad*, Gk. τό, L. *is-tud*
IE *ḱm̥tóm* 'hundred', Sk. *śatám*, Gk. ἑκατόν, L. *centum*
IE *kǝp-/kōp-* 'seize', Lett. *kampju*, Gk. κώπη 'handle', L. *capiō*
IE *sekw-* 'follow', Sk. *sácatē*, Gk. ἕπομαι, L. *sequor*.

c (2) The Pure Voiced Stops, **b d g**; *b* was extremely rare, but *d* and *g* (the latter of several varieties, see **11**) were frequent sounds:

IE *bel-/bol-*, Sk. *bálam* 'strength', Gk. βελτίων 'better', L. *dē-bilis* 'weak', Russ. *bolšiy* 'stronger'
IE *deḱm̥(t)*, Sk. *daśa*, Gk. δέκα, L. *decem* 'ten'
IE *dwōu*, Sk. *dvāu*, Gk. δύω, L. *duo* 'two'
IE *domo-/u-*, Sk. *dámas*, Gk. δόμος, L. *domus* 'house'
IE *ĝenos-*, Sk. *jánas*, Gk. γένος, L. *genus* 'kin'
IE *steg-*, Sk. *sthagáyati*, Gk. στέγω, L. *tegō* 'cover'
IE *gwem-/gwm̥-*, Sk. *gácchati*, Gk. βαίνω, L. *veniō* 'come'.

d (3) The Aspirated Voiceless Stops, **ph th kh** (= *p t k* in English, Scandinavian, and Standard German). Evidence for the existence of these sounds can be found only in Sanskrit and Greek:

Sk. *phálam* 'fruit', Gk. ὄφελος 'use'
Sk. *-tha*, Gk. *-θα*, ending of the second singular perfect (*véttha*, οἶσθα)
Sk. *kákhati*, Gk. καγχάζω 'laugh'.

e (4) The Aspirated Voiced Stops (Sonant Aspirates, Mediae Aspiratae), **bh dh gh**. These appear as genuine aspirated stops (similar to the sound groups in English words like *abhor, adhere, foghorn*) only in the Indic (not Indo-Iranian) group of Indo-European languages, as φ θ χ in Greek, as *f þ h* in Primitive Italic (in Latin, *f f h* initially, *b d h* medially) as *b ð ȝ* in Primitive Germanic (**24**), and as *b d g*, partly alternating with *b ð ȝ*, in the other IE languages:

IE *bher-, Sk. bhárati, Gk. φέρω, L. ferō 'carry'

IE *bhrātēr, Sk. bhrātā, Gk. φράτηρ, L. frāter 'brother'

IE *nebh(os), Sk. nábhas- 'fog', Gk. νέφος 'cloud', L. nebula 'fog'

IE *dhē- 'put', Sk. (dá-)dhāti, Gk. (τί-)θημι, L. fē-cī 'I did'

IE *rudhəró-, Sk. rudhirá-, Gk. ἐρυθρός, L. ruber (Umbr. rufru) 'red'

IE *medhyo-, Sk. mádhya-, Gk. μέσος, L. medius (Osc. mefiaí) 'middle'

IE *ĝheim-/ĝhim-, Sk. himá, Gk. χειμών, L. hiems 'winter'

IE *ĝheu-, Sk. (ju-)hóti 'sacrifices', Gk. χέω, L. fundō 'pour'

IE *weĝh-, Sk. váhati 'drives', Gk. ὄχος 'wagon', L. vehō 'drive'

IE *ĝhengh-, Sk. jaŋghā 'leg', Lith. žengiù 'go', Gk. κοχώνη 'crotch'

IE *ghosti-, L. hostis 'enemy', hospes < *hosti-potis 'host'

IE *ghorto-, OSl. gradъ 'town', Gk. χόρτος 'pasture', L. hortus 'garden'

IE *steigh-, Sk. stighnóti, Gk. στείχω 'go', L. ve-stīgium 'track'

IE *ghwermo-, Sk. ghárma-, Gk. θερμός, L. formus 'warm'

IE *ghwen-/ghwon-, Sk. hánti, Gk. θείνω 'kill', φόνος 'murder'

IE *(s)neighw-/snighw-, Sk. snih- 'melt', Gk. νίφει, L. ninguit 'it
snows'.

The correctness of the reconstructions *bh dh gh* (posited by Curtius, f
KZ 2. 321) and *ph th kh* is doubtful.[1] Sounds of this type (also *mh
nh lh rh*) are very frequent in the Tibeto-Burmese group of languages,[2]
which extends far into India, but they are rare elsewhere, and entirely
lacking everywhere in Europe.   They occur also in the Dravidian and
Munda languages,[3] which occupy a large part of central and southern
India.   It is generally assumed that Indic borrowed from the latter
'cerebral' (supra-dental, point-inverted) *ṭ ḍ ḷ ṇ*, and there is a strong
probability that Indic *bh dh gh* were likewise substitutions for other
Indo-European sounds, taken over from Tibeto-Burmese and Dravidian
languages surrounding, or partly absorbed in, the Indo-European languages of India.[4]   Similarly, *ph th kh* may owe, if not their existence,
at least their continuation and spread to the prevalence of these sounds
in the native languages of India.   They occur in Sanskrit chiefly in
certain emphatic words and in borrowings from native languages, particularly in names of native animals and plants.   Besides, it seems that
p t k after *s* were inclined to become *ph th kh*,[5] but there is also a small
number of words in which these sounds occur under other conditions.[6]
It seems not unlikely that the voiceless aspirates are a remnant from
a period when pure stops and aspirated voiceless stops formed one
phoneme, that is, when the speaker, without being conscious of the
difference, used *p t k* under normal conditions and *ph th kh* under conditions of emphasis and in the neighborhood of certain sounds; this is
more or less the case in present South German.   Subsequently, most

Indo-European languages gave preference to one or the other variety of the phoneme. Only in Greek and Sanskrit both varieties came to be felt as separate sounds. In Sanskrit this was probably due to the example of the native languages. In Greek, conditions are difficult to judge as long as the pronunciation of φ θ χ is not entirely certain. According to the present standard view, these 'letters' had in Classical Greek the articulation of aspirated voiceless stops, so that for Greek as well as for Sanskrit a double system of voiceless stops, pure and aspirated, would have to be assumed. In this, Greek would stand alone among European languages. The arguments for the standard view are weighty, but hardly quite convincing. The inscriptional spellings are ambiguous, and the phonetic arguments insufficient. At any rate, in Christian times Greek φ θ χ were surely pronounced as voiceless spirants, and they *may* have been that since Indo-European times.[7]

To reconcile the treatment of the sonant aspirates in Italic and Greek, it used to be assumed (since Ascoli, KZ 18. 417) that Italic and Greek formed one linguistic group for some time after the separation from the Indo-European stock, and that in this group *bh dh gh* became *ph th kh*, but nothing in the general phonetic character of these languages—their phonetic basis and drift—can be adduced to support this argument. On the whole, it seems that reconstructed IE *bh dh gh* are essentially a remnant from that period of linguistic science, when Sanskrit was considered the fundamental language of the Indo-European group. The claim that the Sanskrit vowel system was practically identical with Indo-European vocalism has been given up since 1878 (cf. **8**), but the Indo-European consonant system as it appears in our standard grammars is still patterned on that of Sanskrit and differs greatly from the 'phonetic pattern' (Sapir, Language 57) of all other Indo-European languages.

g   If these sounds were not sonant aspirates, they almost *must* have been spirants. It is nearly unthinkable that voiced spirants became voiceless spirants in Italic (and possibly in Greek); therefore, only voiceless spirants are left, so that Italic would have preserved the original Indo-European articulation. It would have to be assumed that these spirants were 'lenes' rather than 'fortes' (like *f* in Ger. *Ofen*, rather than in *offen*); this would account for their inclination to become voiced in most IE languages; in fact, it is quite probable that these 'lenes' really were phonemes that could be either voiced or voiceless, perhaps according to emphasis or surrounding sounds. This would be comparable to the treatment of voiceless spirants in English, Norse, and some West Middle German dialects: Gmc. *f þ* between vowels were voiced since OE and ON times (**27**); *f* in words like *Käfer, elf* = [kɛvər, ɛləvə] is voiced, e.g. in Hessian. Our IE *bh dh gh* should therefore be considered phonemes that could appear either as voiceless lenes spirants, or as voiced spirants.

The following sections will show that we arrive at complete phonetic **h** consistency, if we reconstruct the following Indo-European modes of articulation:

(1) *p t k*, the pure voiceless stops, and *ph th kh*, the aspirated voiceless stops, as transitory variations of the same phonemes.

(2) *b d g*, the voiced stops.

(3) Voiceless spirants in lenis pronunciation. For these, the signs *φ θ χ* instead of *bh dh gh* were suggested by the author in Mod. Phil. 16. 102:

*φer-, *φrātēr, *neφos; *θē-, *ruθəro-, *meθyo-, *χeim-, *χeu-, *weχ, *χenχ, *χosti-, *χorto-, *steiχ-, *χwermo-, *χwen-, *(s)neiχw-, instead of **bher-, *bhrātēr, *nebhos, *dhē-, *rudhəro-, *medhyo-, *ĝheim-, *ĝheu-, *weĝh-, *ĝhengh-, *ghosti-, *ghorto-, *steigh-, *ghwermo-, *ghwen-, *(s)neighw-* (**qᵘhermo-, *qᵘhen-, *(s)neiqᵘh-*).

Whoever prefers to consider Indo-European reconstructions as for- **i** mulae pure and simple, without any phonetic connotation, may treat these symbols merely as a simplified way of writing *bh dh gh*; certainly, it is simpler to write **χwermo-* than **ghwermo-*, or, with Brugmann's symbols: **qᵘhermo-*. If IE *φ θ χ* are accepted as the original sounds, we find the following: Certainly in Italic, and possibly in Greek, they remained voiceless spirants. Everywhere else they became voiced spirants. This is the condition that we find in primitive Germanic (**18**), and that we may safely assume for prehistoric Celtic, Slavic, Iranian, etc. In all of these languages, they became in time partly or entirely voiced stops (**24**). In Sanskrit, however, under the influence of native languages, voiced aspirates were substituted.

Detailed arguments for this view are given by Prokosch, Die indogermanische "Media Aspirata", Mod. Phil. 15–18 (1918–20).[8] However, for the sake of conformity with all standard grammars and etymological dictionaries, the established symbols *bh dh gh* are used in the present book.

11. Places of Articulation. According to the place of contact in the mouth, we distinguish the following groups of Indo-European consonants:

(1) The Labials, *p b bh*. Under ordinary circumstances, all three **a**

were bilabial (formed with both lips), but *bh* later became labio-dental *f* (formed by contact of lower lip and upper teeth) in Italic (medially, *b* in Latin), and, much later, also in Germanic, in those dialects and positions in which it remained a spirant: E. *give*, but Ger. *geben* < **ghebh-*; cf. **24**. In Greek, *φ* remained bilabial.

b (2) The Dentals, *t d dh*. Whether these were pure dentals, as in French, or alveolars, as in German, or even post-alveolars, as in American English, can hardly be ascertained. In Italic, *dh* became *f* (medially, *b* or *d* in Latin: *verbum, medius* < **wṛdhom, *medhjos*), see **10 e**. The same transition is frequently noticed in individual English pronunciations, like *fimble* for *thimble*; Russian has regularly *f* for *θ* in borrowings from Greek: *Marfa, Feodor, fita* for Μάρθα, Θεόδωρος, θῆτα.

(3) The 'Gutturals'. This somewhat inept term is generally used in
c comparative grammars to designate consonants that are articulated either against the hard or the soft palate, and it may well serve as a collective term of expedience. The stops *k g* and the corresponding spirants generally, though by no means always, approach the articulation of neighboring sounds. Thus, *k* in *king, car, cool*, and *g* in *give, garden, good*, are articulated at the front, middle, or back palate respectively. Ger. *ch* is a pre-palatal spirant [ç], in *ich, echt*, but a velar (post-velar) spirant [χ], in *Dach, doch, Tuch*; North German intervocalic *g* is palatal [j], in *liegen, legen*, but velar [ʒ], in *lagen, bogen, trugen*. Indo-European comparative grammar distinguishes Palatals (= Pre-Palatals), Velars, and Labio-Velars. The latter are back-palate sounds, which are accompanied by lip-rounding—a frequently observed tendency of articulation in sounds that are pronounced by raising the back of the tongue, such as the typical *u*- and *o*-vowels. Authorities differ greatly as to the transcription of these sounds. The most widely accepted symbols are those used by Karl Brugmann (in his Grundriss der vergleichenden Grammatik der indogermanischen Sprachen, Kurze vergleichende Grammatik der indogermanischen Sprachen, etc.):

Palatals: *k̂ ĝ ĝh*—**k̂ṃtóm, *ĝénos-, *ĝheim-*
Velars: *q g̒ qh*—**qǝp-, *steq-, *qhosti-*
Labio-Velars: *qᵘ g̒ᵘ qᵘh*—**seqᵘ, *qᵘem-, *qᵘhermo-*.

The letters *k g gh* are, in Brugmann's transcription, reserved for those cases where it is uncertain which articulation prevailed in a given Indo-European word, such as OSl. *gǫsь*, Lith. *žąsìs* 'goose' = **ghǝns-* or **ĝhǝns-?*; Lith. *akmuõ*, Sk. *aśman-* = **aqmen-* or **ak̂men-?*; Gk.

ζυγόν, Sk. *yugám* = *juǥom or juǥ^{u}om? Cf. Brugmann, KG 233, Note 3 and 244, Note; Hirt, Idg. Gr. 1. 239 f.

For the purposes of Germanic grammar, the distinction between palatals and velars is immaterial (see below). Labio-velars, however, must be indicated as such whenever there is evidence of the existence of the labial element (lip-rounding). H. Hirt uses in his Handbuch des Urgermanischen *k g gh* for palatals and velars (in his Indogermanische Grammatik he uses *k' g' g'h* for palatals, and *k g gh* for velars), but *k^w g^w gh^w* for labio-velars. Streitberg, UG and Loewe, GS use *k̂ k, ĝ g, ĝh gh g^{v}h*; Bethge, Altg. Dialekte, *k̂ k q, ĝ g ǥ, ĝh gh q̇h*. This book transcribes ordinarily palatals and velars by *k g gh* and labio-velars by *kw gw ghw*. But where Germanic must be compared with Eastern Indo-European languages, palatal articulation will be indicated by *k̂ ĝ ĝh*. This is especially necessary in those cases where Gmc. ƕw does not go back to labio-velar *kw* (Brugmann's q^u), but to a palatal followed by an independent labial spirant, as in Sk. *aśva-*, Go. *aihva-* 'horse', from IE *ek̂wo-, not *ekwo- (*eq^{u}o-). The transliteration *kw* is preferable to *q* or q^u, because in Germanic as elsewhere, the labial element disappears under certain conditions (23), and the remaining velar does not differ in any way from a pure velar or a palatal. Cf. L. *sequor—secutus*, Go. *saihvan*, OHG *sehan*—OE (Anglian) *sǣgon*: IE *sekw-; L. *veniō*, Go. *qiman*, OHG *queman, koman*: IE *gwem-, gwm̥-; Gk. ὀμφή 'voice', Go. *siggwan*, OHG *singan*.

KENTUM and SATEM. As stated in section 2, it is customary to distinguish two groups of Indo-European languages according to the treatment of the Indo-European palatals: they became sibilants in the eastern group, but appear as velars in the western group. But the labio-velars also exhibit a difference of articulation in the two groups: In kentum languages they are apt to preserve the labial element—in fact, under certain conditions they even lose the velar articulation; in satem languages, the labial glide always disappears, so that there is no distinction between velars and labio-velars. Thus there is no individual IE language (except perhaps Albanian? Pedersen, KZ 36. 291 ff.) that possesses all three series of gutturals. The kentum languages have palato-velars and labio-velars. The satem languages have sibilants (or, partly, other spirants, such as Sk. *h*) and velars. The following table represents the fundamental developments in the two groups, omitting secondary changes, such as the Indic and Slavic palatalization of velars, Verner's Law in Germanic, etc.

IE	Sk.	OSl.	Lith.	Gk.	L.	Gmc.
$\hat{k}$ $\hat{g}$ $\hat{g}h$	ś j h	s z z	š ž ž	} κ γ χ	k g h (g)	ƕ k z
k g gh	} k g gh	k g g	k g g	{ π β φ[1]		
kw gw ghw				{ τ δ θ	qu (c) v f	ƕw kw zw
				{ κ γ χ		

[1] π β φ before α o ω, τ δ ϑ before ε η ι, κ γ χ before and after υ; *kwel-/kwol-/kwl-'turn': τέλος 'goal' (turning-point), πόλος 'axis, pole', κύκλος 'wheel' ('turn-turn').

$\hat{k}$: *ḱm̥tóm—Sk. śatám, Av. satəm, OSl. sъto, Lith. šим̃tas—Gk. ἑκατόν, L. centum

$\hat{g}$: *ĝen-, *ĝnō- 'know'—Sk. jān-, OSl. znati, Lith. žinóti, Gk. γι-γνώ-σκω, L. co-gnō-sco

$\hat{g}h$: ĝheim- 'winter, storm'—Sk. hima, OSl. zima, Lith. žiema, Gk. χειμών, L. hiems

k: *kr(e)w-—Sk. kravíš- 'flesh', OSl. krъvь 'blood', Gk. κρέας 'meat', L. cruor 'blood'

g: Sk. sthagáyati 'covers', OSl. o-stegъ 'dress', Gk. στέγω L. tegō 'cover'

gh: Sk. -stighnóti 'climbs', OSl. stignǫ 'come', Gk. στείχω 'march', L. ve-stīgium 'track'

kw: Sk. kas 'who', OSl. kъ-to 'who', Gk. πόϑεν 'whence', L. quod 'what'

gw: Sk. gácchati 'goes', Gk. βαίνω 'go', L. veniō 'come'

ghw: Sk. ghnánti 'they kill', Lith. genù, OSl. ženǫ 'drive', Gk. ϑείνω 'kill', φόνος 'murder', L. of-fendō 'wound'.

In spite of this far-reaching and significant contrast in the treatment of 'gutturals', the assumption of these two branches of Indo-European languages merely on this phonological basis hardly seems justified. Phonetically, there need not be any fundamental difference between the change from IE *ḱm̥tóm to Av. satəm and the change from L. centum to Fr. cent. There merely exists the formal difference that in the latter case we know that the transition was due to the influence of the following front vowel, while in the former case we assume that in Indo-European certain k- g-sounds had palatal articulation, regardless of their surroundings, and that in the eastern group they generally became sibilants. But it is entirely possible that the kentum-satem change was also essentially an assimilation, although there is little chance that we shall be able to reach back far enough into prehistoric times to prove it. The word for '100', for instance, had no vowel in the first syllable in the form that we can reconstruct. But it is more than probable that different case forms of this word originally had different vowel grades: *kṃt-, *kemt-, *komt-. In certain languages, then, the consonant belonging to the front-vowel form (k̂) prevailed in all forms of the word, while in others the velar or back-velar articulation was carried through. Roughly speaking, the palatal articulation prevailed mainly in the eastern half of the Indo-European territory, but Albanian, a satem language, is farther west than Greek, while Tocharian, in the extreme east, is a kentum language. Phonetically, it is not at all surprising that languages which in an alternative gave preference to palatal, rather than velar, articulation, should also be inclined to give up the labial glide of the labio-velars, although this is rather frequent in the western group too (23). Therefore, only so much is safe to say, that the various 'guttural' sounds are inclined to be fronted in a number of Indo-European languages, and that in languages that have this tendency the labial glide disappears. In historical times, French and other Romance languages offer perfect parallels. On the one hand, *kentum* became [sã], and on the other, *quod* became [kə].

12. The Sibilant s was frequent in Indo-European: *seks, *septḿ   **a** '6, 7': Sk. ṣaṣ, saptá, L. sex, septem; *stā- 'stand': Sk. sthā-, L. stāre.

Before voiced consonants it became voiced: *ni-sd-o- > *nizdo- = L. nīdus, E. nest; *o-sd-o = Gk. ὄζος = [ozdos], Ger. A st.

In Greek, s disappeared between vowels, and became h or disappeared initially before vowels, semivowels, nasals, and liquids; in Latin, it was voiced, and then became r, between vowels ('Rhotacism'): Gk. ἕξ, ἑπτά = L. sex, septem; Sk. janasas = Gk. *γένεσος > γένους, L. generis.

'Movable s'. Numerous words begin in some IE languages with s + consonant,   **b** and in others without s; sometimes the same variation occurs within the same language: L. taurus, Gk. ταῦρος E. steer; Gk. στέγος, τέγος 'roof', L. tegō 'cover', toga 'covering, cloak', E. thatch; Go. skaidan 'separate', L. caedō 'cut'. The variation is not fully explained, but probably in many cases, s is the remnant of a prefix or preposition; in other cases, an original s- may have been lost in sentence connection (sandhi).

13. Sonorous Consonants. The 'liquids', l r, and the 'nasals', m n (ŋ)   **a** are consonants by articulation, since the air passage through the mouth is obstructed. The liquids are fundamentally spirants, the nasals are stops. But in their pronunciation the air passes through a comparatively large resonance chamber, in the mouth in the case of the liquids, and in the nasal cavity in the case of the nasals. This produces the acoustic effect of vowel resonance, so that these sounds may be said to occupy a position between consonants and vowels. They may have vocalic (syllabic) function, as in E. *middleman* = [middlmæn], Ger. *handeln*, Czech *prst, čtvrtku, vlk.*

Syllabic function of these sounds (Brugmann's liquida sonans and nasalis sonans) is in IE grammar usually indicated by a circle, less frequently a dot, below the letter: *l̥ r̥ m̥ n̥*. Sanskritists generally use the dot, as in the name of the language, *sãskr̥ta*. But it is hardly necessary to use any diacritic mark at all, as Czech spelling indicates. They represent in all cases the reduced form of diphthongs (35), and it is rather an expedient formula than an unequivocal fact, if our reconstruction assumes syllabic consonants rather than liquids or nasals accompanied by reduced vowels. The distinction is merely one between variations of the same phoneme, as in Ger. *rechnete, handelte* = [reçntə, handltə] or [reçnətə, handəltə]. With the exception of *l r* in Sanskrit, where both appear as *r̥*, all IE languages show a vowel before them, more rarely after them. Sanskrit has *r̥, a (am an)*; Greek, *al ar, a (am an)*; Latin, *ol or em en*; Germanic, *ul ur um un*. Cf. **35, 39**.

b   A. In consonantic function:

L. *lūcus* 'forest clearing', Gk. λευκός 'white', Sk. *lókas* 'open space'

L. *linquo*, Gk. λείπω, Sk. *rinákti* 'leave'

L. *ruber*, Gk. ἐρυθρός, Sk. *rudhirá-* 'red'

L. *vir*, Lith. *výras*, Sk. *vīras* 'man'

L. *māter*, Gk. μήτηρ, Sk. *mãtā* 'mother'

L. *magnus*, Gk. μέγας, Sk. *máhant* 'great'

L. *novem*, Gk. ἐννέα, Sk. *náva* 'nine'

L. *(is-)tum*, Gk. τόν < *τομ, Sk. *tam*, pronominal acc. sg. masc.

c   B. In vocalic function:

l̥: Lith. *vìlkas*, Sk. *vŕkas*, OSl. *vlьkъ*, Czech *vlk*, Go. *wulfs* 'wolf'

r̥: L. *vorsus*, Sk. *vr̥tāná-*, Go. *waurþans* < *wurðanaz, past part. of **wert-*

m̥: L. *centum*, Gk. ἑκατόν, Sk. *śatám*, Go. *hund*, Lith. *šimtas*

n̥: L. *in-* < *en-*, Gk. ἀ- (ἀν-), Sk. *a- (an-)*, Gmc. *un-*, negative prefix.

The velar nasal, *ŋ*, did not exist as an independent phoneme, but only by assimilation to a following *k g*; likewise, *m* is the regular form of the nasal before labials, and *n* before dentals: **seŋχw-* (= **seŋghw-*): Go. *siggwan* = [siŋgwan] 'sing'; Gk. ὀμφή < *soŋχwã 'voice'; **km̥tóm*: L. *centum* (but Lith. *šim̃tas*).

14. The Semi-Vowels, *j w*, are essentially vowels as to articulation, since the air passage is, in general, somewhat narrowed, but not sufficiently obstructed to characterize them as spirants. As reduced forms of diphthongs, they appear as pure vowels, *i u* (39); on the other hand, they tend to be narrowed to spirants or even stops, as in *jugóm 'yoke', Gk. ζυγόν = [dzugon]; Sk. dváyōs 'of two', ON tueggia; Gmc. *trewa-, ON tryggr (33 d). The bilabial semi-vowel (E. w) tends to become a labio-dental spirant, v, (cf. E. water: Ger. Wasser). To indicate this double character, the letters i̯ u̯ are frequently used, but there are advantages in the use, in reconstructed IE forms, of j w for true consonantic function, and of i u for pure vowels or diphthongal glides. (However, j v w are used in this book as everywhere, if historical spelling requires it.)

j: L. iugum, Gk. ζυγόν, Sk. yugám, Go. juk 'yoke'
w: L. vestis 'dress', Gk. (verb) ἕννυμι < ϝεσνυμι, Sk. vastra, Go. (verb) wasjan 'dress'.

THE GERMANIC CONSONANTS

A. The Consonant Shift

15. Lautverschiebung 'Sound Shift' was the term coined by Jacob Grimm in the second edition of his Deutsche Grammatik (1822) to **a** designate a very large complex of interrelated phonetic changes through which the Germanic system of stops and spirants developed from the corresponding IE consonants. It is probably the most comprehensive group of sound changes that has been observed in the history of any language. But the individual changes are of such homogeneous character that finally the Germanic consonants constitute practically the same 'phonetic pattern' as the Indo-European consonants, especially if traditional bh dh gh are interpreted as voiceless spirants. Every single genuine consonant (cf. **13, 14**) had altered its mode of articulation, but the fundamental types of the Indo-European and the Germanic consonants are the same.

Rarely in German books, but rather frequently in English and French **b** works, the whole complex of the consonant shift is termed 'Grimm's Law', 'loi de Grimm'. Recently protests have been voiced against that term (e.g. by Jespersen, Language 43, and by R. C. Boer, Oergermaansch Handboek 116). The substance of the facts has been summed up by Collitz, A Century of Grimm's Law, Language 2. 174 ff.:

> Grimm was by no means the first scholar to observe that in the Germanic languages consonants are often at variance with those of the cognate languages. Such discrepancies were especially noted and commented upon by students of Gothic from Franciscus Junius to the Swedish Professor Johannes ab Ihre and James Jamieson, the author of a well-known Etymological Dictionary of the Scottish

language. Yet for a long time observations to this effect remained
isolated, and amounted to little more than a mixture of truth and
errors.

Matters, however, took a different turn when, two years after
the publication of Bopp's Conjugationssystem der Sanskritsprache,
the great Danish philologist Rasmus Rask brought out his prize
essay on the origin of the Icelandic language. Like Franz Bopp,
Rask is one of the pioneers in the field of Indo-European philology.
He began to investigate in a systematic manner the changes which
the Germanic consonants had undergone in comparison with those
of the cognate languages, and arrived at results that have proved—
with few exceptions—reliable. His results are of great interest
to us, the more so, as they have undoubtedly exercised considerable influence on Jacob Grimm's work. Grimm became acquainted
with Rask's essay when he had nearly finished seeing the first edition of the first volume of his Grammar through the press. He
hastened in the preface to that volume to voice his obligations to
the author of the essay in the broadest and warmest possible manner. 'Meanwhile Rask's excellent prize-essay has furnished far-
reaching information as to the many points of contact existing
between the Germanic and the Lettic, Slavic, Greek, and Latin
languages.' As far as the mere facts of the first Germanic shift
are concerned, Rask, no doubt, was acquainted with most of the
single paragraphs of Grimm's Law, and we may readily understand
how the impression could obtain here and there that the law had
actually been discovered by him. Nothing, however, could be a
greater injustice to Grimm. Granted that Rask observed several
consonant changes that play an important part in the shifting, we
cannot possibly speak of Rask's Law in the singular. . . . With
Grimm the stress lies decidedly on the inner reason connecting
the various parts of the shifting. He felt able to set forth a single
law incorporating all its phases. His notion of such a law was
based on the observation of a threefold uniformity:

c   (1) the second or High German shifting proceeds in general on
the same lines as the first or common Germanic shifting;

(2) one and the same general formula is applicable to the various
sets of consonants, whether they be labials or dentals or gutturals;

(3) the shifting proves to imply a fixed sequence of the principal
forms of the shifting, based on the arrangement of the three classes
of consonants involved in the order of media, tenuis, aspirata. . . .

Such then is Grimm's Law: not merely a set of observations on consonant changes resulting from the first Germanic shifting, but rather a general theory as to the mutual relation between certain consonant changes, occurring as a rule in combination with each other. However much Grimm may be indebted for details to his predecessors, the law remains his own, and is something very different from what others had noticed beforehand.

16. The Fundamental Principle. The articulation of consonants is **a** conditioned by two counteracting factors: The current of air issuing from the lungs, and the tension of the vocal cords and the muscles of the mouth (tongue, lips, velum, cheeks) intercepting the flow. In the case of stops, the breath is completely checked in the mouth—by the lips in the case of labials (*p b*), by the tongue in the case of dentals and 'gutturals' (*t d; k g*). In the case of voiced sounds it is checked in the glottis, by the close approach of the vibrating vocal cords. In some languages, e.g. French, the voiceless stops, *p t k*, are frequently pronounced with simultaneous closing of the glottis (glottal stop), so that the audible articulation is due to the release of the muscular tension of tongue or lips. We cannot know whether the articulation of IE voiceless stops was originally the same in all parts of the Indo-European territory. It is quite possible that some of the dialects had the glottal stop articulation, but we cannot postulate this for general Indo-European, in spite of Meillet, Caractères généraux des langues germaniques 36 f. For Germanic, we must assume open-glottis articulation, and it matters little whether it represented there an original type or a later development.

In the case of spirants, the oral occlusion is not complete, so that the **b** flow of air is not stopped, but only impeded, to the extent of causing an audible friction between the lips (or lower lip and upper teeth) or between the tongue and the teeth, or the tongue and the roof of the mouth. Again, before passing through the mouth the breath may have been partly intercepted by the vibrating vocal cords. Thus, there result either the voiceless spirants *f þ ħ*, or the voiced spirants *ƀ ð ʒ*.

FORTES AND LENES. Both stops and spirants vary as to intensity **c** of expiration and muscle tension. Generally speaking, voiceless stops and spirants tend to be fortes, i.e., they are articulated with greater force, and voiced sounds are generally lenes, i.e., the speech organs are relatively relaxed. But a voiced sound can be (relatively) fortis, e.g., *bb gg* in Ger. *Ebbe, Flagge*, while a voiceless consonant is sometimes lenis, as South German *b d g*. In general, it is not necessary to indicate the difference, but where this is required, the following symbols may be used:

p t k for pure voiceless fortes stops, as in French *pas, tasse, cas.*

p' t' k' for the corresponding aspirated sounds, as in North German *Pass, Tasse, Kasse.*

ḅ ḍ g̊ for voiceless lenes, as in South German *bat, da, gar.*

f þ ħ for voiceless fortes spirants, as in Ger. *offen*, E. *thin*, Ger. *machen.*

φ θ χ for voiceless lenes spirants, as in Ger. *Ofen*, E. *cloth*, North German *sagt.*

b d g are the voiced stops, as in E. *bid, did, give.*

ƀ ð ʒ are the voiced spirants, as in Bav. *aber* (Span. *deber*), E. *then*, North German *Tage.*

χ ʒ are really the symbols for velar sounds, but generally may also be used for the corresponding palatals, since, in the Germanic languages, the two groups practically amount to one phoneme. But where necessary, palatal articulation may be indicated by *ç j*: Ger. *nicht, liegen* = [niçt, liːjən] (but *Nacht* = [naχt], *lagen* = [laːʒən].

d All Indo-European stops and spirants pass through a consistent system of changes during the early history of the Germanic languages. In concrete terms, defining merely the actual result, its general course may be described as follows:

In the case of *stops*, the breath is *released.*

In the case of *spirants*, the breath is *checked.*

Both release and check follow the direction of the breath passing from the lungs, i.e., either process takes place first in the glottis, then in the mouth, as far as this is possible. An occlusion is *opened* in the case of stops, and a passage is *closed* in the case of spirants, but of course an open glottis cannot become opened, and a closed mouth cannot become closed. For instance: *t* is a voiceless stop. The glottis is open. Consequently the breath is released between tongue and teeth, and *þ* results. This being a voiceless spirant, the open glottis is closed, so that *þ* changes to *ð*. This voiced spirant requires an occlusion in the mouth, thus changing to *d*, a voiced stop, which then, by release in the glottis, becomes *t*. Doubtless we must assume certain intermediate steps as phonetic probabilities. Thus, *t* was probably in Pre-Germanic, as elsewhere in Indo-European, a pure stop, and at first the air pressure increased so that the aspirate *t'* resulted as a transition between *t* and *þ*; possibly there existed for a certain time, and in certain positions, a further transitional step, the 'affricate' *tþ*. *þ* was probably originally a fortis, being articulated with that force of expiration and counteracting muscle tension that had led to its formation. But this double maximum of intensity was transitory; the sound became lenis. Between *d* and *t* we are bound to assume as a phonetic interpolation the voiceless lenis $ḍ$.   Therefore, the complete series of these changes is the following:

$$t > t' > þ > \theta > ð > d > ḍ > t$$

Grimm's description of the process is generally represented in this **e** form:

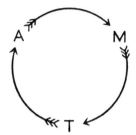

M = media ($b\ d\ g$)

T = tenuis ($p\ t\ k$)

A = aspirata; in this term Grimm includes both the Gmc. spirants $f\ þ\ ?$ and the Gk. 'aspirates', as representatives of what are now termed IE $bh\ dh\ gh$. This nomenclature, while phonetically inaccurate, is natural enough in a chapter that is inscribed 'Lehre von den Buchstaben', and in point of fact there is a certain practical simplicity in the application of this diagram.

The following diagram may, in a sense, be called an adaptation of **f** Grimm's diagram to phonetic facts, but it is correct only if the IE 'sonant aspirates' are assumed to have been voiceless spirants in lenis articulation (the arrows denote the direction of the changes; the figures correspond to the arrangement of the following table):

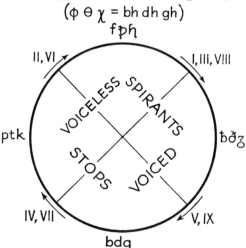

Anticipating sections **18–21** and **24–27,** we obtain on the basis of this diagram, the following chronology of the consonant shift, examples being taken from the dentals, since their shift is carried farthest:

I. Pre-Germanic: θ (= dh) > ð—Gk. θύρα: Gmc. *ðurā- (E. *door*)

II. Germanic: B.C., t > t' > þ—L. *tres*: Go. *þreis*, E. *three*

III. " A.D., 'Verner's Law'—þ > ð—Gk. πατήρ: Go. *faðar* (spelled *fadar*)

IV. " A.D., d > t—L. *edō*: Go. *itan*, E. *eat*

V. Intermediate: ð > d—Gmc. *ðurā- > Go. *daur*; Go. *faðar*: OE *fæder*

VI. High German: t > z—Go. *itan*: OHG *ezzan*

VII. " " d > $ḑ$ (> t)—Go. *daur*: OHG *dor, tor*

VIII. 'German': þ > ð—Go. *þreis*: OHG *dhrī* (Isidor)

IX. " ð > d—OHG *dhrī* > *drī*.

a   **17. The Cause and Time** of the Consonant Shift are moot questions but it is probable that they bear a relation to each other.   It is hardly by mere accident that this strikingly comprehensive and homogeneous group of phonetic changes is contemporaneous with what may justly be called the most momentous national movement in history: the Germanic Migrations ('Völkerwanderung'), which began at least as early as the second century B.C., perhaps much earlier, and ended during the sixth century of our Era, so that its whole duration was not much less than a millennium.

The estimates of the *Time* of the consonant shift show a wide
b difference of opinion.   Kluge represents one extreme (Urgermanisch 52[3]): the second pre-Christian millennium, and Much the other (Btr. 17. 63): the third century B.C.   Between these two estimates stands that of Bethge, Altg. Dial. 176: between 1000 and 400 B.C.   This view is approved by H. Meyer, ZfdA. 45. 126, and Kossinna, IF 4. 49, who fix the date at about 400.   The only concrete arguments consist in loan words and proper names, but the dating of the former is generally uncertain, and the possibility of sound substitution exists in both types of words.   E.g., names like *Cimbri, Teutones*, with L. *c t* for Germanic spirants, do not indicate that the consonant shift had not yet taken place at the time of the Cimbrian migration; rather, these consonants are either Roman or Celtic substitutions.   Cf. Hirt, Indogermanen, 2. 616; Kluge, l. c. 51 f.; Hirt, HU 1. 101 ff.   Apparently the best attempt at a solution is a pragmatic hypothesis that is in keeping with phonetic as well as historical facts, but any such construction must necessarily be uncertain.   In that sense, an analysis of the chronology above leads to the following conclusions:

Step I: IE *bh dh gh* (= $\varphi \, \theta \, \chi$) became *b d g* in all IE languages except c
Italic, Hellenic, and Indic.   In Germanic, where the transition is incom-
plete, an intermediate stage *b ð ʒ* is certain, in the other languages that
have *b d g*, such a phonetic interpolation is very probable.   This transition is such a frequent and obvious physiological process that it does
not entitle us to consider the *b- d- g*-languages as a prehistoric unit.
The change occurred independently, but it is not a part of the Germanic
consonant shift proper, although it must be included in its consideration.   It must be ascribed to 'Pre-Germanic' times, between the separation of the Germanic from the Italic group and the actual consonant
shift, and therefore, at a random estimate, may be said to have taken
place around 1000 B.C.

Steps II and IV: The changes *p t k* > *f þ ħ* and *b d g* > *p t k* represent a surplus of expiration over the counteracting muscle tension,
either in the mouth, or in the glottis.   They seem to be connected, both
as an effect and as a contributing cause, with the Pre-Germanic accent
change: the IE accent was musical (pitch accent), and the Gmc. accent
was dynamic (stress accent) (**43**).   This view was first expressed by
Hirt, Indogermanen, 2. 616, and repeated by R. C. Boer, Neophilologus
1. 103, and Oerg. Hb. 136 f.   The change of *p t k* to *f þ ħ* cannot have
been a sudden transition, but implied a gradual strengthening of expiration that extended over generations, perhaps over centuries.   If we
try to indicate, not its beginning, but its completion, Much's date, the
third century B.C., would seem acceptable.   The unvoicing of the
voiced stops must have been still later; here at least we have fairly
definite evidence from loan words: words like Go. *Krēks* (L. *Graecus*),
Go. *paida* (Gk. βαίτη), Go. *hanaps* (L. *cannabis*), whatever the way of
borrowing may have been, indicate that the transition was not completed before the end of the pre-Christian Era.   Cf. Hirt, HU 1. 102.

Step III: Verner's Law (**20**) must have been almost contemporaneous
with Step IV and may be ascribed to the first generations of the Christian Era—an entirely tentative estimate.

Steps V to IX occurred during the individual history of the several
Germanic languages, although at least Step V started in Germanic
times.   In these changes the following facts of relative chronology
become clearly evident:

(1) The 'Intermediate Shift', i.e., the change from Prim. Gmc. *b ð ʒ*
to *b d g*, took place sooner in initial than in medial or final position.
This change implies an increase in muscular tension, which normally
is greater initially than medially.   Some Romance languages exhibit
a corresponding change in the opposite direction, from stop to spirant.

Go. [siƀun] is the earlier form, and OHG *sibun* the later one, but L. *debēre* became [deƀer] in Spanish, *devoir* in French. Prim. Gmc. *ƀerana*- yielded Go. *bairan*, and *b* in L. *bonus* remained *b* in Standard French, Spanish, Italian. In both groups, then, the stop is more apt to prevail in initial position, the spirant medially, although the Romance languages change the medial stop to a spirant, Germanic the medial spirant to a stop.

The recognition of the Germanic voiced spirants is due to Braune, Btr. 1. 1 ff. (Zur Kenntnis des Fränkischen und zur hochdeutschen Lautverschiebung). The view of Sweet, Meillet, Huchon, that Germanic had voiced stops, which became spirants medially and finally, is clearly wrong.

(2) In the 'High German Shift', *p t k* became spirants in medial or final position, but affricates (*pf ts kh*) in initial or post-consonantal position: E. *open, eat, make* = HG *offen, essen, machen,* but *pound, ten, corn* = *Pfund, zehn* [tse:n], Early *UG khorn* (Standard German *Korn*). The surplus of expiration over tension overcame the occlusion more completely after vowels, where the tension was weaker.

(3) In all phases of the Intermediate and High German Shifts *dentals* change first and most completely, *labials* later and less, and *velars* last and least. This is particularly marked in the High German Shift of *b d g* to *p t k*. Everywhere in Upper German, *d* became *t*, and this change extended also over the larger part of Middle German; the changes *b > p* and *g > k* occurred only in Upper German, but the former was much more far-reaching than the latter. Phonetically, this seems to mean that the ratio of change is proportional to the relative agility of the articulating organs: the tip of the tongue is the most agile, the back of the tongue and the velum are the most inert of the three articulating organs. It is not quite impossible that the relative frequency of sounds may also have played a part, at least in the case of the dentals, which are the most frequent among consonants, but on the other hand, velars are more frequent than labials, which speaks against that assumption.

d   *Residuary Forms* ('Restwörter'). In general, phonetic laws are carried through 'without exceptions' (cf. **9**), but phonetic laws are limited in their duration. For instance, in Greek intervocalic *s* disappeared: *γενεσος > γένους*. Later, intervocalic *t* became *s* under certain conditions, and this new *s* remained: *λυτις > λύσις*. In Germanic as well as in other languages it happened occasionally that a phonetic law came to a standstill before it had covered the entire vocabulary of the language. Especially connectives and other words of relatively neutral semantic contents appear as such linguistic residue. Thus in Gothic, the shift from *d* to *t* did not affect the preposition *du* 'to' and the prefix *dis-* 'asunder', while **dwōi, *deḱm̥(t)* had become *twai, taihun.* In Middle Franconian, postvocalic *t* became regularly *zz*, as in **watar > wazzar;* but in pronominal forms and endings -*t* remained: *that, et, wat, allet.*

The very existence of such residuary forms ('Restwörter'; cf. Prokosch, Mod. Phil. 26. 459 f.) seems to confirm the theory that the consonant shift had its origin in the emphatic articulation of stressed words and syllables, and this is in keeping with the order described above, in which the consonants changed according to their place of articulation and their position in the word. The 'Germanic Consonant Shift' took place in pre-historic times and was virtually completed at the time to which our earliest records belong. But the 'Intermediate' and the 'High German' shifts belong to a period of expansion and migration, the main events of which are sufficiently well known to establish a parallelism with the linguistic changes of that period, and it is fairly safe to assume that the prehistoric developments would show a similar parallelism if the details could be ascertained.

The **Cause** of the consonant shift is even more problematic than its time. Jacob Grimm gave a purely psychological explanation which, in spite of the Romantic exuberance of its wording, may fundamentally contain a good deal of truth. He sees in the consonant shift (the Germanic as well as the High German) an expression of the impetuous character of the Germanic tribes during their early history. H. Meyer(-Benfey) advanced the theory that at least a large part of it was due to an increase in the force of expiration, brought about by life in mountainous districts: the Scandinavian highlands for the Germanic, the Alps for the High-German Shift. His theory has found considerable approval, expressed, for instance, by Osthoff in his lectures, and by Collitz, Language 2. 181. Lately, the 'ethnological theory' seems to be the leading view. According to this, the Germanic as well as the High German Shifts are due to language mixture between Pre-Germanic or Germanic, and Celtic, Finnic, Rhaeto-Etruscan, or the speech of an autochthonous population of North-Central Europe.

In the author's opinion, H. Meyer's view is not without a measure of intrinsic probability. But his factual arguments, showing similar phonetic processes among other mountain tribes, are scattered and insufficient. Moreover, his two chief postulates are highly problematic: *If* the original Germanic home was on the Scandinavian peninsula, it was not upon the high *fjällar*, but in comparatively level southern Sweden. This speaks against Meyer's explanation of the Germanic shift. As to the High German shift, Braune's assumption that it started in the Alps (see below) is a mere hypothesis without historical foundation. Should it happen to be correct, it would be difficult to understand why the Romance languages of the Western Alps, or the languages of the Caucasus or the Himalaya do not show any similar phenomena. Meyer's physiological explanation of certain parts of the consonant shift as the result of increased expiration is a valuable supplement to Grimm and Raumer, but this increase cannot have been due to life in the mountains.

The varieties of the ethnological theory are too numerous to discuss in detail. In spite of some brilliant observations (especially by Kauffmann and Naumann) all of them are weak in principle. On the one hand, voiceless stops are supposed to change to spirants under the influence of absorbed languages (none of which, as far as is known, possessed such sounds to a similar extent), and on the other, for the same reason, voiced stops became voiceless. Moreover, the very multitude of guesses is self-defeating. The phonetic basis of Finnic, e.g., differs radically from that of Celtic; about Rhaeto-Etruscan (if such a language group existed) we know very little, and about the mythical autochthonous language of North-Central Europe nothing at all. Finally, the thorough consistency of this wide complex of phonetic changes is a decisive argument against foreign influence as a determining cause. Any one of the individual steps might, by some stretch of imagination, be ascribed to such—say, the spirantization of occlusives to Celtic,[7] the unvoicing of b d g to Finnic or Rhaetian; but these influences would necessarily have acted independently of each other, and it is quite incredible that the phonetic laws resulting from these separate influences would accidentally have fallen into such a homogeneous pattern as is described in the 'Fundamental Principle', **16.**

f   The following attempt at a solution of the problem is far from adequate, since our knowledge of the historical foundations is incomplete; but it tries to avoid the worst fallacies of the geographical and ethnological theories; the historical details (based essentially on Lamprecht's Deutsche Geschichte) are given by Prokosch, Die deutsche Lautverschiebung und die Völkerwanderung, JEGPh 16. 1 ff.

(1) The Consonant Shift is one continuous process, the duration of which is approximately parallel to that of the Germanic Migration in the wider sense: it began several centuries B.C. and ended about 500 A.D. The Second or High German Shift continues or duplicates in a consistent way the phonetic processes of the Germanic Shift.

(2) The basic trend of the consonant shift developed in and near the Germanic home land: *Scadinavia*, i.e. the West Baltic Basin, and Northern Germany, between Elbe and Oder. In accordance with **7,**

Chronology and Drift, it ceased in each tribe soon after the final settlement in the new home. Accordingly, as the following sections will show, the scope of the shift in each dialect corresponds to the relative period of colonization.

(3) These two statements are based on facts and are merely descriptive of what actually took place. But what was the cause of this 'Basic Trend'? Here we can offer only a hypothetical construction. Linguistic change is largely due to imitation. Every individual departs at times or always from the average norm of speech. To an extent these personal deviations are the result of character and circumstances. Leading personalities are apt to be imitated in their manners, their dress, their speech: they set fashions.

The Germanic Migration was the result of overpopulation of comparatively infertile land, aggravated in the northwest by inundations, and possibly in the east by pressure from Slavs and other nations. Emigration brought temporary relief for some districts, but in general the necessity of emigration continued in the home land through these centuries. Every expedition required years of preparation and organization, and such continued storm and stress could not fail to develop leaders whose personalities influenced the 'behavior' of their followers. It can easily be imagined that in personalities of this type will and contents predominated over reflection and form: the influence of a Boiorix or Ariovistus upon speech as a part of behavior differed from that of a Petronius or Marcus Aurelius. Not only the consonant shift, but also the accent shift, the vowel shift, the Germanic verb system, all reflected a predominance of elements of contents over elements of form.

At any rate, the consonant shift appears to stand in chronological and causal relation to the social, economic, and emotional background of the Völkerwanderung. These chronological facts are certain (cf. **7**): East and North Germanic, the oldest branches from the point of view of settlement in new homes, show only steps I–IV and a small part of step V. West Germanic north of the Benrather Linie (**6 e**) continues step V. High German, particularly Upper German, in the most recent Germanic settlements, completes step V and adds steps VI and VII. The parallelism is too close to be accidental.

The Germanic Shift

18. The IE Spirants, $\varphi\ \theta\ \chi$ = conventional *bh dh gh*, appear in Germanic as voiced spirants, $\delta\ \eth\ \mathfrak{z}$: Step I. For their origin and transcription, cf. **10** (4). It is generally asserted that the shift *ph th kh*

$> f \, \flat \, \acute{\jmath}$ and that of *bh dh gh* $>$ *ƀ đ ʒ* are perfect phonetic parallels. This is by no means the case, in spite of the deceptive appearance of the Schriftbild. In Germanic, voiced and unvoiced sounds move in opposite directions, although the underlying 'drift' is the same. If IE *bh dh gh* had existed and had developed in accordance with the general trend, they would have become *ph th kh*—a transition that is generally, although perhaps wrongly, assumed for Hellenic and Italic, but which certainly did not take place in Germanic.

If we accept $\varphi \; \theta \; \chi$ as tentative reconstructions, we find complete consistency. In accordance with the 'Fundamental Principle' (16) the breath is checked in the glottis, and Gmc. *ƀ đ ʒ* result, exactly as later in step III. This stage is generally assumed for Primitive Germanic ('Urgermanisch'); cf. especially Braune, Btr. 1. 1 ff. But even there the transition to stops had begun, at least in gemination and after nasals: theoretical *ƀƀ đđ ʒʒ*, *mƀ nđ ŋʒ* (24) appear everywhere as *bb dd gg*, *mb nd ng*. The reason is obvious: gemination implies increased tension, and nasals are essentially stops, so that assimilation results. Probably also initial *b d* are to be ascribed to the Germanic period, although possibly some very early Runic inscriptions indicate spirantic pronunciation: *ƀarutʀ*, Björketorp = ON *brȳtr*; *đaʒaʀ*, Einag = ON *dagr*; (Noreen, Aisl. Gramm. 143).

Examples (cf. **10**, 4):

$\varphi = bh$:   **bher-*, Go. *bairan*, ON *bera*, OE OS OHG *beran*

           *bhrátēr, Go. *brōþar*, ON *brōþer*, OE *brōþor*, OS *brōđar*, OHG *bruoder*

           *nebh-, ON *nifl-* 'night', OE *nifol* 'dark', OS *neƀal*, OHG *nebul* 'fog'

$\theta = dh$:   **dhē-*, Go. *ga-dēþs*, ON *dāþ*, OE *dǽd*, OS *dād*, OHG *tāt* 'deed'

           *roudho-, Go. *rauđa-*, ON *rauþr*, OE *rēad*, OS *rōd*, OHG *rōt*

           *medhjo-, Go. *miđjis*, ON *miþr*, OE *mid*, OS *middi*, OHG *mitti*

$\chi = \hat{g}h$:   **ĝhḷtó-*, Go. *gulþ*, ON *gull*, OE *gold*, OS OHG *gold*, OSl. *zlato* 'gold'

           *ĝheu(d)-, Go. *giutan*, ON *giōta*, OE *gēotan*, OS *giotan*, OHG *giozan*

           *ĝheŋgh-, Go. *gaggan*, ON *ganga*, OE *gongan*, OS OHG *gangan*

           *weĝh-, Go. *-wigan*, ON *vega*, OE OHG *wegan*

$\chi = gh$:   *ghosti-, Go. gasts, ON gestr, OE giest, OS OHG gast
*ghorto-, Go. gards, ON garþr, OE geard, OS gard, OHG gart (garto)
*steigh-, Go. steigan, ON stīga, OE OS OHG stīgan
χw $= ghw$: *ghwṇtjā́ 'killing', ON gunnr, OHG gund- 'fight'.

NOTE: The pronunciation of b d g in the various Germanic languages is discussed in **24**. In the Gothic examples given above, ð is used for medial d in Gothic spelling, since its spirantic character is quite certain. After this, d will be used (fadar, instead of faðar).

19. The IE Voiceless Stops, p t k, became Gmc. f þ ħ, with p‘ t‘ k‘ as intermediate stage: Step II. According to **16 c** these spirants were originally fortes, but in historical times they are, relatively, lenes. This is apparent from the following facts: In Gothic they remain voiceless in all positions (broþar, wulfis 'wolf's', taihun 'ten'). In Old Norse and Old English, f and þ in voiced surroundings become voiced, which presupposes lenis articulation; in both languages, the letter f is used for f and v, and þ and ð are used indiscriminately for the voiceless and voiced spirants; cf. **27 b**: OE broþor, ON broþer = broðor, broðer are pronounced with ð, regardless of the spelling. The same is true for OS th (brothar has the sound ð), but the voiced labial is usually spelled ƀ in Old Saxon: neƀo 'nephew'. In Old High German, medial Gmc. f is spelled f or v (nefo, nevo 'nephew') and was probably voiceless, but lenis, sharply distinguished from OHG f < Gmc. p, which is generally spelled ff: offan 'open' (but ovan 'oven'). As to the development of þ in Old High German, see **27 b**. For the Gmc. voiceless velar spirant this book uses the symbol ħ, a modified h: it had originally the value of NHG ch (probably in both pronunciations, according to the preceding or following vowel), but became h or disappeared in most positions. Roman historians of the older period express it by ch: Chariowaldus, Cherusci, or c: Cimbri. In the historical dialects it is weakened to the glottal spirant in initial position (Go. harjis 'Heer'); medially and finally it tends to disappear: Go. taihun, OHG zehan, but ON tīo, OE tīen 'ten'. For details, see **27 d**. It had become voiced ʒ in Prim. Gmc. under Verner's Law (**20**), but in historical times this process was not repeated.

Examples (cf. **10, 1**):

p: *patḗr, Go. fadar, ON faþer, OE fæder, OS fadar, OHG fater
*pōd-, Go. fōtus, ON fōtr, OE OS fōt, OHG fuoz
*penkwe, Go. fimf, ON fimm, OE OS fīf, OHG fimf

t: *treies*, Go. *þreis*, ON *þrīr*, OE *þrīe*, OS *thrie*, OHG *drī*

    tū, Go. ON OE *þū*, OS *thū*, OHG *dū*

    tod, Go. *þata*, ON *þat*, OE *þæt*, OS *that*, OHG *daz*

k̂:   *k̂m̥tóm*, Go. *hund*, ON *hund(raþ)*, OE OS *hund*, OHG *hunt*

    dek̂m̥, Go. *taihun*, ON *tiō*, OE *tīen*, OS *tehan*, OHG *zehan*

    deik̂-, Go. *teihan*, ON *tiā*, OE *tēon*, OS *-tīhan*, OHG *zīhan*

k: *kən-/kōn-*, Go. *hana*, ON *hane*, OE *hana*, OS OHG *hano* 'rooster',
    L. *canō*, *ci-cōnia*

    kāro-, Go. *hōrs*, ON OE OS *hōr*, OHG *huor* 'adulterer, -y', L.
    cārus

    leuk-, Go. *liuhaþ*, OE *lēoht*, OS OHG *lioht* 'light', L. *lūc-s*

kw: *kwod*, Go. *ƕa*, ON *huat*, OE *hwæt*, OS *hwat*, OHG *hwaz*

    sekw-, Go. *saiƕan*, ON *siā*, OE *sēon*, OS OHG *sehan*

    leikw-, Go. *leiƕan*, ON *liā*, OE *-lēon*, OS OHG *līhan* 'lend', L.
    līnquō.

There is no Germanic evidence for IE aspirated voiceless stops.

NOTE: After voiceless spirants, i.e., Gmc. *f þ ƕ* and *s*, this shift did not take place, apparently because the surplus expiration was absorbed by these sounds. In a sense, we can speak of dissimilation: L. *-spiciō*, OHG *spehōn* 'spy', L. *stella*, OHG *stern(o)* 'star', L. *scindō*, Go. *skaidan* 'separate', L. *neptis*, OHG *niftila*, NHG (borrowing from Low German) *Nichte* 'niece', L. *octō*, Go. *ahtau* 'eight'. In some cases, this Gmc. spirant goes back to IE *b bh*, *g gh* before a voiceless consonant, e.g. L. *regō—rēctus*, Go. *raihts* 'right'; IE *ĝhoŋghti-*, Go. *gāhts* 'walk', IE *məghti-*, Go. *mahts* 'might'.—For words like IE *keudh-tó-*, Go. *huzd* 'hoard' cf. **28**.

a   **20. Verner's Law.**   After Step II of the Consonant Shift, Primitive Germanic, like Primitive Indo-European, had four voiceless spirants, namely, *f þ ƕ* < IE *p t k*, and *s* = IE *s*. In voiced surroundings, these tend to become voiced, *ð ð ʒ z*. The same trend is frequently found in other languages. Thus IE *bh dh* are voiceless in Umbr. *tefe, rufru*, Osc. *mefiai*, but voiced in L. *tibi, rubro, mediae*; IE *ĝenesā* > Italic *genezā* > L. *genera*. Gothic has a voiceless spirant in *brōþar, wairþan*, but the corresponding Norse and West-Germanic words show voicing: ON [brōðer, verða], OE [brōðor, weorðan]. In many instances, however, the voicing dates back to Primitive Germanic times: Go. *sibun* [sibun], *fadar* [fadar], *tigjus* [tiʒjus], OE *seofon, fæder, -tig*. The divergence itself had been recognized by Grimm, who coined the term 'Grammatischer Wechsel' (see below) for its most characteristic type. W. Braune, Btr. 1. 513–27 (1873), systematized this group of forms ('Ueber den grammatischen Wechsel in der deutschen Verbalflexion'), without, however, offering any explanation of the apparent irregularity. The rea-

son was approximately recognized by E. Sievers in 1874, who stated it in
a letter to Braune (published by H. Osthoff, Die neueste Sprachforschung
und die Erklärung des indogermanischen Ablauts 13, Heidelberg 1886),
but did not publish it.   In 1877, the Danish linguist Karl Verner found
the cause of the divergence independently and published it in KZ 23.
97 ff., under the title 'Eine Ausnahme der germanischen Lautverschiebung'.   He showed that the Germanic strong verb has voiceless spirants
in medial position in those forms where in Sanskrit the accent is on the
root, but voiced spirants, where Sanskrit has the accent on the ending:
Sk. *vártati* 'I turn', *vavárta* 'I have turned', *vavr̥timá* 'we have turned',
vartāná- 'turned' (past part.)—Gmc. *werþi∂, warþ: wur∂um, wur∂an-.*
Starting with this observation, Verner formulated the following law:
The Germanic voiceless spirants remained voiceless, if the preceding
syllable had the IE accent, but became voiced in voiced surroundings,
if the preceding syllable had been unstressed in IE times.   (Sievers:
'Im Nachlaut der indogermanisch unbetonten Silbe').   Paul (Btr. 6.
538) gave the following wording: 'Die nach Vollzug der germanischen
Lautverschiebung vorhandenen vier harten Reibelaute *h þ f s* sind ausser
in den Verbindungen *ht hs ft fs sk st sp* erweicht, wenn der nächst vor-
hergehende Sonant nicht nach der idg. Betonung den Hauptton trug.'[1]
—This is Step III of the Consonant Shift.
We find the same sound change in Modern English in such forms as
exámine, exért (with *gz*) as compared with *éxit, éxercise* (with *ks*).   In
spite of this well established parallel, the phonetic explanation is difficult.   Probably we have to assume the following: In medial and final
position, the Germanic spirants were relatively weaker than initially;
their articulation may have approached that of IE $\varphi \; \theta \; \chi$ (*bh dh gh*),
but, as in E. *exit*, it was relatively stronger at the end of a stressed
syllable than after an unstressed syllable, as in E. *exert*.   In the
latter position, the lenis spirant was readily affected by the vocal vibrations of the surrounding voiced sounds, and thereby became voiced.
In a later period, this voicing of spirants in voiced surroundings became
general, regardless of accent.   In spite of the title of Verner's article,
Verner's Law is not an exception to the Consonant Shift, but an accel-
eration of it.   (Collitz, Language 2. 177: 'The instances covered by
Verner's Law constitute an exception to Grimm's Law only in the sense
of an accelerated action of the latter, caused by the IE accent.')   The
change of voiceless to voiced spirants follows the general trend of the
Shift in accordance with the Fundamental Principle given in **16 d**.
Spirants being open consonants, an occlusion must take place; the

glottis being open, this occlusion must be formed in the glottis. After an originally unstressed syllable, the lenis development, and accordingly the voicing, took place sooner than in the relatively strong position in the transition from a stressed syllable. But gradually this voicing becomes general. Thus, Verner's Law is a typical instance of the very frequent gradual spread of a phonetic law. It starts under the most favorable conditions, but spreads until it has covered the whole field. In the second Shift and in Early English (partly late Old English, partly early Middle English) we find an apparently different, but really analogous process in the treatment of *th*. It became voiced (in voiced surroundings) in medial position without exception (*clothes, bathing*), but initially only in words which are relatively unstressed in a sentence, or which have little semantic function: *the, that, this, then, there, thou, thee, thine.* Here the whole word is 'lenis', and therefore the weak spirant is voiced; in the case of Verner's Law, the spirant was lenis because it continued the degree of strength of the preceding syllable. —Scandinavian shows a similar development, beginning in the thirteenth century: Initial *þ* appears regularly as *t* (*þing* > *ting*), but as *d* in the same type of words that have *ð* in English (*de, dem, den, det, der, du, dig, din,* etc.).

NOTE: R. C. Boer, Neophil. 1. 110, and Oerg. Hb. 123 f., ascribes Verner's Law to double accentuation in Primitive Germanic. He assumes that the syllable that had been stressed in IE times, but became unstressed through the Germanic accent change (**43**), retained higher pitch. For instance, IE *pǝtér* > Gmc. *faþǽr* > *faðǽr* would, in Germanic, have a dynamic accent of the first syllable, but higher pitch on the second syllable. Inherently, there is nothing impossible in this; we do find similar conditions in modern Swedish and Serbian. But the explanation falls short of explaining Verner's Law in the case of final consonants, as well as the analogous processes of later periods in English, Scandinavian, and Old High German (see **27**).

A similar hypothesis had been advanced by R. Gauthiot, MSL 11. 193-7; Prokosch, JEGPh. 11. 1 ff., tries to show that Verner's Law can be explained on the basis of dynamic accent. Cf. also Kip, MLN 20. 16 f.

b   CHRONOLOGY. Unless Boer's theory be accepted, Verner's Law must have preceded the Germanic accent shift (**43**). This would make the first or second century A.D. the most probable time. At that period, the separation of the Goths from the western and northern Germanic tribes was under way. Now, in Gothic, Verner's Law is much more rare than in the other Germanic languages (see below). It is commonly assumed that it had existed there to the same extent, but was 'leveled out'. But it is more probable that Hirt, HU 1.148 (cf. also 155) is right when he says 'Ich halte es für unmöglich, alles dies auf Ausgleichung zurückzuführen.' He assumes that Gothic had carried out the accent shift sooner than the other Germanic languages, so that only a comparatively small group of rather isolated words were still subject to the law. That is quite possible, and I have held a similar view for many years. The accent shift, like other phonetic laws, was a gradual process. There must have been a time when individual speakers would, in the same word, use sometimes the Germanic, sometimes the Indo-European accent. This was favorable to the development of a semiconscious differentiation between the two accent types, resulting in Verner's Law. But at approximately that time the phonetic drift in Gothic was retarded through its separation from the main stock (cf. **7** and **9**). In general, the spirant remained voiceless in words where the preceding syllable was stressed in some forms, unstressed in others. But it was voiced where the preceding syllable was unstressed throughout. Thus, Gothic has *wairþan, warþ, waurþum, waurþans*, although the root was originally unstressed in the last two forms. But Verner's Law did take effect in words like *sibun* < **septṁ, fadar* < *patér, where the suffix accent had become fixed in IE or very early Gmc. times. Of course, even so we may speak of a sort of leveling, but only in the sense that the analogy of other forms of the same word prevented the change of *waurþun* to *waurdun.——The instances of Verner's Law in Gothic are listed by F. A. Wood, Verner's Law in Gothic, 1895.

INSTANCES:
Due to later consonant changes and to peculiarities of spelling, Verner's Law **c** is not equally traceable in the several Germanic dialects. The table below shows that, in general, only Gothic, Old Saxon, and Old High German are apt to give evidence of V. L. in all four places of articulation. ON distinguished neither the labial nor the dental spirants; OE did not distinguish the labials. However, the table does not take into account some special cases, such as the change of ON *nþ* to *nn* (*finna*: Go. *finþan*) and *lþ* > *ll*, but *lð* > *ld* (*ellre*: *aldenn*); Heusler, Aisl. Elb. §159. In ON and OE *f* denotes both the voiceless and the voiced spirant, according to position, and the letters *þ* and *ð* are used interchangeably, also denoting either the voiceless or the voiced spirant, according to position (**27 b, c**). The table applies to medial or final position only.

Gmc.		Go.	ON	OE	OS	OHG
f	=	*f*	*f*	*f*	*f*	*f*
ƀ	"	*b*	*f*	*f*	ƀ	*b*
þ	"	*þ*	*þ ð*	*þ ð*	*th*	*d*
ð	"	*d*	*þ ð*	*d*	*d*	*t*
ħ	"	*h*	-	-, -*h*	*h*	*h*
з	"	*g*	*g*	*g*	*g*	*g*
s	"	*s*	*s*	*s*	*s*	*s*
z	"	*z*	*r*	*r*	*r*	*r*

In the following instances leveling, including the assumed retention of voiceless spirants in Gothic, is indicated by brackets. For a more complete list, see Streitberg, UG 127 ff., and Noreen, UL 124 ff. Cf. also **63**.

		Non-Gmc.	Go.	ON	OE	OS	OHG	
f > b	Sk.	tarpáyati	þaurban	þurfa	þurfan	thurban	durfan	'need'
	Gk.	ἑπτά	sibun	siau[1]	seofon	sibun	sibun	'7'
	L.	caput	haubiþ	hǫfoþ	hēafod	hōbid	houbit	'head'
þ > ð	Gk.	ἑκατόν	hund	hund	hund	hund	hunt	'100'
	L.	altus	alds (noun)	aldenn	eald	ald	alt	'old'
	Gk.	πατήρ	ȷadar	faþer	fæder	fadar	fater	'father'
ƕ > 3	Gk.	δεκάς	tigus	tiger	-tig	-tig	-zug	'-ty'
	L.	dūcō	[taúhans]	togenn	togen	gitogan	gizogan	'led'
	L.	cunctārī	[hāhan]	hanga	hangian	hangon	hangēn	'hang'
s > z	L.	auris	[ausō]	eyra	ēare	ōra	ōra	'ear'
	Osc.	mais	maiza	meire	māra	mēro	mēro	'more'
	L.	-ōrum	þizē	þeira	þāra	thero	dero	(gen. pl. masc.)

¹ Heusler, Aisl. Elb. §90.

d   GRAMMATICAL CHANGE is primarily the effect of the application or non-application of Verner's Law in different inflectional forms of the same word, due to the movable accent of Indo-European (**43**), but in a wider sense the term is often also applied to the alternation of Gmc. voiceless and voiced spirants in different words of like formation, or in the same word in different Gmc. languages. To the first class belongs, e.g., OE pres. *cēosan* 'choose', past part. *coren*; to the second class, on the one hand, Go. *fadar* < **pǝtḗr* against *brōþar* < **bhrā́tēr*, and on the other hand, Go. *dauþa-* against OE *dēad* 'dead'.

The following types of Grammatical Change are especially important:

(1) For the principal parts of the strong verb the standard view assumes that in all seven classes the first two forms (pres. and singular of the pret.) had in IE root accent, the other two (plural of the pret. and past part.) suffix accent. As shown in **63**, this is probably true only for the first three classes, but through analogical transfer Grammatical Change does occur, more or less sporadically, also in the fifth, sixth, and seventh classes. Gothic retains (or restores?) the voiceless spirant in the regular strong verb, but Grammatical Change is found in some forms of the preterit-presents.

INSTANCES (analogical forms are given in brackets):

I. Go.	leiþan	laiþ	[liþum]	[liþans]	'go'
ON	līþa	leiþ	liþom	liþenn	

	OE	līþan	lāþ	lidon	liden	
	OS	līthan	lēth	lidun	gilidan	
	OHG	līdan	leid	litum	gilitan	
	Go.	sneiþan	snaiþ	[sniþum]	[sniþans]	'cut'
	ON	snīþa	sneiþ	sniþom	sniþenn	
	OE	snīþan	snāþ	snidon	sniden	
	OS	snīthan	snēth	snidun	gisnidan	
	OHG	snīdan	sneid	snitum	gisnitan	
II.	Go.	kiusan	kaus	[kusum]	[kusans]	'choose'
	ON	kiōsa	kaus	kørom	kørenn	
	OE	cēosan	cēas	curon	coren	
	OS	kiosan	kōs	kurun	gikoran	
	OHG	kiosan	kōs	kurum	gikoran	
	Go.	tiuhan	tauh	[tauhum]	[tauhans]	'pull'
	ON	tiōa	—	—	togenn	
	OE	tēon	tēah	tugon	togen	
	OS	tiohan	tōh	tugun	gitogan	
	OHG	ziohan	zōh	zugum	gizogan	
III.	Go.	wairþan	warþ	[waurþum]	[waurþans]	'become'
	ON	verþa	varþ	urþom	orþenn	
	OE	weorþan	wearþ	wurdon	worden	
	OS	werthan	warth	wurdun	wordan	
	OHG	werdan	ward	wurtum	wortan	
	Go.	finþan	fanþ	[funþum]	[funþans]	'find'
	ON	finna	fann	fundom	fundenn	
	OE	[findan]	[fand]	fundon	funden	
	OS	fīthan	[fand]	fundun	fundan	
	OHG	findan	fand	funtum	funtan	
V.	Go.	wisan	was	wēsum	—	'be'
	ON	vesa	vas	[vǫrom]	veret	
	OE	wesan	was	[wǣron]	—	
	OS	wesan	was	[wārun]	—	
	OHG	wesan	was	[wārum]	—	
	Go.	qiþan	qaþ	qēþum	[qiþans]	'speak'
	ON	kueþa	kuaþ	kuǫþom	kueþenn	
	OE	cweþan	cwæþ	[cwǣdon]	cweden	
	OS	quethan	quath	[quādun]	giquedan	
	OHG	quedan	quad	[quātum]	giquetan	

VI.	Go.	[slahan]	slōh	slōhum	[slahans]	'strike'
	ON	[slā]	slō	[slōgom]	slegenn	
	OE	[slēan]	slōh	[slōgon]	slagen	
	OS	[slahan]	[slōg]	[slōgun]	gislagen	
	OHG	[slahan]	sluoh	[sluogum]	gislagan	
	Go.	[hafjan]	hōf	hōfum	[hafans]	'seize'
	ON	hefia	hōf	hōfom	hafenn	
	OE	hebban	hōf	hōfon	hæfen	
	OS	hebbian	hōf	[hōƀun]	gihaƀan	
	OHG	[heffen]	[huob]	[huobum]	gihaban	
VII.	Go.	[fāhan]	faifāh	faifāhum	[fāhans]	'catch'
	ON	[fā]	[fekk]	[fengom]	fengenn	
	OE	[fōn]	[fēng]	[fēngon]	fangen	
	OS	[fāhan]	[feng]	[fengum]	gifangan	
	OHG	[fāhan]	[fieng]	[fiengum]	gifangan.	

Preterit Presents:

I.	Go.	aih	aigum	infin.	aigan	'own'
	ON	ā	eigom	"	eiga	
	OE	āh	āgon	"	āgan	
	OS	*ēh	ēgun	"	ēgan	
	OHG	*ēh	eigun	noun	eigan	
III.	Go.	þarf	þaurbum	infin.	þaurban	'need'
	ON	þarf	þurfom	"	þurfa	
	OE	þearf	þurfon	"	þurfan	
	OS	tharf	thurƀun	"	thurƀan	
	OHG	darf	[durfum]	"	[durfan]	

(2) There existed certain present types with IE suffix accent (**53 a**), notably the aorist presents, the verbs with *n*-infix, and the causatives. In spite of a great deal of leveling, these still give in some cases evidence of Grammatical Change:

AORIST PRESENTS:

I. IE *wéi(n)k-/wi(n)k-* (L. *vīncō*): Go. *weihan* 'fight'—ON *vega, vā* < **waih, vǫgom, vegenn*; OE *wīgan*; OHG *ubar-wehan* 'conquer'; OE OS *wīgand*, OHG *wīgant* 'fighter'

II. IE *bhéuk-/bhuk-* (Lith. *buklùs* 'sly') and *bhéug-/bhug-* (L. *fugiō*): Go. *biugan* 'bend', ON *bogenn* (past part.), OE *būgan*, OS **būgan*, OHG *biogan*, but OHG *buhil* 'hill'

VI. IE *kóp-/kəp-* (L. *capiō*): Go. *hafjan*, OE *hebban*, etc. (see above).

VERBS WITH N-INFIX:

IE *stā̆-/stə̄* (L. *stāre—status*): Go. *standan, stōþ, stōþum, standans*; ON *standa, stōþ, stōþom, staþenn*; OE *standan*, [*stōd*], [*stōdon*], *standen*; OS *standan*, [*stōd*], [*stōdun*], *astandan*; OHG *stantan*, [*stuont*], [*stuontum*], *gistantan*.

IE *trenk̇-*: Go. *þreihan* (transferred to the first class) 'throng', ON *þryngua*, OE *þringan*, OS *thringan*, OHG *dringan* (Gothic generalizes *h*, the other dialects *ȝ* through all forms).

CAUSATIVES:

IE *wért-e-ti* 'he turns', intr., *wort-éje-ti* 'he makes turn, he turns', trans.; cf. Sk. *vártati—vartáyati*: Go. *frawairþan* 'spoil', intr., *frawardjan* 'spoil', trans.

Go. *leiþan*, OE *līþan*, etc. (see above) 'go'—Go. **laidjan* 'lead', OE *lǣdan*, OS *lēdian*, OHG *leiten*.

Go. *ganisan*, OE *genesan*, OS OHG *ginesan* 'recover'—Go. *nasjan*, OE *nerian*, OS *nerian*, OHG *nerien* 'save'.

Go. *lisan* 'know'—Go. *laisjan*, OE *lǣran*, OS *lerian*, OHG *lēran* 'make know, teach'.

(3) Often the same dialect offers different word formations with original accent variation and, therefore, Grammatical Change:

OHG *durfan* 'need'—*darbēn* (Go. *gaþarban*) 'abstain'

OHG *hof* 'court'—MHG *hübesch* 'courtly, pretty'

OHG *fāhan* 'catch'—*fuogen* 'join'

OE *dēaþ*, OS *dōth*, OHG *tōd* 'death'—OE *dēad*, OS *dōd*, OHG *tōt* 'dead'.

(4) In other cases, we find differences of the same type between dialects; in such cases, generally, but by no means always, Gothic shows the voiceless spirant: Go. *ufar* 'over' indicates the accent of Sk. *úpa*, OHG *ubir* that of Sk. *upári*, Gk. ὑπέρ; Go. *alþeis* 'old' shows root accent, ON *aldenn*, OE *eald*, OHG *alt*, suffix accent (**altós*); the stem of the adjective 'dead' is *dauþa-* in Gothic, but **dauða-* in West Germanic: OE *dēad*, OS *dōd*, OHG *tōt* (ON *dauþr* could, theoretically, go with either of the two forms, but doubtless has to be classed with the WGmc. forms). Likewise Go. *ganauha* 'sufficiency', *ganōhs* 'enough', but OS *ginōg*, OHG *ginuog*; also Go. *fraþi* 'sense', *gabaurþi-* 'birth', *gaqumþi-* 'meeting', *hūhrus* 'hunger', and many others have cognates with voiced spirants in West Germanic and Norse. In such cases, the assumption of leveling is not sufficient; we must assume, with Hirt, l. c., that in these words Gothic had root accent sooner than the other Germanic languages.—Variations between the other Germanic languages are less frequent: OHG *haso*, but OE *hara*, ON *here* 'hare'.

Note: According to Bugge, Btr. 12. 399 ff., 13. 167 ff. and 311 ff., Verner's Law, under certain conditions, also affected initial spirants. Probably, this can be accepted only for the second parts of compounds, such as OHG *mezzirahs* (but also *mezzisahs*) 'eating-knife', NHG *Messer* < *mati-sahs*, OS *mezas* < *metsahs*, OE *meteseax*. However, the equation of Gmc. *ga-*, *gi-* with L. *co(n)-* seems to find justification in the assumption of Verner's Law initially, in the same sense in which we may apply the term to E. *the*, *that*, Norse *de*, *det*, etc. (see above). Unstressed Gmc. *ɧa-* had lenis pronunciation at an earlier period than accented syllables with initial *ɧ*, and thereby became subject to the operation of Verner's Law.

21. The IE Voiced Stops, b d g, became voiceless: **p t k**—Step IV. The intermediate stage was doubtless the voiceless lenis, *ḅ ḍ g̊*. Aside from the obvious phonetic probability, this is shown by the parallelism of the second shift (**26**). In general, *p t k* are aspirated fortes in the Germanic languages, but exceptions exist in Dutch and High German.

It is not known why *b* was so extremely rare in Indo-European, but it can hardly have been entirely accidental. Balto-Germanic cognates with IE *b* are fairly numerous, and Slavo-Germanic cognates almost equally so. But there are extremely few reliable etymologies of this kind that can be called 'Indo-European'. Perhaps a consideration like this may, in the course of time, lead to an understanding of the problem: 'Indo-European' is just as little a fixed linguistic system as is 'Germanic', or 'Slavic', or 'Indic'. It had been in flux for an indefinite period before the time of our reconstruction, which is necessarily fixed in an arbitrary way. There are indications that it was going through a pre-historic process similar to the Germanic Consonant Shift. According to **24**, the stop *b* < *b* was rare at a given period in early Germanic, on account of the chronological difference in the development of the three places of articulation. Perhaps something similar had taken place in early Indo-European. The voiced dental spirants, precursors of *d*, had perhaps already completed their transition; the 'gutturals' may still have been in the spirantic stage, so that IE *χ(gh)* would represent an earlier chronological stage than *θ(dh)*, just as NHG *k* does not correspond to *t*, which is a later development (*k* = Gmc. *k*, IE *g*; *t* = Gmc. *d*, IE *θ*). The IE labials may have been approaching the occluding stage at the time of the dialect separation. All of this is admittedly vague and open to some obvious objections, but we can hardly get any farther until new methods are devised.

Instances: (Cf. **19**, 3)

b: IE *skəb-/skāb-*, L. *scabō*, Go. *skapjan*, ON *skape*, OE *scieppan*, OS -*scapan*, OHG *scepfen* 'shape' (but also the root doublet IE *skəbh-*, Go. *skaban*, OHG *scaban* 'scrape'

IE *terb-/trb-*, L. *turba* 'troup', Go. *þaurp* 'field', ON *þorp*, OE *þorp*, OS *thorp*, OHG *dorf* 'village'

IE *dheub-/dheup-*, lith. *dubùs*, Go. *diups*, ON *diūpr*, OE *dēop*, OS *diop*, OHG *tiof* 'deep' (but also ON *dūfa*, OE *dȳfan* 'dive')

d: IE *dek̂m̥*, L. *decem*, Go. *taihun*, ON *tiō*, OE *tīen*, OS *tehan*, OHG *zehan* 'ten'

IE *dwōi* (*dwōu*), L. *duo*, Go. *twai*, ON *tveir*, OE *twā*, OS *twā*, OHG *zwei* 'two'

IE *dom-*, L. *domus*, Go. *timrjan*, ON *timbra*, OE *timbrian*, OS *timbrōn*, OHG *zimbarōn* 'build'

ĝ: IE *ĝeus-*, L. *gustāre*, Go. *kiusan*, ON *kiōsa*, OE *cēosan*, OS *kiosan*, OHG *kiosan* 'choose'

IE *ĝen-*, L. *genus*, Go. *kuni*, ON *kyn*, OE *cynn*, OS *kunni*, OHG *kunni* 'kin'

IE *ĝneu-*, L. *genu*, Go. *kniu*, ON *knē*, OE *cnēo*, OHG *kniu* 'knee'

g: IE *aug-*, L. *augeō*, Go. *aukan*, ON *auka*, OE *ēacian*, OS *ōkian*, OHG *ouhhon* 'increase'

IE *gel-*, L. *gelidus*, Go. *kalds*, ON *kalþr*, OE *ceald*, OS *kald*, OHG *kalt* 'cold'

IE *jugo-*, L. *iugum*, Go. *juk*, ON *ok*, OE *geoc*, OS *juk*, OHG *joch* 'yoke'

gw: IE *gwem-*, L. *veniō*, Go. *qiman*, ON *koma*, OE *cuman*, OS *kuman*, OHG *koman* 'come'

IE *gwenā*, Gk. γυνή, Go. *qinō*, ON *kona*, OE *cwene*, OS OHG *quena* 'woman'

IE *gwīwo-*, L. *vīvus*, Go. *qius*, ON *kuikr*, OE *cwic*(*u*), OS *quick*, OHG *queck* 'alive'.

22. The Germanic Consonant Lengthening. Indo-European possessed no original 'double' or 'long' consonants (geminates), but doubling resulted frequently from composition or derivation: IE *wid-to, wit-to-* 'known' = OHG *giwisso*. The Germanic development of such groups is treated in **29,** but one type is so closely connected with Steps III and IV of the Consonant Shift that it is anticipated here. This is the treatment of Germanic stops and spirants followed by *n*. Such groups occurred chiefly in certain derivative verbs, such as Gk. δάκνω, Sk. *krīṇāmi*, and in the 'weak cases' of the *n*-declension, such as Gk. ἀρνός, gen. sg. of ἀρήν 'ram'. There are so many irregularities and so few non-Germanic equations in these forms that as yet complete agreement has not been reached, but the following must be considered the standard view: IE *p t k* under Verner's Law became identical with IE *φ θ χ* (*bh dh gh*), developing to Gmc. *b ð ʒ*. These voiced spirants became stops, *b d g*, after nasals (**24 b**), and apparently also before *n*. Thus, before an accented *n*-suffix the three series *p t k, φ θ χ* (*bh dh gh*), and *b d g* became identical, namely, *bn dn gn*. Through assimilation of *n* to the preceding voiced stops, *bb dd gg* resulted, which became *pp tt kk* in Step IV. It is clear that this process occurred *after* Verner's Law and *before* the unvoicing of the voiced stops, unless we assume that the latter preceded Verner's Law, and that *bb dd gg* became voiceless through a second process of unvoicing; that is possible but unlikely.

INSTANCES:

(The IE equations are in most cases mere formulae of reconstruction. This was essentially a Germanic process, whether the standard view be accepted in principle or not.)

pn' > *pp*: IE *kup-ná-* (OSl. *kypéti*) Go. **huppōn*, ON *hoppa*, NHG *hüpfen*

tn' > *tt*: IE *snit-nó-* (Go. *sneiþan*, etc.) MHG *snitzen* 'whittle' (intensive formation)

dn' > *tt*: IE *(s)tud-nó-* (L. *tundō*, Sk. *tudáti*, Go. *stautan*, etc.) MHG *stutzen* 'be startled'

kn' > *kk*: IE *l̥k-ná-* (L. *laciō*) ON *lokka*, OE *geloccian*, OHG *locchōn* 'entice'

IE feminine suffix *-ní (-nyá)*, as in Sk. *patní*, Gk. πότνια 'mistress', NHG *Ricke*, fem. of *Reh* (Gmc. *ráiha-*; **rignjá* > *riggja*)

gn' > *kk*: IE *lug-nó-* (Lith. *lùgnas* 'pliable', Gk. λύγος 'twig', λύγινος 'pleated') ON *lokkr* (but *lykna* 'bend the knees'), OE *loc(c)*, OHG *loc* 'lock, curl'

IE *bhəgnó-* (Gk. φώγω) OHG *bacchan* 'bake'

ghn' > *kk*: IE *ligh-ná-* (Gk. λείχω 'lick', λιχνεύω 'taste', L. *linguō*, Go. *bilaigon* 'lick') OE *liccian*, OHG *lecchōn* 'lick'.

But we find Gk. ἰπνός : Go. *aúhns* 'oven' (ON *ogn* and *ofn*, OE *ofen*, OHG *ofan*); Gk. τέκνον 'child' : OHG *degan* 'warrior', in spite of the Greek root accent (the etymology is very uncertain). In the numerous *n*-derivatives of verbs (Gothic fourth weak class) we should expect suffix accent and therefore assimilation of *n*, but at least in Gothic, and partly in Norse, *n* is preserved: Go. *-waknan*, *waknōda*, Norse *vakna*, *vaknada*. Gothic has only two words with *tt* : *atta* 'father', *skatts* 'hoard', both uncertain as to etymology; two borrowed words with *kk* : *sakkus* 'sack' and *smakka* 'fig'; and no words with *pp*.

After a long syllable these geminates were simplified:
Gmc. *haubn‑* > *haupp-* > *haup-* > OE *hēap*, OHG *houf* 'heap'
Gmc. *hwīdn‑* > *hwītt-* > *hwīt-* > Go. *hveits*, OE *hwīt*, OHG *hwīz* 'white'.

ON *sūpa*, OE *sūpan*, OHG *sūfan* 'sip, drink' may on this basis be connected with Sk. *sūpa-* 'soup, gravy': an *n*-formation IE *sūp-nó-* would give Gmc. *sūppa-*, *sūpa-*.

The Germanic gemination explains numerous double forms, such as NHG *schneiden* and *schnitzen, stossen* and *stutzen, Reh* and *Ricke* (also *Ziege* and *Zicke*), given above. Simplification after a long syllable produces a different type of parallels. Gmc. *knuppa-* > NHG *Knopf* 'button', but Gmc. *knauppa-, knaupa-* > MHG *knōp*, NHG *Knauf* 'hilt'. MHG *knübel* 'knuckle' shows that the labial was not IE *b*, but either *φ* (*bh*), or *p* under Verner's Law. In High German, -*p* became *f*, but *pp* became *pf*. It is not always possible to decide whether such double forms are due to the Germanic or to the West Germanic Consonant Lengthening. Cf. **30**.

Probably very few cases of Germanic Consonant Lengthening actually go back to Indo-European forms. A few of these, like IE *lugnós*, may have established a pattern on which many new forms were modeled in the several Germanic languages. Once geminates had been established by assimilation, they could easily become the instrument of sound symbolism; through this, 'bildete schon das Urgermanische partielle Neuschöpfungen durch Dehnung des wurzelauslautenden Konsonanten eines schon vorhandenen Wortes zur Bezeichnung der Intensität, ähnlich wie zu gleichem Zweck das Semitische durch Dehnung des mittleren der drei Wurzelkonsonanten.' (Loewe, GS 77 f.; similarly Braune, Ahd. Gramm. §95 Anm. 2.)

23. The Labiovelars. The most important development of these a sounds in other Indo-European languages have been given in **11**. Their Germanic development is shown in the following table:

IE   Gmc.

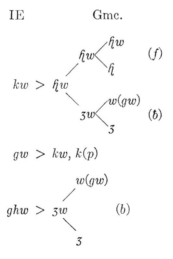

The treatment of the labiovelars in Germanic is similar to that in Latin. Cf. for *kw*, *sequor—secutus—socius*; for *gw*, *veniō* < **gwm̥jō*, *vīvus* < **gwīwos*; for *ghw*, *ninguit—nīcs* = *nīx—nīvem.*

b   The general principle is this: The velar element (*k g gh*) goes through the regular shift, including Verner's Law (indicated where needed by ′ for stressed, ‵ for unstressed syllable preceding). The labial element is retained under certain conditions, lost under others. But Gmc. *ʒw* is a 'phonetic interpolation'—an intermediate stage that must be assumed theoretically, though it is not preserved historically. It appears either as *ʒ* or as *w*; only after *n* (*ŋ*), Gothic and Norse have *gw*. This is exactly like the Latin treatment of IE *χw* (*ghw*, Brugmann's *qᵘh*): IE *neiχw-* (Gk. *νείφει*), *ninχw-* > *nīg-, nīw-, ningw-.*

As in Latin, the labial element disappears before back vowels (IE *u ū o ō*—therefore *secūtus*, but *sequitur*; *sequor* is analogical formation for **secor*, like *equus* for **ecos*). It also disappears before consonants (cf. *socius, secta*), and doubtless too in final position (L. *que* = −*ƕ* in Go. *sah, nih*; Go. *saƕ, laiƕ* are analogical forms).

c   INSTANCES:

IE **kw** > Gmc. *ƕw/ƕ*:

IE *kwe-/kwo-* (interrogative pronoun), Go. *ƕis*, OHG *hwes* 'whose'— OSw. *har*, but also analogical *hwar* = Go. *ƕas* 'who'

IE *kwel-/kwol-* 'turn' (Gk. *τέλος* 'goal', *πόλος* 'axis', OSl. *kolo* 'wheel', L. *collum* < **kwolsom*), ON *huel* 'wheel' (OE *hweogol* < **hweʒla-* < IE *kwe-kwlóm*, reduplicated form similar to Gk. *κύ-κλος*)— Go. *hals* < **kwolsos.*

IE *kwei-/kwoi-* (L. *quies*), Go. *ƕeila* 'while'—*haims* 'home'.

NOTE: Gmc. *ƕw* can also come from IE *k̑w*, as Sk. *śvētas*, Go. *ƕeits* 'white', Sk. *aśvas*, L. *equus*, Go. *aiƕa-* 'horse' (ON *iōr* < **ekwos* > **eƕwaz* > **joƕaz* > **johr, jōr*). In a few instances, it apparently goes back to a plain velar followed by *w*, instead of a real labio-velar, in which the lip-rounding extends over both elements. Our transcription does not indicate this; in Brugmann's transcription, Go. *afhapjan* 'expire' = Lith. *kvépti* 'breathe' would be **qwep-*, while Go. *hals* is represented by **qᵘolso-*. It does not seem expedient to complicate the whole system of transcription for the sake of a very few words.

IE **gw** > Gmc. *kw/k*:

IE *gwem-/gwom-/gwm̥-* (L. *veniō* < **gwm̥jō* = Gk. *βαίνω*; Sk. *gácchati* < **gwm̥sketi*), Go. *qiman*, OHG *queman*—ON *koma*, OE *cuman*, OHG *koman* < **gwm̥-* 'come'; pret. OHG *kam, kāmum* < **gwom-, gwēm-*; Go. *qam, qēmum* are analogical.

IE *gwet-* (L. *vetāre*; the etymology is doubted by Feist, but is probably correct), Go. *qiþan*, ON *kueþa*, OE *cweþan*, OS *quethan*, OHG *quedan* 'speak'

IE *gwen-/gwēn-* (Gk. γυνή, Boeot. βανά), Go. *qinō, qēns*, ON *kuæn*, OE *cwēn*, OS *quān*—ON *kona* (but gen. pl. *kvinna*) 'woman, wife'.

IE **ghw** and ' **kw** > Gmc. ʒw > w, ʒ, (n)gw:

IE *ghwen-/ghwṇ-* (Gk. θείνω, aor. ἔπεφνον 'kill'), ON *gūþ-* (*Gūþrūn*, etc.), *gunnr*, OHG **gundea* 'fight' (*gundfano*, borrowed by French as *gonfalon* 'battle flag')

IE *ghwermos/ghwormos* (Gk. θερμός, L. *formus*), Go. *warms*

IE *lenghw(r)-,lnghw(r)-/lenghw(t)-* 'light, speedy' (Gk. ἐλαφρός 'light', ἐλαχύς 'slight'; L. *levis* < **leghw-*), OE OHG *līht*, ON *lēttr* 'light'— OHG *lungar* 'speedy', OE *lungen*, OHG *lungun* 'lungs'

IE *kneighw-* (L. *conīveō* < **con-cnīgueō*, perf. *conixī* 'close the eyes', *nicto* 'wink'), Go. *hneiwan*—ON *hnīga*, OE OS OHG *hnīgan* 'bend'; Gothic generalizes the forms before *e* (*hneiwiþ*), NWGmc. the forms before *o* (infin. *-onom*)

IE *(s)neighw-/(s)nighw-* (L. *nix, nivem*; *ninguit* with *n*-infix; Gk. νείφει 'it snows', νίφα acc. sg.), Go. *snaiws*, ON *snær*, OE *snāw*, OS OHG *snēo* (< **snoighwos*)

IE *senghw-/songhw-* (Gk. ὀμφή 'voice'), Go. *siggwan* 'read, recite', ON *syngua*, OE OS OHG *singan* 'sing' (perhaps, without *n*-infix, ON *segia*, OE *secgan*, OS *seggian*, OHG *sagēn* 'say').

Through Verner's Law:

IE *akwjá* > Gmc. *aʒwjō* 'watery place, island'—ON *øy, ey* (cf. *Scadinavia*, Latinized form of *Skān-øy* 'Skåne'), OE *ēg, īg, ēglond, īglond* (NE *island* with *s* transferred from Fr. *isle* < L. *īnsula*; cf. *Skeden-īg = Scadinavia*) 'island', OHG *ouwa* 'watery meadow, island'; but with root accent **ákwā* (L. *aqua*), Go. *ahva*, ON *ǫ*, OS OHG *aha* (cf. *Salzach*) 'river'

IE *makwús* 'boy, son', *makwī* (*makwjá*) 'girl' (OIr. *macc*, OCymr. *map* 'son'), Go. *magus*, ON *mǫgr*, OE *mago*, OS *mago*, OHG *maga-*: Go. *mawi*, ON *mær*, OE *mēowle*

IE *sekw-* 'follow' (L. *sequor*), in Gmc. 'follow with the eyes, see'. The forms show a good deal of leveling:

Gmc.	*seḫwana-*	*saḫw*	*sæḫwum*	*seʒwana-, -ena-*
Go.	*saihvan*	*sah*	*sēhum*	[*saihvans*]
ON	*siā*	*sā*	*sǫm*	[*sēnn*]
OE	*sēon*	*seah*	[*sāwon*]	*sewen*
OS	*sehan*	*sah*	[*sāwun*]	*gisewan*
OHG	*sehan*	*sah*	*sāhum*	[*gisehan*], *geseuuen* (Notker)

Go. *siuns*, ON *siōn*, OE *sẏn* 'sight' < **sekwnís* > **seʒwnís*.

NOTE: The OE forms are Saxon; Anglian has *sēgon* (= *sǣgon*), *gesegen*. According to the present standard view (cf. Streitberg, UG 116, 113; Hirt, HU 107 f.), we should expect *g* in the pret. pl., before Gmc. *u*, and in the past part. *g*, if the IE ending was *-ono-*, *w*, if it was *-eno-*. In either case, there are complications. Sievers, Btr. 5. 149, assumed that Gmc. *ʒw* from either source became *w* if the accent followed. This would simplify the explanation of the forms with *w*, but add to the difficulty presented by the forms with *g*. The view is now accepted by few (e.g. by Trautmann, Germanische Lautgesetze 57).

IE *kwetwóres* (Sk. *catvā́ras*, Gk. τέσσαρες, L. *quattuor*, Lith. *keturì*) 'four', Go. *fidwōr*; the other Gmc. forms go back to a **kwekwóres*, with medial *kw* either through the influence of the initial, or by analogy with **penkwe* 'five': ON *fiōrer*, OE *fēower*, OS *fiuwar, fior*, OHG *feor, fior*. The *w* of these forms must be due either to the initial labial, or to a suffix form *-ēres* instead of *-ōres*; Old Norse, however, has the neuter *fiogor*.

Before consonants:

IE *sokwjós* (L. *socius*) 'follower', OE *secg*, ON *seggr* 'companion, man'
IE *sekwti-* 'sight', MHG *sicht*, Eng. *sight*
IE *ghwren-* (Gk. φρήν 'diaphragm, mind'), ON *grunr* 'suspicion'.

In some instances, we find *f ƀ* for Gmc. *ƕw ʒw*. The fact is certain, but the exact conditions are not known; sometimes it seems to be due to assimilation to a preceding *w* or *u*. Cf. Noreen, UL 147, Hirt, HU 108 f.:

IE *wḷkwos* 'wolf', Sk. *vṛkas*, OSl. *vlьkъ*, Lith. *vìlkas*: Go. *wulfs*, ON *ulfr*, OE *wulf*, OHG *wolf*; with Verner's Law,—IE *wḷkwí* (Sk. *vṛkí*), ON *ylgr*, MHG *wülpe* 'she-wolf'
IE *kwekwóres* 'four' (see above), Go. *fidwōr*, etc.; the *f* can also be explained through the influence of Go. *fimf* < **penkwe*.
IE *ukwnos* 'fire, stove' (Gk. ἰπνός), Go. *auhns*, but ON *ofn*, OHG *ofan*
IE *penkwe* 'five' (Sk. *pañca*, Gk. πέντε), Go. *fimf*, ON *fimm*, OE OS *fīf*, OHG *fimf, finf* (*f* may be assimilation to the initial labial, as inversely L. *quinque* shows assimilation of the initial to the medial consonant).

Noreen, l. c., quotes fifty-odd instances, but most of them are quite uncertain.

The Intermediate Shift

(Step V)

The term 'Intermediate' is not entirely apt. The change did not occur *between* the Germanic and the High German Shifts, but began in early Germanic times —probably during the first or second century A.D.—, and continued, in High German, contemporaneously with the earlier stages of the High German Shift. In a sense this Shift might be called 'Overlapping' rather than 'Intermediate'.

24. The Germanic Voiced Spirants, *ƀ đ ʒ*, tended to become voiced **a** stops, in accordance with the 'Fundamental Principle' (**16**). This is virtually the opposite of 'Lenition', a process of common occurrence in Celtic, Romance languages, and elsewhere (e.g. L. *debēre* > Fr. *devoir*, Span. [*deƀer*]), since lenition consists in the change of stops to spirants. But the two processes have at least this in common that a spirant is more apt to be retained or developed medially than initially.

The development of *ƀ đ ʒ* to *b d g* was completed in Upper German, probably also in East Franconian (which by some scholars, e.g. Behaghel, is classed with Upper German). In the other Germanic dialects, the change appears in complete agreement, on the one hand with the chronology of the formation of the dialect units, and on the other with the place of articulation of these sounds and of their position in the words. That is to say: (1) In Gothic and Norse there is least evidence of these changes, more in Old English and Low German, still more in Middle German, while in Upper German the change is complete. (2) Dentals show the widest, velars the narrowest scope of the change. (3) The change appears sooner, and, therefore, more widely, in initial than in medial or final position.

Germanic, Gothic, Norse:

(1) Gmc. *ƀ đ ʒ* after nasals and in gemination are stops in all dialects; **b** therefore, we ascribe this change to Primitive Germanic: Go. ON OE OS OHG *lamb*, Go. gen. sg. *lambis*; Go. OE OS *bindan*, ON *binda*, OHG *bintan*, Go. pret. *band*; Go. *laggs* = [laŋgs], ON *langr*, OE OS OHG *lang*, Go. gen. sg. masc. *laggis*. If *b d* had been spirants, Gothic would have changed them to *f þ* when final as in *hlaiƀis—hlaif*, *rēdan—rairōþ*, but not *lamf *banþ; for the velar, Gothic spelling would not indicate the difference; cf. **31**. Instances of Gmc. *ƀƀ đđ ʒʒ* > *bb dd gg* have been given in **22**.

(2) Initial *ƀ* and *đ* appear as stops everywhere in Germanic, with the exception only of a few isolated forms in early Runic inscriptions, (*ƀarutR* = *brȳtr* 'breaks', Björketorp; *đohtriR* = *dø̄tr* 'daughters', Tune; cf. **18**), for which, however, other explanations might be given. Cf. **18** and Noreen, Aisl. Gramm. 143: Go. *bairan*, ON *bera*, OE OS OHG *beran*; Go. *dauhtar*, ON *dōtter*, OE *dohtor*, OS *dohtar*, OHG *tohter*.

(3) Gmc. *ƀ đ* became stops in Gothic after *l r*, probably also after other consonants, and in Norse *đ* became *d* after *l*: Go. *haldan*, ON *halda*, OE *healdan*, OS *haldan*, OHG *haltan*; Go. *gards*, OE *geard*, OS *gard*, OHG *gart*, but ON *garþr*; Go. *halbis*, gen. sg., *halb*, nom. sg. neut., OHG *halb*, but ON *halfr*, OE *healf*, OS *half*.

The treatment of Gmc. *ʒ* in Gothic and Norse must still be considered a moot question. It is most frequently assumed that it was a spirant medially, but a stop initially; for final Goth. *g*, cf. **31**. But for Gothic the evidence is extremely slight (see especially Dieter, AD 194); for Norse there is no early evidence at all (cf. Noreen, Aisl. Gr. 143, Asw. Gr. 175), and the testimony of the modern languages is conflicting. It is best in keeping with the general trend to assume the following: In Gothic and *early* Norse, Gmc. ȝ was a spirant in all positions, except after nasals and in gemination; before back vowels and consonants it was the velar spirant ȝ (*g* in North German *Tage*), before front vowels, the palatal spirant (*j*): ȝ in Go. *gards*, ON *garðr*, *j* in Go. *giban*, ON *gefa*. This condition remained in Swedish and Norwegian, while in Danish initial ȝ became *g*. But it must be admitted that there is no direct evidence for either Gothic or Old Norse.

Streitberg, GE (5th and 6th ed.) 63, claims stop pronunciation in all positions, not only for *g*, but even for *b* and *d* at the time of Wulfila; in his opinion, based on Sievers's Schallanalyse, 'fordert die Intonation für die Zeit Wulfilas unzweideutig die stimmhaften Verschlusslaute'. In view of the alternation between final *f þ* and medial *b d*, the argument does not seem convincing.

c WEST GERMANIC:

(1) Gmc. ð became *d* in all positions: OE *fæder*, OS *fadar*, OHG *fater*; the change to ð in NE *father*, due to assimilation to the following *r* (as also in *weather*) took place around 1500.

(2) Medial and final *ƀ* remained a spirant (generally voiceless when final) throughout the North: English, Frisian, Saxon, Low and Middle Franconian; it became a stop in the other German dialects: OE *giefan*, OFris. *ieva* (*geva, jeva*), OS *geƀan*, but OHG *geban*. The Germanic spirant *ƀ* had been bilabial, and at least in Gothic and Old Saxon must doubtless still be considered as such. Later it became labio-dental [v] everywhere where it had not become a stop (bilabial in Go. *sibun*, labio-dental in E. *seven*). But since the end of the Middle Ages, medial *b* has been a bilabial spirant in Bavarian, Alsatian, and considerable parts of Middle German, particularly in Rhine Franconian.

(3) The treatment of Gmc. ȝ is not altogether certain. For Old English, it is certain that medial and final ȝ were spirants, and initial ȝ is generally admitted to have been a spirant at least in West Saxon in the earliest period. This is clearly evident from the fact that it alliterates with the IE palatal spirant, as in the first line of Beowulf: *gār* < Gmc. ȝaiza- and *gēar* < Gmc. *jæra-*, IE *jēro-*. But later in the Old English period, initial ȝ before consonants and back vowels (where it had velar articulation) became a stop, as in NE *grass, good*. Before

front vowels (except those that came from the modified vowels *ö* and *ü*) it remained a spirant with palatal articulation: NE *yard, yellow, yield*. But this view is hard to reconcile with such forms as NE *give, get, guest*; since Kluge, Anz. z. Anglia 5. 83, the initial *g* in these words is generally ascribed to Scandinavian influence, but, as said above, there is no real evidence for stop pronunciation of *ȝ*- in Old Norse. It is more likely that the stop forms are of Anglian, the spirant forms of Frisio-Saxon origin.

This is indicated primarily by spelling tradition. In West Saxon the spirantic (palatal) pronunciation of initial *ȝ* is shown by a following *i* or *e*, which are 'silent', having the function of diacritical marks: *ȝiefan, ȝeaf, ȝēafon* = [*jevan, jæf, jǣfon*]; in early MSS forms with *eae* = *eæ*, instead of *ea*, occur, but apparently there developed a tradition against the writing of three consecutive vowels. The macron of *ȝēafon*, when used at all, is a mechanical transfer from the diphthong *ēa* < *au*. The *ē* is silent, and the *a* stands for *æ*. Anglian spelling, as far as it is not influenced by West Saxon tradition, has *gefan, gæf, gǣfon*, with initial stop. (The distinction between two runes for Gmc. *ȝ* in the Ruthwell Cross inscription has nothing to do with this; it refers to palatal versus velar articulation, not to spirant versus stop.)

Modern English dialects offer conflicting evidence. There seems to be a tendency in favor of the stop in the North and in favor of the spirant in the South, but dialect mixture has greatly interfered.

If Anglian did have initial *g* for Gmc. *ȝ*, the shift may date back to continental times. This is suggested by the parallel development in the essentially Anglian territory east and north of the lower Elbe; see below. Apparently, the Saxon and Frisian element of Southern England brought the initial spirant from their continental homes, the Anglians the initial stop, and in both cases that early pronunciation has in a large measure prevailed to this day.

Also in the continental West Germanic dialects, the evidence of spelling is not always sufficient to decide whether Gmc. *ȝ* remained a spirant or became a stop. Often the somewhat uncertain conditions of modern dialects are our only guide. In general, the distribution is as follows:

Initial *ȝ* remained a spirant as far south as Middle Franconian, including the northern part of that dialect, but south of that district became a stop, so that its treatment is essentially the same as that of medial *b*: LG *jeven*, HG *geben*. The spirant is usually palatal (*j*), but velar *ȝ* is found in some districts, especially in Low Franconian (Dutch). Medial *ȝ* remained a spirant (usually voiced, but partly voiceless) everywhere except in Upper German; cf. North German [la:ȝən li:jən]. However, a detached territory in the Northeast has the stop *g* for Gmc. *ȝ* both initially and medially: Initially, *g* is spoken in Schleswig-

Holstein, Mecklenburg-Schwerin, Pommern; medially, in Mecklenburg-Schwerin (Behaghel, GddS 212).

This coincides with the initial stop in neighboring Danish. It is difficult to say whether there is any common cause for this. Might it have anything to do with the proximity of this territory to the Germanic homeland, that the phonetic trend continued somewhat longer in this district than in the older colonial lands? Perhaps it is not quite without importance that at least a part of this territory —chiefly Holstein—is identical with that *Scatenauge Albiae fluvii ripa* (= *Scadinavia*) from which the Langobards emigrated in the second half of the fourth century (Zeuss, Die Deutschen und die Nachbarstämme 471 f.). The consonantism of the Langobards had gone through the High German Shift (cf. Bruckner, Die Sprache der Langobarden 18 ff.; Behaghel, GddS 16), which is entirely in keeping with the theory presented in this book. However, initial *þ* probably did not become *d*, as in German, but *t*, as in Scandinavian.

The High German Shift

a 25. **Chronology and Spread.** The changes described in the preceding paragraphs belong essentially to the period before the geographical separation of the Germanic ethnic unit. Aside from the incompleteness of the 'Intermediate' Shift, these are 'Germanic' changes, affecting more or less all Germanic dialects. After the formation of the East and West Germanic groups, approximately at the beginning of the Christian Era, all three groups possessed the following consonants, in addition to the nasals, liquids, and semi-vowels:

$$b\ \eth\ z;\ p\ t\ k;\ f\ þ\ \hbar;\ s\ z.$$

The consonant changes after the separation show a marked divergence. In Gothic, and especially in Norse, new tendencies set in that led to consonant changes in new directions. In West Germanic, the Germanic Drift, that is, the physiological principle that had dominated the Germanic Consonant Shift, continued for a longer or shorter period, according to the time of emigration; cf. **17**, end. The West Germanic expansion was directed mainly to the east and south, surrounding the East-Elbian homeland like the opening of a fan (cf. **6**). In the northwestern branch, comprising Frisian, Saxon, and Low Franconian, the old trend affected only the voiced spirants in the limited scope described in the preceding section. These dialects, therefore, differ from Gothic and Norse, as far as the Consonant Shift is concerned, only in the change of medial and final *ð* to *d*.

If the trend of the Germanic Shift had continued unabated, the result would obviously have been:

Gmc. $p\ t\ k$ > Ger. $f\ \flat\ \hbar$

Gmc. $\delta\ \eth\ z$ > Ger. $p\ t\ k$ (through $b\ d\ g$)

But these changes took place only in the territory of relatively late expansion south of the 'Benrather Linie', that is, in the High German dialects, and even there with limitations and modifications. For this reason we speak of a 'High German' or 'Second Consonant Shift' in contrast to the 'First' or 'Germanic Shift'. In general, it followed the same trend, but in certain instances the phonetic direction was deflected, so as to lead to slightly different results. Moreover, in certain cases secondary developments counteracted changes that had actually taken place.

The historical order and, therefore, the geographical spread of the Second Shift follows the Fundamental Principle stated in **17**. In the Intermediate Shift, as shown above, the initial or medial (final) position of the consonants was an important factor; it may have been that, temporarily, in the First Shift too, but we have no historical evidence for this. In the Second Shift, particularly in the case of Gmc. $p\ t\ k$, it is of prime importance: the formation of spirants had a wider sway after vowels than initially, after consonants, and in gemination. Since in the Intermediate Shift the development progresses from spirants to stops, but in the Second Shift from stops to spirants, it follows logically that here initial position is unfavorable to the change, while there it was favorable to it.

The maps on the following page (which include the area of later col- b onization east of the Elbe and Saale) outline the spread of the High German Consonant Shift; the shaded areas indicate the territories in which the respective changes took place.

This distribution of the High German Shift is entirely in keeping with the chronological sequence of the West Germanic expansion outlined in connection with the Fundamental Principle of the Sound Shift (**16**). The Germanization of northwestern Germany took place soon after the separation of the East and North Germanic groups from the Central stock. Accordingly, we find that Frisian, Saxon, and Low Franconian continued the shift very slightly beyond the stage reached in the former groups. In Central Germany, the Roman *limes* halted the expansion for several centuries, and the Germans that had reached the middle Rhine before the time of Caesar received strong reinforcements from the central region during that time. This explains the great contrast between Low German and High German. The formation of the Upper German dialects is marked by the final occupation of Southwestern

1.·The Germanic Voiced Spirants
(Intermediate Period)

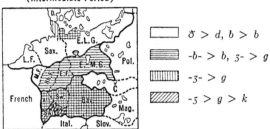

$ð > d, b > b$

$-b- > b, ʒ- > g$

$-ʒ- > g$

$-ʒ > g > k$

2. The H.G. Shift of
Voiceless Stops

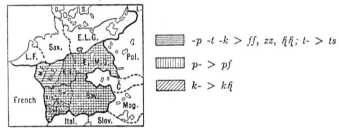

$-p -t -k > ff, zz, ḫḫ; t- > ts$

$p- > pf$

$k- > kḫ$

3. The H.G. Shift of
Voiced Stops

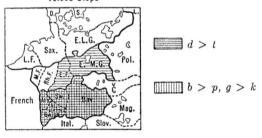

$d > t$

$b > p, g > k$

Germany by the Alemannii, and of Vindelicia by the Baiuvarii
during the fifth and sixth centuries. The parallelism between th‹
tribal consolidations and the stages of the Second Shift can be indi‹
cated as follows:

Occupation of the North Sea coast, last centuries B.C.—$ð > d$
$b- > b$.

Concentration at the *limes*, A.D. to 400—gradual spread of the shift o‹
$p\ t\ k$, continuation of the 'Intermediate Shift'.

Occupation of Upper Germany, 400 to about 500—$b > p$, $g > k$;
$k- > kh$.

A detailed description of the process would go far beyond the limits of this book.

26. Instances and Limitations. The following instances represent the High German Shift in its extreme form, termed 'Streng-Althochdeutsch' by Jacob Grimm. For the sake of convenience, post-vocalic position is indicated by $-p$ $-t$ $-k$, while $p-$ $t-$ $k-$ indicate initial position, position after consonants, and gemination.

(1) Voiceless stops after vowels become voiceless spirants: $-p$ $-t$ $-k$ $> ff$ zz hh. These new spirants are not identical with Gmc. f $\not p$ $\mathfrak h$; these had in the course of time become lenes, while the new ones were fortes. This is generally indicated by double spelling, but after long vowels and in final position simple consonants are commonly used:

Go. *skipis* (gen. sg.), *skip, slēpan*—OHG *skiffes, skif, slāfan* (*slāffan*)
Go. *itan, ētum, þata*—OHG *ezzan, āzum, daz* (*thaz*)
Go. *mikils, bōka, ik*—OHG *mihhil, michil, puoh, ih*.

ff (*f*) was probably labio-dental from the very beginning, since this articulation is better adapted to fortis pronunciation than the bilabial one.

zz (*z*) is used consistently in OHG and MHG MSS (the Isidor MS uses *zss, zs*); grammatical works generally use ȝ to distinguish the spirant from the affricate $z = ts$. Its pronunciation is not known, but it was clearly distinguished from *s*. Perhaps it was originally a slit spirant, a fortis *þ*, which changed to a rill spirant, *s*, towards the end of the MHG time. In most modern High German dialects, the distinction is merely one between fortis and lenis: *lassen—lesen*; voiced *-s-* is a borrowing from Low German.

For *hh* (*h*), *ch* is generally used since the middle of the ninth century. Like ȝ, it is assimilated to the preceding vowel, leading to the distinction between the *ich-* and the *ach-*sound. Alemannian and a part of Southern Bavarian have only the *ach-*sound.

(2) Voiceless stops initially, after consonants, and in gemination change to the corresponding affricates: $p-$ $t-$ $k-$ $> pf$ ts (*z*) kh (*kch*):

Go. *paida*, E. *stamp*, E. *dapper*—OHG *pfeit, stampfōn, tapfer* (but Go. *hilpan*, OHG *helpfan*, since the tenth century *helfan*)
Go. *twai, hairtō, satjan* = WGmc. *sattjan*—OHG *zwei, herza, sezzan, setzan*
Go. *kaurn, -wakjan, drigkan*—OHG (UG) *khorn, wekhan, trinkhan*.

As in the First Shift, this change is prevented by a preceding voiceless spirant: *stein, spil, fisk, naht, luft*. *tr* likewise remains unshifted: Go. *trudan*, OHG *tretan*.

(3) Voiced stops tend to become voiceless stops; to what extent these were lenes or fortes is entirely uncertain; at least for the OHG period, fortes are probable in Upper German.   Medial *b* became *p* in Bavarian only (Bav. *kepan*, Al. *keban*).   *b d g* > *p t k*:

Go. *briggan, haban, gaf*—OHG (Bav.) *princan, hapen, kap*

Go. *dags, fadar, bindan*—OHG *tac, fater, bintan*

Go. *guþ, fugls, dags*—OHG (UG) *cot, focal, tac (tak)*.

These changes are carried through to the following extent:

(a) The shift of *-p -t -k* and *t-* covers the whole High German territory, but Middle Franconian preserves *dat, it, wat*, the ending *-et*, and, partly, the preposition *up*; ('Restwörter' cf. **17 d**).   Also *d* > *t* may be termed general High German, but the voiceless stop was (and is) a lenis in Middle and Rhine Franconian, a fortis (originally) in East Franconian and Upper German.

(b) *p-* > *pf* belongs essentially to East Franconian and Upper German; in Middle Franconian the change did not take place at all, in Rhine Franconian only after *l* and *r* (*lpf, rpf*, later generally *lf, rf*): MFr. RFr. *Pund, Palz*, MFr. *helpen*.

(c) *k-* > *kh̯* is general Upper German in early OHG times, but now the affricate is found only in some southern dialects of Switzerland; in other Swiss dialects and in the Tyrol the spirant *ch* is pronounced: *chalt*.

(d) The shift of *b g* to *p k* belongs to Upper German of the earlier period; the details are not of importance for this brief treatment.

B. Other Consonant Changes

a   **27. The Germanic Voiceless Spirants**, *f þ h̯*, had partly become voiced under the conditions of Verner's Law.   Originally, they were doubtless fortes, since they had developed in the same way as the later High German spirants, but since prehistoric times they showed a progressive tendency towards a weakening in articulation.   This is a natural trend, since the relatively unchecked current of expiration gradually lessens the resistance of the muscles of the lips or tongue, and then, in turn, loses its own force.   Their later development in the several Germanic languages varied according to their place of articulation and their position.

The dental, *þ*, followed the tendency of the Consonant Shift consistently.   Unless it was preserved as a voiceless spirant (see below), it became *ð*, later in part *d*.   The labial, *f*, was perhaps originally bilabial, but there is no certain evidence for this.   (Assimilations like Go. OHG *fimf* < **penkwe* prove nothing.   The *m* may have been labiodental itself; besides, such pronunciations are common even in modern German, which certainly has labio-dental *f*.)   At any rate, its clearness of articulation was enhanced by labio-dental articulation, which we now find in all Germanic languages; in certain positions and in certain languages it became voiced. The velar, for which this book uses the letter *h̩*, (modified *h*, since *h* is the usual spelling in all Germanic languages) had the least stability: being articulated by the relatively inert velum and back of the tongue, it lacked the articulatory intensity that would have favored a further shift; under Verner's Law it had become *ʒ* at a time when it was still pronounced with considerable friction although a lenis. Where it remained voiceless, its physiological character led to further relaxation, resulting in its reduction to actual *h*, the glottal (instead of velar) spirant, and sometimes in complete disappearance. The following is in part a summing-up of statements occurring in former sections.

Gmc. *þ* was preserved in GOTHIC in all positions: *þu, wairþan, brōþar,* **b** *warþ.* In OLD NORSE and OLD ENGLISH it remained *þ* initially, but became *ð* in voiced surroundings: ON *þing—brōðer*, OE *þing—brōðor*; spelling, however, does not indicate this, since the letters *þ* and *ð* are used interchangeably in these two languages. In OLD SAXON and OLD HIGH GERMAN we find *þ* (mostly spelled *th*) in the earliest records in all positions, but gradually this changed to *ð* and soon to *d*, first medially and in habitually unaccented words, e.g., in pronouns and in the definite article. In Bavarian, the process began as early as the eighth century. It gradually spread north, reaching the Low German territory during the late Middle Ages. In MIDDLE ENGLISH, perhaps even in OLD ENGLISH, *þ-* in pronominal forms and similar words of little semantic function became *ð*, and an analogous process took place in Danish, Swedish, and Norwegian where, however, stops resulted: Sw. *ting, tänka,* but *du, De.* ENGLISH and ICELANDIC preserved *þ* initially, English also in strictly final position (cf. *cloth—clothe*; in the latter word *th* was medial in Middle English).

Gmc. *f* was also preserved in GOTHIC in all positions: *fadar, afar, uf.* **c** Like *þ*, it became voiced in voiced surroundings in NORSE and ENGLISH, thus coinciding with IE *bh* and *'p*. In LOW GERMAN (Old Saxon), too, it became voiced. The usual spelling was *ƀ*, but we also find *u*: *wulƀos, fiui.* In HIGH GERMAN it generally remained voiceless, but has been a lenis since OHG times, as its frequent rendering by *u v* in medial position indicates: *nevo, nefor, hevig.*

Gmc. *h̩* was clearly the *ach-/ich-*sound, as is indicated by Latin **d** spellings like *Cherusci, Chatti,* Gk. Χέρουσκοι, Χάττοι. In all Germanic languages it is preserved initially as *h*, but in other positions it must be considered a velar (or palatal) spirant wherever preserved at all: *h* in Go. *haban*, ON *hafa*, etc.; [χ] (or [ç]) in Go. *nahts, raihts, taih*.

However, final *h* in Gothic, while still a velar spirant, must have been decidedly a lenis, while final ʒ, which became unvoiced like final ð and ƀ, was a fortis: *dag, dags* probably had a velar spirant with stronger friction than *taih*, comparable to the difference in the articulation of *ch* in NHG *Bach* and *nach*. In NORSE, *h* disappeared everywhere except initially, in OLD ENGLISH it disappeared between voiced sounds: Go. *himins, hva*: ON *himinn, huat*, OE *heofon, hwæt*; Go. *teihan, saihvan, slahan, ahva, filhan*: ON *tiā, siā, slā, ā, fela*, OE *tēon, sēon, slēan, ēa, feolan*. In both LOW and HIGH GERMAN final and intervocalic *h* is consistently preserved in the older sources, but gradually disappeared, first in Bavarian; cf. NHG *sehen, sah* = [ze:ən, za:]. Before consonants it remained a velar or palatal spirant: *Nacht, Sicht.*—Initially it disappeared before *l r n w* in NORSE as well as in WEST GERMANIC; only English, at least American English, has preserved *hw*: Go. *hlahjan*, ON *hlæja*, OE *hliehhan*, OHG (*h*)*lahhan*—Sw. *le*, E. *laugh*, Ger. *lachen*; Go. *hneiwan*, ON *hnīga*, OE OS OHG *hnīgan*; NHG *neigen*; Go. *hrains*, ON *hreinn*, OS *hrēni*, OHG (*h*)*reini*: NHG *rein*; Go. *hva*, ON *hvat*, OE *hwæt*, OS *hwat*, OHG *hwaz*: Sw. *hvad* = [vad], E. *what* = Brit. [wɔt], LG *wat*, HG *was*.

28. Rhotacism. IE *s* was preserved intact in Germanic where it had not changed to *z* according to Verner's Law. This *z* remained in Gothic, but in North and West Germanic it was intensified to *r*, as in Latin (*genera* < *genezā). This is called Rhotacism from *rho*, the Greek name of the letter *r*. In earliest Norse this *r* is distinct from old *r*: It is expressed by a different rune (transcribed by R in our grammars) and causes *i*-mutation (Go. *kas* 'vessel', ON *ker*). Early Norse loan words in Finnic still show *s* (*rengas, kuningas*). In later Norse and in West Germanic there is no distinction between old and new *r.*—For *s* in final syllables, see **49** D.

INSTANCES:

Go. *maiza*: ON *meire*, OE *māra*, OS OHG *mēro*

Go. *kiusan, kaus*, analogical *kusum, kusans*: ON *kiōsa, kaus, kǫrom, kǫrenn* (*r*-mutation), OE *cēosan, cēas, curon, coren*, OS *kiosan, kōs, kurun, gikoran*, OHG *kiosan, kōs, kurum, gikoran*

Go. *hausjan*—ON *heyra*, OE *hīeran*, OS *hōrian*, OHG *hōr*(*r*)*en*

Go. *huzd*—OE OS *hord*, OHG *hort.*

NOTE: Go. *huzd* goes back to IE *kudh-tó-* > *kud-dhó-, kud·dhó-*, through 'Bartholomä's Law'; it is related to Gk. κύσθος 'concealed place, female organ', L. *custos* 'guardian': similarly **ghadh-tó-*, L. *hasta*, Go. *gazds*, OS *gard*, OHG *gart* 'spike'. IE *z* goes back to *s* before a voiced stop. In such cases, through regular consonant shift, Gmc. *sp st sk* result, as in **ni-zdo-*, L. *nīdus*, OHG *nest*; **o-zdo-*, Go. *asts*, OHG *ast*.

For Gmc. *zm*, see below.

29. Consonant Groups.

(1) s-Combinations.

(a) The IE group *tt* remained as such only in Indic: IE *sed-to-* > **a** *setto-* 'seated' > Sk. *sattá-*. In Iranian, Slavic, Greek it developed to *st*: Gk. *ἄ-ιστος* 'unknown' < IE *n̥-wid-to-*. In Italic, Celtic, Germanic the result was *ss*: L. *sessus*, ON OE OS *sess* 'seat'; Go. *wissa*, ON *vissa*, OE *wisse*, OS OHG *wissa* 'I knew' < IE *wid-tām*; Go. OHG *missa-* 'wrong' < IE *mid-to-* (L. *mitto*, *missus*, OE OS *mīþan*, OHG *mīdan* 'omit'). After a long vowel, *ss* is simplified to *s*; IE *weid-to-*, Go. *un-weis*, ON *vīs-* (nom. sg. masc. *vīss*), OE OHG *wīs* 'wise'; IE *ēdtom* (past part. of *edō*, Go. *itan*), OE *ǣs*, OHG *ās* 'carcass'. It is generally assumed that the transition to *st ss* took place after a sibilant glide had developed between the two *t*'s: *tˢt*; either the first *t*, or both *t*'s were assimilated to this.

Apparently also IE *ts* resulted in Gmc. *ss s*, but evidence for this is very scant: Go. *missō* 'mutually', ON *ȳ-miss* 'alternately' may go back to IE *mit-sām* (Sk. adv. *mithas* 'mutually'), ON *eisa* 'embers' to IE *əidh-s-*, *əits-* (Gk. *αἶθος*).

(b) Inversely, a *t*-glide developed in Germanic and Slavic between *s* and *r*. IE *sreu-/srou-* 'flow', Sk. *srávati*, Gk. *ῥέω*, ON *straumr*, OE *strēam*, OS OHG *strōm*, OSl. *o-strovъ* 'island'; IE *ausro-/usro-* 'bright', Sk. *uṣrá*, L. *aurōra*, Lith. *aušra* 'morning glow', OE *ēastron*, OHG *ōstarun* 'spring festival, Easter'; IE *swesr-*, Sk. *svasár-*, L. *soror*, Go. *swistar*, OE *swester*, OS OHG *swester* (*t* developed in those cases that had originally suffix with zero grade).

(2) **Nasals** and **Liquids** show hardly any independent sound changes **b** (for final *m*, see **49** D), but they are very apt to assimilate other sounds, or to be assimilated to them. The following assimilations are the most important:

(a) The Germanic Consonant Lengthening, *pn' bn' bhn'* > *pp*; see **22**.

(b) Likewise, *ln* > *ll*: IE *pl̥nós*, Lith. *pílnas*, Sk. *-pṛṇa-*, OSl. *plъnъ*, Go. *fulls*, ON *fullr*, OE OS *ful*, OHG *fol*; IE *peln-*, Gk. *πέλλα*, L. *pellis*, Go. *þrūtsfill* 'leprosy', ON *fiall*, OE *fell*, OHG *fel* (gen. *felles*).

(c) *nw* > *nn*: Sk. *riṇváti* 'makes flow', Go. OS OHG *rinnan* 'flow'; L. *minuō* 'diminish', Go. *minniza* 'less'; L. *tenuis*, ON *þunnr*, OE *þynne*, OHG *dunni* 'thin'.

(d) *n*-stop-*n* > *nn*: IE *sent-no-* 'go' (L. *sentiō*, Go. *sinþs* 'walk'; OE *sīþian* < IE *sent-jo-*)—OHG *sinnan* 'go, consider'.

(e) *zm* > *mm*, *zl* > *ll*, *ðl* > *ll*: Sk. *tasmāi* 'him' (dat. sg.), Go. *þamma* (simplified through unstress in OHG *demu*, *demo*; likewise dat. pl. ending IE *-mis* > Gmc. *-miz mz mm m*; see **49** D); IE *es-mi* 'am', Sk. *ásmi*, Gk. **ἐσμι*, εἰμί, Go. *im* < **imm.*—ON *knosa*, OE *cnyssan*, OHG *chnussen* 'strike'; ON *knylla*, OE *cnyllan* 'strike' < **knuz-la-*.— IE *stǝdhlo-*, L. *stabulum*, ON *stallr*, OE *steall*, OHG *stal* (gen. sg. *stalles*) (but IE *stǝtlo-* > OE *stapol*, OHG *stadel* 'shed'); IE *mǝ-tlo-* 'meet', with suffix accent Gmc. *maðla-*, Ger.-L. *mallus* 'place of court', *mallāre* 'sue', *Theotmalli* 'Detmold', but with stem accent, Gmc. *maþla-*, Go. *maþl* 'place of meeting, ON **mahla-* > *māl*, OE *mæþl*, OHG *mahal*, *madal-*.

c   (f) *n* (*ŋ*) before *ƕ* disappears in Primitive Germanic; in Norse, the nasal also disappears before *s* and *f*, and in the Anglo-Frisian group (OE Fris. OS) before *s f þ*; a preceding short vowel is lengthened ('Compensatory Lengthening'); *a* is always lengthened to *ō* in OE, sometimes in ON OFris. and OS:

Gmc. *faŋƕana-*, Go. *fāhan*, ON *fā*, OE *fōn*, OFris. *fā*, OS OHG *fāhan*

Gmc. *þaŋƕta-*, pret. of *þaŋkjana-* 'think', Go. *þāhta*, ON *þātta*, OE *þōhte*,   OS *thāhta*, OHG *dāhta*

Gmc. *þeŋƕana-* 'thrive', Go. *-þeihan*, OE *þēon*, OHG *-dīhan*

Gmc. *þuŋƕta-*, pret. of *þuŋkjana-* 'think, seem', Go. *þūhta*, ON *þōtta*,   OE *þūhte*, OS *thūhta*, OHG *dūhta*

E. *think*, OE *þyncean*, belongs to this verb, but E. *thought*, OE *þōhte*, belongs to Gmc. *þaŋkjana-*, OE *þencean*; thus E. *think—thought* corresponds to NHG *dünken—dachte*; cf. *methinks—mich dünkt*.

OHG *gans*, ON *gǭs*, OE *gōs*, OS **gās*, *gōs*

Go. OHG *uns*, ON *ōs*, OE *ūs*, OFris. OS *ūs*

OHG *wunsken* 'wish', ON *ø̄skia*, OE *wȳscan*

Gmc. *tumft-* 'foundation wall' (L. *domus*, Gk. δόμος) > ON *tōft*, *tōpt*

Go. OHG *fimf*, OE OFris. OS *fīf*; instead of ON **fīf* we have *fimm*,   formed in analogy with the ordinal *fimte* and *fimtān* 'fifteen', in   which *f* had been lost between two consonants.

Go. *kunþs* 'known', OHG *kund*, OE *cūþ*, OFris. OS *kūth*

Go. *anþar*, OHG *andar*, ON *annarr* (*nþ* > *nn*), OE *ōþer*, OFris. *other*,   OS *āðar*, *othar* (but also *andar*—a HG borrowing).

The similar forms ON *ǫþrom*, OE *ōþrum*, dat. sg. masc. of 'other', represent very different phonetic processes; in OE, *n* before *þ* disappeared with the regular compensatory lengthening to *ō*; in Norse, the group *nþ* became *nn* (nom. sg *annarr*), and this became ð(þ) before *r*, as in *kuþr* = Go. *kumþs* (> **kunnr* > *kuþr*).

Some other assimilations are obvious, such as *md* > *nd* : ON *sund* 'swimming' (noun), OE OS OHG *swimman*, ON *symia*.

For Go. *þliuhan* as against ON *flȳia*, OE *flēon*, OFris. *fliā*, OS OHG *fliohan* d 'flee' it is generally claimed that Gothic has retained the original initial, while the other dialects have dissimilated the dentals þ and *l*. But there can really not be any doubt that Zupitza (Germ. Gutt. 131) is right in accepting Gmc. *fl-* as original and considering Go. *þl-* an assimilation. The verb is related to ON *fliūga*, OE *flēogan*, OHG *fliogan*, and is an extension of IE *pleu-* by a *k*-determinant. The simple root occurs in Gk. πλέϝω 'float, swim', OSl. *pluti*, Lith. *plauti*, Sk. *plavatē*, L. *pluit* 'rains', OHG *flouwen* 'rinse', Go. *flōdus* 'flood', OHG *fluot*, etc. With *d*-extension it appears in ON *fliōta*, OE *flēotan*, OS *fliotan*, OHG *fliozzan* 'flow'. Its primary meaning was probably 'floating, even motion, through water, air, or on land'. OHG *fliogan* etc. must be considered an aorist present; the stem vowel was leveled in accordance with the class pattern (instead of **fluȝan* > **flogan*), but Verner's Law was preserved. The same principle applies to Go. *þlahsjan* 'frighten' and *-þlaihan* 'exhort', both of which belong to the family of L. *plangō*. For Go. forms with *fl-* (*flahta, -flaugjan, flauts, flōdus, flōkan*) see Nordmeyer, Language 11. 216 ff.

There are some sporadic dissimilations, for which no definite formula can be e given. The most frequent cases are various types of dissimilation between *m* and *n*: Gk. στόμα 'mouth', IE *stomn-, stemn-*: Go. *stibna* 'voice', OFris. *stifne*— OE *stemm*, OS *stemna*, OHG *stimna* 'Stimme'; IE *nomn-* 'name', ON *nafn*, Go. *namō*, gen. *namnis*; IE *kemn-* 'heaven', OE *heofon*, OS *hevan*—Go. *himins* (while in ON and OE the labial nasal is replaced by a labial spirant, in OHG *himil* the dental nasal is replaced by a dental liquid).

30. The West Germanic Consonant Lengthening. As shown in **22**, *n* was, in Primitive Germanic, under certain accent conditions assimilated to a preceding consonant, resulting in the geminates Gmc. *pp tt kk*. A similar, but by no means identical process took place in West Germanic at a later time: Before semi-vowels and liquids (*j w l r*) consonants were lengthened, but the assimilation of *j w* was gradual, and *l r* were not assimilated. Phonetically the process is not entirely clear, but is apparently connected with a difference in syllable division: In a word like Go. *hal-dan*, *l* belongs clearly to the first syllable; but ð in *bidjan* belongs to the second syllable as well as the first; this may have led to a lengthening of articulation. The type *bidjan*, with a *j*-suffix, is by far the most frequent. The palatal spirant palatalizes the preceding consonant, and a palatal consonant is in its very nature a long consonant (cf. Bremer, Deutsche Phonetik 48; Prokosch, Sounds and History of the German Language 25 f.). The habit of articulation that had developed in this type may then have been transferred to the similar types where other sonorous consonants followed.

INSTANCES:

j: Go. *bidjan*, ON *biþia*—OE *biddan*, OS *biddian*, OHG *bitten*

(Go. *sitan*), ON *sitia*—OE *sittan*, OS *sittian*, OHG *sizzen*

Go. *skapjan*, ON *skepia*, OE *scieppan*, OHG *scepfen*

Go. *sibja*, OE *sibb*, OS *sibbia*, OHG *sippea, sippa.*

  g k after a short vowel were lengthened in Norse too:

(Go. *ligan*), ON *liggia*, OE *licgan*, OS *liggian*, OHG *liggen* (UG *licken*)

Go. *hugjan*, ON *hyggia*, OE *hycgan*, OS *huggian*, OHG *huggen* (UG *hucken*)

Gmc. *bakja-* 'brook', ON *bekkr*, OE *bec(c)*; OHG *bah* < **baki-.*

ON *kk* is generally leveled to *k* through analogy with other forms of the same word, e.g. Go. *wakjan*, ON *vekia* (trans.; intr. *vaka*, pret. *vakþa*), OE *wacian* < **wakajan*, OS *wekkian*, OHG *wecchen*.

r is generally not lengthened:

Go. *nasjan*, OE OS *nerian*, OHG *neren*, but also *nerren*

OHG *skara* 'troup', **skarjo* > *skerjo* 'troup leader', NHG *Scherge* 'bailiff'.

The resulting long consonant is shortened after a long syllable:

Go. *laidjan* 'lead', ON *leiþa*, OE *lǽdan*, OS *lēdian*, OHG *leiten* (early UG *leitten*).

w was more often vocalized to *u o*, but there are a few cases of WGmc. lengthening of labio-velars before *w*:

Go. *naqaþs* 'naked', OHG *nackot*, ON *nokkueþr*, but without lengthening ON *nakenn*, OE *nacod*, OHG *nahhut*

Go. *aqizi* 'axe', OHG *ackus* (but also *ahhus*)

Go. *ahva*, NHG *-ach* in *Salzach*, but *a* in *Fulda*; the Monsee-Wien Fragments of OHG have *kisāhhun* = Go. *-sēhvun*, *nāhhitun* = Go. *nēhvidun*.

Before *l r* a vowel is inserted subsequent to the lengthening:

l: OSl. *(j)ablъko* 'apple', OE *æppel*, ON *eple*, OHG *apful* (and *afful*)

Go. *leitils*, ON *lítell*, OE *lȳtel* (simplified after long vowel), OS *luttil*, OHG *luzzil*

r: Go. *baitrs* 'bitter', ON *bitr*, OE *bittor*, OS OHG *bittar* (*tr-* does not go through the HG Shift)

Go. *akrs*, ON *akr*, OE *æcer*, without lengthening, OS *akkar*, OHG *ackar*

OSl. *dobrъ* 'good', ON *dapr* 'sad', E. *dapper*, OHG *tapfar* 'weighty'.

n is a frequent noun suffix; through different vowel grades in the suffix there arise many parallel forms; if *n* follows the root without a vowel, lengthening takes place. A great deal of leveling has largely obscured the original conditions. In many words the alternation is still clear, but it is not always possible to separate this process from the Gmc. consonant lengthening (**22**), which within paradigms may have been delayed by analogical retention of older forms: Gmc. *knab-* (IE *gnə-/gnō-bh-*), as an *n*-stem, could show the suffix grades *-ŏn-*, *-ĕn-*, *-n-*, *-ō-*; the latter form gave OE *cnafa* (NE *knave*), OHG *knabo* 'Knabe'; forms with zero grade yielded OHG *knappo* 'Knappe'; in either form, the simple or lengthened consonant was leveled through the whole paradigm. Similar *Rabe—Rappe*; E. *drop*—OHG *tropfo* (Gmc. *-p-on-*, *-p-n-*).

31. Secondary Developments. The Consonant Shift had the same trend in all dialects, but it differed in scope, as shown in **18-26**. Beyond this, the development of the consonants presents great variations.

GOTHIC in the form in which we chiefly know it, that of Wulfila's time (4th century), had deviated very little from Germanic consonantism. It shows a **a** preference for voiceless rather than voiced spirants: Verner's Law is carried through very incompletely; final voiced spirants (including position before *-s*, *-t*) are unvoiced: *hlaibis, gōdis, maiza, dagis—hlaif(s), gōþ(s), mais, dag(s)* (voiceless in spite of spelling; cf. **24b**); *giban—gaf, gaft.*—Assimilations are comparatively rare; the doubling of consonants has not progressed beyond the Gmc. conditions; there is no Gothic evidence for the Gmc. lengthening of stops.

Gothic beyond Wulfila is virtually unknown. Neither the smaller documents, nor proper names preserved in historians, nor the fragments of Crimean Gothic offer adequate evidence for later consonant developments. Busbeck's spelling (cf. **5**, Bibliography) seems to point to some changes that remind one of the second consonant shift, such as *plut* 'sanguis', *tag* 'dies', *bruder* 'frater', but the evidence is too contradictory to allow any clear conclusions. Aside from the unreliable spelling, there exists the possibility of dialect mixture; even High German influence is not quite excluded.

NORSE has greatly modified the Germanic consonant system. Its most striking **b** features are the voicing, assimilation, or dropping of medial or final voiceless spirants and the extreme frequency of double consonants, which are in most cases the result of assimilation. Cf. Go. *drigkan, þugkjan, anþar, lagjan,* ON *drekka, þykkia, annarr, leggia.* Voiced stops that were already final in Primitive Norse, became voiceless: **band > *bant > batt.* Whatever the reason, it is a fact that in its final appearance Norse consonantism shows a strange resemblance to Finnish consonantism.

ENGLISH shows in the early period two clearly distinct consonant systems. The northern, Anglian, section hardly differs from continental Anglian: Initial **c** Gmc. *ʒ* is a stop, Gmc. *k* and *g* are not palatalized (see below). The southern territory, which is essentially Frisian (partly Saxon), retains in part an earlier consonant stage, in so far as *ʒ* remains a spirant in all positions (except after *n* and in gemination; initially only before front vowels), in part it develops a new consonant trend that is common in Romance and Slavic, but among the Germanic languages occurs only in Frisian proper, in Southern English, and to a slight extent in later Scandinavian. This is 'Palatalization', a term that, unfortunately, is used with a variety of meanings. In the sense that it has here, it does not refer to variation in the place of articulation of Gmc. *ḫ ȝ* in accordance with neighboring vowels (*ich* and *ach, j* and *ȝ*), but to the change of the stops, *k g* to palatal or dental affricates, *č dž ts dz*. While conditions in English and Frisian are not quite identical, they are sufficiently similar to make us assume that the process was either completed in continental times, or, at least, that *k g* before front vowels had become so decidedly palatal at the time of the Germanic settlement of Southern England that the actual 'assibilation'—the change to the affricates mentioned—was nearly inevitable: OE *cirice*, OFris. *tzerke* (*ziurke*) 'church' (Anglian *kirk*); OE *cytel*, OFris. *szetel* 'kettle' (Anglian; Go. *katils*); OFris. *tsyse*, OE *cīese* 'cheese'; OE *drencean*, OFris. *drentza* 'water' (cf. E. *drench*); OE *licgean*, OFris. *lidza* 'lie'; OE *lǣce*, OFris. *letza* 'leech, physician'; OE *sprǣc*, OFris. *spreze* 'speech'.

d   OLD SAXON virtually retained the West Germanic consonant system; it is still essentially intact in its present-day development, and equally so in Low Franconian, including Dutch. For the change of dental spirants to stops, cf. **24c**.

e   OLD HIGH GERMAN is distinguished from the other Germanic dialects chiefly by the Second Shift, but later consonant changes partly restored former conditions. Rhine Franconian, East Franconian, and Bavarian changed intervocalic *b* to bilabial *v* [*b*]. The Upper German fortes *p t k* became, in general, lenes; Upper German *kḫ* reverted to *k* in most of the territory.

The consonantism of Standard New High German is, in a sense, an artificial structure. As to spelling, it is based on the East Franconian dialect, since its most important home, the East Middle German dialect, is primarily a continuation of East Franconian. But this East Middle German form of the language is interpreted in North German (in fact, almost international) sound values. Thus, German *d* is voiced in the North, voiceless in the South, but Standard German ('Bühnenaussprache') requires the northern pronunciation. German *t* is the South German equivalent of North German *d* (HG *tun*, LG *dōn*), and in its home is pronounced voiceless, mostly as a lenis, partly as a fortis, but never aspirated; still, the 'standard' requires the aspirated pronunciation, which in North German occurs only in those words which in South German have *z*, not *t* (HG *zehn*, LG *ten*). Medial *b* is an entirely artificial introduction; Gmc. -*b*- is a voiceless lenis stop in Alemannian and in the 'Anglian' district east of the Lower Elbe, and a labio-dental or bilabial spirant everywhere else—but Standard German requires a voiced stop. *k*- is practically the only stop that has the same value in Low and High German, partly due to the retrogressive development of *kh* > *k* in Upper German.

C. The Semi-Vowels

32. Articulation. *j* and *w* may be defined as vowels (*i u*) in consonantic function. Brugmann, accordingly, uses the characters *i̯ u̯* for consonantic IE *i u*. In Go. *stigum*, *i* is purely a vowel; in Go. *staig* it is a diphthongal glide which may equally well be designated as a vowel or as a consonant; in IE *dvojō-*, Sk. *dvayōs* 'of two' it is clearly a consonant as to function, and it is inclined to become a consonant in articulation as well: ON *tueggia* (see below). The physiological distinction between vowels and consonants is relative. With a vowel, the current of breath is not impeded in its passage through the mouth; with a consonant, there is an obstruction in the median line of the mouth, be it complete (stops) or partial (spirants). But in the case of the 'high' vowels, *i u*, the back of the tongue is so close to the roof of the mouth that a slight raising is apt to transform them into spirants, or even stops. It is impossible to draw a definite line between vocalic *i u* and spirantic *j w*. English *y* and South German *j* are relatively wide and therefore more nearly vocalic; North German *j* and palatal intervocalic *g* are real spirants (*Jahr, liegen*). In Gmc. words borrowed by Romance languages at various times during the Middle Ages, initial *w* became a stop: LFr. *wardōn*—Late L. *guardāre*, Fr. *guarder*; E. *war*—Fr. *guerre*; Ger. *Welfen, Waiblingen*—Ital. *Guelfi, Ghibellini*.

33. Germanic Developments. Initial *j, w* remained unchanged in a most IE languages; in Greek, *j-* appears either as *h* (') or as ζ; the reasons for the difference are unknown. *w* is preserved as ϝ (Digamma) in many dialects, but had disappeared in (classical) Attic: Sk. *yūyám*, Go. *jus*—Gk. ὑμεῖς 'you'; Sk. *yugam*, L. *iugum*, Go. *juk*—Gk. ζυγόν 'yoke'; Go. *jēr* 'year', Czech *jaro* 'spring'—Gk. ὥρα 'season' (L. *hōra* is borrowed from this), Gk. Ἥρα 'goddess of the seasons'; Sk. *dyáus* 'sky', Gk. Ζεύς, L. *Jūpiter, Diēspiter*, ON *Tȳr*, OHG *Ziu Zio* (from **dejwos*; the Sk. Gk. L. forms from **djēws*); verb suffix *-ejo-*: Go. *nasjan*, OE *nerigean*, OHG *nerian* (*nerren*).—Gk. (ϝ)οῖκος 'house', L. *vīcus*, Go. *weihs* 'town'; Gk. (ϝ)οῖδα, Sk. *véda*, L. *vīdī*, Go. *wait* 'I know'; Sk. *vidhávā*, L. *vidua*, Go. *widuwō* 'widow'.

Initial *j* disappeared in Norse: Go. *jēr, juk*, ON *ār, ok*; initial *w* before *l r* disappeared (gradually) in NWGmc.; in Norse it also disappeared before rounded vowels: Go. *anda-wleizn*, ON *and-lit*, OHG *ant-luzzi* 'face'; Go. *wrikan*, ON *reka*, OHG *rehhan* 'punish, revenge'; Go. *waurþum, waurþans* < Gmc. *wurðum, wurðana-*, ON *urþom, orþenn*.

In NWGmc. we find sporadic loss of *w* after consonants: OE *hwōsta*, OHG *huosto* 'cough'; OE *swēte* < **swoti*, OHG *suozi* 'sweet'. Between consonants it disappeared everywhere: Lith. *leñgvas*, Go. *leihts* 'light'.— For *w* of labio-velars, cf. **23**.

Owing to their semi-vocalic character, *j* and *w* in medial and final b position are apt to alternate with *i* and *u*. The original conditions are largely obscured by secondary changes, but Gothic seems to have preserved the Primitive Germanic forms:

(a) When *j w* became final through the loss of the original final vowel, they appeared as *i u*: Go. *kuni, hari, hairdi* (acc. sg. of *jo*-stems), but *kunjis, harjis* (gen. sg., < **kun-ji-za, *har-ji-za*; for *hairdeis*, see below); *kniu, triu* (nom. acc. sg. neut.), but *kniwis, triwis*. Similarly *hardus* < **hardwaz, sunjus* (nom. pl. < **sun-iw-iz*), but *suniwē*; cf. **49 d**.

The treatment of Gmc. *-ji-* in endings is of special importance. Gothic shows *-ji-* if the stem syllable has a short vowel and a consonant, or a long vowel without a consonant, but *ī* (spelled *ei*) if it has a long vowel and a consonant or is dissyllabic: *satjis* (W V, 2 sg.), *harjis* (gen. sg.), *stōjis* (2 sg.), but *sōkeis* (2 sg.), *mikileis* (2 sg.), *hairdeis* (gen. sg.). This is due to a difference in syllabification. In the former type, the syllable division is between stem and ending: *sat-jis, har-jis, stō-jis*. In the latter type, the final consonant of the stem belongs to the next syllable: *sō-keis, miki-leis, hair-deis*, and interconsonantic *-ji-* = *ii* was contracted to *ī*. ON *hirþis* (*hirþes*), but *niþs, sǽker*, but *setr*, show a further shortening; cf. **49 d**.

From the Gmc. point of view the types *harjis, hairdeis* on the one hand, and *satjis, sōkeis* on the other, are phonetically equivalent. The nouns, however, have the suffix IE *je/jo* (cf. L. *medius*, Go. *midjis*), while in the verbs two types have coalesced; some are *je/jo*-presents like L. *speciō*, Sk. *páśyati* 'he sees', Lith. *stójuo-s* 'I stand up' (L. *stō* < **stājō*) : Go. *bidjis, stōjis, sōkeis*; but the great majority (verbs of Class I W) are causatives in IE *eje/ejo* (cf. **54 d, e, f, g**) with early reduction to *je/jo* : *satjis, lagjis, frawardeis* (cf. Sk. *vartáyati* 'he turns', trans.).

The difference in treatment according to the character of the preceding syllable is not restricted to Germanic, but appears also in Indo-Iranian, Latin (*capis*, but *audīs*), and at least in traces in Greek and Baltic. It may have been Indo-European; this view was first expressed by Sievers (Btr. 5. 129 f.; it is frequently referred to as 'Sievers' Law') and confirmed and extended by F. Edgerton, Language 10. 235 ff. However, the identical development of Gmc. *ji* < IE *je* and Gmc. *ji* < IE *eje* rather seems to suggest independent development in the several languages.

c   HOLTZMANN'S LAW. Intervocalic *j w* after short vowels show in many words strengthened articulation; we may represent the Germanic forms as *jj ww* (Braune, Btr. 9. 545). In West Germanic, the first part of the lengthened semi-vowel forms a diphthong with the preceding short vowel, but in Gothic and Norse it is narrowed to a stop. For *ww* we find *ggw* in both dialects; for *jj* Gothic has the spelling *ddj*, Norse *ggi* (*ggj*), but originally at least the pronunciation was probably the same, namely, a palatal stop followed by a spirantic glide (similar to *gy* in Magyar):

j: Sk. *dváyōs* 'of two'—Go. *twaddjē*, ON *tueggia*: OHG (Isidor) *zweiio*
     Sk. *priyá* 'wife'—ON *Frigg*: OHG *Frīa* < **frijja* (goddess)

Gk. ᾠόν—Go. *addi, Crimean Go. ada (probably pl.), ON egg: OE æg (pron. æy; NE egg is a Norse loan-word), OHG ei.

w: IE drewā—Go. triggwa 'alliance', ON tryggvar (pl.) 'trust': OHG triuwa, treuwa 'faith'

IE ghləwo- (Gk. χλωρός 'light green')—Go. glaggwo 'accurately', ON glǫggr 'clever': OE glēaw, OHG glouwēr 'clever'

IE bhlewo- (bhləwo-, L. flāvus?)—Go. bliggwan: OHG bliuwan 'beat'.

NOTE: Go. ggw in such words is not ŋgw, as in siggwan; bliggwan is a strong verb of the second, siggwan of the third class.

But there is no lengthening in Go. ais (aiz), OHG ēr, ON eir < *ajaz, Sk. ayas 'bronze'; Go. bajōþs 'both'; Go. triwis, kniwis (see above). Sometimes we have parallel forms with and without lengthening, similar to Grammatical Change: ON Frigg, but Go. frijōn 'love'; ON hǫggua 'strike, cut', but Go. hawi 'hay'.

The difference is generally ascribed to IE accent, but the exact conditions are a moot question. Holtzmann, Ad. Gr. 1. 109, assumed lengthening if the accent preceded; cf. Kluge, Urg. 3. 75; QF 32. 127. Lately, strong arguments have been given for suffix accent, especially by Mikkola, Streitberg-Festgabe 267, and Trautmann, Germ. Lautgesetze 40 (with complete material). Also Hirt, HU 1. 113, favors this view. Leveling has so greatly obscured the original conditions that historical certainty can hardly be obtained. Phonetic probability would rather seem to point to root accent as the cause of this strengthening of articulation; cf. Prokosch, JEGPh 11. 7.

In a few cases we find g instead of w in West Germanic too: L. iuventus—OHG jugund, OE geogoþ; L. novem—OS nigun. Probably the following u caused dissimilation in such forms.

For intervocalic w > k, see Hirt, HU 1. 114.

In Norse and West Germanic, with the exception of English, w became a true spirant, before 1000 in Norse, at the end of the Middle Ages in the German dialects. It is bilabial in Dutch (mostly) and High German, labio-dental in Norse and Low German.

VOCALISM

34. The Indo-European Vowels. Until 1878 it had been assumed that Indo-European had essentially the same vowels as Aryan, namely ă ĭ ŭ, and that in the European group ă split up into ă ĕ ŏ. In 1878 and 1879 several scholars showed that the five-vowel system (ă ĕ ŏ; ĭ ŭ) was the original one, and that in Aryan ĕ ŏ had become ă. The priority for this discovery belongs to Hermann Collitz.[1] The Indo-European vowels are best preserved in Greek, but also fairly well in accented syllables in Latin. In Balto-Slavic and Germanic, *a* and *o* on the one hand, and *ā* and *ō* on the other 'fell together', although the treatment was by no means identical in the two groups; see **38**.

IE *ĕ ŏ ă* may be termed the fundamental vowels. They occurred mainly in accented syllables. IE *ĭ ŭ* originally were reductions from diphthongs (**39**) and as such originally occurred only in unstressed syllables. Unstressed simple long vowels were reduced to a slurred vowel which may be likened to the unaccented vowel in Eng. *drama*. It is transcribed by *ə* and termed *shva*, a name taken from Hebrew grammar. Unstressed short vowels were generally dropped, but were sometimes preserved as slurred vowels, perhaps similar to *y* in Eng. *pretty*. This is usually transcribed by the Slavic letter *ъ* (the 'soft sign'), which in present Russian merely indicates palatal articulation of the preceding consonant, but originally expressed short *i*. IE *ə* and *ъ* are distinguished as 'shva primum' and 'shva secundum', but the term 'shva' alone always refers to *ə*.[2]

b INSTANCES:

LONG VOWELS—

ē became *ā* in Sk., *ī* in Celtic, and was preserved in the other IE languages with the exception of Germanic (**37**):

IE *dhē-*—Sk. *dhā-*, Gk. θη- (τίθημι) 'put', L. *fēcī* 'I did', OSl. *dēti* 'put'

IE *sē-*—Gk. ἵημι < *σισημι 'throw', L. *sēmen*, OIr. *sīl*, OSl. *sēmę* 'seed'

IE *rēĝ-*—Sk. *rājan-*, L. *rēx*, Gall. *-rīx* (borrowed in Gmc. *rīk-* NHG *Reich*) 'king'.

ō became *ā* in Aryan, Celtic, and Slavic (also in Lettish, but *uo* in Lithuanian):

IE *dō-*—Sk. *dānam*, Gk. δῶρον, L. *dōnum*, OSl. *darъ* 'gift'

IE *ĝnō-*—Sk. *jñā-*, Gk. γνω-, L. (*co*)*gnō*(*scō*), OSl. *znati* 'know'

IE *dwō* (beside *dwōu*)—Sk. (Ved.) *dvā*, Gk. δύω, (L. *duo*, < *duō*?) OIr. *dā*, OSl. *dъva*.

ā became *ē* in Attic-Ionic Greek, *ō* in Lithuanian (but *a* in Lettish):

IE *māter-*—Sk. *mātar-*, Gk. Dor. μᾱτηρ, Att. μήτηρ, L. *māter*, OIr. *mathir*, Lith. *motė̃* ('wife'), OSl. *matъ* 'mother'

IE *bhrāter-*—Sk. *bhrātar-*, Gk. φρᾱτωρ, L. *frāter*, OIr. *brāthir*, OSl. *bratъ*, Lith. *broter*(*ēlis*) 'brother'

IE *stā-*—Sk. *sthā-*, Gk. ἵστᾱμι, ἵστημι, L. *stāre*, Lith. *stóti*, Lett. *stat*, OSl. *stati*.

SHORT VOWELS—

c *e* was the most frequent IE vowel. It remained *e* in most languages and under most conditions, but became *a* in Aryan.

IE *bhérō*—Sk. *bharāmi*, Gk. φέρω, L. *ferō* 'carry', OSl. *berą*

IE *édō*—Sk. *ádmi*, Gk. ἔδω, L. *edō* 'eat'

IE *deḱḿ*—Sk. *dáśa*, Gk. δέκα, L. *decem*, OSl. *desętь*

IE *ésti*—Sk. *ásti*, Gk. ἐστί, L. *est*,

    o usually alternates with e (Ablaut, **44**; cf. Gk. φέρω 'I carry', φορέω 'I usually carry, I wear'). It remains *o* in most languages, but appears as *a* in Aryan, Lithuanian (*o* in Lettish) and Germanic (**38**).

IE *oḱtó(u)*—Sk. *aṣṭáu*, Gk. ὄκτω, L. *octō*, OSl. *osmь*, Lith. *aštuoni*

IE *ghosti-*—L. *hostis* 'enemy', OSl. *gostь* 'guest'

IE *ghortó-*—Gk. χόρτος 'fenced-in place', L. *hortus* 'garden', OIr. *gort* 'field', OSl. *gradъ* 'city' (from **gord-*, or borrowed from Gmc.; cf. AJPh 32. 431 ff.).

    a was relatively rare. It remained *a* everywhere, except in Slavic, where it became *o*.

IE *aĝō*—Sk. *ájāmi*, Gk. ἄγω, L. *agō* 'lead, drive'

IE *arō*—Gk. ἀρόω, L. *arō*, Lith. *ariù*, OSl. *orją* 'plough'

IE *nas-*—Sk. *nas*, Lith. *nasraĩ*, OSl. *nosъ* 'nose'.

    ə is the reduction of the long vowels *ē ō ā*. It appears as *i* in Indo-Iranian, as *o < a* in Slavic, as *a* everywhere else.

IE *pətér*—Sk. *pitár-*, Gk. πατήρ, L. *pater* 'father' (but normal grade *ā* in *māter*, *frāter*)

IE *stə-*—Sk. *sthitá-*, Gk. στατός, L. *status* 'stood' (past part.), Lith. *stataũ* 'I put', OSl. *stoją* 'I stand'

IE *də-*—L. *datus*, Gk. δοτός 'given' (*o* for *ə* through association with ω in δῶρον 'gift', δίδωμι 'I give'; *a* in δάνος 'gift').

    ъ is the partial reduction of e (**46**) (the full reduction is zero). It can best be attested in Greek and Latin, where it appears as *a* (in Gk. only before nasals and liquids) in syllables that otherwise show alternation between *e* and *o*: *pъt-* (reduced form of *pet-* in Gk. πετάννυμι 'stretch', L. *petō* 'strive') : *pateō* 'stand open'; L. *maneō* 'remain', against Gk. μένω; L. *magnus* 'great' against Gk. μέγας; the Gk. preposition παρά 'about' by the side of περί 'around'.

    i u are 'zero' grades of the diphthongs ei eu (**46**):

IE *bhidh-*, reduced form of *bheidh-* (Gk. πείθω, L. *fīdō*)—Gk. πιθέσθαι 'trust', L. *fidēs* 'faith'

IE *tri-*—Gk. τρι-, L. *tri-* in compounds (full form IE *trejes* in Gk. τρεῖς, L. *trēs*) 'three'

IE *kwid*—Sk. *cid*, Gk. τί, L. *quid* 'what'

IE *yugóm*—Gk. ζυγόν, Sk. *yugám*, L. *iugum* 'yoke' (full form in Gk. ζεύγνυμι 'hitch')

IE *k̂lutós*, (past part. of *k̂leu-* 'hear')—Sk. *śrutás* 'heard', Gk. κλυτός, L. *inclutus* 'famous'.

35. The Indo-European Diphthongs. The fundamental vowels, ă ĕ ŏ, and also the reduced vowel ə, combine with glides to form diphthongs. These glides are either *i u* in semi-vocalic function (written i̯ u̯ by Brugmann and many others), or homosyllabic liquids and nasals. Thus result these diphthongs: *ei eu el er em en; oi ou ol or om on; ai au al* etc. *əi əu əl* etc.; *ēi ēu ēl ēr ēm ēn; ōi āi ōu āu* etc. The ĕ- and ŏ-diphthongs were frequent, the others relatively rare, and it is not always possible to give reliable instances. This is partly due to the fact that in most IE languages long diphthongs either shortened the first element or lost the glide; cf. IE *djēus* '(God of) Heaven'—nom. sg. Sk. *dyāus̩*, but Gk. Ζεύς < *Ζηυς, acc. sg. Sk. *dyām*, Gk. Ζῆν. Probably such double forms go back to Indo-European times.[1]

INSTANCES:

I-Diphthongs:

ei was contracted to *ē* in Sanskrit, to *ī* in (Classical) Latin and Old Slavic.

IE *steigh-*—Gk. στείχω, L. *ve-stīgium* 'track', OSl. *stignǫ* 'reach'
IE *deikō*—Gk. δείκνυμι 'show', L. *dīcō* (early *deicō*) 'say'
IE *bheidhō*—Gk. πείθω 'persuade', L. *fīdō* 'trust'.

oi, the alternation of *ei*, is *ē* in Sanskrit, *ū* in Classical Latin, generally *ē* in Slavic:

IE *oinos*—Gk. οἰνή 'one-spot', L. *ūnus* (early acc. sg. *oino*)
IE *loikwos* (from *leikwō* 'I leave')—Gk. λοιπός 'left behind', OSl. *otъ-lēkъ* 'remainder'.

ai (Sk. *ē*) in Sk. *ēdhas* 'fuel', Gk. αἴθω 'shine', L. *aedēs* 'fire-place, house'.

əi perhaps in Gk. λαιός, L. *laevus*, OSl. *lēvъ* 'left (-hand)'.

ēi in Sk. *āima*, Gk. ἦμεν 'we went'.

U-Diphthongs:

eu is *ou* in early Latin, *ū* in Classical Latin, *ō* < *au* in Sanskrit, *ū* in Slavic:

IE *bheudh-*—Gk. πεύθω, OSl. *b[l]ūdǫ* 'mind'
IE *ĝeus-*—Sk. *jós̩ati* 'he partakes', Gk. γεύομαι 'I taste'
IE *jeug-*—Gk. ζεῦγος 'yoke', L. *iūgera* 'ploughed fields'.

ou is *ō* in Sanskrit, *ū* in Classical Latin and Old Slavic:

IE *louk-*—Sk. *rōcáyati* 'makes shine', *lōkas* 'forest clearing, place', L. *lūcus* 'clearing, grove' (early acc. sg. *loucom*), OSl. *lūča* 'ray', *lūčь* 'light'.

au or əu in Sk. *ōjas* 'strength', Gk. *αὐξάνω*, L. *augeō* 'increase'; Gk. *ταῦρος* 'bull', L. *taurus*; perhaps in L. *auris*, Lith. *ausìs*.

ēu in Sk. *dyāuṣ*, see above.

ōu in IE *gwōus* 'bovine'—Sk. *gāuṣ*, Gk. *βοῦς*, L. *bovem*.

āu in IE *nāus*—Gk. *ναῦς*, L. *nāvem* 'ship'.

Instances for *el er em en* etc. are given in **39**.

36. The Germanic Vowel Shift.

(a) Other Indo-European Languages. In every IE language the **a** vowel development follows more or less clearly discernible directions. Aryan shows a tendency to articulate both short and long vowels with wide mouth opening, so that *ĕ* and *ŏ* change to *ă* (see above). In Attic-Ionic Greek the trend is towards narrowing and fronting: *ā* becomes *ē*, *u* becomes *y* (= *ü*). In late Latin the difference between long and short vowels disappears. Celtic, like Attic-Ionic, has a marked tendency towards vowel narrowing, cf. Gall. *-rīx* (*Vercingetorīx*)—L. *rēx*. In Slavic, *a* became *o*, which requires more articulating energy, while *ō* became *ā*, with lessened energy, and subsequently the difference in quantity was abolished. The significance of this becomes clearly apparent by comparison with the opposite trend in Germanic.

(b) The Germanic Trend.[1] The most outstanding characteristic of **b** early Germanic vowel development is the rigid adherence to the contrast between short and long vowels. As shown above, some other Indo-European languages tend to lessen or eliminate that contrast. In some, as in Aryan, the two types develop on parallel lines. But the early Germanic languages not only preserve, but in fact emphasize the contrast. This becomes clearly apparent by indicating the principal vowel trends in a diagram of the vowel articulations. The conventional 'vowel triangle' is adequate for the purpose and has the advantage of convenience; the 'vowel trapezoid' or the 'vowel ellipse'[2] is more

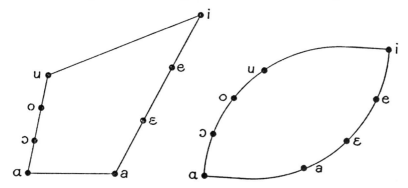

accurately in keeping with the physiological facts. In any case, the place of each letter indicates the place of articulation, that is, the place of highest tongue elevation for each vowel. Cf. D. Jones, Outline of English Phonetics 36.

In the following diagrams arrows indicate the direction of vowel changes in Primitive Germanic and the earliest period after the formation of the several Germanic languages. Broken lines indicate conditional or restricted changes.

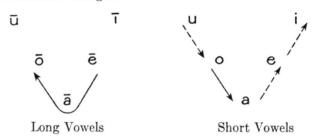

Long Vowels   Short Vowels

From this diagram follows, as a mere, mechanical statement of fact, that long vowels and short vowels tend in opposite directions. With our arbitrary arrangement of the places of articulation (the current of breath following our direction of writing), long vowels may be said to move clockwise, short vowels, counter-clockwise.

Physiologically speaking, in the long-vowel trend the tongue moves away from the position that it assumes when at rest. In the transition from $\bar{e}$ to $\bar{æ}$ to $\bar{a}$ the angle of the jaws is widened and the tongue correspondingly lowered and retracted. Further lowering not being possible, in the transition from $\bar{a}$ to $\bar{o}$ to $\bar{u}$ the tongue is still more retracted, and necessarily raised. (The relative width of the angle of the jaws corresponds, of course, to the position of the tongue.) On the other hand, short vowels tend towards relaxation and a corresponding approach to the position of rest of the tongue. Thus, o and ə become a, and u and e change to o and i, at least under certain conditions.

NOTE: The Slavic change $\bar{o} > \bar{a}$ and a > o represents exactly the opposite tendency. Here, in the case of the short vowel the tongue moves towards a position which is further away from its Ruhelage, while it moves towards the Ruhelage in the case of the long vowel. In the first instance it is relatively tense, in the second, relatively relaxed.

Sievers, Grundzüge der Phonetik 279: 'Kurze und lange Vokale schlagen bekanntlich bei derartigen Verschiebungen häufig entgegengesetzte Wege ein. . . . . . Hiefür liegt der Grund wohl in dem auch sonst zur Anwendung kommenden Gesetz, dass die Artikulationen eines Lautes um so energischer und sicherer vollzogen werden, je stärker derselbe zum Bewusstsein kommt, d. h. je grösser seine Stärke und Dauer ist. Dies erklärt beim langen Vokal sowohl eine Steigerung in der spezifischen Zungenartikulation (nach Stellung und Spannung) als der Rundung, falls solche vorhanden ist. Beim kurzen Vokal dagegen, der nur einen momentanen Zungenschlag erfordert, wird leicht das eigentliche Mass der Entfernung von der Ruhelage wie der Spannung nicht erreicht, d. h. es wird eine Wandlung von Vokalen mit stärkerer spezifischer Artikulation zu Lauten von mehr neutraler Artikulation angebahnt, sowohl was Zungen- und Lippenstellung als was Spannung betrifft.' This is an exact description of the Germanic vowel trend, but is not in keeping with most other IE languages, especially Slavic.

This statement of the physiological fact does not *explain* the Germanic vowel shift, but merely *describes* it. Another factor should not be lost sight of: Acoustically, long vowels move in the direction of lower pitch, short vowels, of higher pitch (*Eigenton*). It is difficult to decide whether this movement in the scale *i-e-a-o-u* was purely accidental or was one of the contributing causes. At any rate, the Germanic vowel shift increases the articulatory contrasts between the two series of vowels, a fact that agrees with the Germanic consonant shift and several aspects of Germanic morphology.

37. The Germanic Long Vowels.   Two changes are generally ascribed to Primitive Germanic: that of *ā* to *ō* and of *ē* to *ǣ*. The latter is largely a 'Phonetic Interpolation', i.e., the assumption of a transitional stage between *ē* and *ā*. In Gothic, *ǣ* reverts to *ē* by a different process of tensing (raising and fronting); in North and West Germanic, *ā* results; this develops secondarily into *ǣ* in Old English, and *ē* in Frisian.

Old English *ǣ* was further narrowed to [e:] in Middle English, and to [i:] in New English: *dǣd* > [de:d] > [di: d]. Gmc. *ō* became [u:] both in New English and New High German. OHG, MHG *uo* is a transitional stage: OE *dōm* > NE [du:m] = NHG *-tum*.

IE *ē*: *dhē-* (Gk. τίθημι, etc., see **34**)—Go. *gadēþs*, OE *dǣd*, OFris. *dēd*, OS *dād*, OHG *tāt* 'deed'

IE *sē-* (L. *sēmen*, etc.)—Go. *mana-sēþs* 'mankind', ON *sād*, OE *sǣd*, OFris. *sēd*, OS *sād*, OHG *sāt* 'seed'

IE *ēd-* (L. *ēdimus*)—Go. *ētum*, OE *ǣton*, OFris. **ēton*, OS **ātun*, OHG *āzum* 'we ate'.

ō: Usually in Ablaut with *ē*.

IE *bhlō-* (L. *flōs*)—Go. *blōma*, ON *blōme*, OE *blōma*, OS *blōmo*, OHG *bluomo* 'bloom, flower'

IE *dhōm-* (Gk. θωμός 'heap')—Go. *dōms*, ON *dōmr*, OE OS *dōm*, OHG *tuom* 'sentence (setting-down)'

IE *plō-* (Gk. πλωτός 'floating')—Go. *flōdus*, ON *flōþ*, OE OS *flōd*, OHG *fluot* 'flood'.

ā was rare; it does not show any ablaut relations, except with its weakened grade ə:

IE *māter*: (L. *māter*, etc.)—Go. **mōdar* (Wulfila uses only *aiþei*), ON *mōþer*, OE *mōdor*, OFris. *mōder*, OS *mōdar*, OHG *muoter*

IE *bhrāter-* (L. *frāter*, etc.)—Go. *brōþar* (Crimean Go. *bruder*), ON *brōþer*, OE *brōþor*, OFris. *brōther*, OS *brōthar*, OHG *bruoder*

IE *stā-* (L. *stāre*, etc.)—Go. ON *stōþ*, OE OFris. OS *stōd*, OHG *stuo(n)t* 'stood'.

ī ū were very rare. They remain unchanged:

IE *su-īno-* (L. *suīnus* 'pork'), Go. *swein*, ON *suīn*, OE OS OHG *swīn* 'swine'

IE *sūro-* (Lith. *sūras* 'salty')—ON *sūrr*, OE OS OHG *sūr* 'sour'.

a **38. The Germanic Short Vowels.**

(1) The changes *o* > *a* and *ə* > *a* are 'unconditional', that is, they are independent of surrounding sounds.

(2) The changes *e* > *i* and *u* > *o* are 'conditional'. The drift is inhibited by an incompatible vowel in the following syllable, but favored by a compatible vowel: *e* remains before a mid- or low-vowel (usually Gmc. *a*), and *u* remains before the high vowels *i* and *u*. But the influence of the following vowel was counteracted by an intervening nasal group ('nx' = *m*, *n* + any consonant), in the Anglo-Frisian group even by a nasal alone. This is due to the fact that a nasal group forms a more effective syllable barrier than other consonants or consonant groups. The result is the following formula (cf. **42 a**):

IE *e* > Gmc. *i*, but *e* + *a* remains *e*; *enx* changes always to *inx* (**pelu* 'much' > OHG *filu*, **kelono-* 'conceal' > OHG *helan*, but **wentos* 'wind' > *wint*)

IE *u* > Gmc. *o*, but *u* + *i*, *u* remains *u*; *unx* remains always (**jugom* 'yoke' > OHG *joh*, but **km̥tóm* '100' > OHG *hund-*).

b NOTES:
1. The conventional formula is virtually the reverse: *e* > *i*, (a) before *i j*, perhaps also *u* (at least in OHG)
 (b) before nasal plus consonant
 (c) when unaccented.
The result is nearly the same, but the new formulation is a clearer expression of the physiological trend. Also, it is more easily reconciled with the apparently irregular treatment of *e* before *u*. In OHG, *e* + *u* > *i* is carried through consistently, but in Norse and Anglo-Frisian this change is easily prevented by leveling of forms or by vowel-lowering consonants: L. *pecu*—OHG *fihu*, but ON

fē, OE *feoh* 'cattle'; IE *pelu-* (Gk. πολύ)—Go. *filu*, OHG *filu*, but ON *fiǫl* < **felu*, OE *feolu* (OE 'breaking', see **42**) 'much'.

It is phonetically improbable that the influence of a following *u* actually *changed e* to *i*. It merely did not exert that restraining influence that we find in the case of a following *a*.

2. In Gothic, *u* and *e* are independent of following vowels: *u* remained *u*, and *e* became *i* everywhere (except before *h*, *r*; **42**).

3. Gmc. *a* in closed syllables became, in general, *æ* in OE, *e* in OFris.: OE *blæd*, OFris. *bled*—OHG *blat* 'leaf'.

4. The change *a* > *e* is treated in **41**.

INSTANCES:

IE e > Gmc. i, unless followed by an IE mid- or low vowel, i.e., *ē ǒ ā*. Leveling has to an extent obscured the original conditions. As far as expedient, such leveled forms are bracketed in the following lists.

(Verb Endings: Infinitive, IE *-onom* > Gmc. *-an*; sg. ind. pres., IE *-ō* > Go. *-a*, NWGmc. *-u*, which disappears in ON and appears as *-e* in OE (West Saxon).)

IE *bher-* (L. *ferō*, etc.)—Go. *bairan, baira, bairiþ*; ON *bera*, [*ber, ber*]; OE *beran*, [*bere*], *bir(e)þ*; OS *beran, biru, birid*; OHG *beran, biru, birit* 'bear'

IE *ed-* (L. *edo*, etc.)—Go. *itan, ita, itiþ*; ON *eta*, [*et, etr*]; OE *etan*, [*ete*], *iteþ*; OS *etan, itu, itiþ*; OHG *ezzan, izzu, izzit* 'eat'

IE *nem-* (Gk. νέμω 'assign')—Go. *niman, nima, nimiþ*; ON *nema*, [*nem, nemr*]; OE *niman, nime, nimiþ*; OS *niman, nimu, nimid*; OHG *neman, nimu, nimit* 'take'

IE *pent-* (Gk. πόντος 'sea', L. *pont-* 'bridge', OSl. *pǫtъ* 'path')—Go. *finþan, finþa, finþiþ*; ON *finna, finn, finnr* (*fiþr*); OE *findan, finde, findaþ*; OS *findan* (*fīthan*), *findu, findid*; OHG *findan, findu, findit* 'find'

IE *deḱm̥* (L. *decem*, etc.)—Go. *taihun*, ON *tīo*, OE *tīen*, OS *tehan*, OHG *zehan* 'ten'.

IE o > Gmc. a:

IE *oktō(u)* (L. *octō*, etc.)—Go. *ahtau*, ON *ātta*, OE *eahta*, OFris. *achto*, OS OHG *ahto* 'eight'

IE *ghosti-* (L. *hostis*, etc.)—Go. *gasts*, ON *gastiʀ* (Runic), *gestr*, OE *giest*, OS OHG *gast* 'guest'

IE *ghorto-* (L. *hortus*, etc.)—Go. *gards*, ON *garþr*, OE *geard*, OS *gard*, OHG *gart* 'yard, house'.

IE a = Gmc. a:

IE *ad* (L. *ad*)—Go. ON OS *at*, OE *æt*, OHG *az* 'to'

IE *agros* (L. *ager*, etc.)—Go. *akrs*, ON *akr*, OE *æcer*, OS *akkar*, OHG *ackar* 'acre'.

IE ə > Gmc. **a**:

IE *pǝter-* (L. *pater*, etc.; full grade in *māter, frāter*)—Go. *fadar*, ON *faþer*, OE *fæder*, OS *fadar*, OHG *fater*

IE *stǝ-* (L. *status*; full grade in *stāre*)—Go. *staþs* 'place', ON *staþr*, OE *stede, stedi* (mutated forms), OHG *stat*

IE *lǝd-* (L. *lassus* 'tired'; full grade in Gk. λησεῖν 'be tired')—Go. *lats*, ON *latr*, OE *læt*, OS *lat*, OHG *laz* 'lazy'.

d   IE ъ (shva secundum) appears in Germanic as *u* at least before and after nasals and liquids, probably as *e* elsewhere; cf. Hirt, HU 1. 62 f.; Güntert, Idg. Ablautprobleme 31.

> According to Sievers, Btr. 16. 236, Streitberg, IF Anz. 2. 48, also shva primum could appear as *u* in Germanic, especially in unaccented syllables, cf. Sk. *vavṛtima* : Go. *waurþum*. The matter is still a moot question. The most probable instance is the Go. preposition *du*, reduced grade of **dē, dō*, which can hardly be explained in any other way. Also *y* in OE *dyde* 'did' is perhaps *u* < ə, with umlaut; but cf. **75 b.**

ъ seems to have become *u* in syllables that were unstressed or weakly stressed in Germanic: OHG *-zug* '-ty' over against Go. *tigjus*; L. *anas*, OHG *anut* (and *enit*) 'duck'; Gk. γέρανος, OHG *kranuh* 'crane'.

IE *ĝhъmōn-* (different ablaut grade in OL. *hemo*; *nēmo* < **ne-hemo*; Class. L. *homō*)—Go., OE *guma*, ON *gume*, OFris. OS OHG *gomo* 'man'

IE *tъl-* (L. *tollo*)—Go. *þulan*, ON *þola*, OE *þolian*, OFris. *tholia*, OS *tholian*, OHG *dolēn* 'suffer'

IE *sъd-* (full form in L. *sedeō*, Go. *sitan*, etc.)—Go. *sitans*, ON *setenn*, OE *seten*, OS *gisetan*, OHG *gisezzan* 'sat'.

IE **i** (reduced grade of *ei/oi*):

IE *bhidh-* (L. *fidēs*, etc.)—Go. *bidjan*, ON *biþia*, OE *biddan*, OFris. *bidda*, OS *biddian*, OHG *bitten* 'ask'

IE *widmén* 'we know' (Gk. ἴδμεν)—Go. *witum*, ON *vitom*, OE *witon*, OS *witum*, OHG *wizzum*.

IE **u** (reduced grade of *eu/ou*):

IE *bhudh-* (Gk. πυνθάνομαι, full grade in πεύθομαι 'find out')—Go. *-budum*, ON *buþom*, OE *budon*, OS *budun*, OHG *butun* 'we offered, ordered'

IE *jugom* (Gk. ζυγόν, L. *iugum*)—Go. *juk*, ON *ok*, OE *geoc*, OHG *joch* 'yoke'.

CHRONOLOGY. The exact time of the Germanic vowel shift can hardly be ascertained, but there are indications that point to the period shortly before and after the beginning of the Christian Era. Germanic loan words in Finnish as well as the earliest Latin renderings of Germanic names have *a* for IE *o*: Finnish *ansas* 'log' = Go. *ans*, L. *onus* 'burden' (?), *Langobardi*, related to L. *longus*; the latter word, like *Ariovistus*, *Chariovaldus*, etc., seems to indicate that unaccented *o* in compounds retained its quality longer than accented *o* (cf. Streitberg, UG §55), but it is more likely that such forms are due to the influence of similar Latin compounds, such as *Ahenobarbus*, which, in turn, may have been imitations of the Greek type ῥοδοδάκτυλος. The shift *ā* > *ō* and *ē* > *ǣ, ā* seems to belong to the Christian Era; Caesar has *Silva Bācenis* (related to φᾱγός, *fagus*) as against OHG *Buochunna* 'beech forest' = Bohemian Forest, and Celtic names that were most probably adopted during the first century A.D. show Germanic *ō*: *Dānuvius*, Go. *Dōnawi*. Cf. Streitberg, UG §59. Gmc. *e* for later *i* is preserved during the first century A.D.: Tacitus has *Segimundus*, *Venedi*; Streitberg, UG §66. Gmc. *ē* is found in Caesar's *Suēvi* for later *Schwaben*, Streitberg, UG §77. Cf. Bremer Relative Sprachchronologie, IF 4. 8 ff., and Trautmann, Germanische Lautgesetze.

39. The Germanic Diphthongs with *i*- or *u*-glides tend to become monophthongs through contraction. See **40**. Aside from this, the regular change of *o ə* > *a*, *e* > *i*, in part also that of *u* > *o*, takes place. Thus, *oi əi ou əu* appear as *ai au*, like *ei* > *ii* = *ī*; *eu* appears normally as *eo* before *a*, as *iu* elsewhere.

In the 'nil grade' (**46**), the first element is lost, so that *i* and *u* appear as genuine vowels. The nasal and liquid glides (**13**) develop in Germanic the vowel *u*, which is treated like *u* as the nil grade of an *u*-diphthong (*u/a* > *o*, **41**). Therefore, we find the following alternations: *ī—ai—i*; *iu/eo—au—u*; *el/il—al—ul/ol*; *er/ir—ar—ur/or*; *em/im—am* —*um/om*; *en/in—an—un/on*.

In the following instances, monophthongized forms except IE *ei* = Gmc. *ī* are given in parentheses. For Go. *ei ai au* see **40 a** and **42 c**.

IE	*steigh-*:	*stoigh-*:	*stigh-*	'climb, go' (Gk. στείχω)
Go.	*steigan*	*staig*	*stigum*	*stigans*
ON	*stīga*	(*stē*)	*stigom*	*stigenn*
OE	*stīgan*	(*stāh*)	*stigon*	*stigen*
OS	*stīgan*	(*stēg*)	*stigun*	*gistigan*
OHG	*stīgan*	*steig*	*stigum*	*gistigan*

IE	*bheudh-*:		*bhoudh-*:	*bhudh-*	'bid' (Gk. πείθομαι)
Go.	*-biudan,*	*-biudis*	*bauþ*	*budum*	*budans*
ON	*biōþa*[1],	*bȳþr*[1]	*bauþ*	*buþom*	*boþenn*
OE	*bēodan*[2],	*bīedst*[2]	*bēad*	*budon*	*boden*
OS	*biodan*[3],	*biudis*[3]	(*bōd*)	*budun*	*gibodan*
OHG	*biotan*[4],	*biutis*[4]	(*bōt*)	*butum*	*gibotan*

[1] **41 d**.   [2] **41 f, 42 k**.   [3] **42 k**.   [4] **42 l**.

IE	wert-:	wort-:	wrt-	(L. vertō)
Go.	wairþan	warþ	waurþum	waurþans
ON	verþa	varþ	urþom	orþenn
OE	weorþan	wearþ	wurdon	worden
OS	werthan	warth	wurdun	giwordan
OHG	werdan	ward	wurtum	giwortan

IE	bhendh-:	bhondh-:	bhndh-	(Gk. πεῖσμα < *φενθ-σμα 'band')
Go.	bindan	band	bundum	bundans
ON	binda	batt	bundom	bundenn
OE	bindan	bond	bundon	bunden
OS	bindan	band	bundun	gibundan
OHG	bintan	bant	buntum	gibuntan.

b   LONG DIPHTHONGS, with the exception of ēi, cannot be recognized as such from Germanic evidence, since they either shortened their first element or, more rarely, lost the second element:

IE ōi > Gmc. ai in ON fleire 'more', L. ploirume 'most', Sk. prāya- 'more'

IE āi > Gmc. ai in Go. aiws 'time', L. aevum, Sk. āyuṣ 'life, time'

IE ēu > Gmc. eu in OHG Ziu, ON Tȳr, Gk. Zeús, Sk. dyāuṣ

IE āu > Gmc. au in ON naust 'boat shed', L. nāvis, Sk. nāuṣ 'ship'

IE ōu > Gmc. au in ON tuau 'two', Sk. dvāu

IE ēn > Gmc. en (in) in Go. winds, L. ventus < IE wē-n-tos (Sk. vāyati 'blows').

Loss of the second element occurs, e.g., in: Go. flōdus 'flood', ON flōþ, OE OS OFris. flōd, OHG fluot, Gk. πλωτός 'floating', alternating with IE pleu/plou- in Gk. πλέϝω 'float', Sk. plávate 'swims', ON fliōta, OE flēotan, OS fliotan, OHG fliozan 'flow'. It is hardly possible in instances of this kind to decide whether we have to deal with original long-diphthongs with shortening of the first element, or with a lengthening of original short-diphthongs.

IE ēi seems to have lost its second element in every case; the resulting Gmc. ē was narrow and is generally expressed by ē², in contrast to IE ē > Gmc. ǣ. In OHG this ē² was further narrowed to ia ie. In Gothic, IE ē and ēi appear as ē. Reliable instances are rare; IE k̂ēi-, lengthened grade of k̂ei- (Gk. ἰ-κεῖ, OS hīr show the normal grade; reduced grade in L. cis, citra, Go. himma, hina, hita) gave Go. ON OE hēr, OHG hiar. IE stēigh-, lengthened grade of steigh- in Goth. steigan, etc., gave OHG stiaga 'Stiege, stair'. IE sk̂ēi-ro- (skei- 'shine') yielded OHG skiari 'clever' (normal grade in Go. skeirs, ON skīrr, OE scīr, OS skīr 'clear', Go. skeinan 'shine').

For the large literature on this moot question cf. Streitberg, UG 65; Hirt, HU 1. 33.

Brugmann, IF 6. 89 ff., and Wood, Germanic Studies, assume IE *ēi* as normal grade of an original long (not lengthened) IE diphthong in the Norse and West Germanic preterites of the *i*-group of those strong verbs that are reduplicating in Gothic, such as ON OE OS *hēt*, OHG *hiaz*, cf. **54**.

In addition to this problematic diphthongal origin of *ē²*, narrow Gmc. *ē* appears in West Germanic as compensatory lengthening for the loss of a following *z*, similar to L. *nīdus* < **ni-zdos*, as in OE *mēd*, OS *mēda*, OHG *miata* 'wages': Go. *mizdō*, Gk. μισθός.

Finally, it generally represents *ē* in loan-words from Latin: OHG *ziagal* < (late) L. *tēgula* 'tile', *briaf* < late L. *brēve* 'letter', *Kriach* < *Graecus* (pron. [gre:kus]).

40. Monophthongization and Diphthongization.

(a) MONOPHTHONGIZATION.

Due to the strong stress accent of Germanic syllables, the first element of diphthongs tended to absorb the semi-vowel glide, so that *ei ai au* easily became monophthongs, *ī ā/ē ō/ā*. Gmc. *eu/iu* resisted this trend longer; being a combination of a front and a back vowel, its component elements were more strongly contrasted.

IE **ei** became Gmc. *ī* everywhere in prehistoric times. The Gothic spelling *ei* is taken over from the Greek spelling of Wulfila's time, in which ει represented [i:]: IE *steigh-*: Go. *steigan*, ON *stīga*, OE OS OHG *stīgan*.

Gmc. **ai au** more or less preserved their diphthongal character into historical times, in part even to the present. For GOTHIC, the standard view assumes that the spellings *ai au* in Wulfila's writing indicated diphthongs where this is indicated by the etymology, but monophthongs [ε ɔ], where they stand for *i u* before *h r* (**42** i). Jacob Grimm introduced the device of spelling *ái áu* for diphthongal, *aí aú* for monophthongal function: *wáit* [wait] = Gk. οἶδα 'I know', *áuso* [auso:] = L. *auris* 'ear', but *baíra* [bɛra] = L. *ferō* 'bear', *daúr* [dɔr] = Gk. θύρα 'door'. Hirt, HU 1. 39 f. presents weighty arguments for the monophthongal character of Wulfila's *ai au* regardless of their origin; of course, there must at least have been a difference in quantity, short vowels representing the original monophthongs, long vowels, [ε: ɔ:] the original diphthongs; Wulfila's *e o* surely denoted the closed vowels [e: o:]. (To Hirt's examples might be added Jordanes' *Oium* < **akwjom*, **aʒwja-*, **auja-* name of a watery place, and *Berig* = *Boiorīx*, **Bajarīks*.) I believe that Hirt is right, but the question is largely one of chronology.

Shortly before Wulfila's time, Gmc. *ai au* were still diphthongs in Gothic, as is indicated by the spelling (*Gutan(e) Iowi) hailag* (R. Loewe's interpretation) on the gold ring of Bukarest and spellings in Latin and Greek historians, like *Radagaisus, Austrogothi* (cf. Streitberg, UG 58 ff.). Shortly after Wulfila, they were monophthongs (*Ostrogothi*). Also in closely related Vandalic, *ai au* had become [ɛ: ɔ:]: *froja, armes* 'domine, miserere' = Go. *frauja, armais* (Streitberg, UG 38). Crimean Gothic has *Broe(t)* 'panis', *Oeghene* 'oculi' = Go. **brauþ, augōna*, where *oe* doubtless stands for [o:] or [ɔ:]; *geen* may possibly correspond to a theoretical Go. **gaian*. In spite of the probability of Hirt's view, it seems expedient to retain the distinction between diphthongal and monophthongal pronunciation in grammatical discussions: *bairan, taíhun, baúrans, taúhans* = [beran, teɧun, bɔrans, tɔɧans], but *áirus, táih, áugo, táuh* = [airus, taih, auʒo:, tauh].

Go. *iu* < Gmc. *eu/iu* was a diphthong.

In OLD NORSE, the Germanic diphthongs in general remained diphthongal (but cf. **42 j**): ON *veit, steinn, auga, þiúfr, gióta* (**41 e**) = Go. *wait, stains, augo, þiufs, giutan*. In modern Norse, they are monophthongs: Norw. *vet, sten, øie, tyv* (Sw. *tjuf* = [ty:f]), *gyte*.

In OLD ENGLISH, *ai* had become *ā* before the time of our earliest documents: *stān, ān* = Go. *stains, ains*. Gmc. *au eu/iu* remained diphthongal until the beginning of the Middle English period; *au* is spelled *ēa* = [æə], *eu* is expressed by *ēo* = [eə] (*cēosan*), *iu* usually by *īo* = [iə] (*līode*—OHG *liuti* 'people'). The macron on the first element, relatively rare in MSS, but used consistently in our editions and grammars, is merely an orthographical device to distinguish these diphthongs from 'broken vowels' (**42 e**). The spelling *ea* for *æa* is due to the scribal tradition mentioned in **24**.—In ME monophthongization continued, so that both Gmc. *au* and Gmc. *eu* finally resulted in [i:]: OE *dēop, hēap*— [di:p, hi:p]. In part, this was deflected by secondary changes: OE *dēad, lēoht* > [dɛd, lait].

In OLD FRISIAN, *ai* became *ē* or *ā*, and *au* became *ā*; in OLD SAXON, *ai* appears as *ē*, *au* as *ō*: OFris. *wēt, stēn, ā* < **aiwa-* 'right', *āgun* = Go. *aigun* 'they have', *āge* 'eye'; OS *wēt, stēn, ōga*. Gmc. *eu* remained a diphthong in both dialects.

OLD HIGH GERMAN ordinarily preserved the diphthongal character of *ai au eu*: *weiz, stein, ouga*; but before certain consonants *ai au* became *ē ō*. Cf. **42 l**.

Toward the end of the Middle Ages, OHG *ie* < Gmc. *ē²* and *uo* < Gmc. *ō* were monophthongized in Middle German, and this was adopted in Standard German while the diphthongs still largely prevail in Upper German: OHG *briaf, brief* > [bri:f], *guot* > [gu:t]. Likewise, the mutated vowel of *uo, üe*, became [y:]: MHG *güete* > [gy:tə].

(b) DIPHTHONGIZATION.   b

Although apparently the opposite of monophthongization, diphthongization in Germanic languages was also a consequence of the strong stress accent. Long vowels tended to increase the energy of their articulation. This had led to the Germanic vowel shift described in **37** and to the later English raising of $\bar{e}$ $\bar{o}$ to [i: u:]. In Old High German, a similar process started during the eighth century, when $\bar{e}^2$ became *ea ia ie*, and $\bar{o}$ became *oa ua uo: briaf, guot*. These diphthongs mark the transition to Middle German [i: u:] (see above).

A more extensive diphthongization took place in English, Dutch, and most of High German before the end of the Middle Ages. The high vowels [i: u: y:] were incapable of further raising. The stress accent seems to have caused further lengthening, resulting in 'slurred' accent (rising-falling accent, circumflex accent, 'Schleifton') and finally in diphthongization. During the articulation of the over-long vowel the tongue reached the highest point only gradually; thus, there developed a glide from a mid-vowel, later even a low vowel, to a high vowel, [i: > ei ai, u: > au]. The new diphthongal element was gradually more or less assimilated to the first part of the diphthong, so that now-a-days English and German generally have the diphthongs [ae ao]: OE OHG *mīn, hūs*, NE NHG [maen, haos], MHG *liute* = [ly:tə], NHG *Leute* = [lɔytə, lɔøtə].

41. Mutation ('Umlaut', a term coined by Jacob Grimm) in the   a
widest sense can be defined as the modification of a vowel under the influence of and in the direction of the articulation of a neighboring vowel. In the Germanic languages the use of the term is essentially restricted to the change of a stem vowel in the direction of the vowel of a suffix or ending. Similar processes are found in many languages. In Russian, *a* is a low-back vowel before a back vowel, but a low-front vowel before a front vowel: *dar(ъ)* 'gift' [dar] < **daro-*, but *danь* 'tribute' [dæñ] < **dani-*. Irish shows a similar trend. In these cases the phonetic process is fairly clear. The intervening consonant is assimilated to the articulation of the following vowel, and the preceding vowel is assimilated to the consonant. This is a corollary to the peculiar plasticity of these languages. In some of the Ugro-Finnic languages there exists a similar process termed 'Vowel Harmony'. But there the stem vowel determines the articulation of the suffix vowel,

requiring front or back articulation respectively, in accordance with its own type: Finn. *huva* 'good', *pähä* 'bad'. In a somewhat mechanical way we may designate the former process as physiological, and the latter as psychological assimilation. The impression of the position of the tongue is retained through the following syllable, regardless of whether the tongue is raised in front or in back.

Germanic mutation, while not identical with either of these two types of mutation, bears a certain relationship to both of them. Its origin is not known, but the following may be an approach to an interpretation of the process. The conditional changes $e > i$, $u > o$ in the Germanic Vowel Shift (**38**) were soon followed by the corresponding conditional change $a > e$ in Norse and West Germanic. But while the former two changes were merely *prevented* by a following incompatible vowel, and therefore occurred also in final syllables, the change $a > e$ *depended* on a following i (j). These three mutations tended in the direction of the general vowel drift. They implied an enrichment of the morphological pattern of the language. Distinctions between forms by gradation (**45**) had been inherited from the Indo-European parent speech. The contrast between OHG *geban* and *gab* was the continuation of the Indo-European alternation between e and o. In consequence of mutation, a new type of interchange between stem vowels developed, e.g., OHG *beran*: *biris*, *hulfun*: *giholfan*, *faran*: *feris*. In some of the Germanic languages this became a grammatical device of great importance. In connection with the weakening of final syllables, which had started before the period of mutation (**49**, A 1), it assumed functional value as an auxiliary means of distinction between singular and plural, indicative and optative, positive and comparative, and other morphological categories. Perhaps this was one of the factors that led to a great extension of the new linguistic device, which no longer followed the general direction of the vowel drift. So far as the endings themselves are concerned, the speech feeling for the phonetic law back of them gradually disappeared. It is obvious, for instance, that in Old English there could not exist any recollection of the fact that the difference between $\bar{o}$ in *fōt* 'foot' and $\bar{e}$ in *fēt* 'feet' was due to the former plural ending *-iz*. All that remained was the functional variation of the stem vowel, which differed in degree in the various Germanic languages. It found its greatest development in High German, particularly in the formation of noun plurals. Through the weakening of endings, Old High German possessed many plural forms that did not differ from the corresponding singulars, e.g. *wort, turi, bruoder, man,* *naht.* In such forms, mutation was introduced during the Middle High German and New High German periods, in imitation of such clear contrasts as *gast—gesti* (analogical mutation), so that the number of mutated plurals in standard New High German is approximately six times as great as in Old High German.[1] A particularly significant feature of this analogical process is the development of [ø]. Phonologically, this sound could not have developed at all. Short *o*, from which it is nominally derived, could exist only as *a*-mutation of Gmc. *u*; but the change *o* > *ø*, as a phonetic transition, would require *i*, not *a*, in the following syllable. Therefore, an alternation of suffixes with *a* and *i* would imply an alternation of the stem vowels *o* and *y*, not *o* and *ø*. We have certain instances of this alternation, e.g., ON *holpenn: hylpe*—NHG *geholfen: hülfe*; OE OHG *gold* < **gulda-*: OE *gylden*, NHG *gülden*. But in most cases this alternation is leveled out (NE NHG *golden*; NHG *hälfe, hölfe*).

In the most extreme form of mutation, which we find in Old Norse, we may say that every back vowel was fronted by a following front vowel, every front vowel rounded by a following back (rounded) vowel. Thus, the following fundamental system results:

Before *i* (*j*):	Before *u* (*w*):
$\breve{a} > \breve{æ}\ e$	$\breve{a} > \breve{o}$
$\breve{o} > \breve{ø}$	$\breve{e} > \breve{ø}$
$\breve{u} > \breve{y}$	$\breve{i} > \breve{y}$

NOTE: In a limited way, *a* caused mutation of *i* to *e*, contrary to the direction of the drift. This seems to indicate that Gmc. *i* and *e* were practically one 'phoneme'; before *i*, both vowels appeared as *i*, before *a*, as *e*. Cf. **36.** IE *wiros* 'man' > OHG *wer*; IE *stighos* > OHG *steg*; IE *ni-zdom*> OHG *nest*. But this change occurred only in comparatively isolated forms. Within the system of the strong verb it was counteracted by the leveling influence of other forms. Thus we find OHG *gestigan*, without *a*-mutation, under the combined influence of *stigun* and *stīgan*. But the change of *u* to *o*, which is in the direction of the drift, resists such leveling: *gigozzan*, in spite of the form *guzzun*.

Mutation on this large scale began perhaps in the fifth or sixth b century and therefore does not exist in Wulfila's Gothic. Visi-Gothic names (*Ega, Egica, Egila, Emila*, cf. Streitberg, UG 2. 78) seem to indicate mutation of *a* to *e*. Crimean Gothic does not happen to offer any clear instances. In Norse and West Germanic, this peculiar fact appears, which I am unable to interpret: The extent of consonant shift stands in inverse ratio to the extent (and, probably, time) of mutation, i.e., the more consonant shift any given dialect shows, the more re-

stricted is the scope of mutation in that dialect. This implies that
Old Norse has the widest, Bavarian the narrowest scope of mutation,
while the intermediate dialects are graded in a most consistent way
in accordance with this principle.

The following outline does not attempt to go into details, but merely
indicates the general trend.

c   In GOTHIC, in addition to the factor of chronology, the narrowing
of *e* to *i* and of *æ* to *ē* were unfavorable to the spread of mutation, and
the widening influence of *h* and *r* also counteracted a change that was
contingent, not on the following consonant, but on the vowel of the
following syllable. Go. *bairis* [bɛris]: *bairan, nimis: niman* do not admit any distinction between Gmc. *e* and *i*.

d   NORSE developed vowel mutation very extensively, virtually to the
limit of the general scheme indicated above. The earliest Runic inscriptions (4th to 6th century) show some unmutated forms: *gastiʀ*
> *gestr*.[2] The following instances illustrate its chief features:

i-mutation: *a* > *e*, **ʒastiz* > *gestr*

   ā > *ǣ*, *lāta* 'let', 2 sg., *lǣtr* < **lātiz*

   o > *ø*, Run. *dohtriʀ* > **døhtr* > *dø̄tr*

   ō > *ø̄*, Go. *dōmjan* 'judge', ON *dø̄ma*

   u > *y*, Go. *þugkjan* 'seem', ON *þykkia*

   ū > *ȳ*, **mūsiz* 'mice', ON *mȳss*

   au > *ey*, Go. *hlaupis* 'you run', ON *hleypr*

   iu > *ȳ*, Go. **þliugis* 'you fly', ON *flȳgr*.

u-mutation:

   a > *ǫ*, Go. *magus* 'son', ON *mǫgr*; Go. *ahva* 'water', ON **ahwu, *ahu*
        > *ǭ* 'river'

   e > *ø*, Go. *riqis* < **rekwes* (Gk. ἔρεβος), ON *røkkr*

   i > *y*, Go. *triggws* 'faithful', ON *tryggr*; OE *Tīu* (L. *dīvus*), name of a
        god, ON *Tȳr*.

e   'Breaking' in Old Norse can be defined as incomplete mutation.
Genuine mutation is caused by the high vowels *i u*. Breaking is caused
chiefly by *a*, less often by *u*; *e* before *a* becomes *ia*, *e* before *u* becomes *io*:

OHG *herza*, ON *hiarta* 'heart'

OHG *bergan*, ON *biarga* 'conceal'

OHG *erda*, ON **erþu* > *iorþ* 'earth'

Go. *hairus*, ON *hiorr* 'sword'.

This leads to considerable variations in paradigms, e.g., *skioldr*
'shield' < **skelduz*, gen. sg. *skialdar* < **skeldauz*, nom. pl. *skilder* <
*skeldiuz.

NOTE 1: *u*-breaking is in competition with *u*-mutation of *e*, which results in *ø* (*røkkr*). Essentially, the former is caused by vocalic *u*, the latter by *u* in consonantic function, -*w*, but the exact conditions are not quite clear; cf., e.g. Go. *fairhus* 'life', ON *fior*, Go. *aiha-* 'horse', ON **ehwa* > **iohu* > *iōr*.

NOTE 2: The term '*breaking*' should be applied only to this form of vowel change, in which actually one vowel is 'broken' in two. At best, it might be extended to the development of a glide in Old English before certain consonants (**42 e**), but it should not be used for forms like OE *giefan, geaf, gēafon, geoc*, in which *i* and *e* do not denote any actual vowel sounds, but are diacritical marks, indicating spirantic pronunciation of g. Cf. **24.** Least of all should the term 'breaking' be used in the meaning for which Jacob Grimm coined it. Since in his 'Lehre von den Buchstaben' he had letters, not sounds, in mind, he used it for Go. *ai au* = [ɛ ɔ] before *h* and *r*, and then transferred it to OHG *i* > *e*, *u* > *o*. Cf. Geschichte der deutschen Sprache 183.

NOTE 3: While the direction of mutation in Norse is the opposite of Finnish vowel harmony (see above), its result is the same in principle. It is, therefore, not quite impossible that the considerable Finnish element that must have been absorbed by the Germanic Scandinavians had some influence on this remarkable spread of mutation.

ENGLISH mutation in all dialect groups seems to belong either to the **f** late continental, or to the earliest insular period. *ă ŏ ŭ* became *e ǣ ø̆ y̆*, but the latter two were unrounded during the Old English period, becoming *ĕ ĭ*; Northumbrian preserved *ø̄* as late as the eleventh century:

a > e, Go. *nasjan* 'save', *satjan* 'set', OE *nerian, settan*

ā > ǣ, Go. *laisjan* 'teach', OE **lārjan* > *lǣren*

ǣ = ǣ, Go. *-dēþs* 'deed', WGmc. *dādiz*, OE *dǣd*

o > ø > e, **dohtri*, dat. sg. of *dohtor* 'daughter' > *dehter*

ō > ø̄, ē, Go. *dōmjan* 'judge', OE *dø̄man, dēman*

u > y, **guldīna-* > *gylden* 'golden'

ū > ȳ, Gmc. *mūsiz* 'mice' > *mȳs*

au > īe, Go. *galaubjan* 'believe', OE *gelīefan*

iu > īe, Go. *kiusan, kiusiþ* 'choose', OE *cēosan, cīesþ*.

Mutation by *u* occurs chiefly in Anglian. It takes the form of genuine 'breaking', that is, incomplete mutation: *a* (*æ*) and *e* develop a glide before *u*, especially if a liquid intervenes; some West Saxon examples are *ealu* 'beer' < **alu* (but *magu* 'boy', *sacu* 'quarrel'), *heorot* 'hart', *geolo* 'yellow', *seofon, sefon* 'seven'.

In OLD FRISIAN *ă* before *i* (*j*) was mutated to *ĕ*, *ō* to *ē*, *ŭ* > *y̆* > *ĕ* **g** (also in Kentish mutation of *ŭ* had resulted in *ĕ* instead of *y̆*). *ē* as mutation of WGmc. *ā* cannot be distinguished from unmutated *ā*, since this, too, was narrowed to *ē*:

a > e, Go. *harjis* 'army', OFris. *here*

ā > ē, OE *dǣd* (see above), OFris. *dēd*

$o > e$ cannot be definitely ascertained; *gelden* 'golden' had better be
interpreted as $u > e$ mutation

$\bar{o} > \bar{e}$, Go. *dōmjan* 'judge', OFris. *dēma*

$u > y > e$, OHG *kuri* 'choice', OFris. *kere* 'privilege'

$\bar{u} > \bar{y} > \bar{e}$, Go. *rūmjan 'make space', OFris. *rēma*

$au > e$, Go. *hausjan* 'hear', OFris. *hēra*.

A type of breaking occurs sometimes before u, as in *siugun, niugun*
= Go. *sibun, niun* < IE *septm, newm.*

h   OLD SAXON, so far as spelling is an indication, mutated only a to e,
but doubtless $\bar{a}$, $\breve{o}$ and $\breve{u}$ were also mutated by i, although orthography
rarely expresses this:

$a > e$, Go. *harjis, lagjan,* OS *heri, leggian*

$\bar{a} > \bar{e}$, OS *lēti, gēfi,* as occasional spellings for the usual *lāti, nāmi.*

$\bar{o} > \bar{e}$ is found in *bētian* for *bōtian* 'atone'

$u > y$ in *andwirdi* 'answer' for *andwurdi*

$\bar{u} > \bar{y}$ in *fīsid* 'inclined' for *fūsid* (*fūsian* 'endeavor').

i   OLD HIGH GERMAN shows considerable dialectic variations.   In all
Franconian dialects the change $a > e$ appears in our earliest records,
that is, since the middle of the eighth century.   In Alemannian it
sets in somewhat later, and in Bavarian it occurs latest.   Moreover,
certain consonants or consonant groups (**42**) inhibit this mutation more
widely and effectively in the southern than in the northern dialects.
As in Old Saxon, we can be sure that the $a > e$ mutation was not the
only type, but we have very scant orthographical evidence of the mutation of o and u.

$a > e$, *faran: ferit,* Go. *lagjan,* OHG *leggen.*

Before $h\ l\ r$ (**42**) we find dialect variations: Franc. *wehsit, heltit,
gerwen,* UG *wahsit, haltit, garwen.*

$\bar{a} > \bar{æ}$ is sometimes indicated by $\bar{e}$ e, e.g., *quēme* for regular *quāmī,
sundere* for *sundāri;* for $\bar{o} > \bar{\phi}$ we find *troistet,* for $u > y$, *antliute* for
antluzzi; for $\bar{u} > \bar{y}$ Notker frequently has *iu,* e.g., *liute, chriuter.*

42. Influence of Consonants.   In many Indo-European languages,
particularly Slavic and Romance, consonants were frequently modified
by the influence of neighboring vowels.   This is rare in the Germanic
languages.[1]   The Frisian and West Saxon palatalization of k and gg
is almost the only instance.   On the other hand, in Germanic, as in
other languages, vowels are frequently modified by following, rarely
by preceding consonants.   The most important types of such changes
are these:

a   (1) *Nasals* exert an influence on preceding vowels in Primitive Germanic times. *e* before a nasal group follows the trend to *i* regardless of the vowel of the next syllable, and *u* before a nasal group remains *u* regardless of the following vowel: IE *bhendh-* > ON *binda*, Go. OE OS *bindan*, OHG *bintan*; Go. *bindis*, ON *bindr*, OE *bindest*, OS OHG *bindis*; IE *bhṇdh-* > Go. *bundeis*, *bundans*, OE *bunde*, *bunden*, OHG *bunti*, *gibuntan*. It is not likely that nasal groups were really the impelling cause of this vowel treatment. As indicated in **38**, they merely formed a syllable barrier that prevented the influence of the following vowel. True, *i* followed the general vowel drift, while *u* merely remained unchanged. This is explained by the fact that *i* had always existed by the side of *e*, being virtually another form of the same phoneme, while *o* was a new vowel, developing from *u* under favorable conditions, namely, when the 'pull' of the following low or mid vowel was not counteracted by a nasal group. IE *onx* had become *anx*; *ṇx* > *unx* remained regardless of the following vowel, while *uxa* became *oxa*; IE *tong-* > * þank-*, IE *tṇg-* > *þunk-*, Gmc. *ʒuta-* > NWGmc. *ʒota-* (Go. *þagkjan*, *þugkjan*, ON *gotenn*, OE *goten*, OHG *gigozzan*).

In Anglo-Frisian, single nasals formed a sufficiently effective syllable barrier to prevent a following vowel from influencing *i* or *u*: OE *niman*, OFris. *nima* (*nema*), OS *niman* (*neman*), but ON *nema*, OHG *neman*; OE *numen*, OS *ginuman* (*-noman*), but ON *nomenn*, OHG *ginoman*.

NOTE 1: Loewe, GS 1. 39 f., assumes Gmc. *ol or om on* < IE *l̥ r̥ m̥ n̥* and consequently formulates a law Gmc. *onx* > NWGmc. *unx* (43). The same law is necessary for Collitz's similar assumption, MLN 33. 328.

NOTE 2: The term 'nasal groups' includes *mm nn*: OHG *giswumman*, *gispunnan*. NHG *o* in such forms seems to have developed in Middle German during the 15th century. Cf. Paul, Deutsche Grammatik 1. 208 f.

While Primitive Germanic *seems* to point to a development of *enx onx* to *inx unx* (the latter only if we accept the view of Collitz and Loewe), Old Norse shows the opposite, and far more probable, effect of nasal groups. Nasals before certain consonants nasalize the preceding vowel, lowering both its acoustic effect and its actual articulation, and then disappear: OE *rinc*, ON *rekkr* 'man', OE *drincan*, ON *drekka* 'drink', Go. *sigqan*, ON *søkkua* (*u*-mutation) 'sink'; *Þōrr* (name of the God) < *Þunrar*, Go. *sugqans*, ON *sokkenn*.

In Old English and Old Frisian, partly also in Old Saxon, *a* before nasals is nasalized (*ą*), and this is frequently expressed by the spelling *o*: *man/mon*. This is especially marked when *n* disappeared before a voiceless spirant (cf. **29 c**): OE *ōþer*, OFris. *ōther*, OS *ōthar*.—Gmc. *ǣ* < IE *ē*, which is regularly *ā* in WGmc., changes to *ō* before nasals in OE: OHG *nāmum*, OE *nōmon*.

(2) Other Consonants.

b   Certain other consonants influence preceding vowels with a graded
consistency similar to that of the scope of mutation. Again, Gothic
stands by itself. But for Norse and West Germanic we observe, although less clearly, the same general trend: The degree of consonant
shift in any given dialect stands in inverse ratio to its tendency towards
vowel change. Moreover, there is great consistency in the degree to
which different consonants influence vowels. Arranged in accordance
with this, the active consonants are: $ƕ$ r l, *dentals*; w exerts similar
influences, but can hardly be assigned a definite place within this scale.
The form of influence varies considerably in the several dialects, but the
general agreement is too significant to be considered accidental. The
effect of these consonants consists essentially in a lowering and backing
of the articulation of the preceding vowel. A glance at D. Jones's
vowel ellipse, **36 b,** will show that this implies a trend of i towards ε,
a trend of u towards $ɔ$. This must mean that in all Germanic languages
these consonants were pronounced, more or less, with a marked retraction of the tongue. With $ƕ$ (the 'ach-sound'), and w this is self-
evident. For r l, and the dentals we must assume that they were at
least strongly post-alveolar, perhaps even point-inverted ('domal',
'cerebral'), as in American English, especially in New England, and in
many Scandinavian and some German dialects. Modern English offers
obvious parallels to the effect of r and l on preceding vowels. We
should expect Germanic $ʒ$ to have a similar effect as $ƕ$, but this extremely
yielding consonant adapts itself to the articulation of the preceding
vowel, becoming palatal after a front vowel. The same is the case with
High German *ch* ('ich-sound' and 'ach-sound'). Only Germanic $ƕ$ has
the effect referred to, not *ch* < Gmc. *k*.

We must distinguish between the influence of these consonants on
single vowels and on diphthongs, and their effect in preventing i-mu-
tation.

(a) Simple Vowels:

c   In Gothic, h ($ƕ$) and r lower (and retract) preceding high vowels,
i.e., i u/h r > [ε $ɔ$], now spelled *aí aú*, e.g., *gíban*, but *saíƕan, síbun,*
but *taíhun, gutun, gutans,* but *taúhun, taúhans, waúrþun, waúrþans.*

NOTE: Collitz, l. c., ascribes this vowel change to Primitive Germanic. 'The
mid vowels *e* and *o* developed a tendency to pass into the high vowels *i* and *u*.
They succumbed to this tendency everywhere except when followed by one of
the two consonants *r* or *h*' . . . 'The same consonants *r* and *h* which prevented
the old *e* and *o* from turning into *i* and *u* gained the power also to change the
old *i* and *u* to *e* and *o*' . . . 'Gothic has actually preserved the Prim. Germanic

vocalism.' While the theory is by no means without foundation, it is difficult to accept it in full in view of numerous forms of the type of OHG *fihu* like *filu*, but *beran* like *stelan*, where the difference is clearly due, not to *h* or *r*, but to the vowel of the following syllable. It would require a most elaborate system of analogical cross currents to reconcile this with Collitz's theory.

NORSE presents a fairly close approach to Gothic. It also lowers the **d** high vowels to mid vowels before *h* (which disappears with lengthening of *ĭ ŭ* to *ē ō*): A. M. Sturtevant, Notes on the x-sinking in Old Norse, JEGPh 31. 407. Cf. also Pipping, Inleding §23 a. **rihtjan*, OHG *rihten* 'straighten': ON *rētta*, OHG *līhti* 'light': ON *lēttr*, OHG *sucht* 'disease': ON *sōtt*, Go. *þūhta* 'seemed': ON *þōtta*. The effect of R is difficult to interpret. While Gmc. *r* has no effect on the preceding vowel, R < z (**28**) lowers *ĭ u* to *ĕ o*, but on the other hand palatalizes a preceding back vowel (R-mutation): Go. *mis* 'to me', *weis* 'we', *us* 'out': ON *mēr, vēr, ōr*; OHG *glas*: ON *gler*; **kurun* 'they choose', **kūr* 'cow' > *kø̄ro, kȳr* (but acc. sg. *kū*) show both lowering and mutation. Apparently, the process of rhotacism consisted in a raising and retraction of the tip of the tongue behind the alveolae, as in a transition from z or ð to American *r*; this transition is unfavorable to high vowels, but also unfavorable to extremely low vowels. That Gmc. *r* did not influence *i* and *u* is seen from instances like *hirþer* 'shepherd', *þurfa* 'may', NHG *dürfen*.

In OLD ENGLISH, the effect of these consonants appears chiefly as **e** 'breaking', similar in result, but not in character, to Old Norse breaking (**41**). The front vowels *æ e i* developed a glide similar to that in Swiss [iəχ] = HG *ich*. The 'broken vowels' are spelled *ea eo io*, for [æə eə iə].

æ > *ea* before *h*, and before *r l* followed by any consonant:

    Go. *ahtau, sahv*: OE *eahta* 'eight', *seah* 'saw'
    Go. *hardus, gards*: OE *heard* 'hard', *geard*[2] 'house'
    Go. *barn, haldan*: OE *bearn* 'child', *healdan* 'hold'.

e > *eo* before *h*, before *r* followed by any consonant, and before *l* if 'backed' (velarized) by a following *c* or *h*:

    Go. *aihva-, faihu*: OE *eoh* 'horse', *feoh* 'cattle'
    Go. *airþa, fairhvus*: OE *eorþe* 'earth', *feorh* 'life'
    OHG *elaho, melkan*: OE *eolh* 'elk', *meolcan* 'milk'.

i > *io* before *h* and before *r* plus consonant:

    Go. *maihstus*: OE *miox, meox* 'manure'
    *lirnōjan > OE *liornian, leornian* 'learn'.

WGmc. *ā* < Gmc. *ǣ* was prevented from being fronted by a following *w*: OE (WS) *sāwon* = OS *sāwun* 'they saw'. Gmc. ʒ followed by a back vowel has the same effect: *mǽg* 'son', gen. sg. *māgas*, dat. pl. *māgum*.

f   OLD FRISIAN shows traces of breaking, insofar as *-icht-* becomes *-iuht-*: *liuht* = OE *leoht*, *kniuht* = OE *cneoht* (*cnieht*, *cniht*). Old Frisian is contemporaneous with Middle English, in which breaking had disappeared.   It is therefore not unlikely that pre-literary Frisian had breaking to an extent similar to that of West Saxon. (In the Anglian dialects breaking was more restricted).

a, which normally became *e* in closed syllables, remained *a* before *h* plus consonant, *l* plus consonant, and partly also before *r* plus consonant: *achts, all, warm*.

g   In OLD SAXON *ar al* are sometimes found for *er el*: *arthe* 'earth', *farah* 'life', *walda* 'would'.   But this is rare.

h   In OLD HIGH GERMAN, simple vowels are not affected by following consonants.

(b) Diphthongs.   The lowering of the second element is a first step towards the monophthongization of *ai au*.

i   GOTHIC.   If Hirt is right in assuming that *ai au* were monophthongs everywhere, it would seem possible that they became that first before *h* and *r*, and later in all other positions, but that can hardly be proven.

j   OLD NORSE monophthongizes *ai au* before *h r* to *ā ō*: Go. *aih*—ON *ā* 'I have'; Go. **waih*—ON *vā* 'I fought'; Go. *air*—ON *ār* 'early'; Go. *þlauh*—ON *flō* 'I fled'.   With *i*- mutation, ON *ǽtta* < **aiħtjōm* 'I had' (optative); with *u*-mutation, ON *tǫ* < **tāhu* 'toe'.

iu before dentals is lowered to *iō*: Go. *siuns*—ON *siōn* 'sight'; *biōþa* 'bid', but *fliūga* 'fly', *kliūfa* 'split'.

k   OLD ENGLISH, OLD FRISIAN, OLD SAXON do not show any influence of consonants on diphthongs, due in part to their early monophthongization.

l   OLD HIGH GERMAN has significant features.   *ai* became *ē* before *ħ r w*, and *au* became *ō* before *ħ* and *dentals*.   Before other consonants they appear as *ei ou*.   Doubtless, lowering of *i u* to *e o* was the direct cause of this monophthongization.   In this respect at least, although not in the case of the simple vowels, Collitz's generalization of the Gothic lowering of *i* and *u* is justified.   The front vowel *i* was retracted and lowered by those consonants only that have the strongest tendency to produce that effect (see above), but the back vowel *u* was affected by all of them, except *w*.   That *au* before *w* was not monophthongized (MHG *ouwe* 'Au', Go. **aujō*) is due to the fact that the articulation of *u* and *w* is virtually the same, so that *w* could not have a lowering, but rather a stabilizing effect on *u*.

ai > ē. We find the spelling *ae* in some Bavarian eighth-century documents, otherwise we have *ē*: Go. *air*, **gaiza-*, **laiza-*, *taih*, *aihts*, **taiha*—OHG *ēr* 'before', *gēr* 'spear', *lēra* 'teaching', *zēh*, pret. of *zīhan* 'accuse', *ēht* 'possession', *zēha* 'toe'; Go. *saiws*, *snaiws*, *saiwala*—OHG *sēo* 'lake', *snēo* 'snow' (gen. *sēwes*, *snēwes*), *sēola* 'soul'.

au > ō. Upper German, especially Bavarian, has *ao* during the eighth century; in Bavarian names this is found until 821. Otherwise, *ō* is general: Go. *hauhs*, *ausō*, *nauþs*, *auþs*, *launs*, *laus*, *stautan*—OHG *hōh* 'high', *ōra* 'ear', *nōt* 'need', *ōdi* 'waste', *lōn* 'reward', *lōs* 'empty, -less', *stōzan* 'push'.

Gmc. **eu** appears at first in all dialects except Gothic as *iu* or *eo* according to the following vowel (**39**). But in Old High German there is found a significant difference between the dialects: *eu* before *a* becomes *eo* (later *io ie*) in Franconian regardless of the intervening consonant, but in early Alemannian and Bavarian this takes place only before *ƕ* and *dentals*, i.e., under the same conditions as those in which *au* became *oo* = *ō*. Again, then, we find that in Upper German the vowel development sets in later than in Franconian.—*iu* < *eu* + *i, u* is not affected by the following consonant.

General OHG	Franconian only	Upper German only
biotan—biutu, biutis	*liob*	*liub*, later *liob*
fliohan—fliuhu, fliuhit	*liogan—liugu, liugit*	*liugan*, later *liogan, liugit*

NOTE: This is the reason of the alternation between *ie* and *eu* in New High German: Go. *þiuda-reiks* 'Dietrich', **þiudiska-* 'deutsch'; *fliegen*, *kriechen—er fleugt, kreucht.*

(c) Mutation by following *i* is apt to be prevented by intervening **m** consonants of this type. In Norse, Frisian, and Old English this was not the case, probably because in these dialects mutation was older than the effect of these consonants. In Old Saxon, *a* > *e* mutation was prevented by *h* when supported by a following dental (*ht hl hn hr*), often also by *r* or *l* and consonant: *haldid* 'holds', *mahti* 'he might', *trahni* 'tear', *wardian* 'ward'.

Old High German again shows the usual difference between the dialects: *hs ht* and *consonant* + *w* prevent *a* > *e* mutation everywhere, *l r* + *consonant* only in Upper German: *mahtīg* 'mighty', *wahsit* 'grows', *garwen* < **garwjan* 'make ready'; Franc. *heltit* 'holds', *eltiro* 'older', *wermen* < **warmjan* 'warm'—UG *haltit*, *altiro*, (Bav.) *warmen*. This dialect difference has been largely preserved in modern times, although the mutated forms have gained ground, partly by analogy.

ACCENT AND ITS EFFECTS

a   **43. Indo-European and Germanic Accent.** Accent, as an inherent quality of every syllable, presents two aspects that are termed *stress* and *pitch*. Neither of these ever exists alone, but according to the predominance of either element we speak of dynamic (stress) accent and musical (pitch) accent. With the former the dominating factor is the degree of loudness, which depends primarily on the strength of expiration, with the latter, the rate of vibrations of the vocal cords, depending basically on their tension. Either factor may prevail to such an extent that our acoustic reaction leads us to distinguish between languages of the stress type and the pitch type. Generally speaking, the Germanic languages belong to the former, the Romance and Slavic languages more or less to the latter. It is quite likely that in Indo-European, too, the preponderance of the two aspects of accent varied chronologically, perhaps also geographically. Hirt, HU 1. 51, assumes four accent periods. During the first two periods unstressed vowels were reduced and then, partly, dropped. The third period was marked by qualitative gradation (change of *e* to *o*) and further vowel reduction, and during the fourth period the vowels were stationary. This points to a predominance of stress accent during the earlier, of pitch accent during the later periods.

But at all times that are within our reach, Indo-European accent was 'free', that is, the variation of stress or pitch did not necessarily depend on the morphological character of a syllable (root, suffix, ending, prefix), nor on its rhythmical position (first, penult, etc.). For instance, the Greek word for 'man' shows these accent forms: Nom. sg. ἀνήρ, gen. sg. ἀνδρός, acc. sg. ἄνδρα, with the accent on the suffix, the ending, and the root respectively; one infinitive form of the verb 'to leave' is λείπειν, another, λιπεῖν. All Indo-European languages went through some form of accent regulation. In Italic, Celtic, Germanic, the accent was, in prehistoric times, essentially fixed on the first syllable, which points to stress accent in those languages. Later, Latin substituted a rhythmical accent depending on quantity: **in-ˈcapiō* at first became ˈ*in-cipiō*, the change *a > i* being due to loss of stress, and later *inˈcipiō*. Neither of these two accent shifts need be ascribed to any language mixture any more than the Indo-European accent periods presuppose any variation in ethnic structure. They may have been an incidental feature of the general drift of the language, quite as much as, for instance, the transformation of the verb system in these languages.   The same thing is true of the Germanic accent shift.

The Germanic stress was not necessarily shifted to the first syllable. b Compound verbs stressed the stem syllable, while compound nouns and adjectives stressed the prefix, with the exception of the prefix *ga-*, which was probably always unstressed: Go. *us-*'*leiþan* 'go out', but '*us-liþa* 'paralytic'; *ga-*'*leikon* 'compare', *ga-*'*leiki* 'likeness', *ga-*'*leiks* 'like'. The reduplicating syllable was originally unaccented, as is shown by Verner's Law in Go. *saizlēp*, but was doubtless stressed in historical times: ON *rera* 'rowed' < **rerō* shows weakening of the stem syllable; Go. *saisō* 'sowed' has either leveled or not carried through Verner's Law.

NOTE 1: It is not always possible to distinguish between genuine compound verbs and verbs derived from compound nouns, nor, on the other hand, between genuine compound nouns and nouns derived from compound verbs. Go. *usfulleins* probably is derived from *usfulljan* (cf. NHG *Erfüllung* from *erfüllen*) and therefore has the accent on the stem; on the other hand, Go. *andawaurdi* 'answer' corresponds to NHG *Antwort*, NE *answer* with prefix accent, but *andwaurdjan*, with loss of the vowel of the second syllable, seems to require stem accent, different from NHG *antworten*, NE *answer* (verb).

NOTE 2: Streitberg, UG 168, GE 160, Kieckers, HGG 100 f., assume for Gothic nouns stressed *ga-*, on account of double compounds like *ga-galeikōn* 'das *ga-leiks* "aehnlich"' . . . voraussetzt. Wie die Intonation lehrt, war das Praefix zur Zeit Wulfilas noch durchweg akzentuiert.' The argument is not convincing.

NOTE 3: Loewe, GS 1. 32, explains the accent difference between compound verbs and compound nouns as follows: 'Es lag das daran, dass zur Zeit der Akzentzurückziehung Präposition und Verbum noch nicht zu einem einheitlichen Worte verschmolzen waren, wie dieselben denn auch noch got. durch enklitische Partikeln, z. B. in *ubuhwōpida* "und schrie auf" (*uh* "und"), *usnugibiþ* "gebt nun her" (*nu* "nun") voneinander getrennt werden konnten. So begreift es sich auch nur, weshalb die got. Präposition *and* "entlang, entgegen" in nominalen Zusammensetzungen, z. B. in *andawaurd* "Antwort", noch in ihrer älteren Gestalt **anda*, in verbalen aber gleichfalls nur als *and-*, z. B. in *andwaurdjan* "antworten" erscheint: -*a* war got. nur ausl., nicht auch inl. geschwunden. Wie hier so war auch sonst in den Nominalkomposita, die schon idg. einheitliche Wörter gewesen waren, der Akzent stets auf die Anfangssilbe des ersten Bestandteils zurückgezogen worden. Diese Verschiedenheit der Betonung führte ahd. auch zu Verschiedenheiten der Laute, indem die Vokale vortoniger Silben verändert wurden, die hauptoniger unverändert bleiben; daher z. B. *intlāzan* "entlassen, loslassen" neben *antlāzi* "Loslassung" und noch nhd. *erteilen* aus ahd. *irteilen* neben nhd. *Urteil* = ahd. *urteil*.'

Both the Indo-European and the Germanic accent had far-reaching effects on the structure of the language.   The former resulted primarily in *Gradation*, the latter primarily in the *Weakening of Unstressed Syllables* (and, later, in the Standardization of Quantity of stressed syllables). But the difference between these two concepts is rather one of degree, direction, and chronology, than of principle. On the one hand, quantitative gradation (**46**) implies weakening of unstressed syllables in the IE period, and on the other hand, the Germanic vowel drift is somewhat akin to qualitative gradation. Still, the two processes are fundamentally separate historically and must be treated without reference to one another.

Gradation

44. Ablaut (Jacob Grimm's term) or *Gradation* is a reflex of the two accent types of Indo-European. *Pitch* accent led to an alternation between front and back vowels. Since *i* and *u* did not function as genuine vowels in Primitive Indo-European, except as the result of the reduction of diphthongs (**35**), this type of gradation is restricted to the alternation between the mid vowels *e* and *o*. *Stress* accent resulted, on the one hand in the weakening or loss of unstressed vowels, on the other hand, under certain circumstances, in a lengthening of overstressed vowels. We call the result of pitch accent *qualitative* gradation or *Abtönung*, that of stress accent, *quantitative* gradation or *Abstufung*.

Gradation is by no means a peculiar characteristic of Indo-European. It is doubtful whether there exists any language that does not show some form of quantitative gradation, but also qualitative gradation is frequent. Of the linguistic groups adjacent to Indo-European, Finno-Ugrian possesses it only in rudimentary traces (e.g. Finn. *pala-* 'burn', trans., *poltta-* 'burn', intrans.; Ostyak *mort-* 'to break', *mirta* 'I break', *murtəm* 'I have broken'). But the Semitic languages possess highly developed ablaut systems of a more consciously functional character than Indo-European in the form that science has been able to reconstruct: Arab. *qatala* 'kills' shows quantitative gradation in the conative form ('Zielstamm') *qātala* 'tries to kill' and the causative form *'aqtala* 'makes kill', qualitative gradation, e.g., in the passive form *qūtila* 'is killed'; a stem like *qatala*, with the middle vowel *a*, has transitive meaning; intransitive verbs have, in general, a front vowel in the middle syllable to denote temporary condition, a back vowel to denote permanent condition (*i u* in Arabic, *e o* in Hebrew): Arab. *hasuna* 'is beautiful', but *sakira* 'is (now) drunk', *yabisa* 'is (now) dry'. These few types of ablaut are far from conveying an adequate picture of the great wealth and consistency of those Semitic systems, in comparison with which Indo-European gradation seems very restricted and irregular.

Among the Indo-European languages, Germanic, like all others, has greatly decreased the number of phonetic variations, but it has greatly increased their functional importance. In particular, gradation has been systematized as the structural mechanism of the German 'Strong Verb'.

45. Abtönung, Qualitative Graduation, is the alternation between $\check{e}$ and $\check{o}$. It is frequently explained as the result of the loss of accent.[1] But only a small part of the material can be reconciled with this, such as Gk. φέρω 'I carry': φορέω 'I am in the habit of carrying'. In general, there is no evidence that e was the original and o the secondary vowel, but the two vowels rather seem to alternate as equals, as in Gk. λέγω 'I speak': λόγος 'speech', although such derivatives as φορέω were doubtless secondary developments. It is hardly possible at present to venture any definitive explanation. But the obvious parallelism between Indo-European and Semitic ablaut may point the way. In the Semitic verb system, as illustrated above, the front vowel indicates temporary condition, a passing fact, as it were, while the back vowel denotes permanent condition, a state of rest. In Indo-European, the most characteristic sphere of the front vowel is the form of present action, as in λέγω. The fundamental connotation of the back-vowel o is condition: λόγος 'the condition of speaking', λέ-λοιπα '(I have brought about) the state of leaving behind', λοιπός 'left behind', against λείπω 'I am leaving'. True, it is only in root syllables that we find such significant traces of what may have been the origin of Abtönung, and even there Indo-European is very far from showing a regular, clearly definable alternation between e and o (cf. ped-, pod-, pōd- without perceptible difference in L. ped-, Gk. ποδ-, Go. fōtu- 'foot'), and in formative syllables very few rules can even be attempted. But if the parallelism between Indo-European and Semitic ablaut has any significance at all, it must imply some sort of sound symbolism ('Ausdrucksbewegungen'). Acoustically, the interchange between front and back vowels means an interchange between high and low oral resonance ('Eigenton'). But it is an empiric fact that high oral resonance is apt to be accompanied by high tension of the vocal cords, low resonance by their relaxation, so that resonance and vocal pitch generally, though not necessarily, coincide. This can easily be tested by asking persons without phonetic or musical training to pronounce 'high' and 'low' vowels. While interpreting these terms as referring to vocal pitch, not to oral resonance, they almost invariably select i or e (very rarely a) for the former, u or o for the latter, although physiologically it is quite

as easy to articulate *i* in a low voice and *u* in a high voice.   Now, muscle
tension implies interest, and in speech this holds true especially for the
tension of the vocal cords.   It would seem, then, that the IE 'present
tense' is fundamentally the expression of interest in an action going on
and is expressed by articulation with tense vocal cords, favoring the
selection of a front vowel.   Inversely, forms of rather abstract, remote
meaning, such as verbal nouns, tend towards relaxation of the vocal
cords and, indirectly, towards back vowels.

NOTE: Some fifteen years ago, experiments with Felix Krueger's device for
testing the larynx vibrations seemed to indicate to me that in some modern
languages, at least in German and English, the present tense forms have higher
pitch than the past tense forms, although various emotional factors frequently
interfere with this general trend.   Normally, the trend appears not only in forms
like *give—gave, sing—sang, sleep—slept*, where the present has an acoustically
higher vowel, but also in forms where the opposite is the case, like *hold—held,
schlafen—schlief, rufen—rief*, and in forms that are identical for the two tenses,
like *cut, cast, put*.   External conditions compelled me at the time to interrupt
those experiments, and I have never been able to take them up again.   The
preliminary results cannot be considered reliable.

American nursery talk offers an amusing illustration.   A little steam engine
tries to climb a hill and says cheerfully, 'I think I can, I think I can.'   But the
hill is too steep, the poor little engine slides back and says sadly, 'I thought I
could, I thought I could.'   The front vowels [ɪ æ] aptly characterize the active
interest in the successful performance, the back vowels [ɔ u] the melancholy
retrospect to what might have been.

Recent experiments in 'phonetic symbolism' by E. Sapir and others (see J.
Exp. Psych. 12. 225–39 [1929]; Stanley Newman, Am. J. Psych. 45. 53–75 [1933])
tend to lay a statistical foundation for this view.   Newman's statistics show a
definite trend to associate back vowels with concepts of large or dark, front
vowels with concepts of small or bright.   Obviously, this can be observed only in
paired nonsense words, since in actual languages the action of phonetic laws
has greatly modified the original conditions.

The **e-Grade** is characteristic primarily of the present tense of thematic verbs of light bases: L. *ferō, legō, deicō > dīcō, *deucō > doucō >
dūcō*.   But it also occurs in nouns of various types, especially in *s*-
stems and root stems: L. *genus, ped-*.—The lengthened *ē*-grade appears
in certain aorist types, such as L. *lēgī, vēnī*, Go. *sētum, qēmum*, OSl.
sēdъ, which are originally athematic aorists (see **46** and **55**), L. *vēxī,
tēxī* (*s*-aorists), but also in some root nouns, like L. *lēg-, rēg-*, in which
the long vowel is probably due to analogical transfer from the nominatives *lēx, rēx*.

The **o-Grade** belongs chiefly to the singular of the perfect and to
various types of verbal nouns and root nouns: Gk. λέλοιπα, πέπονθα,

δέδορκα, λόγος, ποδ-, L. noct-. Also causative verbs have generally the o-grade: Sk. vartáyati, Go. -wardeiþ 'makes turn' < *wortéyeti. Lengthened grade in φώρ 'thief' (from φέρω 'carry'), L. vōx 'voice' (cf. Gk. ϝέπος); Gk. ἡγεμών 'leader' (gen. -όνος).

Apparently, also IE a could alternate with o, but a was rare and in many cases cannot be distinguished from ə, for the latter became a everywhere except in Indo-Iranian, where it appears as i. Therefore, Indo-Iranian evidence is the only certain criterion of IE a: Sk. pitár- 'father', sthitá- 'stood' (past part.) as against Gk. πατήρ, L. pater, Go. fadar, Gk. στατός, L. status, Go. staþs 'stead' prove IE ə, but Sk. ájati 'drives', ápa 'off' indicate IE a for Gk. ἄγει, L. agō, ON aka 'drive', Gk. ἀπό, L. ab, Go. af. The rare a-o alternation is found in ἄγω: ὄγμος 'furrow', ἄρχω 'rule'—ὄρχαμος 'leader', L. acer 'sharp': ocris 'pointed'. The alternation ā-ō is still rarer, but can hardly be doubted for Gk. (Dor.) φᾱμί 'speak': φωνή 'voice' and perhaps one or two other instances.

46. Abstufung, Quantitative Gradation, consists in reduction or in-   a
crease of vowel quantity.   Vowels that are short under normal accent conditions may be weakened or dropped when unaccented, or lengthened when over-accented.   Normally long vowels may be reduced to slurred vowels, but do not disappear entirely.   This statement may be accepted as a general working principle for quantitative gradation, but it is far from comprehensive.   It is perhaps safe to say that we are even further from an accurate understanding of quantitative than of qualitative gradation.   Nor is this surprising.   Even in living languages that can be observed experimentally, phenomena akin to *Abstufung* often resist scientific definition.   We cannot postulate uniform phonetic values for French 'silent' e, for the German or English article (definite or indefinite), for the medial syllables of Ger. *handelte, rechnete*.   In spite of the great methodical value of historical and comparative analysis, which is sometimes more reliable than even experimental phonetics, we cannot expect absolute consistency in our reconstruction of vowel reduction in reconstructed Indo-European.   However, certain schematic contrasts as indicated below form an indispensable and trustworthy working hypothesis, even though some problems remain unexplained.

The distinction between normally short and normally long vowels is based on the assumption of two types of 'Bases', that is, syllables subject to gradation.   A base may be a root syllable, a prefix, a suffix, an ending, or an independent particle.   If, under conditions of ordinary stress, its vowel is short we speak of a *Light Base*, if, under like conditions, it is long, we speak of a *Heavy Base*.   Thus, the Latin present tense *ferō* has a light base as its root, but *rērī* has a heavy base.   Likewise, Gk. λόγος has a light base, but δῶρον, L. *dōnum* a heavy base. An explanation *why* certain bases are light and others heavy is not available at present, but the distinction as such is of the greatest importance. It might be desirable to use different diacritic marks for the two kinds of long vowels, e.g., to write **lēg-* for L. *lēgī* (lengthened grade of a light base), but **kêp-* for L. *cēpī* (normal grade of a heavy base); but unfortunately this is hardly feasible on account of the large number of forms where the classification is uncertain. Also, such marking might lead to the misunderstanding that there existed a phonetic difference between the two kinds of long *e*, which of course is not the case: they are different genetically, but identical phonetically.

b A. Light Bases.

1. The *Normal Grade, Vollstufe, Normalstufe*, is generally *e/o*: Gk. φέρω—φόρος, λέγω—λόγος, L. *tegō—toga*. For rare cases with *a*, see above.

2. When unstressed, short vowels are either dropped: *Zero Grade, Schwundstufe, Nullstufe*, or weakened (slurred, **34, 38**): *Reduced Grade, Reduktionsstufe*. For Indo-European, we can hardly draw an entirely sharp distinction between the two grades, but within the several IE languages, analogy and varying habits of speech seem to have standardized their use. The 'Strong Aorist' offers typical examples of the Zero Grade: Gk. πέτομαι 'I fly', ἐ-πτόμην 'I flew', ἔχω < **σεχω* 'I have', ἔ-σχον 'I had', but it is also found in other categories: L. *sedeō* 'I sit', *nīdus* < **ni-zd-os* 'nest' (the place for sitting down), Gk. ὄζος < **o-zd-os* 'branch' (the place to sit upon, the perch); Gk. δόρυ 'spear', but Go. *triu* 'tree'; *genu*, Gk. γόνυ, but Go. *kniu* 'knee'.

The Reduced Grade, ə = 'shva secundum', is especially frequent before suffixes with long vowels, as in L. *manēre, patēre, habēre* as against Gk. μένω, L. *petō*, Gk. πέτομαι, OHG *geban*, but frequently takes the place of the Zero Grade if this would result in a consonant group that is out of keeping with the phonetic habits of a given language, or that would interfere too much with the phonetic resemblance of grammatically connected forms. Thus, initial combinations of stops, as in Gk. πτέσθαι (infin. of πέτομαι), or in Czech *pták* 'bird', are incompatible with the phonetic pattern of Germanic; *st-*, as Zero Grade of *set-*, would be phonetically unobjectionable, but a past part. Go. **stans* instead of *sitans* would be too remote from the acoustic impression of *sitan*. This seems to account for the fact that the first three classes of the Germanic strong verbs, where the diphthongal glide assumes vocalic function, have Zero Grade in the past part.,

while the monophthongal fourth and fifth classes show Reduced Grade:
OHG *gistigan, gibotan* < *-buðana-, giwortan* < *-wurðana-* < *-wrtonó-*,
but *ginóman* < *-nъmonó-*, *gisezzan* < *-sъdonó-*.

The Zero Grade of a diphthong is obviously the glide in vocalic
function: *ei eu el er em en* alternate with *i u l r m n:* cf. Go. *steigan staig*
—*stigum stigans; giutan gaut—gutum gutans.* The liquids and nasals
in vocalic ('syllabic') function developed supporting vowels (*u* in Germanic) in accordance with **13**: OHG *helfan, werdan, swimman, singan—
hulfum giholfan, wurtum giwortan, swummum giswomman, sungum
gisungan.*

NOTE: The Reduced Grade of *i-, u*-diphthongs can hardly be established with
certainty. It is often assumed[1] that *ъi ъu* became *ī ū* in early Indo-European, at
least under certain circumstances (perhaps before consonants and in pausa).
The 'aorist presents' of the second class (*lūkan, sūpan, sūgan*) may be explained
in this way (but cf. **54**), and possibly some of the *ī*-presents of the first class, e.g.,
OE OS *wīgan* 'fight', OHG *wīgant* 'fighter', which phonetically, as far as the
vowel is concerned, are indistinguishable from normal grades, have the same
origin. Before vowels, however, *ъi ъu* appear certainly as *ij uw*, and it is hardly
ever possible to assign such forms with certainty to either normal or reduced
grade.

3. On the other hand, short vowels can be lengthened. The origin
and nature of the *Lengthened Grade* (*Dehnstufe*) is still a moot question.
The 'Streitberg-Michels Theory',[2] which may be considered the prevailing view at present, ascribes it in all cases to the loss of a vowel of
the following syllable, e.g., Gk. φώρ 'thief' < *φορος, πώς, L. *pēs*
< *ποδος, *pedos, rēx* < *regos, πατήρ < *πατερε or *πατερο. The
possibility of such compensation must be admitted, but its generalization seems unjustified. A representative of the opposite view, which
favors spontaneous lengthening, is R. Loewe (G. Sprw. 1. 49): 'Die
idg. Dehnung war meist lautsymbolischer, speziell dynamischer Natur,
indem die Intensität der Vorstellung durch Längung des Vokals wieder-
gegeben wurde.' Spontaneous lengthening of strongly stressed syllables is so frequent in many languages that its occurrence in Indo-
European seems at least probable—particularly in that very category
of forms for which Streitberg devised the most elaborate compensation
theory, namely, the preterits of the type of L. *sēdimus, vēnimus*, Go.
sētum, qēmum, OSl. *sēdъ, nēsъ.* The standard view explains these as
contractions of IE reduplicated perfects of the type *sésdəmen, sézdəmen*
> *sédəmn̥.* While this particular form is assured by Sk. *sēdimá*, its
extension over the whole category is far less plausible than spontaneous lengthening. The functional use of this process in Semitic has

been mentioned above (**44**). Monosyllables like Ger. *der, du, so,* E. *the, he, we* are regularly short or long according to emphasis. The standardization of quantity in the later development of the Germanic languages implies spontaneous lengthening of a phonetic, non-functional character. In Lithuanian, short *e* and *a* are lengthened when accented (*gēras* 'good', *tākas* 'path', instr. *gerù, takù*). It is often hardly possible to decide definitely whether lengthening is due to compensation or to spontaneous overstress, but for the type of Go. *qēmum* the latter assumption seems better founded.

c   *Lengthened Diphthongs.* Like simple vowels, diphthongs are subject both to reduction (see above) and to lengthening, so that IE *āi āu ēi ēu ōi ōu āl ēl ōl ān* etc. can either be original long diphthongs or lengthened short diphthongs. But in Germanic, as in most IE languages, long diphthongs of whatever origin shorten their first element (with the exception of *ēi* > *ē²*, **39**). Therefore, Germanic does not offer any direct evidence for the lengthened grade of short diphthongs, since the few fairly clear cases of *ē²* < *ēi* seem to be originally long diphthongs. However, it does furnish indirect evidence in cases where the *i*- or *u*-glide was absorbed in the lengthened vowel so that, e.g., we find alternations between IE *oi* and *ō* < *ōi*, *ou* and *ō* < *ōu*, etc. It is not known just under what circumstances these long diphthongs were monophthongized instead of shortened, but the fact itself is certain:

> *ei* : *ē*—Sk. *váyati* 'blows', L. *ventus*, Go. *winds* 'wind' < **wēntos*
> *oi* : *ō*—Go. *haims*, Gk. κώμη 'village'
> *eu* : *ou* : *ō*—OHG *fliozan* 'flow': Go. *flōdus* 'flood', Gk. πλωτός 'floating'.

Other cases are very uncertain. Thus, Lith. *leidù* (*leidžù*) 'I leave' points to a diphthongal root, but the evidence of Go. *lētan*, Gk. λήδο-μαι, L. *lassus* < **ləd-tos* is too strongly in favor of *ē/ə* (heavy base, see below). It is more likely that we have in *leidžù* a contamination, due to similarity of meaning, with *liekù* 'I remain, I leave' = Gk. λείπω.

HEAVY BASES are syllables whose normal grade shows a long vowel.
d Generally, this is *ē* or *ō*, more rarely *ā*; *ē* and *ō* sometimes alternate; qualitative gradation of *ā* with *ē* or *ō* is very rare. The reduced grade is *ə*; rare instances of zero grade of heavy bases are probably due to analogy with light bases. Lengthened grade of heavy bases does not exist; where the circumflex accent in Greek or Lithuanian would seem to indicate it, we have to deal with secondary developments of rhythmical accent in those languages.

ē/ō/ə—Go. *tēkan* 'touch', pret. *taitōk*; ON *taka* 'take', pret. *tōk*

    Go. *lētan* 'let', ON *lāta*, OE *lǣtan*, OHG *lāzzan*, Gk. λήδομοι;
    L. *lassus* < *ləd-tos*, Go. *lats* 'lazy', ON *latr*, OE *læt*, OHG
    laz

    Go. *gadēþs* 'deed', OE *dǣd*, OHG *tāt*, Gk. τί-θημι 'I put',
    L. *fēcī* 'I did'; Gk. θῶμα 'heap', ON *dōmr*, OE *dōm*, OHG
    tuom 'judgment, sentence'; OE *dōm*, OHG *tuom* 'I do'

    L. *cēpī* (possibly analogy to *fēcī*), Gk. κώπη 'handle'; Go. *hōf*
    'I lifted'; L. *capiō*, Go. *hafjan* (pres. of *hōf*)

    L. *rērī* 'think', Go. *-rēdan* 'provide', *rōdjan* 'talk'; *-raþjan*
    'count', *raþjō* 'accounting', L. *ratus*, past part. of *rērī*

ō/ə—L. *dōnum* 'gift', Gk. δί-δωμι 'I give', L. *dare* 'give'

ā/ə—L. *stāre* 'stand', Gk. (Dor.) ἵ-στᾱμι 'I stand', Go. *stōþ*, OHG
    stuot 'stood'; Gk. στατός, L. *status*, Sk. *sthitá-*, past part.,
    Go. *standan* 'stand'

    L. *scabō*—*scābī* 'shave' = Go. *skapjan*—*skōp* 'shape'

    L. *vādō* 'I am walking', *vadō* 'I go through', late denominative
    from *vadum* 'ford'—Go. *wadan*—*wōþ*, ON *vaþa*—*vōþ* (*ōþ*)
    'wade'

    L. *sāgiō* 'scout', *sagax* 'clever', Go. *sōkjan* 'seek' (perhaps
    also Go. *sakan* 'quarrel')

ā/ō/ə—Gk. (Dor.) φᾱμί 'I speak', φωνή 'voice', -φατός 'spoken'.   e

DIPHTHONGAL HEAVY BASES with *ēi ōi āi ēu ōu āu ēl ōl āl* etc., should
theoretically show the reduced grades *əi əu əl* etc. Taking into account
the usual shortening or monophthongization of long diphthongs, we
should expect in Germanic the normal grades *ē²*, *ai/ō*, *eu* (> *eo iu*)/*ō*,
el al etc., and the reduced grades (*ə* > *a*, **38**) *ai au al*, but the material
is scanty and for the most part etymologically uncertain. Morphological considerations (**54**) make it probable that the verbs of the Germanic seventh class come closest to this condition. As far as etymologies are clear, they are predominantly heavy bases: Go. *lētan*
belongs to L. *lassus* (see above), *-rēdan*, *-raþjan* to *rērī*, *ratus*, *saian* =
[sǣan] or [sǣjan] to *sēmen*, *satus*, *fāhan* to *pāx*, *pangō*, *blēsan* to *flāre*,
aukan to *augeō*, *tēkan*, ON *taka*, to Gk. δάκτυλος. Go. *lētan*—*lailōt*—
lailōtum (analogically for *lailatum*) contains in principle the same gradation as light bases like Go. *steigan*—*staig*—*stigum*, namely, *ē/ō/ə* over
against *e/o/-*. Many verbs of this class have reduced-grade presents
('Aorist Presents', like OE *cuman* < *gwm-*), e.g., L. *capiō*, *faciō* <
kəp-, *θək-*. Accordingly, the following parallels seem justified (Gothic
forms are given, where not otherwise marked):

Monophthongs	*i*-Diphthongs	*u*-Diphthongs
ē: Pres. *lētan*	WGmc. Pret. *hēt* < *kēid-	OHG *stioz* < *stēud-
ō: Perf. sg. *lailōt, hōf*	Perf. sg. *haihait* (*ōi*)	*staistaut* (*ōu*)
ə: Perf. pl. *lailatum	Perf. pl. *haihaitum* (*əi*)	*staistautum* (*əu*)
Aor. Pres. *hafjan*	Aor. Pres. *haitan*	*stautan*

West-Germanic preterits of the type of *hēt* are on a level with the normal-grade present forms of the type *lētan*, and diphthongal presents of the Germanic seventh class, like *haitan*, have the same structure as a number of monophthongal presents of the sixth class, like *hafjan*, namely, reduced grade. The relation of this distribution of ablaut grades to the general system of the Germanic strong verb is discussed in **54**. But this must be admitted: in spite of its systematic consistency, this interpretation is at best a good working hypothesis. The small number of instances points to the probability of analogical leveling. Thus, the plural *haihaitum*, instead of coming from *-*kəid*-, may be leveling from the singular *haihait* < *-*kōid*-. Besides, not one of the diphthongal verbs in this class can definitely be proved to be a heavy base. The only more or less valid argument for their being that consists in their morphological parallelism with monophthongal heavy bases like *lētan, tēkan* (ON *taka*, aorist present with reduced grade). The matter is still further complicated by the fact that *əi əu* as reductions of *ēi ēu* are not universally accepted. Hirt, for instance, (Idg. Gr. 2. 66 ff., HU 1. 61) assumes that their regular reduced grade was *ī ū*. This would yield an alternation *ēi ēu/ī ū*, as in Sk. *dhāyas* 'nourishing', OHG *tāju* 'suckle' : L. *fīlius*; Gk. *oὖθαρ* < *ōudhr- : Sk. *ūdhar*, L. *ūber*, OHG *ūtar* 'udder'—or even *ē/ī ū*, since long diphthongs are apt to lose their glide: *θηλή* 'breast', L. *fēlāre* 'suckle', *fēmina* 'woman' : L. *fīlius*; Go. *fōn*, gen. *funins* : Gk. *πῦρ*, OHG *fuir* = [fy:r] 'fire'; Gk. *ἥλιος*, Dor. *ἀέλιος* < *sāu-elijos, Go. *sauil* = [sɔːil], ON OE *sōl* : Sk. *sūryas* 'sun'. I cannot consider it definitely proved that *ī ū* are necessarily the reduced grades of *ēi ēu*. In some of the instances given by Hirt (*l. c.* and HU 1. 67) we really have to deal with short diphthongs that are lengthened in certain forms, e.g., in OSl. *nitъ* 'thread' < *neiti- we have the normal grade, in Go. *nēpla* 'needle' the lengthened grade, with *ēi* > *ē*, while Lith. *nýtis* [niːtis] 'fuller's teasel' has *ъi* rather than *əi*; cf. **klei-/kloi-/klъi-/kli*- in Lith. *šlejù* 'I lean', *šlaĩtas* 'slope', *pa-šlýti* 'stumble', *šlìtìs* 'pile of sheaves'. The alternation *ēi/əi/ī* = Gmc. *ē²/ai/ī* for heavy bases is quite as likely as the alternation *ei/ъi/i* = Gmc. *ī/ī/i*, which for light bases is now generally admitted. Besides, transition from light to heavy bases and vice versa was doubtless quite frequent.

f   DISYLLABIC BASES are formulae necessary to account for parallel forms like L. *genu*, Gk. *γόνυ*: Go. *kniu* 'knee'; Gk. *δόρυ* 'spear' : Go. *triu* 'tree'; L. *augeō*, Go. *aukan* 'increase' : Go. *wahsjan* 'grow'; Sk. *távas* 'strength' : Gmc. *þūs*- in Go. *þūs-(h)undi* '1000', WGmc. *Thūsnelda*; L. *plēnus* : Go. *fulls* 'full'; L. *gnō*-, Gk. *γνω*-, OE *cnāwan* 'know' < *ĝnē- : Go. *kann, kunnum* 'can'. We have here to deal with double gradation, for which the customary formula is *ere, erā*. The former type is called a disyllabic *light* base, the latter a disyllabic *heavy* base. Either of the two syllables is subject to gradation, so that we may find *ere/re/er/ēr/rē* and *erā* (*ā* = *ē* = *ō*)/*erə* (*ʋrə*, if both syllables are unaccented)/*rā*. E.g., **ĝeneu* shows the form **ĝenu* = L. *genu* and **gneu* = Go. *kniu*; **pelē-* appears as **plē-* in *plēnus*, as **plə-*, with secondary loss of *ə* in Germanic, in *fulls* < **plənos*. Sanskrit grammar, preserving the functional value of these parallel types, distinguishes between *sēṭ*-bases and *aniṭ*-bases, i.e., bases with or without *i* < *ə* (*sa-* 'with', *an-* 'without'). An instance of the former is *caritum* 'to move' < **kwerə-* (**kwelə-*, Gk. πέλομαι); of the latter, *vártum* 'to choose' < **wer-* (**wel-*, L. *velle*), which may equally well be considered a reduction from disyllabic **were-* (**wele-*), or a monosyllabic light base, **wer-* (**wel-*). In a great majority of cases disyllabic gradation results in a metathesis of *l r m n i u*. The Germanic languages have not preserved it in grammatical function. Generally, it can be recognized only by comparison with other languages, as in Gk. δόρυ : Go. *triu*, but there are some rare cases of internal Germanic evidence, such as Go. *aukan* : *wahsjan* < **awg-* : **wog-*.

For bibliography and history of the theory, see Hirt, Idg. Gr. 2. 106 ff.

47. The Germanic Ablaut Series. Gradation was a factor of funda- a mental importance in Indo-European and has as such been particularly well preserved, perhaps even extended, in the Gmc. Strong Verb. Its types have been arranged by grammarians as 'classes' or 'series' varying in number and character, depending principally on the gradual advancement of knowledge concerning the IE vowel system. Jacob Grimm, Deutsche Grammatik I (1819) set up fourteen 'Conjugationen'; in their OHG forms they are the following: *heizan, stōzan, faltan, bindan, lesan, neman, werfan,* (*zeran* = Go. *tairan*), *gripan* (sic; Go. *greipan*), *zīhan,* (Go. *teihan*), *gizan, slahan* (Grimm's spellings). The present arrangement by seven classes, which had not been possible before Collitz's reconstruction of the IE vowel system (**34**), developed through the cooperation of the Leipzig Neo-Grammarians. It was, I believe, first printed in Braune's Gotische Grammatik (1886). Hirt, HU 1. 75, says rightly about it: 'Die Anordnung ist durchaus willkürlich. Sie ist aber eingebürgert, und man ersetzt sie besser nicht durch eine andere.'

The seven classes are, in Gothic forms:

   I. *steigan—staig—stigum—stigans* (*i*-diphthongs)

  II. *giutan—gaut—gutum—gutans* (*u*-diphthongs)

 III. *hilpan—halp—hulpum—hulpans* (*liquid* or *nasal* diphthongs)

 IV. *niman—nam—nēmum—numans* (monophthong before *liquid* or *nasal*)

V. *sitan—sat—sētum—sitans* (monophthong before *stop* or *spirant*)

VI. *hafjan—hōf—hōfum—hafans* (Gmc. *a/ō* series)

VII. *lētan—lailōt—lailōtum—lētans* (Reduplicating Class).

For the sake of historical continuity this arrangement is retained in the chapter on strong verbs. A more logical classification, however, would be the following:

Light Bases with monophthongs: I a, *sitan*, I b, *niman*

Light Bases with diphthongs: II a, *steigan*, II b, *giutan*, II c, *hilpan*

Heavy Bases with monophthongs: III a, *hafjan*, III b, *lētan*

Heavy Bases with diphthongs: IV a, *haitan*, IV b, *stautan*, IV c, *haldan*.

b   While we generally associate these classes with the strong verb, they include, of course, all categories of words and syllables. Some Germanic instances follow:

		Go.	ON	OE	OS	OHG	
I a,	e:	*giban*	*gefa*	*giefan*	*geban*	*geban*	'give'
		giba	*giof*	*giefu*	*geba*	*geba*	'gift'
		in	*ī*	*in*	*in*	*in*	'in'
		-is	*-(i)r*	*-es*	*-is*	*-is*	2 sg. pres. ending
	o:	*gaf*	*gaf*	*geaf*	*gaf*	*gab*	'I gave'
		gabeigs 'rich'		*gafol* 'tribute'			
		-and	*-a*	*-aþ*	*-ath*	*-ant*	3 pl. pres. ending.
	ē:	*gēbum*	*gǭfom*	*gēafon*	*gābun*	*gābum*	'we gave'
			gǣfr 'healing'			*gāba*	'gift'.
	ъ:	*gibans*	*gefenn*	*giefen*	*gigeban*	*gigeban*	'given'
	—:	*sind* < *s-enti*		*sind*	*sind*	*sint*	'they are'.
I b,	e:	*niman*	*nema*	*niman*	*niman*	*neman*	'take'
		filu	*fiol*	*feolu*	*filu*	*filu*	'much'.
	o:	*nam*	*nam*	*nom*	*nam*	*nam*	'I took'
		-an	*-a*	*-an*	*-an*	*-an*	infin. ending.
	ē:	*nēmum*	*nǭmom*	*nōmon*	*nāmun*	*nāmum*	'we took'
			-bǣrr	*-bǣre*		*-bāri*	'bearing'
		qēns	*kuǣn*	*cwēn*			'woman'.
	ъ:	*numans*	*nomenn*	*numen*	*ginuman*	*ginoman*	'taken'
			koma	*cuman*	*cuman*	*comen*	'come'
		faura		*for*	*fora*	*fora*	'before'
	—:	*fadrum*	*feþrom*	*fædrum*			'to the fathers'
		triu	*trē*	*trēo*	*triu*		'tree'.
II a,	ei:	*steigan*	*stīga*	*stīgan*	*stīgan*	*stīgan*	'climb'
		weihs	*vē*	*wīg*	*wīh*	*wīh*	'temple, idol'.
	oi:	*staig*	*steig (stē)*	*stāh*	*stēg*	*steig*	'I climbed'
		stains	*steinn*	*stān*	*stēn*	*stein*	'stone'
		þai	*þeir*	*þā*	*thē*	*dē* (?)	'they'.

		Go.	ON	OE	OS	OHG	
	i:	stigum	stigom	stigon	stigun	stigum	'we climbed'
			stigr			steg	'path'.
II b,	eu:	-biudan	biōþa	bēodan	biodan	biotan	'bid'
		diups	diūpr	dēop	diop	tiof	'deep'.
	ou:	bauþ	bauþ	bēad	bōd	bōt	'I bade'
		daupjan	deypa	dīepan	dōpian	touffen	'baptize'
		dauþs	dauþr	dēad	dōd	tōt	'dead'.
	u:	budum	buþom	budon	budun	butum	'we bade'
			boþe	boda	bodo	boto	'messenger'.
II c,	el+:	hilpan	hialpa	helpan	helpan	helfan	'help'
		hilms	hialmr	helm	helm	helm	'helmet'.
	er+:	wairþan	verþa	weorþan	werthan	werdan	'become'
		hairda	hiorþ	heord		herta	'herd'.
	en+:	bindan	binda	bindan	bindan	bintan	'bind'
		drigkan	drekka	drincan	drinkan	trinkan	'drink'.
	ol+:	halp	halp	healp	halp	half	'helped'.
		balgs	belgr	belg	balg	balg	'skin, bag'.
	or+:	warþ	varþ	wearþ	warth	ward	'I became'.
		frawardjan		āwierdan		frawartan	'spoil'.
	on+:	band	batt [bant]	bond	band	bant	'I bound'
		dragkjan	drekkia	drencan	drenkan	trenkan	'make drink'.
	l+:	hulpum	hulpom	hulpon	hulpum	hulfum	'we helped'.
		wulfs	ulfr	wulf	wulf	wolf	'wolf'.
	r+:	waurþum	(v)urþom	wurdon	wurdum	wurtum	'we became'
		baurgs	borg	burg	burg	burg	'fortification'.
	n+:	bundum	bundom	bundon	bundum	buntum	'we bound'.
III a,	ō:	hōf	hōf	hōf	hōf	huob	'I lifted'.
	ā:	stōþ	stōþ	stōd	stōd	stuo(n)t	'I stood'.
	ə:	hafjan	hefia	hebban	heffian	heffan	'to lift'
		standan	standa	standan	standan	standan	'to stand'.
III b,	ē:	lētan	lāta	lǣtan	lātan	lāzan	'to let'
		slēpan		slǣpan	slāpan	slāfan	'to sleep'.
	ə:	lats	latr	lǣt	lat	laz	'lazy'
			lata = lāta	LG	slap	slaf	'weak'.
IV a,	ēi:		hēt	hēt	hēt	hiaz	'I called'.
	ōi:	haihait					'I (have) called'.
	əi:	haitan	heita	hātan	hētan	heizan	'to call'.
IV b,	ēu:		hliop	hlēop	hleop	(h)liof	'I jump, run'.
	ōu:	haihlaup*					'I (have) jumped'.
	əu:	hlaupan	hlaupa	hlēapan	hlōpan	(h)loufan	'to jump, run'.
IV c,	ēn+:		fekk [fing] feng		feng	fenc [fiang]	'I caught'.
	ān+:	faifāh < fānχ < -þānk-					'(have) caught'.
	ən+:	fāhan < þank-		fōn	fāhan	fāhan	'to catch
		fangans*	[fengenn]	fongen	gifangan	gifangan	'caught .

Unstressed Syllables

48. Quantity of Final Syllables. All morphological types of syllables—roots, prefixes, suffixes, endings—could be either long or short. In the case of long syllables, Greek and Lithuanian orthography uses two forms of accent signs, the acute, ′, and the circumflex, ∼: ποιμήν 'herdsman', ἡγεμών 'leader', but Lith. akmuõ 'stone' (nom. sg.), θεῶν 'gods' (gen. pl.): Lith. stóras 'thick', kója 'foot', but gẽras 'good', duktė̃ 'daughter'. In modern Lithuanian, and probably also in classical Greek, the acute denotes even pitch (Stosston), the circumflex changing pitch (Schleifton): In stóras, the pitch rises or falls evenly during the articulation of the vowel, in gẽras, it either rises and then falls, or it falls and then rises. This is particularly marked in the case of diphthongs: gáuti 'get' has Stosston, gaũsti 'resound' has Schleifton. Syllables with the circumflex accent, especially those with diphthongs, are noticeably longer than those with acute accent. We find a similar contrast between the American and the Standard German articulation of diphthongs: Ger. Mai, Haus, neu are distinctly shorter than Am. my, house, boy, and the latter may be said to have Schleifton. Certain German dialects distinguish between (er) haut, braut and (die) Haut, Braut by a circumflex accent on the former, an acute on the latter words.

The Greek and Lithuanian accents can by no means be identified with IE conditions, but are largely due to secondary changes. However, in final syllables at least they do reflect IE conditions. The vowels of IE endings clearly show three types: short, acute-long, and circumflex-long. It is virtually certain that the circumflex accent of endings was in all cases due either to contraction or to compensation: the ending of the nom. pl. masc. of o-stems was -õs < o + es; the gen. sg. of ā-stems had -ãs < -ā + so; the nom. sg. of certain n-stems ended in -õ < -ón.

In Germanic, endings with a circumflex accent show more resistance to weakening (**49**) than long-vowel endings with an acute accent. This fact, as well as the Greek-Lithuanian parallels and the origin of endings with a circumflex accent, indicates that these were really longer than endings with an acute accent. At any rate, it is a convenient, if somewhat mechanical, device for the purpose of Germanic grammar to classify endings as having one, two, or three 'morae' (time units), equivalent to short syllables, long syllables with an acute accent and long syllables with a circumflex accent. E.g.:

Nom. sg. masc. *dhwesos, 2 pl. pres. *nemete have final syllables of one mora: Gk. θεός, νέμετε.

Nom. sg. fem.   *dhwesā, 1 sg. pres. *nemō have final syllables of two
     morae: Gk. θεᾶ, νέμω.

Gen. pl. *dhwesōm < o-om, ā-om⎫ have final syllables of three morae:
Gen. sg. *dhwesās < ā-so   ⎭   Greek. θεῶν, θεᾶς.

49. The Germanic Weakening of Unstressed Syllables. The strong a
stress accent on the stem (or first syllable) (**43**) caused in Germanic a
progressive weakening of unaccented syllables, which is particularly
marked in the case of final syllables.   Roughly speaking, this may be
said: during the first two or three centuries A.D., i.e., soon after the
Germanic accent shift, final syllables lost one mora.   About five hundred years later a second mora was lost; another five hundred years
later, a third.   Naturally, this is an over-mechanical statement and a
good deal of allowance must be made for deviations.   But the following
instance may serve to characterize the trend:

The noun termination -ō, as in Lith. *akmuõ* 'stone', has three morae.
It appears in Go. *tuggō, namō* (**48**) as a long vowel with two morae.
With a corresponding ending, though a different gender, OE *nama* has
one mora; this was lost towards the end of the ME period, resulting in
NE [*neim*].   The Scandinavian languages as well as Dutch and most
German dialects approach this, but Standard German, being highly
artificial and largely the product of spelling pronunciation, lags far
behind.

The following outline intends to show merely the general trend.
Numerous details are added in the Morphology.

A. SHORT VOWELS.

(1) In *Final Syllables* they tend to disappear.   Unless followed by b
consonants, they are not preserved anywhere; the low and mid vowels
e o a disappear very early even before consonants, but the high vowels,
i u, show more resistance.

a: Gk. οἶδα 'I know' ⎫
                           ⎬ Go. *wait*
e: Gk. οἶδε 'he knows' ⎭

Sg. imper. Gk. νέμε, pl. imper. νέμετε—Go. *nim, nimiþ* 'take'.
o: Gen. sg. -*so* (Gk. θεοῦ < *θεοσο)—Go. *wulfis*, earliest OE -*æs*.

Before consonants, *a* < *o* is preserved in very early Runic inscriptions (4th to 6th cent. A.D.) and in Norse loan words in Finnish: Run.
Holtingaʀ, staina (acc. sg., < *stainam), horna*, Finn. *ringas, kuningas*
= Go. *Hultiggs, stain, *haurn, *kuniggs.*—Before -*ns*, however, all
short vowels are preserved: Go. *wulfans, gastins, sununs*, OHG *wolfa,
gesti, sunu*, etc.

The greater resistance of high vowels (*i u*) may be ascribed to the c

clearer muscular consciousness during their articulation.   Probably the
same law originally applied to all Germanic dialects: after a long syllable, or after two syllables (which phonetically, or metrically, amounts
to the same thing) they disappear sooner than after a short syllable.
This law, which seems to express a general trend of Germanic towards
accented syllables of two morae, is clearly preserved.   In Norse, early
Runic retains *i u* after long as well as short syllables, but in literary
Norse they have disappeared in both cases, and only the chronology of
mutation (**41**) reflects the original condition: Run. *Saligastiʀ, magu,*
Go. -*gasts, magu,* ON *mǫg, giof* < *ȝeƀu.*   In Gothic, it would seem that *i*
disappeared, but *u* was preserved regardless of the quantity of the preceding syllable: *gasts, baur* 'son' (*i*-stems), but *handus, sunus.*   However, forms like *agis* 'terror', *hatis* 'hate', *riqis* 'darkness' clearly indicate that for *i* the law was the same as in NWGmc., but had been
obscured through leveling in the *i*-stems.   A parallel treatment of *u*
is made highly probably by *tagr* 'tear' = Gk. δάκρυ.

   Instances for *i u*:

i: *ghostis 'guest, enemy'—Go. *gasts,* OE *giest,* OS OHG *gast*
    *nemeti 'he takes'—Go. *nimiþ,* OE *nim(e)þ,* OS *nimid,* OHG *nimit*
    *nemonti 'they take'—Go. *nimand,* OE *nimaþ,* OHG *nemant*
    Go. *hatis* 'hate', ON *hatr,* OE *hete,* OS *heti,* OHG [*haz*]
    Sk. *upari* 'above'—Go. *ufar,* Run. *uƀar,* OE *ofer.*

· u: *sunus 'son'—Go. *sunus,* ON *sunr,* OE OS OHG *sunu*
    **peku̯* 'cattle'—Go. *faihu,* ON *fē,* OE *feoh,* OS *fehu,* OHG *fihu*
    Go. *dauþus* 'death', ON *dauþr,* OE *dēaþ,* OS *dōth,* OHG *tōd.*

   NOTE: WGmc. -*u* < IE *ā ō* (see below, B) shows the same treatment: nom,
pl. neut. OE *fatu* 'vats', OS *fatu,* OHG [*faz*]; OE OS *word,* OHG *wort* 'words'.
but Go. [*waurda*].   In the OHG inst. sg. *wortu* < -*ō, u* is retained through analogy
with words like *tagu, hofu.*   Also in the 1 sg. pres., WGmc. -*u* < -*ō* is preserved
everywhere by analogy: OHG *bintu* like *nimu.*

d   When *a* disappeared after *j w,* these became vocalic (**33**):

   j > *i* in *kunjam > Go. *kuni,* ON *kyn* 'kin', *rīkjam > Go. *reiki,*
ON *rīke,* OE *rīce,* OS *rīki,* OHG *rīchi.*   OE *cynn,* OS *kunni,* OHG
chunni are analogies from the oblique cases, with doubling of *n* before *j*
(which would not have taken place before *i*).   ON *kyn* as against *rīke*
is due to the chronology of the loss of *i.*   At the time when *i* was
dropped after a long syllable, about 700 A.D., the forms were still
**rīkja,* **kunja,* which then became *rīki,* **kyni.*   Somewhat later, but
before 900, *i* disappeared after a short syllable, *kyni > *kyn,* but this
did not affect the long stems.   Cf. Heusler, Aisl. Elb. 39.   Likewise

*herdja(m) 'herdsman' (acc. sg.) became Go. hairdi, ON hirþe, OE hyrde, OS hirdi, OHG hirti. The Go. nom. sg. hairdeis, harjis 'army' are analogies from the gen. sg. hairdeis, harjis < -jeso (see below). The phonetic forms would have been *hairdis, *haris.

w > u: *knewam 'knee' > Go. kniu, ON knē (explanation as for kyn; for lengthening of e, see Heusler, l. c. 31), OE cnēo, OS kneo, OHG chniu. In Gothic and Old English, w is preserved after a long or an unstressed syllable, but that is probably analogy after the oblique cases: Go. hlaiw 'grave' (Run. hlaiwa-), OE hlāw, but OS OHG hlēo; Go. snaiws 'snow', OE snāw, but ON snǽr, OS OHG snēo; in Go. waurstw 'work', gaidw 'lack', þiwadw 'servitude', w may have been merely orthographical.

(2) In *Medial Syllables* conditions are so irregular that a general rule e
working with uniform consistency can hardly be established. Leveling of forms and chronological differences have greatly interfered with regular development. Besides, frequently the original quality and quantity of medial vowels cannot be definitely ascertained. The general trend seems to have been that not only i u, but also a, were more apt to be dropped after a long syllable than after a short one. Cf. for a Go. anahaitan 'invoke', andhaitan 'praise', allwaldands 'omnipotent', allawērei 'honesty', þiudangardi 'kingdom', allawaurstwa 'entire', ainfalþs 'simple', managei 'multitude', manasēþs 'mankind', samaleiks 'like'. For i, cf. Go. brūþ-faþs (compound of two i-stems) 'bridegroom', but Run. Saligastiʀ (name), Go. riqizis, gen. sg. of riqis 'darkness', hatizōn 'be angry'; for u, OHG Hadubrant, Haduwig, but Go. handuwaurhts 'handmade', handugs 'skillful', ON hǫndugr, OE hendig; Go. qiþuhafts 'pregnant'.

The treatment of medial i in the first class of weak verbs is especially f
important.[2] According to 'Sievers' Law of Syncopation' (Btr. 5. 23–61, 78 f.; 7. 141 f.) medial i disappeared in West Germanic after a long stem syllable, but was preserved after a short syllable:
Go. nasida   OE nerede   OS nerida   OHG nerita
Go. sōkida   OE sōhte   OS sōhta   OHG suohta
The chronology of mutation relative to the time of syncopation of the g
middle vowel led to the condition termed 'Rückumlaut' by Jacob Grimm ('Unmutation' by Curme, Grammar of the German Language[2] 315). Evidently, wherever i had disappeared before the period of mutation, the stem vowel had to remain unchanged. In Old Norse we find the same development as in the case of i-stems (salr : gestr, 41), e.g., telia 'count', pret. talþa, but heyra 'hear', pret. heyrþa. The WGmc. condi-

tions are greatly complicated by the fact that the periods of the two phonological events more or less overlapped. In Old English, we find *nerian, nerede* 'save', *fremman, fremede* 'perform', *dēman, dēmde* 'judge' (Go. *nasjan, *framjan, dōmjan*), in which mutation preceded syncopation; but in *tellan, tealde* < **taljan, *tal(i)ða* 'count' (about 20 verbs of this or similar type) syncopation had occurred earlier than mutation. Similarly, Old Saxon has *nerian, nerida*, but *tellian, talda*. Old High German shows more mutation in the Franconian dialects than in Upper German: RFr. *zellen, zelita*, but UG (and EFr.) *zellen, zalta*. Analogy has largely done away with unmutation so that, as an effect of syncopation, Standard NHG has preserved it only in *brennen, kennen, nennen, rennen, senden, wenden* (*brannte*, etc.). In *denken* and *bringen* and the preterit presents it must be traced back to Germanic times, cf. Go. *þagkjan, þāhta, briggan, brāhta, kunnan, kunþa*; these preterits never had *i*.

h   The development of medial *je* depends on the quantity of the preceding syllable. The difference was probably general Germanic or even Indo-European, but it is clearly preserved in Gothic: Gen. sg. of *jo*-stems, **harjisa* > *harjis*, but **herðjisa* > *hairdeis*; 2 sg. pres. of *jo*-verbs, **nasjisi* > *nasjis*, but **sōkjisi* > *sōkeis*. The problem has been treated frequently, but doubtless the difference is due to a difference in syllabication (cf. **33 b**), which is in keeping with the principles of Gmc. metrics, and also with the 'Standardization of Quantity' (**50**). The nominatives *harjis, hairdeis*, for phonological **haris, *hairdis* are analogical transfers from the genitives (see above). In *hairdjam* (dat. pl.), *sōkjam* (1. pl.), etc. there was obviously no basis for contraction, and it is likewise quite improbable that *-jis, -eis* could go back to Gmc. *-jaz* < IE *-jos*.

i   (3) PREFIXES in general retain their vowels. But there is some evidence of a tendency towards weakening in isolated cases. Thus, Go. *at-augjan* 'show' is doubtless cognate with OHG *zougen* 'show'. OHG has accented *fora, ur-, zuo*, but unaccented *fir-, ir-, zi-*; *bī-* appears in nouns, *be-* in verbs. English has given up *ge-* as a verbal prefix, aside from archaisms like *yclept*. German shows weakened prefixes in words like *Glück, Glaube, bleiben*. In Norse, verbal prefixes were lost entirely.

B. LONG VOWELS (and diphthongs) of two morae.

(1) Final syllables shorten long vowels:

j   IE *ē* > *a* in Gothic, > *e* elsewhere (spelled generally *i* in earlier Norse):

Gk. πατήρ—Go. *fadar*, ON *faþer*, OE *fæder*, OS *fadar*, OHG *fater*

Gk. (ποιμ)ήν—Go. *hana*, ON *hane*, (the Gothic form may also go back to -*ōn*)

IE -*ēt* (3 sg. pret. of weak verbs), Go. *nasida*, ON *talþe*.

IE *ā ō* > Gmc. *ō* became *a* in Gothic, but *u* in NWGmc. This indicates that in the latter group the usual trend of the long-vowel drift was anticipated in final syllables, while in Gothic the vowel shortening must have happened relatively earlier.—NWGmc. -*u* < IE -*ā* is treated like -*u* < IE -*u*; it disappeared sooner after long than after short syllables, cf. OE *ār* < **aisā* (Gothic would have **aiza*) 'honor', as against *giefu*, Go. *giba* 'gift'. For Norse this is not so certain, unless we consider words like *sǫg* as analogical, or assume that the chronology of the *u*-mutation coincided with that of the *i*-mutation— which, of course, is quite likely. -*u* < -*ā* is preserved in Run. (*giƀu*) and in Norse loan words in Finnic (*panku* 'bracelet', ON *spǫng*).

Gk. θεά—Go. *giba*, ON *giof* < **geƀu*, OE *giefu*; OS *geba*, OHG *geba* are accusatives.

Ved. *yugā́* 'yokes'—Go. *waurda*, ON *bǫrn*, OE OS *word*, OHG *wort*; but OE *hofu*, OS *graƀu*.

Gk. στείχω—Go. *steiga*, ON *stīg*, OE **stīgu*, OS OHG *stīgu*.

(OE -*u* remained fairly late in Anglian, but in West Saxon it was early replaced by -*e*, which was probably a subjunctive ending).

But before nasals, IE -*ā* -*ō* were shortened to -*a* everywhere. This is hard to explain, but may perhaps be linked up with the fact that elsewhere, too, nasals seem to tend to preserve the quality of the preceding vowel (**42**). Thus we find:

Acc. sg. fem. -*ā́m*—Go. *giba*, OE *giefe* < -*æ*, OS *geba*, OHG *geba*.

Nom. sg. of *n*-stems, -*ón* (Gk. ἡγεμών)—Go. *guma* (can also go back to -*én*), OE *tunge*, OS *tunga*, OHG *zunga*; ON *gume* may correspond to this, or to WGmc. forms in -*a*, -*o* (see below); but Finnic loan words of this type, like *haka* 'field' (ON *hage* 'Gehege'), as well as Runic forms in -*a* rather seem to point to -*én*. Run. *tawiðō* 'I did' indicates that -*óm* became -*o* > -*a*. The ending of Go. *guma*, anyway, is not identical with the WGmc. forms OE -*a*, OS OHG -*o*, which surely go back to -*ō*; see below.

Diphthongs are monophthongized earlier in unstressed than in k stressed syllables; in fact, it is doubtful whether historical Germanic has preserved any unstressed diphthongs. While it is methodically defensible to pronounce diphthongs in Go. *anstai*, *sunau*, *habaida*, Hirt is very probably right in assuming that at least in Wulfila's time *ai au* were [ε ɔ]. In final syllables we have the usual reduction by one mora: 3 sg. pass., Gk. φέρεται = Go. *bairada*.

The Gothic dat. sg. of *o*-stems, *daga*, is usually explained as an instrumental or as an ablative (**79**). Both explanations are possible, but unnecessarily separate the form from the other classes and the other Germanic languages. It is more satisfactory to consider *daga* a locative, like other 'datives',—**dhogho + i > *ðaȝai > daga*.

1   (2) In Medial Syllables long vowels and diphthongs are more resistant than in final syllables. Thus we find:

IE *ā > ō* is preserved as a long vowel in Gothic and Old High German, shortened in the other Gmc. dialects: Go. *salbōda*, OHG *salbōta*, ON *kallaþa*, OE *sealfode*, OS *makoda*.

In OHG medial *ō* is not diphthongized to *uo*. This may indicate that it had undergone at least a slight shortening before the period of diphthongization. Before nasals, however, it became *ū* in OHG, *u* in ON: *zungūn, tungu (tungo)*: Go. *tuggōn* (oblique cases of *tuggō* 'tongue'). This is in keeping, on the one hand, with the usual treatment of *u* before nasal groups or nasals in general (cf. OHG *gisungan*, OE *-numen*), and, on the other hand, with the analogous treatment of final *-ā*, but the matter is far from clear.

Medial *ē* in the third class of weak verbs goes back partly to IE *ei/əi* and partly to IE *ē*. From the Germanic point of view the two types cannot be distinguished. Gothic has *ai*, which is almost certainly [ε:], OHG has *ē*, and in the other dialects the preterit of this class probably never had any medial vowel (Sievers, Btr. 8. 90 ff.): Go. *habaida*, OHG *habēta*, ON *hafþa*, OE *hæfde*, OS *habda*.

Gradually, medial long vowels are shortened everywhere. In the living Germanic languages, long medial vowels do not exist.

m   (3) Prefixes (and prepositions, which may be considered akin to nominal prefixes) show the tendency towards shortening mentioned under A. Theoretically, we should expect preservation of long vowels in nominal compounds, but shortening in verbal compounds, according to **43**. But this is only partly the case. Apparently, the unstressed forms spread from verbs to nouns, but we may in part have to deal with IE double forms going back to a time before the Gmc. weakening of unstressed syllables. This possibility is indicated especially by the fact that Gothic does not offer any evidence of long vowels in the prefixes Gmc. *bī/bi, ūs/us, tō/tu*. It has only *bi* 'by', while OE OS OHG have both *bī* and *bi* (*be*): Go. *bistugq* 'shock', like *bistigqan* (verb), but OHG *bīspel* 'example', *bīwurti* (and *biwort*) 'parable', as against *bigangan* 'pass through'; Go. *us* (*ut*) in *ussindō* 'extremely', almost certainly with short *u*, like *ussatjan* 'found', *urruns* 'East', but ON preposition *ōr, ūr*,

OHG prep. *ūz* (and *ur*, *ir*, *ar*): *ūzlāz* 'end' against *irtrinkan* 'drown'; Go. preposition and prefix *du*, *duginnan* 'begin', OE OS *tō*, *te*, OHG *zuo*, *ze* (*zi*, *za*), *zuohelpha* 'support', *zigangan* 'perish'.

NOTE 1: Go. *ut* (*ūt?*) = *us* = *ur*, ON OE OS *ūt*, OHG *ūz* = *ur* go back to IE *ŭd* (Sk. *ud*) 'out of'. These doublets arose in sentence connection from Indo-Hittite ablative forms in *-tos*, similar to Gk. ἐκ (ἔκτος) = ἐξ, οὕτω(τ) = οὕτως.

NOTE 2: The vowel of Go. *du* is problematic. We must probably assume, with Delbrück, IF 21. 355 f., that in Gothic ō in proclitic position became *u*, but since it is an isolated form no definite explanation seems possible. For the consonant, cf. **17**, under 'Residuary Forms'.

C. THREE MORAE existed only in final syllables. They are preserved **n** as long vowels or as diphthongs in Gothic and partly in Old High German, but are short elsewhere. Some of the most important types are the following:

Contraction: Nom. pl. of *o*-stems (masc.), *o-es* > *ōs*, of *ā*-stems (fem.), *ā-es* > *ās*, in Go. *dagōs*, *gibōs*, OHG *tagā*, *gebā*, but ON *dagar*, *giafar*, OE *giefe* < *-æ*, OS *geba*.

Gen. pl., originally only of *o*- and *ā*-stems, but transferred to all classes, masc. and neut. *e-om* > *ẽm* for Gothic, *o-om* > *ōm* elsewhere, *ā-om* > *ōm* in all dialects: Go. *dagē*, OHG *tagō* (original length certain, although not indicated by spelling), OS *dago*, ON *daga*, OE *daga*; Go. *gibō*, OS *gebo*, ON *giafa*, OE *giefa*.

Compensation for IE loss of final vowel: gen. sg. fem. *-ā-so* > *ās* (θεᾶς), Go. *gibōs*, OHG *geba*, ON *giafar*, OE *giefe* < *-æ*, OS *geba*.

Compensation for loss of *n* in sentence connection: The nom. sg. of *n*-stems, *-ón*, probably lost *n* before *s* (and before *bh dh gh*, if these were really voiceless spirants, φ θ χ), but retained it before other consonants and vowels, so that we find the doublets *ō/ón*, as in Gk. ἡγεμών, but L. *homō*: Go. *tuggō*, *hairtō*, ON *tunga*, *hiarta* (feminines and neuters), OE *guma*, OS *gumo*, OHG *gomo* (masc.) go back to *-ō*, but Go. masc. *guma*, ON *gume*, OE fem. *tunge*, OS *tunga*, OHG *zunga* go back to *-ón* (or *-én*, in the case of Gothic and Old Norse).

NOTE: Similar in phonetic principle, but different in chronology is the treatment of *-ons* (acc. pl. ending) in Anglo-Frisian (OE OS OFris.). In these dialects *n* disappeared before *s*, with compensatory lengthening of the vowel: OE *dagas* < *-ōs*, OS *dagos* are really accusatives, which, however, function also as nom. pl.

DIPHTHONGS. The optative suffix of thematic verb forms is *o-ī* > *oī*: Go. *bairais*, *bairai*, ON *berer*, *bere*, OE *bere*, OS *beres*, *bere*. OHG *berēs*, *bere*.

Gen. sg. of *i*- and *u*-stems, *oi-so, ou-so,* Go. *anstais, sunaus,* OHG *fridoo.*

o D. FINAL CONSONANTS in unaccented syllables disappear in Primitive Gmc. with the exception of *s* and *r*; *r* remains in all dialects, *s* remains as *s* in Gothic, as *r* (rhotacism) in Norse, but disappears in WGmc.:

-*r*: Go. *fadar*, ON *faþer*, OE *fæder*, OS *fadar*, OHG *fater*.

-*s*: Go. *dags*, ON *dagr*, OE *dæg*, OS *dag*, OHG *tag*.

-*ns* remains intact in Gothic and preserves the preceding vowel: *dagans, gastins, sununs,* but OHG *taga, gasti, sunu**. In the Anglo-Frisian dialects, where *n* was lost, with compensatory lengthening (see Note above), *s* was preserved. This seems to indicate that *n* was partly assimilated to *s*, strengthening its articulation. We have a parallel in Italic: *-ons* > *-ōs* in Latin, but *-úss* in Oscan: *hortōs* 'gardens', *feihúss* 'walls'; the nom. pl. of the latter word is **feihus* < *-ōs*, corresponding to Go. *dagōs*, OHG *tagā*.

-*t*: Secondary ending *-nt*: Go. *budun*, ON *buþo*, OE *budon*, OS *budun*, OHG *butun* (but Go. *-and*, OHG *-ant*, 3 pl. pres., < *-onti*).

-*n*, -*m*: acc. sg. Go. *dag* < *-om*, *giba* < *-ām*; nom. sg. of *n*-stems: Go. *guma* < *-ón* (see above).

-*m* first became -*n*, which disappeared in endings, but was preserved in monosyllables: Go. *þan* 'then'—L. *tum*; *þana* = *þan-a*.

50. Standardization of Quantity. The combination of pitch and stress accent had resulted in gradation (**44**). The Germanic stress accent led to the weakening or loss of unstressed syllables, and it was a contributing factor in monophthongization and diphthongization (**40**). A continuation of its effect is seen in a standardization of the quantity of accented syllables that took place in all Germanic languages during the 13th and 14th centuries. The details differ considerably in the several languages, but the principle is the same everywhere: short accented vowels in open syllables are lengthened. In Dutch, the contrast between long and short vowels is least noticeable; it is largely superseded by the contrast between *volkomen* (tense) and *onvolkomen* (lax) vowels. In English, the influence of the following consonant greatly obscured the underlying principle. It is seen most clearly in German, where the process is fundamentally the following: In MHG, accented syllables were of four types: open-short, *ne-men*, open-long, *nā-men*, closed-short, *dahte* 'covered' (NHG *deckte*), closed-long, *dāhte* 'thought'. Towards the end of the MHG period, the first and fourth types disappeared; *nemen* became *nehmen*, *dāhte* became *dachte*. This means that MHG accented syllables had either one or two or three time units—short vowel without consonant, short vowel with consonant, long vowel without consonant, long vowel with consonant. In Standard NHG, leaving aside complicated details, it may be said that every accented syllable has two time units—short vowel with consonant, or long vowel without consonant.

PART THREE

INFLECTIONS

51. Word Structure. The component elements of IE words are pri- a
marily: *root, suffix, ending, prefix, infix.* A root with certain types of
suffixes is generally termed *stem.* The combination of certain suffixes
with grammatical endings is often designated as termination. But all
of these concepts are abstractions arrived at by comparative analysis
of the only real linguistic realities, the word and the sentence.

The Latin words *fundō, fūdī, effundō, fūsiō* have, in various phonetic
variants, one element in common, the sound group *fŭd*, which furnishes
the semantic common denominator, the idea of 'pouring'. This is the
root of these words, but there is no evidence nor, indeed, any probability that it ever had any independent existence, that it ever functioned as a 'word' *per se.* Its grammatical character is determined and
its meaning modified or specialized by *suffixes,* such as *e/o/ō,* to which
are linked grammatical endings, as in *fund-i-s, fund-u-nt* < *-e-s, -o-nt.*
The group *fund-e/ŏ-* constitutes the *stem; -is, -unt* are *terminations.*
The meaning of this verb is modified by the *prefix ex-* in *effundō* 'I
pour out'. Comparison between the present *fundō* and the perfect *fūdī*
reveals an additional *n*-element in the former, called a nasal *infix.* The
addition of a *-ti*-suffix forms a noun stem *fūd-ti-* > *fūsi-*, and this is
assigned to a specific type of declension by the further suffix *-ōn-,* to
which are attached the various case endings, as in *fūsi-ōn-is* < *-es.*

If we further compare these Latin words with cognates in other IE b
languages, we do find the same 'root' *fŭd* < IE *ĝheud-* in Go. *giutan*
(*gaut, gutum, gutans*), but elsewhere it appears without the final *d,* or
with other final consonants: Sk. *hu-,* Gk. χέω < *ghewō,* χεῦμα 'pouring', χύδην 'abundantly', ON *giōsa* 'pour forth', *geyser* 'hot spring'; in
Latin itself we have the root without final consonant in the adjective
fū-tilis 'to be poured, worthless'. So we have several forms of the root,
such as *gheu-/gheud-/gheus-.* The *d-* and *s*-variants (and any other final
consonant may constitute such variants) are said to be formed by
'determinants'. While the existence of determinants is certain, the
concept is an extremely elusive one, and it is hardly possible to give a

141

clear and unambiguous definition that would sharply distinguish them
from suffixes.[1] The functions of these elements are constantly changing,
and all that can be said is this, that 'determinants' form, relatively
speaking, a very close unit with the primary root, while in the cases of
suffixes the connection seems more transparent. But that is essentially
a matter of subjective feeling. Even 'suffixes' are not always easily
distinguished from second parts of compounds, unless we have historical
evidence. Most of them never were independent words, but were
always mere root or stem variations; others had developed from words.
We can see this process clearly enough in historical times. E. *-ly*, Ger.
-lich is now a mere suffix with barely perceptible meaning, but it goes
back to a noun, Go. *leik* 'body'. E. *-ty*, Ger. *-zig* can now hardly be
termed more than a suffix with arithmetical function, but in Gothic
it is still a noun, *tigjus* 'decades'. But where we have no such historical or comparative evidence, the etymological explanation of determinants, as well as suffixes, remains guess work with varying degrees of
probability. Thus, L. *crēdō* doubtless is a compound, **k̑red-* 'heart'
(= *cord-*) + **dhē-* 'put one's heart on some one'; this is shown by the
close parallel with Sk. *śrad-dhā* 'confidence', *śrad-dadháti* 'he trusts'.
But are we safe in likewise reconstructing *fundō* as **ghum-dhē-*, Go.
standan as **stəm-dhē-* (or *stām-dhē-*) 'to make a pouring, a stand'? It
has been suggested, but without such foundation as in the case of
crēdō; as to *standan*, the parallel of forms like L. *statuō* practically re-
futes the idea. Perhaps intermediate between the virtual certainty of
crēdō and the utter improbability of the analysis of *fundō*, *standan*
are forms that can be approached on the basis of analogous developments in the same or other languages. Thus, there is a frequent
formative element *-bh-* which seems to have collective or typifying
significance. *Suebi* (**Swǣbjōz*) is best interpreted as an extension of
*swē- (akin to L. *suus*), 'the own people' or 'the people themselves, as
a whole'. This *bh*-determinant may well belong to the root **bhewe-*
(Gk. φύω, L. *fui*). It may be contained in Gmc. **wība-* (E. *wife*, Ger.
Weib) < **wei-bh(w)om*. The primary root of this is identical with the
plural pronoun of the first person, Go. *weis*, Sk. *vay-ám*, so that **wība-*
seems to mean 'the typical person of our group, our tribe' (cf. **78**), in
contrast to *wĭ-ros* (Ger. *wer-*, L. *vir*, Sk. *vĭras*) 'the individual person of
our tribe' (of course, other etymologies have been suggested). The
bh-determinant is also found in similar function in **gwol-bh-es/os-* >
E. *calf*, Ger. *Kalb*, literally 'der Wurf, litter', related to Gk. βάλλω
'throw', δελφύς 'womb', ἀ-δελφός 'co-uterinus, brother'.

There is a good deal of uncertainty and arbitrariness still inherent in the whole subject of determinants, but the following can be said with some assurance:

(1) MONOPHTHONGAL LIGHT BASES (Gmc. fourth and fifth classes) c have no determinants. Their last consonant is an integral part of the root, so that *nem-, sed-* cannot be further dissected. But *diphthongal light bases* lend themselves very readily to variation by determinants. Go. *-leiþan* 'go' rests on a primary root *lei-* 'slide, move easily': Sk. *líyati* 'adhere', *līnas* 'snug', L. *lino* (perf. *lēvī*) 'smear', *līmus* 'slime', *līra* < **leisā* 'furrow' and many other words show the same root partly with, partly without determinants of various types. For Go. *giutan*, see above. **wer-* 'turn, bend' occurs without determinant perhaps in Lith. *vìrti* 'bubble', with *m* in L. *vermis* 'worm', Go. *waurms*, *g* in Sk. *várjati* 'turns', L. *vergō* 'bend', Go. *waurk* 'work', *n* in OE *wringan* 'wring', *wrong* 'wrong' (originally perhaps 'twisted'), *t* in L. *vertō* and its numerous cognates, *b* in Go. *wairpan* 'hurl, throw', L. *urbs* 'mit geflochtenem Zaun geschützte Niederlassung' (WP 275).

It is doubtful whether the final consonant of a DIPHTHONGAL LIGHT d BASE can *ever* be considered an integral element of the root. The process of extension or variation started, to be sure, in IE times, so that some extended roots, like **wert-* (S. *vártati*) must be classed as Indo-European. It progressed least in Indo-Iranian and Greek, where primary roots such as *hu-*, χέ(ϝ)- are quite frequent. It spread farther in Balto-Slavic, still farther in Italic, and shows its most extensive development in Germanic, where it is probably safe to say that nearly all diphthongal roots are extended, i.e., for etymological purposes the final consonant must in principle be considered a determinant. This statement has to be qualified in the case of roots ending in nasal + consonant, since there the nasal may be an infix, which caused a transfer from or to some other class. E.g., if Go. *finþan* 'find' is related to L. *petō*, it belonged originally to the Gmc. fifth class and was transferred to the third by the nasal infix; if Go. *siggwan*, OHG *singan* 'sing' is a cognate of OHG *sagēn*, the same is true; we certainly have infixes in OHG *klimban*, OE *climban* 'climb', Go. *sigqan*, OHG *sinkan* 'sink'; for the first verb, OHG *klīban*, ON *klīfa* show that it belonged to the first class, < **glei-bho-/glei-po-*; for the second, OHG *sīhan* 'sift', OE OHG *sīgan* 'drip' (Go. *saiws* 'sea'? < **sei-kwo-/seighwo-*) are evidence for the same. (WP *496 assumes *sengw-*; in that case, *ī* in *sīhan* indicates a variant **senkw-* > Gmc. *sinh-* > *sīh-*, **29**).

(2) MONOPHTHONGAL HEAVY BASES frequently have determinants, e

but the final consonant forms an integral part of many roots: Go. *rēdan* 'think', *blēsan* 'blow' have determinants, as is shown by L. *rē-rī*, *flā-re*. Perhaps we may assume this also for *slēpan*, with uncertain etymology. *standan* (pret. *stōþ*) has a *t*-determinant and a *n*-infix, which in OHG is extended to the preterit (*stuont*). Go. *saian* 'sow', *waian* 'blow', *faian* 'reproach', *bauan* 'dwell', *bnauan* (OHG *nūa*) 'reproach' are without final consonants. But with most verbs of the type of *lētan* 'let', *grētan* 'wail', *tēkan* 'touch', *hwōpan* 'boast', or *hafjan* 'lift', *skapjan* 'shape', *graban* 'dig', *wakan* 'wake' (in fact, probably with all verbs of the sixth class), the final consonant is an integral part of the root.

f   Since most Diphthongal Heavy Bases have so far resisted successful etymological interpretation (**46**), no general statement concerning their relation to determinants should be attempted, but very probably most, or all, of them should be judged like diphthongal light bases. Go. *aukan* 'increase' (which may equally well be considered a light or a heavy base) probably has a primary root, **aweg-/aug-* (unless we assume connection with Go. *audags* 'happy' and its numerous cognates); but determinants are more or less certain in *haitan, haldan, falpan, saltan*; it is certain that *fāhan* and *hāhan* possess a nasal infix; the same thing is possibly true of *gaggan*.

THE VERB

a   **52. Tense and Aspect.** The German term for verb is 'Zeitwort'— tense word. This implies the attitude of the Germanic, largely also of the Romance speaker towards this type of words: We consider 'tense' the fundamental category of the verb. The six tenses of Latin grammar, present, imperfect, perfect, pluperfect, future, and future perfect, are likely to be considered logical necessities, and at least the speaker of a Germanic language is apt to be somewhat disconcerted by the existence of the Greek aorist and the French passé défini. In a sense, those types may be said to exist in Germanic too, but in a greatly modified form, and the speaker is less clearly conscious of them. Still, there are many languages that get along without tenses. Semitic grammar speaks of an imperfect and a perfect, but these are not tenses in our sense of the word, but represent completed and incompleted action: Arab. *qatala* 'he slays, slew, will slay' is called a perfect; *yaqtulu* 'he is slaying, was slaying, will be slaying', an imperfect. The Finno-Ugrian present and preterit (really verbal nouns with various determinants, especially *k* and *j*) originally had the same functions. The Slavic languages possess a well-defined preterit (a verbal noun, e.g., Russ. *on dal* 'he is giver = he gave'), but in colloquial speech this is quite commonly superseded by the present.

This does not mean that such languages are unable to express differences of chronology quite as well as classical Latin or standard English or German. When necessary they can do so by various means, such as adverbs of time or, in Finno-Ugrian, a multitude of verbal nouns. Moreover, many of them have, in historical times, developed compound tenses similar to those of the Germanic and Romance languages. But quite often the speaker's consciousness does not require those tense distinctions that we consider indispensable because another set of distinctions is more essential to him: the system of *aspects* or modes of action (Aktionsarten). It is possible to speak or write a Slavic language tolerably well without having recourse to any tense forms but the present. But it is impossible to get along without a correct grasp of the aspects, especially the forms for the 'perfective' (momentary) and 'imperfective' (durative, continuous) action. Russ. *kričat'* means 'to be crying'; *kriknut'*, 'to give a yell'; *dat'* 'to give', *davat'* 'to distribute'. Semitic verbs, in addition to the distinction between 'perfect' and 'imperfect', have theoretically as many as ten stem forms, which are essentially aspects, especially the first four stems: *qatala* is merely perfective action, without qualification; *qattala* is iterative (frequentative) or intensive, something like 'he slays and slays'; *qātala* is conative, 'he tries to slay'; *'aqtala* is causative, 'he causes to slay'.

It would be wrong to ascribe to Indo-European the complicated tense **b** system of Sanskrit, Greek, or Latin. A good deal of this is secondary innovation. All we can be sure of is this, that IE had verb *forms* that correspond to the Gk. present, aorist, and perfect. But to what extent *tense* function should be ascribed to these forms, is an open question. A certain tense nucleus is implied in their primary meanings. The present form is normally durative and therefore most apt to be used for that which is going on at the time of speaking, although it can be made to refer to continuous action in the past: λείπειν 'to be leaving', λείπω 'I am leaving', ἔ-λειπον 'I was leaving'; the prefix ἐ, called the augment, is probably a temporal particle, meaning 'then'. The aorist expresses momentary action, and this type of action by its very nature can never coincide in time with its verbal expression. Ger. *Das Kind fällt* is really a future, *Es blitzt* is really a past tense; Gk. λιπεῖν 'to leave' has no tense connotation, but ἔ-λιπον 'I left' is past tense; δείκνυμι 'I am showing' is present, δεῖξαι 'to point' is a tenseless aorist, ἔ-δειξα 'I pointed' is past aorist, δείξω 'I shall point' is future. In the last three forms, which have the stem *deik-s-*, the momentary aspect is indicated by the *s*-suffix ('*s*-aorist'), while in the case of *lip-* Abstufung has that function. In the Slavic languages the present form of a perfective verb, which corresponds in function, though not in form, to the Greek aorist, has automatically future meaning: *kriknú* 'I shall cry out'. The perfect, finally, denotes completed action and the state resulting therefrom. According to the predominance of either of the two factors it may refer primarily to the past or to the present: λέ-λοιπα 'I have left (and am gone)', but (ϝ)οῖδα 'I know (because I have seen)'. It is possible that the reduplication λε- implies particularly the reference to past action.

In spite of numerous secondary developments, the general principle of the combination of tense and aspect in Greek and Sanskrit probably represents fairly closely the conditions of primitive Indo-European. Balto-Slavic emphasized more and more the comparatively objective element of aspect, while the Western languages, particularly Italic and Germanic, developed the more subjective tense factor to such an extent that the aspects were largely obscured, although later partly reintroduced by secondary formations. The procedure in the two groups was fundamentally almost the same, although the details differed: the durative form which with most primary (= not derived) verbs was characterized by the root vowel *e*, was the main foundation of the present system, although other present types developed. This is essentially a part of the Latin Third Conjugation and the Germanic Strong Verb of the first five classes. The functional distinction between aorist and perfect disappeared. They were fused into a combination tense, which by contrast to the present was basically a past tense, called 'perfect' in Latin, 'preterit' in Germanic (and Celtic) grammar. The future in both groups is a later formation. The forms of the preterit (it would be better to use this term for Latin too) were taken partly from the aorist, partly from the perfect; its function combined the two. A characteristic difference between Latin and Germanic was this: In Latin, each verb of this type used *either* the perfect *or* the aorist in this combined function: *cecĭdĭ* is a genuine perfect, *dīxī* (and probably *lēgī*) an aorist. (Occasionally we find alternative forms: *pangō* used, without difference in meaning, both the perfect type *pepigī* and the aorist type *pānxī*, or even the analogical *pēgī*.) The preterit of the Germanic Strong Verb combines the two forms into a mixed paradigm in which, roughly speaking, the singular is based upon the perfect, the plural upon the aorist.

The Present

53. The Stem Classes. The Sanskrit grammarians distinguished ten a
classes of primary verbs, which they named after traditional paradigms.
While the arrangement does not exactly represent IE conditions, and
in particular differs greatly from Gmc. conditions, it is based on such
acute observation that it deserves a place even in a Gmc. grammar.
The classes are:

1. *bhū-* (*bhávāmi* 'I am', Gk. φύω)	accented root	thematic vowel
2. *ad-* (*ád-mi* 'I eat, Lith. édmi)		without thematic vowel
3. *hu-* (*ju-hómi* 'I sacrifice')		reduplicated, without thematic vowel
4. *div-* (*dívyāmi* 'I play')		*jo*-suffix
5. *su-* (*sunómi* 'I press')	unaccented root	*neu*-suffix
6. *tud-* (*tudámi* 'I push')		thematic vowel
7. *rudh-* (*ruṇádhmi* 'I hinder')		nasal infix
8. *tan-* (*tanómi* 'I stretch')		*neu*-suffix*
9. *krī-* (*krīṇámi* 'I buy')		*nā*-suffix
10. *cur-* (*córáyāmi* 'I steal')		*ejo*-suffix

* Really identical with class 5; the Hindu grammarians considered -*n*- a part
of the root and -*ō*- as the suffix. The correct analysis is **ḷṇ-neu-mi (IE *ṇ* >
Sk. *a*).

To these are added five secondary stem forms, the causatives, the
intensives, the desideratives, the denominatives and the passive voice.
The causatives belong in form, though not in meaning, to class 10.
The denominatives have various forms, for which the *ā*-type is of special
importance in Germanic: Sk. *dōlá* 'a swing'—*dōláyatē* 'he is swinging'
(like Gk. τιμάω from τιμά 'honor', L. *plantō* < **plantājo* from *planta*
'plant').

This system has been reorganized in many ways, both for Sanskrit
and for the purposes of general IE grammar.[1] From the point of   b
view of Germanic grammar we can set up the following groups:

I. Thematic presents with root accent = class 1. These form the
bulk of Germanic Strong Verbs.

II. Thematic presents with suffix accent = class 6. These are the
Germanic 'Aorist Presents'.

III. Various types of presents with *j*-suffixes = classes 4 and 10.
These are primarily certain verbs of the Gmc. classes V and VI S and
the majority of the Weak Verbs.

IV. Athematic verbs = class 2; a few isolated verbs like OHG *tuom* 'I do' and, from the point of view of conjugation, the verbs of classes II and III W.

Verbs with present reduplication do not form an established type in Germanic. OHG *bi-bēt* = Sk. *bi-bhēti* 'he is afraid' (ON *bifa*, OE *biofian*, OS *bibon*) and OHG *zittarōn* (ON *titra*) < *ti-trō-*, perhaps also Go. *reiran* < *rī-rai-* are probably the only remnants of this class, either preserved or newly formed by sound symbolism; the meaning of all of them is the same, 'tremble'.

V. Verbs with nasal suffixes = classes 5, 8, and 9. Here belong certain verbs of the Gmc. class III S (-*nw*- became *nn*, as in Go. *rinnan* if a cognate of Sk. *r̥ṇváti* 'arises') and the Gothic and Norse verbs of class IV W.

VI. Presents with nasal infixes = class 7; a few scattered verbs of the type *fāhan, standan, windan.*

VII. Denominatives, for Germanic principally those in -*ā*- (class II W, Go. *salbōn*) and -*nā*- (class IV W, Go. *fullnan*).

Certain verbs may be classed with several types, according to the point of view; *salbōn* < *salbōjan-* belongs to group III because it has a *j*-suffix, but also to group VII because it is a denominative; cf. also III and IV, I and V, VI.

a **54. The Germanic Present Types.** The present system of the Gmc. verb has been greatly standardized. The thematic type has been generalized to include virtually all strong verbs. 'Thematic' are those verbs that use the vowel *e/o* as a connecting link between root and ending, like Gk. λείπ-ε-τε, λείπ-ο-μεν (Sk. class 1) and ἐ-λίπ-ε-τε, ἐ-λίπ-ο-μεν (class 6: in these Gk. forms the accent is secondary, but the root has nil grade; the infinitive λιπεῖν shows the original accentuation). We have to distinguish, in accordance with the preceding paragraph:

b I. Durative Presents, type *bhávati* < *bhéw-e-ti*. They appear in the following forms, according to the ablaut classes of the strong verbs:

  I. *stéigh-e/o*—Go. *steigan*
  II. *ghéud-e/o*—Go. *giutan*
  III. *wért-e/o*—Go. *wairþan*
  IV. *ném-e/o*—Go. *niman*
  V. *sékw-e/o*—Go. *saihvan*
  VII. *lēd-e/o*—Go. *lētan.*

It is certain that many of these verbs were originally athematic, cf. *lētan*—Lith. *léidmi, itan*—Sk. *ádmi*, Lith. *édmi*.

These verbs are durative in the sense that in their most frequent, so to speak natural use, they express continuous action, 'to be climbing, pouring, turning (becoming), distributing (taking), seeing, relaxing (letting)'. Theoretically, every verb can be durative or momentary, ('to reach the top, pour, make a turn, give out, notice, let go'), but in Germanic there is a definite tendency to use for the present exclusively that form of the stem that is predominant in use. The other stem form is either given up entirely or, in certain types, used as a substitute preterit. Thus, Go. *slēpan* 'sleep', *rēdan* 'meditate' are normally durative, and the *bhávati*-form is used for the present, while the *tudáti*-form (see below), **slapan*, **radan*, has disappeared. On the other hand, ON *vaþa* 'wade, pass through', *taka* 'take' are *tudáti*-forms, and the normal grade forms, *(v)ōþ*, *tōk* are used as preterits.

II. Aorist Presents, of the type of *tudáti*, were doubtless more fre- c quent in Pre-Germanic than in the historical forms of the Gmc. languages. Most of them were either changed to the form of the durative verbs by leveling in accordance with the model of the great majority of strong verbs, or they lost their original form by phonetic laws and were transferred to other classes because of a resemblance between the form that had developed and forms already occurring in those classes. The original suffix accent is indicated either by the reduced grade of the root, in so far as this is not obscured by phonetic laws, or by Verner's Law, unless this is leveled. Some of the clearest cases are:

Class I: **wik-e/o-* (L. *vincō*) 'slay' or 'sacrifice', ON *vega*, OE *wegan*, *wigan*, OHG *-wehan*, MHG *-wigen*, OS OHG (part.) *wīgand* 'fighter'. Suffix accent is chiefly indicated by Verner's Law. *-ī-* is due to leveling with the other verbs of the first class. Go. *weihan* may be considered either a survival of the old durative form or, what is more likely, completely leveled. OHG *-wehan* has leveled the consonant. *e* in ON OE OHG is 'a-umlaut' of *i*. ON *vega* shifted to class V on account of the identity of three of its forms with class V verbs: *vega* < **wigana-* = *gefa*, *vā* < **waih* = *vā* < **wah* 'I weighed', past part. *vegenn* < **wiganaz* = *gefenn*. This led to the substitution of 3 pl. pret. *vǫgom* = *gǫfom* for **wigom*.—Other verbs of this type are Go. *digan* 'form', L. *fingō*, **dheigh/dhigh*; OS *stekan*, OHG *stehhan* 'sting', L. *in-stīgō*. Probably also Go. *bidjan* (ON *biþia*, etc.) = Gk. πείθω belongs here, in spite of its *j*-suffix which would rather point to iterative meaning; without *j*, Go. imperative *us-bida*. This verb shifted to class V, *stekan stehhan* to class IV.

Class II. A number of verbs (from four to twelve in the various dialects) have the stem vowel *ū*. This is explained either as 'nebentonige Tiefstufe',[1] = ƀu, or as reduced grade of a long diphthong,[2] = əu. The first explanation is contradicted by *wigan (if ƀu gave ū, ƀi would surely become ī), the second by the past participles with short u. Probably the forms are analogical, following this proportion:

> steigan staig stigum stigans = lŭkan lauk lukum lukans.

An analogical leveling of *lŭkan to lūkan is required to make the parallelism complete. Some verbs of this type are:

Go. lūkan	ON lūka	OE lūcan	OHG lūchan	'lock'
	sūpa	sūpan	sūfan	'drink'
	sūga	sūgan	sūgan	'suck'
		brūcan	brūchan	'use'.

Class II or III (?). Go. trudan, ON troþa, OE OS tredan, OHG tretan is difficult to judge because the etymology is not certain. Cf. WP 796. In the Gmc. languages this verb belongs to various classes, IV in Gothic and ON, V in WGmc., but possibly all of this is analogical transfer. If it belongs to Sk. drávati 'he runs', < *dréw-e-ti, we have to reconstruct *dru-tó, and the WGmc. forms are analogical.

Class IV. ON koma, OE OS cuman, OHG comen < *gʷm- (L. veniō, Gk. βαίνω).

Durative forms in Go. qiman, OHG queman (cf. E. 'he is coming').

Class VI. As far as we have accepted etymologies, about one half of the verbs of the sixth class are aorist presents of heavy bases. It is fairly certain that the following may be thus regarded:

Go.	ON	OE	OS	OHG	
hafjan	hefia	hebban	hebbian	heffan, -hevan	'lift'
hlahjan	hlæia	hliehhan	(hlōgun, pret.)	hlahhan	'laugh'
raþjan			(redia)*	(redia)*	'count'
sakan	saka	sacan	sakan	sahhan	'quarrel'
skaban	skafa	scafan		scaban	'shave'
standan	standa	standan	standan	stantan	'stand'
skaþjan	skaþa	sceþþan		skadōn	'harm'
(tēkan)	taka				'take'
	vaþa	wadan		watan	'go through'.

Proof that they are reduced grades of heavy bases (ə > a) is furnished by their alternation with forms containing ē ō ā, such as L. (capiō) cēpī (perhaps for *cōpi, in analogy with fēcī, Sommer, LLFL 551), Gk. κώπη 'handle', (status) stāre. For details, consult etymological dictionaries.

Class VII offers etymological difficulties that have so far proved insurmountable. Among monophthongal roots, Go. fāhan, hāhan <

*pənk-, *kənk- may be considered original aorist presents. But since the *n*-infix generally implies reduced grade, and also for other reasons, this is uncertain.

Among the diphthongal roots of this class, according to **62** there is not one that has been explained with certainty. Personally, I believe that Brugmann and Wood[3] are right in considering them reduced grades of heavy bases, and therefore aorist presents. Cf. **56**.

The clearest cases (and that does not mean much) might be the following:

Go.	ON	OE	OS	OHG	
haitan	*heita*	*hātan*	*hētan*	*heizan*	'call'
hlaupan	*hlaupa*	*hlēapan*	*hlōpan*	*hloufan*	'run'
skaidan		*scādan*	*skēthan*	*sceidan*	'separate'
staldan		*stealdan*			'provide'
stautan	*stauta*		*stōtan*	*stōzan*	'push'
waldan	*valda*	*wealdan*	*waldan*	*waltan*	'manage'.

It would be useless in this place to go into the etymological problems of this class. For the systematic justification of this view, cf. Prokosch, JEGPh. 20. 468 ff.

For verbs with Gmc. *a* < IE *o* and *ō* < IE *ō*, cf. below, III b.

III. Verbs with *j*-suffix. This was fundamentally a dissyllabic base **d** which, according to the accent, appears either as *je/jo* (*dív-ya-ti*) or as *eje-ejo* (*coráyati*), or as *ēje/ējo*, or *ī*, reduced grade of *ēi*, that is, either or both syllables can show the nil grade, and the first syllable can also show lengthened grade; the second syllable appears as *ō* in the 1 sg. pres. In Germanic, the first two types have fallen together, probably partly by weakening of the medial syllable, partly by analogy. But the *ēje/ī* type is preserved.

(a) When the root was accented the suffix was reduced to *je/jo*. In that case we should expect normal grade of the root, and occasionally we do find it, as in Gk. τείνω 'stretch' < *ten-yō, L. *sāg-iō* 'track'. But there must have been analogical cross-currents at an early time, since the root often appears in the reduced grade, as in L. *capiō*, Sk. *lúbh-ya-ti* 'he desires'.

(b) When the suffix has the normal grade, *éje/éjo*, the root as a rule shows the *o*-grade, and the meaning of the verb is causative or intensive (iterative): L. *moneō* 'admonish' < *mon-éjō, root *men-* (*me-min-ī, mēns*), Gk. φορέω 'I wear' < *bhor-éjō, from φέρω 'I am carrying'. Also lengthened grade often occurs, as in Sk. *svāp-áya-ti* 'puts to sleep' from *sváp-a-ti* 'sleeps'.[4] In Latin, shva secundum is frequent: *maneō* 'I remain', cf. Gk. μένω.

(c) The $\bar{e}i/\check{\imath}$ type is most evident in Balto-Slavic, but it is also of importance in Greek and can be traced in Germanic by the comparison of dialects. Verbs in $-j\bar{o}/\bar{e}iti$ = OSl. $-j\d{a}/\bar{e}ti$, Lith. $-iu/\acute{e}ti$ (1 sg. and infin.) form a well-established type in Balto-Slavic:

Lith. $v\acute{e}izd\check{z}u$ 'I see' $<$ $*veid-j\bar{o}$, infin. $veizd\acute{e}ti$; OSl. $vi\check{z}d\d{a}$ $<$ $*veid-jom$, infin. $vid\bar{e}ti$

$s\acute{e}d\check{z}u$ 'I sit' $<$ $*sed-j\bar{o}$, infin. $sed\acute{e}ti$; OSl. $se\check{z}d\d{a}$ $<$ $*sed-jom$, infin. $sed\bar{e}ti$

Gk. $\mu\alpha\acute{\iota}\nu o\mu\alpha\iota$ 'I rave', aor. $\dot{\epsilon}\mu\acute{\alpha}\nu\eta\nu$, infin. $\mu\alpha\nu\hat{\eta}\nu\alpha\iota$, $\varphi\alpha\acute{\iota}\nu o\mu\alpha\iota$ 'I shine', $\dot{\epsilon}\varphi\acute{\alpha}\nu\eta\nu$, $\chi\alpha\acute{\iota}\rho\omega$ 'I rejoice', $\dot{\epsilon}\chi\acute{\alpha}\rho\eta\nu$.

If this type were preserved in Latin, it would appear as $*vidi\bar{o}$, $vid\bar{e}re$, $*sedi\bar{o}$, $sed\bar{e}re$, but the $\bar{e}i$-type ($\bar{e}$-type, through loss of the diphthongal glide) has been extended to the present, $vid\bar{e}mus$, $vid\bar{e}tis$. In fact, we can say that this type and the causatives were merged in Latin, so that $vide\bar{o}$ took its form from $mone\bar{o}$, while $mon\bar{e}mus$, $mon\bar{e}tis$, $mon\bar{e}re$ are transfers from $vid\bar{e}mus$, etc. Quite accidentally, a close approach to the original conditions developed in Gallic Latin, since French ($per-$, $re-$)$çevoir$ requires a reconstructed form $*cap\bar{e}re$. But this is, of course, secondary, and not a survival of an old form.

(d) Denominatives are formed by jo from a variety of noun stems, most frequently from nouns in $-\bar{a}$. These are represented by the Latin first conjugation, $plant\bar{o}$ $<$ $*plant\bar{a}-j\bar{o}$.

The following are the Germanic parallels:

e (a) Although the difference between types (a) and (b) has disappeared, it is probably sound method to consider them separately and to consider the $-jan$ verbs of the classes V S and VI S as formed with IE $-jo-$ suffix. But these verbs represent several types. Those of class V have roots with e (Gmc. $sitjan-$ $<$ $*sed-jo-$, see above), except Go. $bidjan$, which is a transfer from class I, with reduced grade. The stem vowel of class VI is partly ∂ (e.g., $hafjan$, L. $capi\bar{o}$), partly o ($farjan$, by the side of $faran$, Gk. $\pi o\rho\epsilon\acute{u}o\mu\alpha\iota$). But it must not be assumed that all of them had root accent. The voiceless spirants in Go. $hafjan$, $hlahjan$, $skaþjan$, $fraþjan$ are an insecure foundation for such a theory,[5] since Gothic did not carry through Verner's Law within the regular strong verb and the other Germanic dialects furnish evidence both for and against it. At least the first three of these verbs, and possibly the fourth one too, have heavy bases ($capi\bar{o}$—$c\bar{e}p\bar{\imath}$, $\kappa\lambda\acute{a}\zeta\omega$ 'sound'—$\kappa\lambda\acute{\omega}\zeta\omega$ 'yell', $\dot{a}-\sigma\kappa\eta\theta\acute{\eta}s$ 'unharmed'), with ∂-grade in the present which a priori points to suffix accent; also $bidjan$ indicates this. Voiced spirants are at least partly preserved in other Germanic languages: OE *hebban*, OFris. *heva*, OS *hebbian*; it is not surprising that the influence of the other classes has introduced voiceless spirants (respectively, their derivatives) in OFris. *skathia*, OHG *skadōn*, ON *hlæja*, OE *hliehhan*, OHG *hlahhan* (OS pret. pl. *hlōgun*, past part. *bihlagan* show grammatical change).

The number of verbs of this type varies in the several Germanic dialects. The following are most widely represented:

Go.	ON	OE	OS	OHG	
bidjan	*biþia*	*biddan*	*biddian*	*bitten*	'ask'
(*ligan*)	*liggia*	*licgan*	*liggian*	*liccen*	'lie'
(*sitan*)	*sitia*	*sittan*	*sittian*	*sizzen*	'sit'
hafjan	*hefia*	*hebban*	*hebbian*	*heffen*	'lift'
hlahjan	*hlæia*	*hliehhan*	(*hlōgun*)	(*hlahhan*)	'laugh'
skapjan	*skepia*	*scieppan*	*skeppian*	*scephen*	'shape'
(*swaran*)	*sueria*	*swerian*	*swerian*	*swerjen*	'swear'

Scattered instances are: Go. *fraþjan* 'understand', *skaþjan* 'harm', *wahsjan* 'grow'; ON *þiggia* 'receive', *deyia* 'die', *geyia* 'bark'; OE *þicgan* 'receive', *fricgan* 'ask', *stæppan* 'step'; OS *af-sebbian* 'perceive'.

These verbs, then, belong to the type of L. *capiō*, Sk. *dívyati*. Originally some of them, at least *sit(j)an*, belonged to group c, L. *sedēre*.

(b) CAUSATIVES in *éje/éjo* (Sk. class 10) form the bulk of Gmc. f class I W. Their number is large, and only a few instances are given below. The alternation of root vowel *e* for the strong, primary verbs and *o* for the weak, causative verbs is carried through consistently. In general, we have to deal here with light bases, but there are a few heavy bases with *ē/ō* (or *ə/ō*):

Primary Verb in the Go. form	Go.	ON	OE	OS	OHG	
drigkan	*dragkjan*	*drekkia*	*drencean*	*drenkian*	*trenken*	'make drink'
ligan	*lagjan*	*leggia*	*lecgan*	*leggian*	*leggen*	'lay'
lisan	*laisjan*		*læran*	*lērian*	*lēren*	'teach'
-nisan	*nasjan*		*nerian*	*nerian*	*nerian*	'save'
sinþan	*sandjan*	*senda*	*sendan*	*sendian*	*senten*	'send'
-rēdan	*rōdjan*	*rǿþa*				'make think, talk'
hlahjan		*hlǿgia*				'make laugh'

The intensive or iterative meaning appears in:

bidjan	*baidjan*	*beiþa*	*bǣdan*	*bēdian*	*beiten*	'force, demand'
dreiban	*draibjan*					'drive, bother'
kiusan	*kausjan*					'test'.

For denominative verbs in *je/jo*, like Goth. *dōmjan, hailjan, salbōn*, see below, VII.

g (c) The gradation *ēi* (*ē*) *ĭ*, which is fully preserved in Balto-Slavic, has also left clear traces in Germanic.[6] Such verbs as OSl. (infin.) *sēdēti* 'sit', *volēti* 'wish', *slyšati* < **slyšēti* 'hear', *stojati* < **stojēti* 'stand', *vidēti* 'see', Lith. *gulěti* 'lie', *lyděti* 'accompany', *sravěti* 'flow', *veizděti* 'see', *mylěti* 'love', *girděti* 'hear', *seděti* 'sit', *steběti* 'wonder' have in the present the connecting vowel *i*, which in Slavic must go back to *ī*, in Lithuanian to *i*: 1 and 2 pl., OSl. *sēdimъ, sēdite*, Lith. *sědime, sědite*.

Go. ON OHG show the same type as Gk. ἐμάνην and the Latin second conjugation, that is, *ē* is carried through the paradigm, except where analogically replaced by forms from other classes. Go. *ai* in *habais*, etc. is clearly [ε], shortened from *ē*; *haba, habam, haband* are best interpreted as transfers from most other verbs (strong verbs and I W), although attempts have been made to explain them from *-ē-mi, -ē-mos, -ē-nti*.[7] The same holds true for ON *hǫfom, hafa*, but ON *e* in *hefe, hefer, hefeþ* is shortened *ē*. On the other hand, the OE OS forms clearly show reduction to *i* (*j*) in *hæbbe* (analogical stem vowel instead of **hebbe*), OS *hebbiu*, etc.; OS *habes*, etc. = OHG *habēs*. The endings with *a* are taken over from class II W, Go. *-ōs*, etc. This was quite natural since several verbs can be classed with either type: OE *lifian* : *libban*; OE *þolian*, OS *tholoian, tholon* : OHG *tholēn*; OS *tilian*, OHG *zilōn, zilēn*; OS *haton* : OHG *hazzēn*. The paradigms are:

Go.	ON	OE	OS	OHG
[haba]	hefe	hæbbe	hebbiu	habēm
habais⎫	hefer	[hafast]	habes, [-as]	habēs
habaiþ⎭		[hafaþ]	habed, [-ad]	habēt
[habam]	[hǫfom]			habēmēs
habaiþ	hafeþ	habbaþ	hebbiad	habēt
[haband]	[hafa]			habēnt.

h IV. ATHEMATIC VERBS are those that form the *mi*-conjugation in Greek. The term refers to their most conspicuous characteristic, the ending of the 1 sg. Thematic verbs have no real ending in that form, but lengthen the thematic vowel *o*; athematic verbs end in *-mi*: φέρω, but τί-θη-μι.

Athematic verbs originally show root Abstufung—normal grade in the singular, reduced grade in the plural: Sk. *ásmi, ási, ásti—smas, sthá, sánti; juhómi, juhósi, juhóti—juhumás, juhuthá, júhvati; dádhāmi, dádhāsi, dádhāti* (accent is secondary, as in Greek)—*dadhmás, dhatthá, dádhati*.

Germanic has preserved the athematic type in the following verbs:
(1) *és-mi 'I am' (cf. **75 a**):

Go.	ON	OE	OS	OHG
im	em	eom		
is	es			
ist	est	is	is(t)	ist
sijum		⎫	⎫	
sijuþ		⎬ sind,	⎬ sind,	
sijun		⎭ sindon	⎭ sindun	sind, sindun.

(2) Three verbs that were originally 'reduplicating' are 'do' = τίθημι, 'stand' = ἵσταμι, 'go' = κίχημι 'arrive'. In Germanic, both reduplication and root gradation have disappeared. The athematic type is still apparent in the WGmc. first person sg., but otherwise the endings are the same as with other verbs:

OE (Angl.)	OS	OHG
dōm (Later and WS dō)	dōm	tōm, tuom
	(infin. stān,	stām stēm
	gān)	gām gēm.

Various substitutes for these verb forms occur in all dialects, e.g., Go. taujan, standan, gaggan.

OE OS dōn, OHG tuon (infin.) show ō-grade, as in Gk. θωή 'punishment', θῶμα 'heap', OE dōm, OHG tuom, Go. dōms 'judgment'. ē-grade appears in Go. ga-dēþs, OE dǣd, OS dād, OHG tāt 'deed' and in the OHG pl. pret. tātum. For OE 1 sg. dōm we should expect *dēm (umlaut), corresponding to 2, 3 sg. dēst, dēþ; it is an analogical form from the pl. dōþ < *dō-anti and the infin. dōn. The reduced grade ə perhaps appears in the pret. dyde, which may really be an optative, *dudi; for ə > u, cf. **38 d**. A different hypothesis is given **75 b**.

The rare OS forms gān, stān are probably borrowings from Old High German.

In Old High German, the forms with ā are Alemannian, those with ē Franconian (Rhine Franconian also ā) and Bavarian. The IE forms are *stā-, *ghē-. The two verbs show mutual influence in several languages, e.g., Gk. ἔβην for *ἔβημα, *ἔβηνα < *e-gwēm-m, cf. L. vēnī, in analogy with ἔστην; Sk. ágām in analogy with ásthām (I do not believe in an original root *gwā- 'come', which is frequently assumed for these and other Gk. and Sk. forms). stān is formed after gān; the original vowel appears in Go. stōþ, etc. (pret.). The Franconian and Bavarian forms with ē have been treated frequently. OHG ē has three sources: from ēi (ē²), but this is diphthongized at an early time (**40**):

from $ai + h\ r\ w$ (**42**); and from ai in unstressed syllables (**49**). None of the three possibilities covers the case, so we must have to deal with analogy. Do we find a conjugation *-ēm -ēs -ēt* elsewhere? Yes, in class III W: *habēm, habēs, habēt,* infin. *habēn*; perhaps *folgēn* was the starting point, wrongly interpreted as *fol-gēn*; cf. OE OS *ful-gangan,* OE *ful-ēode* 'follow', OS *ful-gān* 'fulfill', by the side of OE *fylgan, folgian,* OS *folgon*. This meets all requirements, so that it may safely be accepted as the origin of *stēn* and *gēn*. Otfrid has 2, 3 sg. *steis, steit.* For this, Streitberg's explanation as $ai < \partial i$ is possible, but it may also be a mere extension of *stēs, stēt* in analogy with the great majority of verbs, like *grīfis, neris*.

For verbs with present reduplication cf. **53 b,** IV Note.

(3) The OHG weak verbs with long suffix vowel, although not athematic, if we take this term in the widest sense (verbs without any connecting vowel) can be classed with this group, since the 1 sg. is *salbōm, habēm*.

These four types of present stems may be said to have morphological function. To a greater or lesser extent they are a part of the conjugational system. The other types have in Germanic essentially etymological foundation:

i   V. (a) Some of the verbs in *nn* of class III S doubtless have the same suffix *neu/nw* that we find in the Sk. class 5. The clearest example is Go. *rinnan* = primary root *rei-* + *nw* > *nn*. Go. *fraihnan,* OHG *gafregin* (1 sg.) has a *ne/no* suffix, like Gk. δάκνω, ἔδακον 'bite', OSl. *stanǫ, staneši* (1, 2 sg.) 'stand', *sъchnǫ* 'become dry'.

(b) The suffix *nā/nə* (Sk. class 9) forms class IV W in Gothic and Norse. These verbs have inchoative meaning and are derived either from verbs (mostly strong) or from adjectives, e.g.:

Go. *wakan,* ON *vaka* 'wake'—Go. *-waknan,* ON *vakna* 'wake up'
Go. *giutan* 'pour'—*usgutnan* 'be poured out'
Go. *qius,* ON *kuikr* 'alive'—Go. *-qiunan,* ON *kuikna* 'revive' (intr.)
Go. *fulls* 'full'—*fullnan* 'fill up' (intr.)
Go. *weihan* 'consecrate'—*weihnan* 'become sacred, be hallowed'.

In the present tense, originally the singular had *nā,* the plural *nə,* cf. Gk. δάμνᾱμι—δάμναμεν. But this has been standardized: in Gothic, these verbs have the same inflections as strong verbs (doubtless starting with 1, 3 pl., *-am -and* < *-əmos -ənti*), in Old Norse they have been transferred to the second class:

Go. *wakna   waknis   wakniþ   waknam   wakniþ   waknand*
ON *vakna   vaknar   vaknar   vǫknom   vakneþ   vakna.*

But the preterit shows $n\bar{a} > n\bar{o}$ clearly: Go. *waknōda*, ON *vaknaþe* (medial $\bar{o}$ shortened to a).

In Gothic and Norse these verbs are numerous, but in WGmc. we find only traces, which no longer form an independent type: OS *mornōn* = *mornian* 'mourn' belongs to class II W, OHG *mornēn*, Go. *maurnan* to class III W. OHG *reganōn* 'rain' is a denominative. The English verbs in *en* (*awaken*) are borrowed from Norse; they tend to become transitive (*blacken*).

Through the Germanic gemination (**22**) the *n*-suffix is sometimes assimilated to the preceding consonant: *pn* > *pp* in ON *hoppa*, NHG *hüpfen, hupfen* 'jump' (OSl. *kypēti*) < IE *kup-nā-*; *dn* > *tt* in MHG *stutzen*, to Sk. *tudáti*, L. *tundere*, Go. *stautan*, OHG *stōzan*; *kn* > *kk* in OHG *zocchōn*, NHG *zucken, zücken* 'give a start', to L. *dūcō*, Go. *tiuhan*; *gn* > *kk* in OHG *stecchēn* 'sting', < *stig-nā(nēi)-*. Many of these may really have *j*-suffixes (WGmc. lengthening, **30**), or spontaneous consonant strengthening.

VI. Nasal Infixes are less frequent in Germanic than in most other IE languages, cf. L. *tundō, scindō, fingō, pangō*, Lith. *tenkù* 'suffice', infin. *tèkti, limpù* 'stick', *lìpti* (Sk. *limpámi* 'smear'), *bundù, budĕti* 'wake up'—OSl. *bǫdǫ, byti* 'become'; OSl. *lęgǫ, lēšti* 'lie down', *sędǫ, sēsti* 'sit down'.

The most evident case in Germanic is probably Go. OE OS *standan*, ON *standa*, OHG *stantan*. The cognate of Lith. *tenkù*, Gmc. *þinhana-* > *þīhana-* (**29**) shifted to class I on account of the formal identity with verbs like Go. *weihan: þeihan, þaih, þaihum, þaihans*. *h* is analogical for *g*, since verbs with nasal infixes as a rule have suffix accent (cf. the reduced vowels in the Latin examples given above). The same is true for Go. *fāhan, hāhan*. The two verbs have doubtless influenced one another, perhaps, due to their frequent juxtaposition in legal language. *fāhan* (*fā, fōn, fāhan, fāhan*) is a heavy base and must go back to *pǝk/pǝnk-* (L. *pangō*; normal grade in *pāx*); *hāhan* (*hanga, hōn, hangon, hāhan = hangēn*) is a light base, L. *cunctor* (< *concitor*?). The present forms with *h* instead of *g* must have withdrawn the accent to the root before the time of Verner's Law, in analogy with the great majority of strong verbs, which had original root accent.

Other fairly certain cases of *n*-infix are Go. *windan, sigqan, stigqan, wringan*. For details consult WP.

VII. DENOMINATIVES have been in part referred to in some of the preceding groups. The most important type is the verbs of class II W. These are *je/jo*-derivatives, primarily from feminine *ā*-stems, like Gk.

τιμάω, L. *plantāre, multāre* 'punish' (from *multa* 'fine'); but the type spread, so that we find such verbs derived also from other noun stems and even without any etymological connection with nouns. The original forms are most clearly preserved in Lithuanian: *pã-saka* 'story', *pã-sakoju, -sakoti* 'relate'; *kartas* (masc.) 'time', *at-kartóju* 'I repeat'; **sauga* 'care', *saugóju* 'I am careful'. In Germanic, the full form occurs in some OS infinitives, like *ahtoian* (*ahton*) 'respect', *geƀoian* (*geƀon*) 'present'. Otherwise, the *ōja/ōji* suffix is contracted to *ō* (a process akin to the loss of the second element of long diphthongs in IE) or *ō* disappears, so that the forms resemble those of class I W, differing from them, however, by the lack of WGmc. *j*-gemination (**30**) and of mutation. The former is the case in Go. ON OS OHG, the latter in OE (see below). While this is clearly in keeping with the general weakening of unstressed syllables, it cannot be reduced to a concrete phonetic formula because parallels in other word categories are lacking. Analogical forms are abundant. Thus, in Gothic the 1 sg. and 3 pl. should have *a* (law of final syllables in the 1 sg., shortening of the diphthong *ōn* to *on, an* in the 3 pl.). In OE, the 2 and 3 sg. have taken over the forms of the athematic type with *ō*, while the other persons, as far as the suffix is concerned, do not differ from the *je/jo*-type.

These forms characterize the group in the several Gmc. languages:

	Go.	ON	OE	OS	OHG
Infin.	salbōn	kalla	sealfian	salbon	salbōn
1 sg.	salbō	kalla	sealfie	salbon	salbōm
2 sg.	salbōs	kallar	sealfas	salbos	salbōs
3 pl.	salbōnd	kalla	sealfiaþ	salboþ	salbōnt.

Instances:

OE *sealf*, OS *salƀa*, OHG *salba*: Go. *salbōn*, etc.

Go. OHG *kara* 'care, mourning': Go. *karōn* 'take care', OE *cearian* 'wail', OS OHG *karon* 'mourn'

Go. *paida* 'dress': *gapaidōn* 'to dress'

Go. *sunja* 'truth': *gasunjōn* 'justify'.

From *a*-stems:

Gmc. *fiska-* 'fish': Go. *fiskōn*, OE *fiscian*, OFris. *fiscia*, OS *fiskon*

Gmc. *wairþa-* 'worth': Go. *wairþōn*, OE *weorþian*, OS *giwerðon*, OHG *giwerdōn* 'estimate'.

From *n*-stems:

Go. *frauja* 'master'—*fraujinōn* 'rule'. (In Gothic, *-inōn* became a productive suffix which was transferred to other stems: *skalkinōn* 'serve' from *skalks* 'servant', *hōrinōn* 'commit adultery' from *hōrs* 'adulterer', *leikinōn* 'compare' from *leiks* 'like'.)

For many verbs in *ōn*, nouns are not attested, and probably did not exist, e.g.:

Go. *mitōn* 'consider', OHG *mezzōn* 'moderate', with similar meaning

    Go. *mitan*, ON *meta*, OE *metan*, OHG *mezzan* 'measure, estimate'

Go. *laþōn*, ON *laþa*, OE *laþian*, OS *ladon ladoian* 'load'.

NOTE 1: In part at least these non-denominative verbs may go back to an old type which appears in many languages, but is not frequent anywhere. Go. *mitan/mitōn* corresponds exactly to L. (Old) *lavere/lavāre, dūcere/educāre, cumbere/cubāre, capiō/occupāre.* Such verbs are especially important in Slavic, where they have regular morphological function, e.g., *berǫ* 'I carry', infin. *bъrati, derǫ* 'I flay', *dъrati*; in certain derived forms, especially in denominatives, the *ā*-suffix is carried through the whole paradigm. e.g. *strada* 'suffering', *stradajǫ, stradati* 'suffer', *dělo* 'work', *dělajǫ, dělati* 'make'.

NOTE 2: It is not possible to draw a definite line between suffixes that form clearly established present classes such as *neu/nw, nā/nə*, and those suffixes or determinants that have purely lexical significance. Different languages show different conditions. In Latin, *-sko-* forms inchoatives: *adolescō* 'I grow up'; in the Gmc. languages it occurs in a few scattered instances, like OHG *forskōn* 'search' = L. *poscō* < *porĝskō*, without definable connotation. The suffix *-to-* is in Latin intensifying, as in *clamitō* 'cry loud', but has no clear semantic function in Germanic (OHG *flehtan*, Gk. πλέκτω, πλέκω 'braid'). For a morphological function of *-to-* in Germanic, see **69.**

The Preterit

55. Strong and Weak Verbs. The distinction between the two fundamental types of the Gmc. verb is not based on the present stem, as in Sanskrit or Balto-Slavic grammar, but on the forms of the preterit. 'Strong' verbs form it by gradation of the root syllable; 'weak' verbs, by a dental suffix. The terms were coined by Jacob Grimm, who justified them in a characteristic way in his Deutsche Grammatik 1. 558 (1819):

Die starke Conjugationsform verdient so zu heissen: 1) weil sie lauter einfache kräftige Wurzeln enthält, die schwache hingegen meistens Ableitungen (auf *-jan, -ilon, -iron* etc.), also spätere, aus jenen Wurzeln erst entsprungene Verba..... 2) Weil sie des Ab- und Umlautes fähig ist, die schwache in der Regel keines von beiden, sondern behilft sich mit äusseren Mitteln. Sie muss der Lautveränderung aus derselben Ursache verlustig seyn, aus welcher in dem Sprachbildungsgesetz überhaupt einmal veränderte und verdoppelte Wurzellaute ihre innere Kraft und Bewegung ein- büssen..... 5) Da die Zahl der starken Verba beständig abnimmt, die der schwachen dagegen steigt; so folgt auch daraus unwiderleglich die edlere Natur der ersteren. Steigt ein schwaches Verbum aufwärts in die starke Form, so muss dies als unorganische Ausnahme; sinkt ein starkes in die schwache herab, so muss dies als der natürliche Gang der Sprache betrachtet werden. .... 7) Die zunächst folgende Betrachtung einer anomalischen Conjugation lehrt, dass, nach Erschöpfung der starken Form, erst gleichmässig gezwungener Weise zum Hülfsmittel der schwachen gegriffen wird.

Aus allem diesem erhellt deutlich, mit welchem Unrecht die gewöhnlichen Grammatiken die schwache Conjugation als Regel, und die starke als unorganische Ausnahme betrachtet haben.

The Strong Preterit

a **56. The Standard View,** if the consensus of opinion expressed by the great majority of historical grammars of the Germanic languages may be thus designated, considers the strong preterit essentially a direct continuation of the IE perfect tense. By implication this view may be ascribed to Jacob Grimm (cf. esp. l. c. 554 f.). Quite logically his first four 'strong conjugations' are those that show reduplication in Gothic. The several IE languages do not entirely agree in the formation of the perfect. The clearest characteristics are these:

(1) The singular ENDINGS are -a -tha -e: οἶδα, οἶσθα, οἶδε. The plural endings are not so certain. The first person had an m-element (ἴδ-μεν, Sk. vavṛtimá), the ending of the second person perhaps did not differ from that of other tenses (ἴστε), and the third person, at least in Aryan, Italic and Celtic, was characterized by an r-element (Sk. vidúr 'they know', OIr. -leldar 'they remained behind', L. fuēre 'they were').

(2) The ROOT has o-grade in the singular, reduced grade in the plural: οἶδα—ἴδμεν < *ἰδμέν. This postulates root accent as against termination accent, as in Sk. vavárta—vavṛtimá, which is confirmed by Verner's Law: OHG zēh—zigum, zōh—zugum, ward—wurtum.

(3) A large group of perfect forms is characterized by REDUPLICATION, that is, the initial consonant or consonant group + e is prefixed, Gk. λέλοιπα for earlier *λελοίπα, Sk. vavárta.

b To what extent is this fundamental perfect formation in keeping with the Germanic preterit?

(1) The singular endings are clear. Go. wait, ON veit etc. are identical with οἶδα, οἶδε, and the Go. ON ending of the 2 sg., waist, gaft, agrees with Gk. οἶσθα. Cf. **19.**

But the WGmc. 2 sg. ends in -i: OE tige, tuge, wurde, gǣfe, OHG zigi, zugi, wurti, gābi. Grammatical change indicates suffix accent.

It is now generally accepted that these forms are aorists of the type of
ἔ-λιπ-ες (without augment, however). -z is lost in WGmc., -i remained after short stems, so that the long-stem forms are analogical.
This explanation is entirely adequate, but it raises the question: Is this
the *only* aorist form in the Germanic preterit?

(2) The singular root vowel is Gmc. *a* in the first five classes, and in
part also in the seventh class.   Class VI consists of several types, but
all of them show Gmc. *ō* throughout the preterit: Go. *hafjan, hōf,
hōfum, skaban, skōf, skōfum, faran, fōr, fōrum.*   This *ō* may, of course,
go back to IE *ō* or *ā*, or it may represent analogical transfer.

The plural vowel agrees with the accepted theory in the first three
classes, but nowhere else.   For the seventh class, it may be assumed
that this rapidly disintegrating type was particularly susceptible to
analogy, so that *lailōtum* was substituted for **lailatum.*   Class VI,
again, is such a heterogeneous conglomeration of types that we need
not expect a uniform origin of all of its verbs.

But classes IV and V constitute a well-defined type with root vowel
IE *ē*: Go. *sētum* etc.   In order to reconcile this with the traditional view
that every Gmc. preterit must necessarily be an IE perfect, Michels
and Streitberg[2] developed this theory: IE *ghé-ghebh-men, ghé-ghebh-nt*
(with *accented* reduplication) became **ghéghbhmm, ghéghbhnt* in accordance with Streitberg's Dehnstufen theory (similar to Vedic forms with
long vowel in the reduplication), and through some consonant assimilation or simplification this resulted in Go. *gēbum, gēbun.*   Streitberg
considers the connection with the IE perfect an inescapable postulate
of method: 'Der Ursprung des "schwundstufigen" *ē* ist im schwachen
Perfektstamm (perf. plur. act. usw.) zu suchen.   Alle Erklärungsver-
suche, die ihn nicht zum Ausgang nehmen, müssen a priori aus method-
ischen Gründen als verfehlt betrachtet werden.   Denn es kann kein
Zufall sein, dass nur der Plural des Perfekts, nicht der vollstufige Singular, (aber auch nicht das schwundstufige part. perf.) den Vokal *ē* kennt.'
A weighty parallel is L. *sēdimus*; as in *nīdus* < **ni-zd-os*, this may
contain compensatory lengthening, going back, phonologically, to **se-
zd-əmos*, Sk. *sēdimá.*

To what extent the assumption of Verner's Law for *all* classes (except,
of course, class IV) is in accordance with the facts is discussed in **63**.

(3) The lack of reduplication in the first six classes is explained as
'haplology' (fusion of two similar syllables into one, as in 'interpretive'
for 'interpretative'), which may have started with the type *sētum* <
*sēzd-men, sēstum.   Its preservation in the Gothic seventh class and a

few ON and OE forms is considered an archaism ascribed to the lack of vowel contrast between the present and preterit with most of these verbs, e.g., Go. *haitan—haihait, haihaitum.*

This standard theory is presented most clearly, in spite of the extreme brevity of the treatment, by Loewe, GS 2. 73–9. But it can hardly be considered quite adequate. The first breach was made by Fierlinger's convincing explanation of OHG *zigi*, etc. as aorists (see above). The assumption of aorist elements was considerably extended by Prokosch, Sounds and History of the German Language (1917) and Inflectional Contrasts in Germanic, JEGPh 20, 468 ff. It is stressed by Hirt, HU 2. 152 ff. ('Der Aorist im Präteritum') and treated systematically and in detail by Sverdrup, Der Aorist im germanischen Verbalsystem und die Bildung des starken Präteritums, Falk-Festschrift 296 ff. Cf. also Collitz, Das schwache Präteritum und seine Vorgeschichte 199. Hirt, l. c.: 'Es ist zu beachten, dass die 3. Pluralis nicht dem Perfektsystem angehören kann. Denn die Endung dieser Form ist im Ind. *-ur*, im Griech. *-nti*, also primär, während die germanische Form sekundär ist. . . . Jedenfalls ist das germanische Präteritum ebenso aus dem Perfekt und Aorist gemischt wie das lateinische, nur dass im Lateinischen der *s*-Aorist die Rolle spielt, die im Germanischen der starke Aorist übernommen hatte.' Collitz, l. c.: '. . . so wird man dahin geführt, den Ursprung des *ē* ausserhalb des eigentlichen Perfektstamms zu suchen. Auf Grund des Lateinischen liegt es nahe, an einen alten Aorist zu denken. Das könnte nur der alte einfache Medial-Aorist gewesen sein, dessen 3 sg. im RV. *sād-i*, mit Augment *á-sād-i* lautet. Wie lat. *sēd-ī*, got. *sēt-um* an (*á*)*sād-i*, lassen sich lat. *vēn-ī* für *(*g*)wēm-ī*, got. *qēm-um* an die 3 sg. Aor. me. *á-gām-i* anknüpfen.' Sverdrup furnishes valuable evidence from other IE languages and considers not only OHG *sāzi*, but also Go. *sētum* as aorists, corresponding to Sk. (passive aorist) *ásādi*.

a   **57. Syncretism in the Strong Preterit.** The following considerations appear to be valid arguments against the current view:

(1) The Streitberg-Michels Theory is evidently a petitio principii. To explain *ē* in *gēbum*, it is from the outset taken for granted, for inadequate reasons of method, that the form *must* be a perfect. Then, the equally unproven Dehnstufentheorie is applied to the accented (?) reduplication, and the single consonant is ascribed to simplification of the heavy consonant group. The latter point is acceptable enough, in spite of the lack of phonological parallels, but the two unproven premises are not. The parallel of L. *sēdimus* and Sk. *sēdimá* is deceptive, since

the two forms are by no means identical (though some, e.g., Johannes Schmidt, KZ 25. 60 ff., have defended that view). Sk. sg. *sasā́da* < *sesóda, pl. *sēdimá* < *sezdimá, *sezdəmé, is a regular IE perfect type, since **sezd-* had to become **sēd-* by phonetic law (Thumb, Hdb. Sk. 362: 'Dass ai. *sēdimá* nicht dem got. *sētum* gleichzusetzen ist, muss heute als ausgemacht gelten'). L. *sēdimus*, taken alone, could go back to *sezdəmos (see above), but this would isolate the form entirely in the Latin verb system, separating it from obviously parallel forms like *lēgimus, vēnimus*. Moreover, the Germanic forms do not lend themselves to such an explanation. *se-zd-mén would have given Go. *sistum (cf. OHG *nest*). The Sk. type *sasā́da—sēdimá* cannot be considered Indo-European. Its resemblance to Go. *sat—sētum* is accidental. It developed in Sanskrit, starting with forms where phonetic law required *ē*, such as *yayā́ma—yēmimá* < **ya-im-*, like *sēd-* < **sezd-*. From this type it spread to other verbs, such as Ved. *paptimá—*Sk. *pētimá, tēnimá*, etc.

(2) The lack of reduplication in classes I–VI makes it difficult to identify the Gmc. strong preterit entirely with the IE perfect. If Streitberg's explanation of *sētum* were probable, the lack of reduplication could conceivably have spread from classes IV and V to the other classes. But even then it would be difficult to account for the presence of reduplication in *lailōt, haihait*, but its absence in *fōr, staig* (however, cf. above, under 3; it should be kept in mind that not only the 'reduplicating class' VII, but also class VI has the same vowel in the singular and the plural).

(3) Verner's Law is quite generally considered as definitely required for all classes of strong verbs (except, of course, class IV). But this is not borne out by the facts. As shown in **63** it is remarkably regular in classes I, II, III, but in classes V, VI, VII it is either·entirely missing, or it appears sporadically and in irregular distribution over the tenses. This indicates that the assumed distribution of the accent (root accent in the singular, suffix accent in the plural) is valid only for the first three classes, while the other four classes had different accent conditions. (Streitberg's assumption of accented reduplication in classes IV and V is probably accepted by few.)

(4) The endings do not agree with the standard view. The WGmc. 2 sg. in *-i* and the Gmc. 3 pl. in *-un* cannot be perfect endings, and the 1 pl. in *-um* need not be one; the 2 pl. in *-uþ* is surely analogical. These endings are identical with those of the aorist (secondary endings, with thematic vowel after reduced grade root, without it after lengthened

grade root): Gk. ἔλιπ-ε-ς, *ἔβηναν (for which analogical forms, chiefly ἔβησαν, were substituted) < -ṇt. The thematic type spread from classes I–III to IV–VII, the athematic type inversely from IV, V to the other classes. The root vowels, too, coincide with certain aorist forms: OHG zigi, zigun, zugi, zugun with Gk. ἔλιπες, ἔφυγες, nēmun possibly with *ἔβηναν and certainly with L. vēn-, sēd-.

b   These considerations indicate that the Gmc. strong preterit is not a homogeneous development from one source, but a combination of several types. Go. gaf, gaft, gaf (class V) and the corresponding forms in classes I–IV as well as the reduplicated forms of class VII (haihait) are genuine perfects. The plurals stigum, gutum, hulpum show reduced grade of the root, which is common to the perfect plural and the aorist of diphthongal roots, but the endings of these forms and of the WGmc. 2 sg. point clearly to the latter alternative. At best, it might be admitted that the identity of the root syllable in the two forms may have been a contributing cause for the fusion of the perfect and aorist paradigms. The long vowel forms of classes IV and V are definitely aorists. Thus we have in the first five classes syncretistic preterits, representing aorists everywhere in the plural, in WGmc. also in the 2 sg.; the 1 and 3 sg. are perfect forms everywhere, in Gothic and Old Norse also the 2 sg.

The parallel of this combination of paradigms with Latin conditions is obvious. As in Germanic, the functional distinction between perfect and aorist was abandoned and a new type was created, which combined both functions: L. vēnī = Gk. ἔβην (for *ἔβηνα) (aorist, 'I went') + βέβηκα (perfect 'I have gone'). But while Germanic combined both types in every preterit of classes I–V, in Latin, any given verb (aside from numerous new formations) used for its 'perfect' either the one or the other. An assumed Latin paradigm pepigī, pepigisti (= pēgisti), pepigit—pēgimus, pēgistis, pēgerunt would be an approximate analogon to Go. gaf, gaft (= WGmc. *gābi), gaf—gēbum, gēbuþ, gēbun.

The Classes

(Cf. **47**)

58. The Diphthongal Light Bases = classes I, II, III.

Pres. has e-grade: ei > ī, eu > Go. iu etc., el+ er+ em+ en+ > Go. il aír im in etc., according to the phonetic laws of the several dialects.

Pret. sg. has o-grade: ai au al etc.

Pret. pl. and, in WGmc., 2 sg. have zero grade: i u ul etc.

Past part. has zero grade.

For the development of diphthongs cf. especially **42**; for *h* also **27**.

Class I   a
   Pres.

Go.	*steigan*	*beitan*	*leiþan*	*-reisan*	*-teihan*	*þeihan*
ON	*stīga*	*bīta*	*līþa*	*rīsa*	*tiā*	——
OE	*stīgan*	*bītan*	*līþan*	*rīsan*	*tēon*	*þēon*
OS	*stīgan*	*bītan*	*līthan*	*rīsan*	*-tīhan*	*thīhan*
OHG	*stīgan*	*bīzan*	*līdan*	*rīsan*	*zīhan*	*dīhan*
	'climb'	'bite'	'go'	'rise'	'accuse'	'thrive'

   Pret. Sg.

	staig	*bait*	*laiþ*	*rais*	*taih*	*þaih*
	stē[1]	*beit*	*leiþ*	*reis*	(W, *tiāþa*)	——
	stāh	*bāt*	*lāþ*	*rās*	(II, *tēah*)	*þāh*
	stēg	*bēt*	*lēth*	*rēs*	*-tēh*	*thēh*
	steig	*beiz*	*leid*	*reis*	*zēh*	*dēh*

   Pret. Pl.

	stigum	*bitum*	*liþum*	*risum*	*taihum*	*þaihum*
	stigom	*bitom*	*liþom*	*risom*	(W)	——
	stigon	*biton*	*lidon*	*rison*	(II, *tugon*)	*þigon*
	stigun	*bitun*	*lidum*	**rirun*	**tigun*	**thigun*
	stigum	*bizzum*	*litum*	*rirum*	*zigum*	*digum*

   Past Part.

	stigans	*bitans*	*liþans*	*risans*	*taihans*	*þaihans*
	stigenn	*bitenn*	*liþenn*	*risenn*	*tigenn*[2]	——
	stigen	*biten*	*liden*	*risen*	*tigen*	*þigen*
	gistigan	*gibitan*	*gilidan*	**giriran*	**gitigan*	*githigan*
	gistigan	*gibizzan*	*gilitan*	*arriran*	*gizigan*	*gidigan*[3]

[1] for **stā*, through analogical formation of **steih*, in accordance with *beit* etc.
[2] 'excellent'.   [3] cf. NHG *gediegen*.

Transfers to other classes (for ON OE pret. forms of *tiā*, *tēon*, see above): Go. *bidjan* (**54,** II) 'ask' and the corresponding forms in the other Gmc. languages to V; but the durative form *beidan* 'wait', ON *bīþa*, OE *bīdan*, OHG *bītan* remained in class I.

Go. *weihan* 'fight' remained in class I, but ON *vega* was shifted to V.

Probably Go. *lisan* 'read, gather', ON *lesa* 'read', OE *lesan* 'gather', OHG *lesan* 'read, gather', historically in class V, originally also belonged to class I. It is in form identical with the pret. pres. *lisan—lais* 'I know' and may be explained as an *s*-extension of the widespread base *lei-* (*t*-extension in Go. *leiþan* etc.), like L. *līra* 'furrow' < **lei-s-ā*, de-

līrus 'insane'.   Lith. *lesù* 'pick up, gather' would in that case have to be considered not a cognate of *lesan*, but a borrowing from German (term of agriculture).

wei-to- (L. *vītis*, Ger. *Weide* 'willow') appears in Gothic as *-widan* 'bind'; it belongs in class V according to the evidence we have, but it is a transfer from class I; OHG has *wetan*, class V.   With nasal infix this verb shows transfer to class III: Go. *-windan* (ON *vinda*, OE OS *windan*, OHG *wintan*) 'wind'.   (Originally this is a heavy diphthongal base, *wēi-*; different etymology in Feist, GEW 72).

Similarly Go. *rinnan* etc. 'run' if connected with IE *rēi-*, Sk. *rīyatē* 'begins to flow', L. *rīvus* 'brook'.   Cf. Feist, GEW 300.

Go. *digan* 'need, shape' (see **54**, II) may have belonged to I or to V. Etymological evidence connects it with class I, but in the verb proper Gothic has only forms with ĭ.

b Class II

Pres.

Go. -*biudan*	*þliuhan*	*giutan*	*kiusan*	*liugan*	*tiuhan*
ON *bioþa*	*flȳia*[1]	*giōta*	*kiōsa*	*liūga*	*tiōa*[2]
OE *bēodan*	*flēon*	*gēotan*	*cēosan*	*lēogan*	*tēon*
OS *biodan*	*fliohan*	*giotan*	*kiosan*	*liogan*	*tiohan*
OHG *biotan*	*fliohan*	*giozan*	*kiosan*	*liogan*	*ziohan*
'bid'	'flee'	'pour'	'choose'	'tell lies'	'draw'

Pret. Sg.

bauþ	*þlauh*	*gaut*	*kaus*	*laug*	*tauh*
bauþ	*flō*	*gaut*	*kaus*	*lō[laug]*[3]	(W, *tōþa*)
bēad	*flēah*	*gēat*	*cēas*	*lēah*	*tēah*
bōd	*flōh*	*gōt*	*kōs*	*lōg*	*tōh*
bōt	*flōh*	*gōz*	*kōs*	*loug*	*zōh*

Pret. Pl.

-*budun*	*þlaúhum*	*gutum*	*kusum*	*lugum*	*taúhum*
buþom	*flugom*	*gutom*	*kǫrom* (etc.)	*lugom*	(W, *tōþom*)
budon	*flugon*	*guton*	*curon*	*lugon*	*tugon*
budun	**flugun*	*gutun*	*kurun*	*lugun*	*tugun*
butum	*fluhun*	*guzzum*	*kurum*	*lugum*	*zugum*

Past Part.

budans*	*þlaúhans*	*gutans*	*kusans*	*lugans*	*taúhans*
boþenn	—	*gotenn*	*kǫrenn*	*logenn*	*togenn*
boden	*flogen*	*goten*	*coren*	*logen*	*togen*
gibodan	**giflogan*	*gigotan*	*gikoran*	*gilogan*	*togan*
gibotan	*giflohan*	*gigozzan*	*gikoran*	*gilogan*	*gizogan*

[1] analogical from pres. ind. *flȳr*.   [2] 'suffice'.   [3] analogical.

Aorist Presents with $\bar{u}$ (cf. **54,** II):

Go.	-lūkan							
ON	lūka	sūga	sūpa	lūta				
OE	lūcan	sūgan	sūpan	lūtan	brūcan	būgan	hrūtan	dūfan

OS	*slūtan[1]	sūgan			brūkan	*būgan[1]		
OHG	lūchan	sūgan[2]	sūfan		brūchan		(h)rūzan	*tūchan[1]

    'lock'   'suck' 'swallow' 'bend 'use'   'bend' 'snore' 'dive'.
                                      down'

Further OE *scūfan* 'shove', *slūpan* 'slip', *strūdan* 'pillage', *þūtan* 'howl', *smūgan* 'creep', ON *flūga* = *fliūga* 'fly'.

---

[1] to be inferred from MHG.   [2] also *sūcan*.

Transfers to other classes: Possibly Go. *trudan* etc. < **dreu-to-* (class IV in Go. and ON, V in WGmc.; cf. **54,** II).

Go. *bugjan*, ON *byggia*, OE *bycgan*, OS *buggian* 'buy', which probably belongs to *biugan* 'bend', was transferred to the weak conjugation, forming a preterit without connecting vowel: Go. *baúhta*, OE *bohte*. The transfer of meaning may be explained from the connotation 'turn over', cf. Gk. πέλω 'turn', πωλέω 'sell', or from the use of arm rings (which were 'bent off', i.e. broken from spirals) for gifts or purchases; cf. Hildebrandslied 33 (*want her do ar arme wuntane bouga*). For other explanations, see Feist, GEW 82.

Go. *stautan* 'push' (ON *stauta*, OS *stōtan*, OHG *stōzan*) belongs to Sk. *tudáti*, L. *tundō* (perf. *tutudī*), with o-present like *faran* etc. (class VI, cf. **60**); it was transferred to class VII.

Go. *bliggwan* (OHG *bliuwan*) < **bhleu-*, Feist, GEW 74, was not transferred to class III, as assumed by Braune, Gotische Grammatik 85, Kieckers, HGG 212, but belongs to class II, as stated correctly by Streitberg, GE 144, with *ggw* through Holtzmann's Law, as in *triggwa-*.

Class III   c
    Pres.

Go.	-bindan	drigkan	finþan	hilpan	sigqan	wairþan[1]
ON	binda	drekka[2]	finna[2]	hialpa[3]	søkkua[2,3]	verþa[3]
OE	bindan	drincan	findan[4]	helpan	sincan	weorþan[1]
OS	bindan	drinkan	fīthan[2]	helpan	sinkan	werthan
OHG	bintan	trinkan	findan	helfan	sinkan	werdan
	'bind'	'drink'	'find'	'help'	'sink'	'become'

Pret. Sg.

-band	dragk	fanþ	halp	sagq	warþ
bant	drakk²	fann²	halp	sǫkk²	varþ
band	dranc	fand	healp	sanc	wearþ¹
band	drank	fand⁵	halp	sank	warth
bant	trank	fand	half	sank	ward

Pret. Pl.

-bundum	drugkum	funþum	hulpum	sugqum	waúrþum
bundom	drukkom²	fundom	hulpom	sukkom²	urþom⁶
bundon	druncon	fundon	hulpon	suncon	wurdon
bundun	drunkun	fundun	hulpun	sunkun	wurdun
buntum	trunkum	funtum	hulfum	sunkum	wurtum

Past Part.

-bundans	drugkans	funþans	hulpans	sugqans	waúrþans
bundenn	drukenn²	fundenn	holpenn	sokenn²	orþenn⁶
bunden	druncen	funden	holpen	suncen	worden
gibundan	gidrunkan	gifundan	giholpan	gisunkan	wordan
gibuntan	gitrunkan	gifuntan	giholfan	gisunkan	giwortan

¹ **42, 2.**   ² **29, 2 f.**, Note and **31.**   ³ **41** and Heusler, Aisl. Elb. 74 and Note 1.
⁴ for *fīþan.   ⁵ for *fōth.   ⁶ **33.**

NOTE: To this class belong a few verbs with stems ending in other consonant groups than liquid or nasal + consonant. Most of them have r before the stem vowel so that, in a sense, we may speak of a metathesis of r, avoiding groups of three consonants; in a more systematic way, we may class these verbs as dis-syllabic roots with consonant determinants and zero grade in the first syllable: Go. þriskan 'thrash', e.g., is best explained as *tere- (L. terō 'rub') + sko- (as in L. crē-scō). The most important verbs of this type are: Go. trudan (see above); ON bresta 'burst', bregþa 'brandish' (pret. brā < *brahþ)—verbs in pp tt kk like sleppa 'glide', spretta 'sprint', drekka 'drink' seem to belong in this irregular group of class III, but since their double consonants come from mp nt nk there is nothing irregular about these verbs at all; OE brestan 'burst', bregdan 'brandish', þrescan 'thrash', stregdan 'scatter', feohtan 'fight', frignan 'ask'; OS brestan, bregdan, fehtan 'fight', flehtan 'pleat', fregnan; OHG brestan (also IV: brāstun), brettan, hrespan 'pluck', arleskan 'extinguish', fehtan, flehtan. Verbs of this type tend to go over to class IV or V: Go. trudan (no preterit form preserved; probably *traþ, *trēdum, trudans); Go. brikan, brak, brēkum, brukans; OE tredan, træd, trædon, treden; OHG tretan, trat, trātum, gitretan; OE brecan, bræc, bræcon, brocen and brecen; OHG brehhan, brah, brāhum, gibrohhan, etc. For details consult the special grammars of the several dialects.

Also bringan belongs to class III and may be grouped with this type (< *bher[e] + nkó-), but has gone over to the weak conjugation (however, OE in poetry, part. *brungen*, OHG (Otfrid) *brang brungun*, UG part. *prungan*).

Aorist Presents: Go. *trudan* (but durative forms in the other dialects: OE *tredan*, OHG *tretan*); OE OS OHG *spurnan* 'kick' (chiefly weak forms); Go. *finþan* etc. might be suspected of being an analogical substitute for an earlier *fundan, since its meaning is essentially momentary. OE *findan* may either be considered a survival of the older form with vowel leveling, or it may be due to consonant leveling with the plural preterit and the participle.

-*ginnan* (Go. *du-*, OE *ā-*, *be-*, *on-*, OS *bi-*, OHG *bi-*) (for etymology see **65 d**) has a weak preterit in OHG: *bigunda, begonta, bigonsta*.

In the sense of **51 d**, every verb of this class may be considered a transfer from some other class, either through extension by a determinant, or through a nasal infix. Some of the clearest examples are the following (cf. WP, and Dunham, Class Shifting in the Gothic Strong Verb, Yale Dissertation 1932):

DETERMINANTS:

From class IV:

Go. *wairþan* 'become', *wairpan* 'throw', *swairban* 'turn' from root *wer* + *t-*, *b-*, *bh*-determinant; *swairban* with movable *s*.

NOTE: For the sake of convenience, root and determinant are given in a hypothetical IE form, but this should not imply the assumption of actual existence of these forms in IE times. In the case of *wairpan*, e.g., we have clearly to deal with a new Gmc. formation of which we cannot know whether it originated before or after the consonant shift; it will, therefore, be just as correct to speak of 'Gmc. *p*' as of 'IE *b*'.

hilpan = *kel-* 'hold' + IE *b* or Gmc. *p*; other determinants in Go. *hilms*, E. *helm* (in both meanings: that which holds = protects the head, and that by which one holds = steers a boat), Ger. *Halm* (that which holds the ear of grain), Go. *haldan* (transfer to class VII, which contains essentially heavy bases); without determinant (class IV) in OE OS OHG *helan* 'conceal' (Go. *huljan*), L. *cēlō* (lengthened grade). *oc-culō* < *ob-celō 'conceal'.

filhan 'bury', ON *fela* < **felhana-* 'conceal', root *pel-/pol-* 'much'. In Go. *filu*, Gk. πολύ, with *n*-determinant (suffix) in *fulls*, L. *plēnus* (meaning: to fill a hole, to cover with earth).

bairgan 'conceal, protect', *bher* + *gh*, without determinant in *ferō*.

at-þinsan 'draw near', to L. *teneō* 'hold', *ten-dō* 'stretch'.

NASAL INFIX:

From class I:

windan 'wind', root *wei-wi-* + *n*-infix + *t* '; without infix in L. *vītis* 'vine', Ger. *Weide* 'willow'.

stiggan 'collide' = *sti[n]g-wo-*, L. *in-stīgāre* 'incite', Gk. στίζω 'prick'. Ger. *stechen*, **stikana-* > *stekana-* (*a*-umlaut) has been transferred to class IV instead of V, in analogy with similar forms like *sprechen, brechen* (see above).—For *windan, rinnan*, see class I.

The following two verbs belonged originally to the fifth Gmc. class. The nasal infix disappeared with compensatory lengthening before Gmc. ħ, while it was preserved before ʒ (Grammatical Change); in the former case the resulting *ī* caused transfer to class I, while the forms with ʒ belong to class III:

Go. *þeihan*, OE *ge-þēon*, OS *thīhan*, OHG *dīhan* 'thrive' < **té[n]ko-*: OE *ge-þungen*, OS *gi-thungan* 'stately' < **t|n]kó-*; ʒ also in Ger. *gediegen* 'excellent'; Lith. *tenkù, tèkti* 'have enough'.

Go. *þreihan** 'press' < **tré[n]ko-*: ON *þryngua*, OE *þringan*, OS *thringan*, OHG *dringan* < **tre[n]kó-*; Lith. *trenkiù, treñkti* 'shake', L. *terō* 'rub'.

(Normal grade instead of zero grade in the suffix-extended forms is analogical restoration; on the other hand, Gothic doubtless carried through **þihans* > **þaihans*, **þrihans* > **þraihans* as against OE *geþungen*, OHG *gidrungan*. The hypothetical Gmc. present forms would be either **þīħana-* or **þungana-*—possibly the former in durative function, the latter in perfective (aoristic).

59. The Monophthongal Light Bases = Class IV, V.

Present has *e*-grade: *el er em en* (no example with *en*) = Go. *il air im*.

Pret. sg. has *o*-grade: *al ar am*, as in classes I, II, III.

Pret. pl. and in West Germanic 2 sg. have lengthened grade: *ǣl ǣr ǣm* > Go. *ēl ēr ēm*, NWGmc. *āl ār ām*.

Past part. has reduced grade, now usually termed 'shva secundum' (ɞ), which appears as *u* before liquid and nasal, as *e* before stop or spirant. This constitutes the only difference between class IV and class V. The older formula considers *i* < *e* in Go. *gibans* a restoration of the stem vowel in analogy with the present, since forms like **ʒɞana-* do not agree with the phonetic structure of Gmc., and forms like **stana-* might give rise to ambiguities (Go. **stans* would seem to belong rather to *standan* than to *sitan*); *u* in *numans* was explained as due to a form **nṃ-óno-*; syllabic nasal or liquid generally stands before consonant or in pausa, but here syllable division would have had the same function.

Class IV

Pres.   a

	steal	bear	take	come	be fitting	destroy
Go.	stilan	bairan	niman	qiman	-timan*	-tairan
ON	stela	bera	nema	koma[1]		
OE	stelan	beran	niman	cuman		teran
OS	-stelan	beran	niman	kuman		
OHG	stelan	beran	neman	queman, cumen, coman	zeman	zeran*
	'steal'	'bear'	'take'	'come'	'be fitting'	'destroy'

Pret. Sg.

	stal	bar	nam	qam	tam*	tar
	stal	bar	nam	kuam, kom[2]	—	—
	stæl	bær	[nōm]	[cōm, cwōm][3]	—	tær
	stal	bar	nam	quam	—	—
	stal	bar	nam	quam	zam	zar*

Pret. Pl.

	stēlum	bērum	nēmum	qēmum	tēmum*	tērum
	stǫlom[4]	bǫrom	nōmom[5]	kōmom[5]	—	—
	stǣlon	bǣron	nōmon	cōmon	—	tǣron
	stālun	bārun	nāmun	kāmun	—	—
	stālum	bārum	nāmum	kāmum	zāmum	zārum

Past Part.

	stulans	baurans	numans	qumans	tumans*	taurans
	stolenn	borenn	numenn[6], nomenn[7]	komenn	—	—
	stolen	boren	numen	cumen, cymen	—	toren
	stolan	giboran	numan	kuman	—	—
	gistolan	giboran	ginoman	gikoman	gizoman*	gizoran

[1] aorist present, see below; for disappearance of w, cf. **23 b**.   [2] cf. Heusler, Aisl. Elb. §82, 2.   [3] Analogy from the pl.   [4] Heusler, Aisl. Elb. §72.   [5] **42 f.**
[6] Icel.   [7] Norw.

Aorist Present. Gmc. *qem-/kum- is the clearest survival of double forms according to aspect. Gothic has only the durative present, qiman, ON OE OS have only the aoristic forms, koma, cuman, kuman, and OHG has both: queman 'to be coming', quomen, komen, kuman 'arrive' (of course, the original difference in meaning is no longer observed in OHG literature).

Class V

b   Pres.

	'give'	'speak'	'see'	'pick, read'	'be'	'ask'	'eat'
Go.	giban	qiþan	saihvan[1]	lisan[2]	wisan	bidjan[2, 3]	itan
ON	gefa	kueþa	siā[4]	lesa	vesa, vera	biþia	eta
OE	giefan[8]	cweþan	sēon[4]	lesan	wesan	biddian[5]	etan
OS	geban	quethan	sehan	lesan	wesan	biddian[5]	etan
OHG	geban	quedan	sehan	lesan	wesan	bitten[5]	ezzan

Pret. Sg.

	gaf	qaþ	sahv	las	was	baþ	ēt*[6]
	gaf	kuaþ	sā[7]	las	vas, var	baþ	āt
	geaf[8]	cwæþ	seah	læs	wæs	bæd	æt
	gaf	quað	sah	las	was	bad	āt*
	gab	quad	sah	las	was	bat	āz, az

Pret. Pl.

	gēfum	qēþum	sēhvum	lēsum	wēsum	bēdum	ētum
	gǭfom	kuōþom, kōþom	sǭm	lǭsom	vǭrom	bōþom	ǭtom
	gēafon	cwǣdon	sāwon[9]	lǣson	wǣron	bǣdon	ǣton
	gābun	quādun	sāwun	lāsun	wārun	bādun	ātun
	gābum	quātum, quādum	sāhum	lārum, lāsum	wārum	bātum	āzum

Past Part.

	gibans	qiþans	saíhvans	lisans	*wisans	bidans	itans
	gefenn	kueþenn	sēnn	lesenn	veret (neut.)	beþenn	etenn
	giefen[8]	cweden	sewen[9]	lesen	wesen	beden	eten
	gigeban	giquedan	gisewan	gilesan	giwesan	gibedan	etan
	gigeban	giquetan	gisehan	gileran, gilesan	giwesan	gibetan	gezzan

---

[1] **42 i.**   [2] probably transfer from class I, see above.   [3] **53 b, 54 d.**   [4] **27 d.**
[5] **30.**   [6] only the pl. *ētun* occurs, but on the basis of *frēt*, from *fra-itan* 'fressen' and in keeping with other Gmc. languages the existence of *ēt* is certain. The long vowel is probably due to leveling from the plural, on account of the 'unsubstantial' character of *at*, although some consider it a contraction of reduplication and stem vowel (*e-ed-* or *e-od-*?; we cannot know what the result of either contraction would have been).   [7] **27 d.**   [8] **24 c.**   [9] Angl. *sǣgon, gesegen*, **23 d.**

Transfers: Go. *gawidan*, OHG *wetan* 'bind'; Go. *lisan* etc. and ON *vega* < *wiʒana-*, to Go. *weihan* etc. are originally aorist presents of class I (see above).—ON *vega* really represents two different verbs: in the meaning 'slay' it corresponds to Go. *weihan*, OHG *wegan*, in the meaning 'lift' to Go. *gawigan*, OHG *wegan* (class V).

60. Monophthongal Heavy Bases.

The long normal grades *ē ō ā* alternate with the reduced grade *ə*. The majority of verbs of this type is apt to express primarily momentary action: *catch, strike, injure, chip off, pass through* (Go. *hafjan, slahan, -skapjan, skaban, *wadan*—ON *vaþa*). A few, however, express preferably continued action, such as *sleep, meditate, bewail* (Go. *slēpan, rēdan, grētan*). The former tend toward the use as aorist presents with *ə-*, the latter toward the use as durative presents with *ē, ō*. With some verbs we find both alternatives in actual use: Go. *tēkan* 'touch' versus ON *taka* 'take'; Go. *-rēdan* 'provide', ON *rāþa* etc. 'advise', as against Go. *garabjan* 'count', OS *reðiōn*, OHG *redōn* 'talk' (these, however, are not aorist presents but denominatives connected with Gmc. *-raþjōn-*, L. *ratiō*). We find clear parallels in L. *capiō, faciō, scabō* as against *rē-rī*, Gk. λήδομαι 'be tired', and an interesting sidelight is thrown on the problem by Latin double forms like *lăbō* 'waver'—*lābor* 'glide', *vădō* 'pass through'—*vādō* 'wander'. With this type of verbs the reduced grade forms have more or less momentary, 'perfective' meaning, while normal grade forms have durative function. With the *capiō*-type, however, the normal present substitutes tense function for aspect function and thereby becomes a preterit merely by force of contrast to the present, while with the *rērī*-type the process is the reverse. With *capiō* momentary action is predominant, and therefore the *ə*-form appears in the present, the *ē-(ō)*-form in the preterit; *rē-rī* has primarily durative aspect, therefore the normal grade is the present and the reduced grade (*rătus*) functions as preterit; cf. also L. *lassus* < *ləd-tós* 'tired' with Gk. λήδομαι.

Class VI consists of two or possibly more different types that have coalesced (**54 b** and **d**), heavy bases with *ə*-present and light bases with *o*-present, corresponding on the one hand to L. *căpiō, scăbō, vădō*, on the other hand to Gk. πορεύομαι. In the present the two types are virtually identical in Germanic; a *j*-suffix is frequent with either of them: Go. *hafjan, hlahjan, raþjan, skapjan* have heavy bases with *j*, *skaban, standan, sakan* (L. *sagiō, sāgax*, Go. *sōkjan*), ON *taka, vaba*, without it; of light bases, ON *sueria*, OE *swerian*, OS OHG *swerian* (but Go. *swaran*) and Go. *wahsjan* have a clear *j*-suffix; Go. OS OHG *malan*, ON *mala* show *j* in OSl. *meljǫ* (as against L. *molō* < *melō*);

Go. *farjon** 'travel, especially by boat' (but *faran** 'travel') belongs to I W and was probably originally a causative from **ferana-* (Gk. περαίνω 'go through' etc.). But *graban, wakan* and others of uncertain etymology have no *j*. Brugmann, Grdr. 2. 3². 122 and IF 32. 179, believes that light base iteratives in *-j-* of the type of ON *sueria*, Go. **swarjan* were the starting point, and Hirt, HU 2. 149, seems to agree with him; in that case the preterit Go. *swōr* was originally a reduplicated perfect with *ō*, like Sk. *cakăra* 'have done', *babhăra* 'have carried'. But the absence of gradation between singular and plural rather speaks against this. The Sk. plurals *cakṛmá, babhṛmá* have zero grade, and in Germanic the pattern of the first five classes would have tended to preserve some sort of difference in the stem vowel between the two numbers. In spite of this, the theory is possible; but the majority of the class rather suggests that the type L. *scabō—scābī, capiō—cēpī* (possibly for **cōpī*) formed a new preterit by analogy due to the identity of the present forms. The original preterit of *far(j)an, dragan, graban* was probably **far-fērum, *drag-drēgum, *graf-grēfum*, but this was replaced by *ō-forms* in keeping with *hōf—hōfum* etc.

Pres.

Go.	*hafjan*	*-skapjan**	*standan*	*faran**	*dragan*	*graban*
ON	*hefia*	*skepia*	*standa*	*fara*	*draga*	*grafa*
OE	*hebban*	*scieppan*[4]	*standan*	*faran*	*dragan*	*grafan*
OS	*heffian,*	**skeppian*	*standan*	*faran*	*dragan*	*graban*
	hebbian					
OHG	*heffen,*	*skepfen,*	*stantan*	*faran*	*tragan*	*graban*
	-hevan[2]	*skaffan*				
	'lift'	'make'	'stand'	'travel'	'carry',	'dig'
					OE	
					'draw'	

Pret. Sg.

	hōf	*-skōp*	*stōþ*	*fōr**	*drōg*	*grōf*
	hōf	*skōp*	*stōþ*	*fōr*	*drō*[2]	*grōf*
	hōf	*scōp*	*stōd*	*fōr*	*drōh*	*grōf*
	hōf	*skōp*	*stōd*	*fōr*	*drōg*	*grōf*
	huob	*skuof*	*stuo[n]t*	*fuor*	*truog*	*gruob*

Pret. Pl.

	hōfum	*-skōpum*	*stōþum*	*fōrum**	*drōgum*	*grōbum*
	hōfom	*skōpom*	*stōþom*	*fōrom*	*drōgom*	*grōbom*
	hōfon	*scōpon*	*stōdon*	*fōron*	*drōgon*	*grōbon*
	hōbun	*skōpun*	*stōdun*	*fōrun*	*drōgun*	*grobun*
	huobun	*skuofum*	*stuo[n]tum*	*fuorum*	*truogum*	*gruobum*

Past Part.

hafans	-skapans	*standans¹	farans*	dragans*	grabans
		(or *stadans)			
hafenn	skapenn*	staþenn	farenn	dregenn³	grebenn
hæfen⁵	sceapen⁴	standen	færen⁵	drægen⁵	græben⁵
gihaban	giskapan	(gi)standan	gifaran	gidragan	gigraban
gihaban	giskaffan	gistantan	gifaran	gitragan	gigraban.

NOTE: hafjan, -skapjan, standan are heavy bases (**60**; **54 b** and d): L. capiō —cēpī, scabō—scābī, stătus—stāre. Go. skaban is probably also a cognate of L. scabō (root doublets IE *skǝb.skǝbh). faran, dragan, graban are light bases and may, with Brugmann, l. c., be considered original j-iteratives that have lost the suffix by leveling: Gk. περάω περαίνω, OSl. drъžati 'hold', IE *dhregh-, OSl. grebǫ. ¹ not preserved. The WGmc. forms point to *standans, the ON form to *staþans. The question cannot be decided with certainty.   ² **27 c.**   ³ e for a is generally ascribed to the influence of g or k after e, as in tekenn 'taken', dreke 'dragon' (OE draca); Heusler, Aisl. Elb. 23.   ⁴ **41 f** and **24 c.**   ⁵ or hafen, dragen, graben; a in closed syllables becomes æ (**38 c**), but in open syllables we seem to have regularly æ before an original front vowel (fæder, < -ēr), a before an original back vowel (faren = Go. farans); but this matter is still problematic.

Class VII contains a number of monophthongal heavy bases with normal grade in the present: Go. lētan, hōpan, bauan; cf. **60**. These are treated in section **62**.

61. Diphthongal Heavy Bases within the Germanic verb system have not yet been proven conclusively (cf. **54 c**) but they offer a practical working hypothesis through which the verbs of class VII can be linked up with the rest of the strong verbs, showing a parallelism between light and heavy bases. Theoretically we obtain the following possibilities of alternation:

		Light Bases	Heavy Bases	
I	(i-diphth.)	ei oi i	ēi ōi ǝi	= Gmc. ē² ai ai
II	(u-diphth.)	eu ou u	ēu ōu ǝu	= Gmc. eu au au
III	(l, n-diphth.)	el ol ēl ḷ	ēl ōl ǝl	= Gmc. el al al
IV, V	(monophth.)	e o ē ъ	ē ō ǝ	= Gmc. ē¹ ō a

Cf. **39 b.**

The distribution of these vowel grades in class VII is indicated in the following section. Class VI, on the basis of this table, represents one alternative of the heavy-base type of classes IV and V: alan—ōl, hafjan—hōf have ǝ—ō (ā?), corresponding to ъ—o in numans—nam, gibans—gaf. The other alternative is represented by lētan—lailōt, like giban—gaf. The reduced grade presents are aorist presents, the normal grade presents are durative. This accounts for the appearance of the same verb in either the sixth or the seventh class: ON *taka* : Go. *tēkan* (60). The present type decided for membership in either of the two classes.

a   **62. The 'Reduplicating Verbs'** (Class VII) present one of the most difficult problems of Germanic grammar. Gothic stands in sharp contrast to NWGmc. The former has reduplicated preterits which are obviously old perfects: *haihait, haihlaup**, *haihald, faifāh, saislēp*; the latter have unreduplicated forms: OE *hēt, hlēop, hēold, fēng, slēp.* Since Jacob Grimm it has been taken for granted that Gothic had preserved the old form and that the NWGmc. forms were contractions, **heh[ai]t, he[h]ald* etc. True, the exact phonetic process had never been explained on the basis of phonetic laws, but the view seemed to gain support from the actual existence of a few remnants of reduplication in NWGmc.:

ON *rōa* 'row'—*rera, sā* 'sow'—*sera* (< *seza or analogical), *snūa* 'turn' —*snera* (< **snez[n]a* or analogical), *grōa* 'grow' *grera, gnūa* 'rub'—*gnera.*

OE *hātan* 'be called'—*heht, lācan* 'jump'—*leolc, lǣtan* 'let'—Angl. *leort* (dissimilation from *leolt or analogy; WS *lēt*), *rǣdan* 'advise'— Angl. *reord* (WS *rēd*), *ondrǣdan* 'be afraid'—*ondreord* (WS *ondrēd*).

OHG has a few forms with medial *r* which seem to be analogical modifications of reduplicated preterits, starting from some verb like *scrōtan* 'cut'—*kiskrerot* (2 pl. pret.): *būan*—*biruun, stōzan*—*steroz, stirz* etc., *plōzan*—*capleruzzi.* Cf. Joh. Schmidt, *KZ* 25. 598.

But the existence of these forms speaks rather against than for equating the *hēt*-type with the *haihait*-type. If *heht* was the regular phonetic development of *hehāt = Go. *haihait*, it seems improbable that at a comparatively late period it should have gone through the altogether irregular development to *hēt*; if the form had been preserved at all, it would have remained *heht* in Anglian, as in *reht, cneht*, or become *heoht in West Saxon, as in *reoht, cneoht*. There was no starting point for an analogical deflection since *lēt, rēd* present the same difficulties or even greater ones. Besides, it is not absolutely certain that these isolated forms are reduplicated. The prevalence of *r* might be more than merely accidental. ON *rera* etc. might be considered an extension of abnormally short forms like *rō (*ra*), for which there are no parallels. In OE *reord, ondreord*, the initial *r*, in *leolc* the initial *l* might have led to a sort of assimilation ('Fern-Assimilation'). But admitting tentatively that we have here to deal with reduced forms, this would not necessarily prove more than that for a time two preterit types existed side by side in this class, one with reduplication and one without it, as in L. *pepigī—pēgī*. W. Schultze (Die reduplizierten Präterita des Tocharischen und des Germanischen, Sitzungsbericht der preussischen Akademie der Wissenschaften 1924, 166 ff.) lays stress on a parallelism with Tocharian, where dialect A has the reduplicated type, *cacäl* 'has lifted', dialect B the type with a long vowel without reduplication, *cāla*. But as long as both types are frequent in Indo-European, this parallelism is hardly more than a coincidence.

In 1895 Brugmann and Wood (**39 b**) presented simultaneously but **b** independently the view that the NWGmc. forms do not correspond to the Go. reduplicated preterits, but represent a different type of IE gradation, namely the alternation between normal grade (*ē ō ā*) and reduced grade (*ə*) of heavy bases, both of the monophthongal and the diphthongal type. This view met with a good deal of approval at first (Hofmann, Janko, Feist, Karstien, Swerdrup;—cf. Hirt, HU 2. 143 footnote), but gradually strong opposition to it developed. The phonetic side of the older view is plausibly defended by Heusler, Aisl. Elb.[2] 105: *fe-fall* could become *fell*, (1) to avoid the repeated *f*-articulation, (2) because in the related form *he-halt h* had disappeared by phonetic law, (3) because the speaker, under the influence of the great number of unreduplicated preterits, was inclined to use monosyllabic forms. But these are merely arguments for the possibility of the process, not for its actual occurrence. Hirt (l. c. 144 note) attaches great importance to Heusler's argument against the Brugmann-Wood theory, 'dass sich das *ē*[2] und *eo* nur im Präteritum, nicht aber in den Verbalableitungen (Kausativen) und Nominalbildungen findet. Es gibt kein aisl. *grēta* "weinen machen", *hlōpa* (< *hleopjan*) "laufen machen", kein *hēt* "Geheiss" oder *fell* "Fall".' But this apparently convincing argument is a fallacy. True, with light base strong verbs, causatives and nouns are often formed with the *o*-grade, and so is the singular of the preterit. But this is not tantamount to saying that they are formed from the preterit. The *ō*-grade is quite common with heavy bases as well, e.g. Go. *rōdjan*, ON *rø̄pa* 'talk' (verb and noun) from *-rēdan*, OE *behāt* 'promise' from *-hātan*, like *belāf* 'remainder', from *lēon* (Go. *leihvan*), with *ō*-grade.

It does not seem at present that either of the two theories can be proved or disproved, but the older theory, in spite of Heusler's sensible reasoning, is very difficult to reconcile with the standard views of phonetic laws. On the other hand, the new hypothesis agrees with them very well. Both systems must have recourse to a good deal of leveling, but the new one much less so than the old one. Moreover,—and this is perhaps the decisive factor—the Brugmann-Wood theory is so well in keeping with the general drift from aspect to tense in Germanic that I consider it best to use it as the basis for the listing of instances of this class.

With some slight modifications, to adapt the theory still better to the general system, the NWGmc. preterits of this class are explained in the following way:

c   (1) As explained in **60**, the leading verbs of class VI are aorist presents of monophthongal heavy bases:
hafjan = capiō, *wadan = vădō. Their preterit is originally nothing but the form of the durative aspect, transferred to preterit meaning by mere force of contrast, since it was the only (or almost the only) other ablaut variation:
hōf = *cōpī, cēpī, *wōþ = vād(ō).

d   (2) The same is true for the Gmc. present and the NWGmc. preterit of the diphthongal heavy bases—except for the unfortunate fact that the instability of long diphthongs prevents the same degree of certainty that we have in the case of class VI. For this reason, no effort is made here to follow this up etymologically. The pragmatic probability of systematic consistency is all that can be offered. We arrive at the following distribution of vowel grades:

	ē-Grade	*ō*-Grade	Reduced Grade
	NWGmc. Pret.	Go. Pret. (Sg.?)	Gmc. Pres. (Go. Pret. Pl.)
I. *i*-Diphth.	*ēi*: OE *hēt*	*ōi* > *oi*: Go. *haíhait*	*əi*: Go. *haitan*, OE *hātan*
II. *u*-Diphth.	*ēu* > *eu*: OE *hlēop*	*ōu* > *ou*: Go. **haíhlaup*	*əu*: Go. -*hlaupan*, OE *hlēapan*
III. *l*-, *n*-Diphth.	*ēl* > *el*: OE *helt*	*ōl* > *ol*: Go. *haíhald*	*əl*: Go. *haldan* OE *healdan*.

The Go. pret. pl. *haíhaitum*, etc., may equally well be considered original *ə*-forms, or levelings from the *ō*-singular.

The past participles are not included in the table because they always have the same vowel as the present forms, possibly by analogy.

In class III we find many analogical forms: OE leans to leveling according to class II (*hēold*), OHG according to class I (*hialt*).

e   THE REDUPLICATION IN GOTHIC. The vowel of the IE reduplication was *e* which would have given Go. *i* except before *h* and *r*. It was originally unaccented (cf. *saizlēp*, but analogically also *saislēp*, ON *sera* < **se-zō*) but probably the accent was shifted to the first syllable in primitive Germanic times. It is generally assumed that Go. *ai* for *i* is leveling, but this is not quite likely since there are only five verbs of this type that begin with *h* (*haitan, hlaupan, hāhan, haldan, hōpan*) and one with *r* (*rēdan*). Probably Hirt (HU 2. 143) is right in assuming that pretonic *e* became Go. *ai* regularly. Verbs that begin with *st, sp* (and, of course, *hv*) repeat the whole group: *staistaut*.

The stem vowel of the Go. reduplicated preterits is the same in the singular and plural. *ō* in *lailōt* is transferred analogically to the plural, *lailōtum* for **lailatum* with *a* < *ə*. *haihaitum*, etc. can, of course, be explained equally well from *əi* and from (analogical) *ōi*, and forms of this type may have been the starting point for the leveling between singular and plural.

(3) Monophthongal heavy bases with primarily durative meaning **f** form the remainder of this class. Consistently, we would expect preterits like **lat, rap* < **lad-, rət-* to Go. *lētan, rēdan* (cf. L. *lassus, ratus*). But for some reason, at which we can only guess, we find throughout secondary formations that clearly show their analogical character by the fact that for the most part they cannot be reconciled with the ablaut series of the stem vowel. In general, the *ēi*-type has intruded (ON OE OS *hēt*, OHG *hiaz*), but to an extent also the *ēu*-type (OE *blēot*, OHG *riof*). This is partly accounted for by the fact that the verbs of the *ēi*-type are especially numerous and frequent. It is possible that the verb *lētan* formed the bridge. As Lith. *léidmi* seems to indicate, it was probably originally diphthongal (*lēid-*), but appears as monophthongal, by absorption of the glide in IE times, in Gk. λῃδεῖν, Go. *lētan*, OHG *lāzan*. The assumption of the doublets *lēd-/lēid-*, would account for the monophthongal present and the diphthongal preterit, and *rēdan, slēpan*, for which we have no evidence of diphthongal origin, may have followed this pattern.

In the following tables only the present and preterit sg. are given, **g** since the other two forms do not contribute anything new, even in grammatical change:

I. *i*-Diphth.

Pres.

Go.	*haitan*	*maitan*	*skaidan*	*laikan*
ON	*heita*			*leika*
OE	*hātan*		*scādan*	*lācan*

OS	hētan		skēdan, skēðan	
OHG	heizan	meizan	skeidan	
	'call'	'cut'	'separate'	'leap'

Pret.

	haihait	maimait	skaiskaiþ	lailaik
	hēt			lēk
	hēt		scēd	lēc
	hēt		skēd	
	hiaz	miaz	skiad	

II. u-Diphth.

Pres.

Go.	stautan	hlaupan	aukan	
ON		hlaupa	auka	
OE		hlēapan		
OS	stōtan	hlōpan	(past part. ōcan 'pregnant')	
OHG	stōzan	(h)loufan		
	'push'	'leap'	'increase'	

Pret.

	staistaut	haihlaup	aiauk
		hliōp	iōk
		hlēop	
	steot	hleop	
	stioz	(h)liof	

For treatment of diphthong, cf. **39 b,** and **42.**

III. l-, n-Diphth.

Pres.

Go.	haldan	gaggan[1]	fāhan[2]	hāhan[1]
ON	halda	ganga	fā	hanga
OE	healdan	gangan	fōn	hōn
OS	haldan	gangan	fāhan	hāhan
OHG	haltan	gangan	fāhan	hāhan
	'hold'	'go'	'catch, get'	'hang'

Pret. Sg.

	haihald	(iddja)	faifāh	haihāh
	helt	gekk	fekk	hekk
	held, heold[3]	gēong[4]	feng	heng
	held	geng	feng	heng
	hialt	giang	fiang, feng	hiang

Pret. Pl.

haíhaldum	(iddjēdum)	faífāhum	haíhāhum
heldom	gingom, -e-	fingom, -e-	hengom
heldon, -eo-	gēongon	fengon	hengon
heldun	gengun	fengum	hengun
hialtum	giangum	fiangum	hiangum

Past Part.

haldans	gaggans	fāhans	hāhans
haldenn	gengenn	fengenn	hangenn
healden	gangen	fangen	hangen
gihaldan	gigangan	gifangan	gihangan
gihaltan	gigangan	gifangan	gihangan

[1] *gaggan* and *hāhan* are transfers from light bases: Lith. *žengiù* 'I step', Gk. κοχώνη < *χοχώνᾱ, Sk. *jaghánas* 'crotch'; L. *cunctōr* 'hesitate' < *conc-itōr* (intensive).   [2] *fāhan* shows a good many analogical cross currents. Phonologically, it would have the ablaut forms *pāk-/pǝk-, cf. L. *pāx—pangō*, or, with nasal infix, *pānk-/pǝnk-; the long diphthong would be shortened in Gmc., so that both forms would become identical, aside from Verner's Law: *fanχ- > *fāχ-/fang-. So it would appear that the pres. *fāhan* has normal grade, but its meaning would point to an aorist present, and *h* in *fāhan* might be leveling with *hāhan* < *kónk- > hanχ-, hāh-, with which it is frequently associated in legal phrases. For the disappearance of *h* in ON and OE, see **27 d**, for *n*, **29 c**.—The preterit vowel also shows analogical interference, which cannot be traced with certainty. Probably *e* and *i* (the latter a secondary change before nasal + consonant) go back to the same source as *ia* in OHG, < *ēi*, shortened before the consonant group; in OE a secondary lengthening may have occurred, cf. Sievers, Angelsächsische Gramm. 395, Anmerkung 1, and 129.   [3] OE *heold* by the side of *held* may be due to leveling with the second class, but cf. Sievers, l. c. 81, Anmerkung 1: 'Ob die *eo* im reduplizierten Präteritum wie *weoll, heold* etc. als Brechungsdiphthonge oder als ältere Langdiphthonge anzusehen sind, ist ungewiss.' Perhaps the regular scope of breaking (**42 e**) was extended under the influence of the *ēo*-forms.   [4] OE *gēong* must be leveling from the second class.

IV. Monophth.   (a) Present Vowel $\bar{e}$ = Gmc. $\bar{æ}$
   Pres.

Go.	lētan	-rēdan	blēsan
ON	lāta	rāþa	blāsa
OE	lǣtan	rǣdan	blāwan
OS	lātan	rādan	—
OHG	lāzan	rātan	blāsan
	'let'	'advise'	'blow'

Pret.

lailōt	rairōþ	baiblēs*
lēt¹	rēþ¹	blēs¹
lēt¹	rēd (rǣdde W)¹	bleow²
lict¹	riad¹	—
liaz¹	riat¹	blias¹

¹ analogical from class I.   ² from class II.

(b) Present Vowel ō = IE ā or ō

Pres.

Go.	flōkan¹	bauan²	blōtan³	
ON	—	būa	blōta	
OE	flōcan 'applaud'	būan	blōtan	hrōpan
OS	flōcan 'strike'	būan		hrōpan
OHG	fluohhan	būan	bluozan	(h)ruofan
	'condemn'	'dwell'	'sacrifice'	'cry'
Pret.				
	faiflōk(un)	(bauida W)	baiblōt	—
	—	biō	blēt	—
	flēoc⁴	(būde W)	blēot⁴	hrēop⁴
	—	(buida W)	—	hriop
	—	(būta W)	plioz, pleruzzun	(h)riof⁴
		(biruun etc.)		

¹ plāg- (πληγή, L. plāga—borrowed from Dor. Gk. ?—'blow').   ² pron. [bɔ·an], like saian = [sɛ·an]; lengthened o-grade of IE bheu-, bhōu, monophthongized to bhō-; ON biō is regular e-grade, so that we have here a light base that was shifted to a group of heavy base verbs through phonetic resemblance.   ³ extension from bhlā- (L. flāre 'blow', flāmen 'praise').   ⁴ analogy from class II.

63. Grammatical Change. In sections **58** to **62** bold-face type indicates instances of 'grammatical change', i.e. the effect of Verner's Law within the verb system. A brief survey of the tables suggests the statement of **20 d**: that in the first three classes the change is very regular, in classes V, VI, VII very irregular. 'Regular' means Gmc. voiceless spirants, f þ ƕ s, in the first two forms (pres. and pret. sg.) and Gmc. voiced spirants, ƀ ð ȝ z, in the last two forms (pret. pl. and past part.). The reason for this is stated in **20 a, b**. All standard grammars assert, or at least imply, that this regularity originally belonged to all classes, but that internal leveling (leveling within the several forms of a given word) had interfered with it. It is likely that this axiomatic belief in the comprehensive scope of Verner's Law has greatly retarded the recognition of the great importance of the aorist for the Gmc. preterit.

It is not very easy to disprove the current view by statistical facts. A certain amount of analogical disturbance must be expected even in early documents, and it is really surprising that in spite of it the conditions are as transparent as we find them. But there are a number of weighty elements of uncertainty. External analogy ('Systemzwang', the influence of established grammatical types upon verbs of different type) had been a very important factor in the Gmc. verb system since earliest times. Scribes are not always consistent and often contradict one another. Finally, the evidence of the several Gmc. dialects is very unequal in scope and importance. In Gothic, 'Systemzwang' had either leveled out or prevented grammatical change in the regular strong verbs; the only exception is *standan—stōþum*, which, by the way, supports rather the first than the second of these alternatives: *d* after *n* presupposes the existence of Gmc. ð. The alternation *s* : *z* (*r*) is evident both in Norse and West Germanic, but for the other spirants we find the following differences: Norse spelling can give evidence only for the velars, with the exception of very few cases such as *finna*. In Old Saxon and Old English Verner's Law can be detected in the case of velars and dentals, but the latter is not always certain, since the scribes are often careless in distinguishing *d* and ð (our grammars normalize in this respect). Only in Old High German all three series of consonants are kept distinct. This should, therefore, be the starting point for a statistical analysis. These are the facts (for details, consult the special grammars of the several dialects):

Old High German: Class I. Up to 900 A.D., 12 verbs show grammatical change consistently, only Otfrid wavers slightly. Of 3 other verbs we know only the participles but not the preterits.

Class II. 5 verbs show regular change. Only *fluhun* 'they fled' is leveled; this is doubtless due to the contrast to *fliogan*, with which it was originally identical (**29 d**). On account of OE *flugon* we may safely assume that it formerly showed the change.

Class III. 3 verbs show the change, *findan, werdan, swelhan*, but *findan* is sometimes leveled in Tatian (where, however, the distinction between *d* and *t* is inconsistent anyway), and *werdan* begins to show leveling in several documents. *hwerfan* sometimes introduces *b* into the present, and vice versa, *f* into the preterit plural. *felhan* has no change, perhaps on account of its semantic contrast to *folgēn*.

In these three classes, then, we have 20 (or 21, including *fliohan*) verbs with regular change, 1 or 2 without change, and 1 with early crossing of the two forms.

Class V. *s/z*: with *lesan, lārun* occurs, but *lāsun* is more frequent in every century. *jesan, kresan, ginesan* have no change (except for the very rare *ginārun*). *wārun*, however, is used everywhere (but the participle in *giwesan* has *s*, although here we surely should expect Verner's Law). This points to early contamination. The following explanation is likely: lenis articulation is a basic condition of Verner's Law (**20**); the verbum substantivum has as a rule little sentence stress and therefore lenis articulation. Thus, we may expect voicing of the spirant exactly as in E. *the, that*, etc. and their Scandinavian cognates. In the participle *s* must be due to leveling with the infinitive which has the same stem vowel.

þ/ð: with *quedan, quātun* occurs, but as early a writer as the scribe of Isidor uses it rarely; the same thing is true in Ludwigslied. Tatian has *quādun* regularly. Otfrid has this oftener than *quātun*.

ƕ/ʒ: grammatical change hardly occurs at all. We do find *gisewan*, but not **sāwun*. *gifehan, fnehan, jehan, giscehan* have only *h*.

Thus: in the preterit of this class, 8 verbs never show the change, 3 show some uncertainty, and only in 1, *wesan*, is the change fixed.

Class VI. Of this class Braune, Ahd. Gramm. 346, Anm. 2, says characteristically: 'Die auf *h* ausgehenden verba *dwahan, lahan, slahan, giwahan* haben im Ahd. grammatischen wechsel, der nicht nur vollkommen fest ist, sondern sogar sein *g* (statt *h*) auf den sg. prät. ausgedehnt hat.' This is a perfect example of contradictio in adjecto. Hartmann (in Dieter, AD) says (490): 'doch ist ... der konsonant des pluralis stets auf den singularis übertragen.'

We have here four verbs with *h/ʒ*, where the standard view would assume Gmc. *slaƕan, slōh—slōʒum, slaʒan*, while the vowel grades point to *slaʒan—slōƕ, slōhum—slaʒan*. The OHG conditions are quite irregular, showing great uncertainty in the language of the period. The same is true of *heffen*. *stantan* has *t* in all forms, but this is without a doubt later leveling. Gothic has the original condition: *standan, stōþ, stōþum, *standans* or **stadans*.

Class VII. Only *fāhan* and *hāhan* are subject to Verner's Law. We have *fiang, fiangum, hiang, hiangum*, clear products of leveling. *blāsan, skeidan, zeisan, houwan* have no change.

In these three classes then, only 1 verb has regular grammatical change, 8 never show it (in the preterit) and about 2 have irregular distribution of the consonants, indicating secondary development.

To sum up, in classes I, II, III we have 20 regular changes and 2 or 3 irregular cases.

In classes V, VI, VII, 1 regular change, about 8 irregular cases.

Or: Among some 3 dozen verbs that can show the change, it is quite regular in classes I, II, III, but occurs in what is considered its standard distribution in only 1 verb of classes V, VI, VII.

Old Saxon has leveled so widely that it has no value as evidence.

Old English: The frequent confusion between ð and *d* lessens the reliability of the evidence, but the figures are approximately these:

Class I.   8 verbs show regular grammatical change, 3 do not; but of the latter, *mīþan* and *wrīþan* are uncertain.

Class II.   7 verbs have the change, only *ābrēoþan* shows leveling.

Class III.   *findan* is leveled in accordance with *bindan*, the other 2 available verbs (*weorþan* and *feolan* < **feolhan*) have the change, but also analogical *fǽlon*, *fūlon*.

In these three classes 17 verbs have regular change, 4 do not (3 of them have ð/*d*).

Class V.   4 verbs have the change regularly: *sēon*, *gefēon*, *wesan*, *cweþan* (the last is not quite certain on account of the confusion between ð and *d*). *genesan*, *lesan* do not change.   For *sēon*, *gefēon*, the desire for contrast to the present may have been a contributing factor, since the unchanged forms of the preterit plural would have been *sōn*, *gefōn*.

Class VI.   No regular change.   The 5 verbs with *h* 'carry over' the *g* into the singular (*slōg*) as in Old High German.   Again, desire for contrast to the present may be in part responsible.   *hebban* is irregular.

Class VII.   *fōn*, *hōn* have *feng*, *heng*, as in Old High German, a leveling that doubtless goes back to Prim. Gmc. times.

The result for Old English is approximately this: Classes I, II, III, 17 to 20 verbs with grammatical change, 1 to 4 without it.   V, VI, VII: Only 10 fairly regular changes; the others either do not change at all, or do so very irregularly.

Old Norse: There is scanty evidence of any sort, partly because only *h s* and *nþ* could show grammatical change, partly because several otherwise available verbs were transferred to the weak conjugation.

Class I offers no evidence, in class II there are 3 verbs which show the change (*kiōsa*, *friōsa*, *flȳia*, in the older language or poetry *kørom*, *frørom*, *flugom*).   In class III *finna* has change.   There are then 4 verbs in favor of the standard view, none against it.

Class V.   *vesa* has the change, which later is transferred to the present and preterit singular (*vera*, *var*, *vǫro*), probably due to lack of sentence stress; as in West Germanic, *siā* has *sōm* in the preterit plural.

But in East-Norse (OSw.), the pret. pl. *sågho*, with analogical grammatical change, is found, later transferred to the sing., *sågh* for *sā*; cf. Sw. *såg, sågo*.

Class VI. *standa*, as in Gothic, provides evidence for our theory; the 5 *h*-verbs have change, *slā, slō, slōgom, slegenn*; but *slō* may just as well go back to **slōȝ* as to **slōƕ* (like *draga—drō*).

Class VII. *fā* and *hanga* have irregular change, *ausa* and *blāsa* no change at all.

The ON evidence is not sufficient support for either theory.

Gothic has grammatical change only in *standan* (aside from some preterit presents which are not included in this analysis).

These statistical facts offer a strong argument in favor of the view that Verner's Law in the 'regular' distribution belonged originally only to the first three classes. In the last three classes the vowel grade is an indication of the location of the accent, and therefore we should expect the voiceless spirants in the first three forms of class V, and in the second and third forms of class VI, and this is just what we find, almost without exception. Class VII is a combination of several accent types and is correspondingly irregular in regard to Verner's Law.

NOTE: In so far as the transmitted vocabulary can be considered, if not as complete, at least as representative, there is a peculiar difference between Gothic and West Germanic in the number of strong verbs with roots ending in spirants. Gothic has 14 such verbs in classes I, II, III, and 16 in classes V, VI, VII. In Old English there are 21 against 15, in Old High German 23 against 20. The weight of the second group is further increased in Gothic by the fact that the reduplicated preterits gave to class VII the stamp of a unified type, but it is decreased in West Germanic by the widely differing appearance of the several subtypes of that class. In Old English, the loss of *h* in the 5 verbs of class VI still more weakens the leveling influence of this group. Perhaps the numerical difference is not large enough to allow any confident conclusion, but if it means anything at all, we may assume this: grammatical change is chiefly a question of the preterit plural. In Gothic, the 16 verbs of the type *sēhum, slōhum (faifā-hum)* not only retained their forms, but the type was extended over the 14 verbs of class I, II, III. In Old High German, the original conditions were largely preserved, but the pattern of the 23 verbs with 'regular' grammatical change seems to have had some slight influence on some of the other 20. In Old English the influence of the 21 verbs on the 15 was stronger, but by no means sufficient to bring about anything like regularity in the scope of Verner's Law.

This numerical difference may have been one of the causes for the absence of Verner's Law in the Go. strong verb.

64. Later Developments. In the later history of the Gmc. languages there is a trend towards leveling in several directions. Where the two numbers of the preterit have different stem vowels, one of them is leveled out; grammatical change is more and more eliminated, and many strong verbs are shifted to the weak conjugation. The trend is strongest in English, weakest in Dutch. The details belong to the historical grammar of the several languages, but comprehensive treatments in dissertations and other monographs are highly desirable. Only a few illustrations are given here to characterize the directions.

In NORSE, the two forms of the preterit in the first five classes appear consistently as one. The old plural forms disappear and Verner's Law is leveled completely so that there is no longer any difference whatso-ever between singular and plural: Norw. *drive—drēv* 'drive', *gyte—gjøt* 'pour', *drikke—drakk* 'drink', *bære—bar* 'bear'. Transition to the weak conjugation is frequent: *skapde* (Ger.) 'schuf', *læsde* 'las', *svømmede* 'schwamm', *fangede* 'fing' (from *fange*; also *fā—fik*), *skede* 'geschah'.

In ENGLISH, the number of strong verbs has been greatly reduced by replacements from Norman French. Among those remaining, the trend is virtually the same as in Norse, but some classes (and dialects) give preference to the vowel of the singular, others to that of the plural. The former is the case with Standard English *rode, drove, ran, sang*, the latter with *bit, found, gave; bore, stole, broke* have introduced the vowel of the participle into the preterit. The only preterit that retains two vowels and grammatical change is *was—were*. Among the many trans-fers to the weak conjugation are *chew, help, laugh, fold*.

GERMAN and DUTCH are more conservative. German has also, in various ways, given up the double stem vowel of the preterit, with the exception of *ward—wurden*, but has retained several instances of gram-matical change; however, singular and plural of the preterit have always the same consonant so that the alternation is only between present and preterit (and past participle): *schneiden—schnitt, leiden—litt, ziehen—zog* etc. Transfers to the weak conjugation are, e.g., *neigen, bellen, schmerzen, kneten, fluchen*.

Dutch has not only retained the two preterit vowels to a large extent, but also until rather recently some grammatical change, like German: *tijgen, teeg, tegen, getegen* (Middle Dutch still *tien, teech*) 'show'; (*tien* >) *tiegen, toog, togen, getogen* 'lead'. Transfers to weak verbs are frequent, e.g., *dijen* 'thrive', *helen, beren, waden, waken* etc. *was—waren* still shows grammatical change.

65. The Preterit-Presents. The IE reduplicated perfect denoted a completed action, resulting in a present state. But in addition to this, there existed a perfect of identical morphological structure but without

reduplication. With these the psychological emphasis lay on the state
attained and not on the action of which it was the result. Only one
perfect of this type shows a fairly wide currency among the IE languages in the forms in which we know them: Sk. *vĕda—vidmá*, Gk.
(ϝ)οῖδα—(ϝ)ἴδμεν (for *ἰδμέν), OSl. *vēdē*, Go. *wait—witum* 'I know',
is the unreduplicated perfect of a root *weid- (L. *video*, Go. *-weitan*).
These forms have been given the appropriate name 'Preterit Presents'.

   The Gmc. languages have preserved this perfect type to a much
greater extent than any other IE language. In fact, they doubtless
added to this group in prehistoric times. Thus, Go. pl. *kunnum* is an
n-formation to the IE root *ĝen(ē)-* (L. *gnō-*, Gk. γνω-, OSl. *zna-*, Lith.
žinōti < *ĝn̥nō*). It was probably a present with zero grade (*ĝn̥-no-* or
-nwo-), but fell in line with verbs of the type *rann—runnum* and thus,
forming a new singular, became identical in form with the preterits of
the third class; the similarity in meaning of *wait* and *lais* may have
contributed. It is impossible to tell to what extent we should assume
such new formations. In a small isolated group like this, irregularities
are bound to occur, and we cannot hope to explain all of them. We
simply must take the Gmc. facts as we find them.

   The conjugation of the forms with present meaning is entirely that
of the regular preterit in Gothic and Norse as far as the endings are
concerned (**73 a**), but West Germanic shows a difference: The second
singular of the 'regular' strong verbs is an aorist (**56 b**) (OHG *zigi*,
zugi, *wurti* etc.), because their preterit is a syncretistic paradigm in
the sense of **57**. But the 'present' of the οῖδα-type of verbs is not
syncretistic. It has no association with the aorist, and therefore the
second person singular has in West Germanic the same form as in
Gothic and Norse, namely, the genuine perfect form, and has preserved
this remarkably well in English up to the present time (*thou shalt*), in
German into a rather late period of early New High German (Volkslied:
du solt).

   These verbs formed a new preterit for which there is no IE equivalent
of clearly definable meaning, although the type as such is common
enough. It is a *t*-formation, such as L. *plectō*, Gmc. *flehtan* 'pleat', as
against Gk. πλέκω; L. *pectō* 'comb', Gmc. *fehtan* 'fight' (Gk. πέκτω
and πέκω). This is discussed in **66**.

   (The examples are arranged in the order present sg., present pl.,
preterit, past participle. The infinitive has everywhere the vowel of
the present pl., e.g., Go. *witan** etc.).

Class I.

Go.	wait	witum	wissa	wiss	'certain', -weis 'knowing'	b
ON	veit	vito	vissa	vīss	'certain'	
OE	wāt	witon	wisse	wīs	'wise'	
OS	wēt	witun	wissa	wīs		
OHG	weiz	wizzum	wissa	wīs.		

Gk. (ϝ)οῖδα, ἴδμεν etc., see above. For ss in wissa, cf. **29 a**. In OE wista, OHG wista, westa, t was added analogically.

The regular strong verb with normal grade in the present occurs in Go. in-weitan 'pay homage', fra-weitan 'avenge', OE wītan 'reproach'. With ēi̯-suffix (verb of class III W), Go. witan 'watch, observe'; active past part. weitwōþs 'witness' (suffix -wĕs-/wŏs-/wŏt- : εἰδώς, fem. ἰδυῖα < *weid-wŏt-s, *wid-us-yə, cf. Go. bērusjōs 'parents', plural of fem. *bērusi 'having borne').

wiss < *wid-to-; with normal grade, -weis and its cognates in the other Gmc. dialects, < *weid-to-, with simplification of ss after the long vowel; ON vīss has ss < sR.

Go. *lais lisum* lista*.*

Root *lei-, with t-determinant in Go. leiþan; s-determinant as in Go. lais, in L. līra < *leisā 'furrow', de-līrus 'insane', OSl. lēcha ('garden)-bed'; causative (class I W): Go. laisjan, OE lǣran, OFris. lēra, OS lērian, OHG lēren 'teach'.

Go.	áih	áigum, áihum[1]	áihta	áigans*	'have, own'
ON	ā	eigo	—	—	
OE	āg, āh	āgon	āhte	ǣgen, āgen	'own'
OS	ēh*	ēgun	ēhta	ēgan	
OHG	ēh*	eigum	—	eigan.	

*oiḱ-/iḱ- (Gmc. ai in plural is leveling), Sk. ícē 'have power over'.

[1] grammatical change, h by analogy.

Class II.

Go.	daug (impersonal)	—	—	'suffice'	c
ON	—	—	—		
OE	dēag	dugon	dohte		
OS	dōg	dugun	—		
OHG	toug 'is useful'	tugun	tohta		
Lith.	daũg 'much'.				

It is highly probable that originally E. buy also belonged to this group. Go. bugjan, bauhta, ON byggia, bygþa, OE bycgan bohte, OS buggian are related to Go. biugan. The present seems to have been a j-formation with iterative meaning, from an aorist present *bugan.

Such iterative-momentary verbs (verbs that denote repeated momentary happenings) are a standardized type in Slavic; e.g. *u-mirati* 'to be on one's deathbed' is a regular iterative of the momentary verb *u-mrēti* 'to die'. For the semantic development cf. **58 b.**

d   Class III.

Go.	kann	kunnum	kunþa[1]		kunþs[1]	'known'
ON	kann	kunnom	kunna[2]		kunnat, kūþr[3]	
OE	can(n)	cunnon	cūþe		cūþ, on-cunnen	
OS	kan	kunnun	konsta[4]		—	
OHG	kan	kunnum	konda, konsta[4]	kund.		

kunnan belongs to the root *ĝnō-* (γνω-, L. *-gnōscō*, Sk. *jā-nāti* 'know', OSl. *znāti*), zero grade *ĝn-* + *neu/nu*-suffix; *ĝnē-*, ablaut variation to *ĝnō-*, yields OHG *bi-knāen* 'recognize' (I W).

uf-kunnan 'recognize' follows in general III W, but the preterit is either *uf-kunnaida* or *uf-kunþa*; past part. *ufkunnaiþs*. Similarly *ga-kunnan* 'experience, read', *at-kunnan* 'grant', *ana-kunnan* 'read'. But *fra-kunnan* 'despise', *sik gakunnan* 'surrender' are preterit presents.

ON	ann		unnom	unna[2]		unn(a)t
OE	an(n)		unnon	ūþe[3]		ge-unnen
OS	—		—	3 sg. gi-onsto[4]		—
OHG	an 'love, gönnen'		unnum	onda, onsta		— .

[1] Obviously an analogical formation, since zero grade in the first syllable would require Verner's Law. The accent must have shifted before Verner's Law, probably on account of the frequent use of this verb as a modal auxiliary, which led to the falling-rising sentence rhythm ⸜ x x ⸍, for which the falling-falling rhythm ⸜ x ⸍ x was substituted: **rǽðana kunþō* > **rǽðan kúnþa*. Probably the form was further supported by the participle **kunþa-*, which is a frequent type; in adjectives secondarily accented zero grade occurs both in Germanic and elsewhere: Sk. *ríkta-* 'empty', as an adjective, but *riktá-* in participial function. Probably sentence rhythm was here too the reason for this abnormal accent.
[2] **31 b.**   [3] **29 c.**   [4] *st* analogical (cf. *wista*).

Old High German has also the compound *gi-unnan* > *gunnan* = MHG *gunnen, gonde*, NHG *gönnen*, now a regular weak verb.

Go. *duginnan*, OE *beginnan*, OS OHG *biginnan* are probably related to this verb. While in historical times regularly a verb of III S, we find weak preterits: OHG *bigonda*, MHG *begonde, begunde*, early NHG (occasionally as late as the 18th century, cf. Paul, Deutsche Gramm. III §188, Anm.) *begun(n)te, begon(n)te*. The Gmc. root *an-* (e.g., Go. *uz-anan* 'expire', VI S) is related to Gk. ἄνεμος, L. *animus, -a*, and the meaning of the latter word seems to have been the starting point in Germanic. Transferred from class VI to class III under the influence of *kann kunnum, ann* meant 'I have put my mind, my heart, on somebody or something; I love'. *ga(gi-)-an* came to be used in a more concrete sense, 'I have put my mind on some work, I am starting it'. To this was formed a regular present of class III (*-ginnan*) and various other prefixes were added: *du-* in Gothic, *bi-* in Old High German, Old Saxon, Old English, *on-*, *ā-* in Old English, *in-* in Old High German. A preterit present *-gann*, *-gunnum* then assumed the usual preterit function of such forms, but the old preterit *-gi-onda* > *-gonda* continued to exist for many centuries.

Go.	*þarf*[1]	*þaurbum*[1]	*þaurfta*	*þaurfts*	(adj. 'useful')
ON	*þarf*	*þurfom*	*þurfta*	*þurft*	
OE	*þearf*	*þurfon*	*þorfte*	—	
OS	*tharf*	*thurƀun*	*thorfta*	—	
OHG	*darf*	*durfun*	*dorfta* MHG *durft*	'necessary' (adj.).	

Root *terp-*: Gk. τέρπω 'satisfy', τέρπομαι 'enjoy', Lith. *tarpà* 'welfare', Sk. *tárpati* 'is satisfied'.

(*sik*) *gaþarban* (III W) 'abstain', ON *þarfa* 'be necessary', OE *þearfian* (II W), OS *tharƀōn* (II W), OHG *darbēn* (III W) 'be in need'.

[1] Like *aih—aigum*, one of the few instances of grammatical change in Gothic.

Go.	*ga-dars*	*gadaursum*	*gadaursta*
OE	*dearr*	*durron*	*dorste*
OS	*gidar*	**gidurun*	*(gi)dorsta*
OHG	*gitar*	*gidurrum*	*gidorsta*
	'dare'.		

Gk. θαρσέω 'I am courageous', θαρσύς 'bold', Lith. *drᶒsù* 'dare'.

Class IV. The 'regular' strong verbs of class IV and V have Gmc. *e* *ǣ* in the plural. These are aorist forms, but the preterit presents are perfects pure and simple, without aorist admixture, and have therefore in the plural the regular ablaut grade of the perfect, namely, zero grade: *skulum* as against *stēlum*, *munum* as against *nēmum*. Cf. also (see above) the perfect ending *-t* in the 2 singular in West Germanic, instead of the aorist forms *stāli*, *nāmi*.

Go.	*skal*	*skulum*	*skulda*[1]	*skulds*	(adj. 'guilty')
ON	*skal*	*skulom*	*skulda*[1], *skylda*[2]	*skyldr*	'necessary'
OE	*sceal*	*sculon, scylon*[2]	*sc(e)olde*	—	
OS	*scal*	*sculun*	*scolda*	—	
OHG	*scal*[3]	*sculum(ēs)*	*scolta*	*giscolit.*	

[1] Verner's Law.   [2] *y* from optative.   [3] also forms without *k*; in the zero grade *skl̥-*, *k* is apt to disappear before the development of *u*, to lighten the heavy consonant group, but the change is not carried through consistently   *o* for *a* (*sol*) is probably due to the following *l*, as in *holōn* for *halōn*; but it appears in the OHG period almost only in Alemannian.

L. *scelus* 'guilt, crime', Lith. *skeliù* 'I am guilty', *skolà* 'guilt'.

Go.	*man*	*munum*	*munda*	*munds*
ON	*man*	*munom*	*munþa*[1], *munda*	—
OE	*man*	*munon*	*munde*	*gemunen*
OS	*-man*	**munun*	*-monsta*	—

'believe'.

munan (III W) 'intend'.

OE *manian*, OS *manōn* (II W), OHG *manōn* (III W) 'admonish'.

Root *men-*: L. *me-min-ī*, Sk. *man-yatē* 'believe', Gk. μαίνομαι < *μανjομαι 'I am inspired, insane', L. *moneō*.

[1] Gmc. *ð*, not *þ*; the latter would have given **munna*; *munda* is a later form.

Class V.

f	Go.	*ganah*	—	—	*binaúhts* 'permitted'
	OE	*ge-neah*	*genugon*	*genohte*	—
	OHG	*ganah*	—	—	—

'is enough'.

Streitberg, GE 156 f. and Kieckers, HGG 264, prefer to put this verb into the fourth class, on account of the vowel grade of Go. *binaúhts*, 'der in der fünften Reihe keinen Platz hat.' That is merely a matter of terminology; the vowel is like that in Go. *trudan*, *brukans*, which may equally well be put into class III, IV, or V. The lines between the classes are not as sharp as that. The lengthened grade of the derived adjective Go. *ganōhs*, ON *gnōgr*, OE *genōh* (NE *enough*), OS *ginōh*, OHG *ginuog(i)* points to a regular *e/o*-base with the usual vowel reduction in the perfect plural, and we have to assume that shva secundum became in Germanic *u* (Go. *aú* before *h*) not only before but also after liquid (*trudan*) or nasal; the same assumption is necessary for *skulum*, *munum*.

Cf. L. *nancīscor* 'obtain', Sk. *náśati* 'he obtains'.

Class VI.

g	Go.	*mag*	*magum*	*mahta*	*mahts*
	ON	*mā*	*megum*[1]	*mātta*[2]	*mātt*
	OE	*mæg*	*magon*	*meahte, mihte*	—
	OS	*mag*	*mugun*	*mahta*	—
	OHG	*mag*	*mugum*[3]	*mahta, mohta*[3]	—

[1] *e* from the optative *mega*.　　[2] < *mahta*, **31 b**.　　[3] the forms with *u*, *o* are due to the influence of *kunnan*, *skolan*.

This is a heavy base, like Go. *tēkan, standan*, ON *taka, standa*. Normal grade *māgh-* appears in Gk. μῆχος, Dor. μᾶχος 'contrivance', reduced grade *məgh-* in OSl. *mogǫ* 'I can', Lith. *magóti* 'be helpful'. Regular strong verbs of class VI do not show any genuine perfect forms. We may assume that the pl. *magum* was the starting point for this preterit present and that the singular, theoretically perhaps *mōg*, was replaced by *mag* under the influence of *kann, skal* etc.

Go. *ōg* *agum* or *ōgum?*[1] *ōhta*.
The causative 'to frighten' appears with both vowel grades: *ōgjan* and *-agjan*. Cf. Gk. ἄχομαι 'I am sad', heavy base.

[1] the present participle *un-agands* 'fearless' points to *agum*.

Go.	gamōt	'have room'		gamōsta
OE	mōt	'be allowed'	mōton	mōste
OS	mōt	'be allowed, be able'	mōtun	mōsta
OHG	muoz		muozum	muosa, later muosta.

A light base which belongs to class VI in the same sense as *faran, graban* etc. Gk. μήδομαι 'I contrive', L. *meditāri* 'consider', Go. *mitan* 'measure'. *st* in the preterit has been taken over from Go. *gadaursta*, OS OHG *konsta* etc.

The Weak Preterit

66. The Dental Suffix. The present stems of the weak verbs have a been discussed in **54**. Gmc. grammar distinguishes the following classes:

I. Stems in *ja/ji/i* (**54 f**), Go. *nasjan, sōkjan*.
II. Stems in *ō* (**54 k**), Go. *salbōn*.
III. Stems in *ai ē* (**54 g**), Go. *haban* (pret. *habaida*), OHG *habēn*.
IV. Stems in *nō* (**54 i**), Go. *fullnan* (pret. *fullnōda*).

With the exception of preterits of the type of *baúhta* (see below), the preterit is formed by the addition of a suffix with Gmc. ð: Go. *nasida, salbōda, habaida* (OHG *habēta*), *fullnōda*.

The personal endings of those classes, including preterits of the type b of *baúhta* as well as those of preterit presents (*kunþa* etc.) are the same in any given dialect. Preterit of Gmc. *laʒjana-* 'lay', causative of *liʒjana-* 'lie':

Go.	lagida	lagidēs	lagida	lagidēdum	lagidēduþ	lagidēdun
ON	lagþa	lagþer	lagþe	lǫgþom	lǫgþoþ	lǫgþo
OE	legde	legdes	legde	legdon	legdon	legdon
OS	legda	legdes (-os)	legde	legdun	legdun	legdun
OHG[1]	legita	legitōs	legita	legitōm (-um)	legitōt (-ut)	legitōn (-un).

[1] the plural forms with ō are Alemannian and partly Rhine Franconian; those with u are Bavarian and Franconian.

Likewise:

Go.	kunþa	kunþēs
ON	kunna	kunner
OE	cūþe	cūþes
OS	konsta	konstes (-os)
OHG	konda	kondōs etc.

c   The origin of the dental suffix and some associated problems of conjugation (endings) are the most debated topic of Gmc. grammar, and we are still far from a complete solution of the problem, even though Hirt (HU 2. 160) says: 'Ich halte somit das schwache Präteritum im wesentlichen für aufgeklärt.' The bibliography up to 1912 is given very fully in Collitz's admirable monograph 'Das schwache Präteritum und seine Vorgeschichte', Hesperia 1, (1912); later publications are listed by A. W. M. Odé, 'Das schwache Präteritum in den germanischen Sprachen' (Amsterdam 1926) and by Collitz, "Das schwache Präteritum als Mischbildung", PMLA 43. 593 ff. (1928).

The main questions are these: What is the origin of the dental? What is the explanation of the Go. endings, -dēdum, -dēduþ, -dēdun? What is their relation to the endings of the other Gmc. languages? As Collitz points out in the last named article, the chief obstacle in reaching a solution has been the attempt to find a single key for all of these questions.[1] Since Franz Bopp (Das Konjugationssystem der Sanskrit-Sprache 151–7 [1816]) and Jacob Grimm (Deutsche Grammatik 1. 563 [1819]) the view, which had been suggested as early as 1718 by Diederich von Stade (cf. Collitz, l. c., 1), has persisted that the Gmc. weak preterit is a combination of the verb-stem plus the auxiliary *dhē-/dhō- 'do' (Gk. τί-θη-μι, L. fē-ci, OE dōn, OHG tuon). Among recent defenders of this view are Boer, OH 263 [1918]: 'kan er bij der hoofdmassa wel geen twijfel over bestaan, dat het gevormd is door samenstelling met vormen van den wortel idg. dhē-/dhō-'; Hirt, Idg. Gr. 4: 'Was das

schwache Präteritum bei den schwachen Verben betrifft, so ist die
Zusammensetzungshypothese einfach das Gegebene. Bei got. *salbō-da*,
salbō-dēs, Pl. *salbō-dēdum* liegt sie auf der Hand, und es bedarf eines
ganzen Rattenkönigs von Analogiebildungen, um eine andere Hypothese
an die Stelle der alten Bopp'schen zu setzen.'; HU 2. 56: 'Diese Erklärung liegt auf der Hand. Sie wird durch die besten Parallelen
gestützt, dass sie sich trotz aller Angriffe doch wieder aufdrängt. Ich
habe sie stets vertreten.'; Loewe, KZ 45. 334 ff. (1911); Chr. Rogge,
'Die Entwicklung des schwachen Präteritums im Germanischen als
psychologische Form-Angleichung', Btr. 50. 321 ff. (1926); Sverdrup,
'Das germanische Dentalpräteritum', NTS 2. 5 ff. The adherents of
this view consider the NWGmc. forms (partly also the Go. singular)
as contractions of the compound forms for which the exact procedure
cannot be ascertained and probably does not need to be. The preterit
forms of the preterit presents (Go. *kunþa—kunþēdum*) and a small
number of other weak verbs without a connecting vowel (Go. *waúrhta*
etc.; see below) do not lend themselves to the *dhē*-theory. They must
be *t*-forms; so they are generally ascribed to the influence of the verbal
adjective (participle) in -*to*- (*kunþs*, *þaurfts*, *waúrhts*). Cf. especially
Sverdrup, l. c., 94 and Hirt, HU 2. 158. It is difficult to see why this
group of verbs, most of which are of particularly frequent occurrence,
should carry out such an unusual type of leveling, but the possibility
must be admitted.

Combinations of stem and auxiliary verb are frequent in other IE
languages, e.g., the following imperfect forms: L. *amābam* 'I loved',
OSl. *delěachъ* 'I did', Lith. *dìrbdavau* 'I worked', and perhaps the Gk.
passive aorist, ἐτιμήθην 'I was honored'. The second elements of
these compounds are: L. -*bam* < -*bhwām*, Ital. *-f(u)ām*, a subjunctive
of the root *bheu-* 'to be'; OSl. -*achъ* < -*ēsom*, a regular imperfect of the
root *es-* 'to be'; Lith. -*davau*, a preterit either of the root **dhē-*, or,
more likely, of the root **dou-* (Go. *taujan* 'do'; Gk. δοῦλος 'slave';
Hirt, l. c., 158); Gk. -θην perhaps also from the root *dhē-*, but see
below. Perhaps the closest parallel to the Gmc. forms are Oscan
forms such as *aa-manaffed* 'posuit' which Brugmann, Grdr.[2] 2. 3. 149,
explains from **-fefed*, reduplicated perfect of **dhē-* = OHG *teta*.

Of other explanations the following are especially important: Wackernagel-Behaghel (in W.'s Miszellen zur griechischen Grammatik, KZ
30. 313): 'Sodann macht mich Behaghel auf die Möglichkeit aufmerk-
sam, von -*thēs* aus das germanische schwache Präteritum zu erklären.
Soweit ich die Sache übersehe, scheint mir ein solcher Zusammenhang

grosse Wahrscheinlichkeit zu haben; germ. *vuldēs* deckt sich Laut für
Laut mit altind. *vṛthā́s* (Whitney, Sanskrit Grammar §824 a); *waúrhtēs*
= ig. **vṛkthḗs.*' This statement is made in connection with Wacker-
nagel's explanation of the Gk. passive aorist, ἐλύθην, ἐλύθης, ἐλύθη, etc.:
He considers the second singular as the starting point of the whole
paradigm, identifying it with Sk. *-thās*, the secondary ending of the
medial second singular (e.g., ἐ-δό-θης = Sk. *a-di-thās* < IE **é-dǝ-
thēs*). Collitz (Sch. Prät. 19) believes 'dass der zweiten Singular hier
ein Einfluss auf die Gestaltung des ganzen Paradigmas zugewiesen wird,
der schwerlich im Einklang mit dem tatsächlichen Gebrauch dieser
Form steht.'

Collitz (l. c., 138 ff., but stated as early as 1888 in AJPh 9. 42 ff.,
and BB. 17. 227 ff.): The starting point is the third person singular of
the IE medial perfect:

Go. *nasj-a-da* (3 sg. pres. pass.): *nasi-da* (weak preterit) = Gk. λύ-ε-ται
(3 sg. pres. pass.) : λέ-λυ-ται (perf. pass.).

In his above-mentioned article, 'Das schwache Präteritum als Mischbildung', Collitz still attaches great weight to this explanation, but em-
phasizes the probability that other forms have contributed to the
gradual development of the weak preterit. He refers especially to IE
root aorists like Sk. *á-sthā-m*, *á-sthā-s*, *á-sthā-t*, Gk. ἔ-στη-ν; he considers the 3 sg. IE (*e-*)*stā-t* as identical with Go. *stōþ* and believes that
the dental spread from this form over the whole preterit; 'Es kann
keinem Zweifel unterliegen, dass als urgerm. Formen 1. und 3. sg.
stōþ, 1. pl. *stōdum*, 3. pl. *stōdun* anzusetzen sind. Die Pluralformen
stehen auf einer Linie mit westgerm. Formen wie *salbōdum* und *dēdum*.
Im Gotischen fehlt *dēdum* als selbständige Verbalform, während es
anscheinend in Pluralformen wie *salbo-dēdum*, *hausi-dēdum* usw. (also
im regelrechten Paradigma der schwachen Verba) enthalten ist.'

Each of these suggestions is plausible to a certain extent, and Collitz
may be right in considering a combination of them as a practical working
hypothesis. They have one weakness in common, that of assuming the
extension of a single personal ending over the whole paradigm, and the
fact that three different endings are taken as possible starting points
aggravates this weakness rather than lessens it. It must be admitted,
however, that in itself such a spread of a personal ending need not
arouse objection. Its assumption for the Greek passive aorist may or
may not be correct, but it is quite certain that in the modern Norse
languages the ending of the 2 sg., *-r* < *-si*, has been extended over the
whole present: Norw. *jeg elsker, du elsker, han elsker, vi elsker* etc.).

In the author's opinion the general principle of the explanation given by Brugmann, Btr. 39. 84 ff. (1914), is more convincing than any of these hypotheses. He considers the weak preterit 'als umbildung eines vorgermanischen themavokalischen präteritums auf *-to-m -te-s -te-t. Dieses gehörte zu der klasse der aus uridg. zeiten stammenden mit -to- gebildeten präsentia, deren formans dasselbe ist wie das der adjektivischen und substantivischen nomina auf -to- (-tā-)' (cf. Grdr. 2². 3. 282 ff.). Thus he connects Gk. imperfects like ἔπεκτον or aorists like ἔβλαστον with such Gmc. weak preterits as Go. *munda, baúhta* (with suffix accent as in Sk. *sphutá-ti*, Gk. βλαστεῖν; for the root accent of *kunþa* cf. **65 d**). Of the instances that he quotes the most interesting and convincing is perhaps Go. *ōg—ōhta* 'be afraid'; aside from the vowel grade this is the exact equivalent of Gk. ἄχομαι— ἄχθομαι (< əgh-—əgh-t-; ght > χθ by 'Bartholomae's Law') 'be sad, be in pain'; there is no perceptible difference in meaning between the two Gk. forms, but ἄχθομαι may have been an intensive at some time. In Gothic, the ə-grade appears in the part. *un-agands* 'unfearing' and in causatives: (*af-, in-, us-*)*agjan* 'frighten'.

Thus Wackernagel-Behaghel, Collitz (in two forms) and Brugmann derive the suffix of the Gmc. weak preterit from IE *t*, and Brugmann states (l. c., 85), 'Jeder versuch, der für die dentale des schwachen präteritums von . . . uridg. *t* ausgeht, hat . . . , was das rein lautliche betrifft, unbedingt freie hand.'

Brugmann's hypothesis is materially strengthened, if the -tā-form of the suffix rather than the -to-/-te-form is used as a starting point. This occurs in L. intensives (frequentatives, conatives) like *clamitāre* 'cry aloud', *iactāre* 'throw frequently', *captāre* 'try to catch'. These express modes of action (aspects), and it would be well in keeping with the general trend of the Gmc. verb system, if the -tā-suffix (or, for that matter, the -to-/-te-suffix) should there assume temporal function.

The following considerations may be helpful:

(1) The Go. -dē-d-forms should, at the start, be left out of consideration. Their contraction to the shorter NWGmc. forms presents such phonological difficulties that it should be admitted only if very strong arguments were brought forward—which so far has not been the case. Wilhelm Scherer considered them an innovation as early as 1868.

(2) The endings of the plural, OHG (Bav.—Franc.) -um, -ut, -un need not concern us. Unless a thoroughly convincing phonological explanation of their alleged contraction from -dēd-forms is offered, we may safely consider them as transfers from the strong preterit.

(3) This makes the Alemannian forms with -ō- the logical starting point. The plural endings are usually ascribed to the influence of the 2 sg. which has -ō- in all OHG dialects, but this needs explanation itself. To explain it as coming from the root *dhē-/dhō-* brings us back to the phonological anomaly of *þaurfta, kunþa, baúhta,* etc. Besides, there is such a strong trend in the Gmc. verb to have the same personal endings for any given tense in all, or nearly all, verb types that it is far more likely that the *u*-forms, as stated above, followed the pattern of the strong preterits, replacing older -ō-forms, than that the -ō-forms have replaced older -*u*-forms.

If we consider the Alemannian forms as original, we have an exact parallel to the L. -*tā*-verbs, and for this dialect no further explanation is necessary. The paradigm is IE -*tā́m, -tā́s, -tā́t, -tā́men, -tā́te, -tā́nt,* rather than Brugmann's -*tom, -tes, -tot,* etc.

For Old High German this hypothesis meets all requirements, and it also explains most of the forms of the other NWGmc. dialects as well as the Go. 1, 3 sg. *lagida.* But some of the forms (Go. *lagidēs,* ON *lagþer, lagþe,* OS *legdes, legde*) require the assumption of IE *ē*, which would become NWGmc. *ā* in accented syllables, but *e* in endings (Streitberg, UG 187 f.). An ablaut alternation of *ā* with *ē* does not exist, but a remote parallel may possibly be found in the L. subjunctive, where we have *ē* in the first conjugation (*laudēs, laudēmus*), but *ā* elsewhere (*agās, agāmus*). Of course, this parallel is by no means an adequate explanation; the origin of this *ē* must be admitted to be obscure. If we assume that Gmc. *ō* goes back to IE *ō*, we have regular ablaut alternation, as in the NWGmc. gen. pl. in -*ō* against Go. -*ē*; but an IE verb formation in -*tō*- does not exist elsewhere. At any rate, if IE *ē* of uncertain origin be assumed in interchange with *ā*, as in the L. subjunctive, the explanation of those NWGmc. forms that do not go back to *ā* is simple enough.

The plural forms of Old Norse and Old English can be either the result of leveling from the strong preterit, or can be traced to IE -*ā*-. The 2 sg. everywhere except in Old High German goes back to -*ēs* (OS -*os* is probably a borrowing from Old High German). The 1 sg. points to -*ām* (Run. *tawiðo, worahto,* etc.); Collitz traces it back to the medial ending -*ai,* which is phonologically possible for literary Norse (cf. BB 17. 1–53), but needlessly separates it from the Run. forms; OE -*e* < -*ām,* like acc. sg. fem. *giefe* < **ghebhām.* The 3 sg. must go back to -*ét* (Old English could also go back to -*āt,* but there is no reason to assume that).

These reconstructions do not explain the Go. dual and plural forms, but they are adequate for the Go. singular, if we assume that the quantity of $\bar{e}$ in the 2 sg. was preserved through the leveling influence of the dual and plural forms. But the -$d\bar{e}d$-forms clearly go back to the root $dh\bar{e}$- and must, therefore, be considered a Gothic innovation. A parallel to this secondary composition is offered by L. $d\bar{e}scendid\bar{\imath}$ for $d\bar{e}scend\bar{\imath}$, $respondid\bar{\imath}$ for $respond\bar{\imath}$. These followed the pattern of $condid\bar{\imath}$, from con-$d\bar{o}$, etc., and Brugmann (l. c., 94 f.) suggests that the Gothic innovation may likewise have started in imitation of compounds like OHG $untart\bar{a}tum$. Probably the 2 sg. in -$d\bar{e}s$ exerted some influence, being felt as a form of IE $dh\bar{e}$-, Gmc. $\eth\bar{æ}$-. The perfect of this verb was IE dhe-$dh\bar{e}$-a, -tha, -e, pl. dhe-$dh\vartheta$-men (the 2 and 3 pl. as well as the dual cannot be reconstructed with any certainty) > Gmc. $\eth e\eth\bar{æ}, \eth e\eth\bar{æ}\flat, \eth e\eth\bar{æ}, \eth e\eth am$ (or $\eth e\eth um$?); (Collitz, Sch. Prät. 145, assumes *dhe-dh-ai, the medial perfect, for WGmc. $deda$). The singular is preserved in West Germanic: OE $dyde$ (with irregular stem vowel, cf. **75 b**), OS $deda$, OHG $teta$; the OHG and OS plural was remodeled in accordance with the plural of the fifth class: OHG $t\bar{a}tum$, OS $d\bar{a}dum$ (but also $dedun$). The stem of the Go. forms of the dual and plural (-$d\bar{e}du$, -$d\bar{e}duts$, -$d\bar{e}dum$, -$d\bar{e}du\flat$, -$d\bar{e}dun$) corresponds exactly to this $d\bar{a}d$-, $t\bar{a}t$-, and there is no reason to doubt their identity. Starting with a misinterpretation of the 2 sg. in -$d\bar{e}s$, the verb 'to do' assumed the function of an auxiliary for the Gothic dual and plural. That Gothic, as we know it, does not possess the verb Gmc. *$\eth\bar{æ}$- as an independent verb, -$taujan$ being used instead, does not weaken but strengthens the probability of this view: It is quite frequent that words disappear from a language where they have come to be used as mere functional elements; thus in Romance -$mente$ became an adverbial suffix and was subsequently given up as a noun; similarly E. -$hood$ = Ger. -$heit$ (Go. $haidus$ 'manner, way'), Ger. -$schaft$, -tum (E. -dom as suffix, $doom$ as noun) lost their nominal character; L. $hom\bar{o}$ became an indefinite pronoun in the Romance languages, and later disappeared as a noun in several of them. Of course, this process is not consistently carried out; Old Norse also lost the verb $\eth\bar{æ}$-, substituting for it $g\phi rua$, although it had not made use of the lost verb to form a compound weak preterit.

67. The Connecting Vowel.

Class I. Syncopation and 'Rückumlaut' (cf. **49**). In addition to **a** the 'regular' four classes of weak verbs (**66 a**), Germanic possessed a number of verbs that had t-preterits without any connecting vowel. They are listed with an abundance of related material by Collitz, Sch.

Prät. 29–98 (literature, 29). They are primarily the preterit-presents (*þaurfta*, *kunþa*, etc.). Besides, the following verbs had preterits of this type probably since Prim. Gmc. times.

Pres.

Go.	*briggan*	*brūkjan*	*bugjan*	*sōkjan*	*þagkjan*	*þugkjan*	*waúrkjan*
ON	—	—	*byggia*	*sø̄kia*	*þekkia*	*þykkia*	*yrkia*
OE	*bringan*	(*brūcan*)[1]	*bycgan*	*sēcan*	*þencan*	*þyncan*	*wyrcan*
OS	*brengian*	(*brūkan*)[1]	*buggian*	*sōkian*	*thenkian*	*thunkian*	*wirkian*
OHG	*bringan*	*brūhhan*[2]	—	*suohhen*	*denken*	*dunchen*	*wurchen*
	'bring'	'use'	'buy'	'seek'	'think'	'seem'	'make'

Pret.

	brāhta	*brūhta*	*bauhta*	[*sōkida*][3]	*þāhta*	*þūhta*	*waúrhta*
	—	—	*bugþa*	*sōtta*	*þātta*	*þōtta*	*orta*
	brōhte	(*brēac*)	*bohte*	*sōhte*	*þōhte*	*þūhte*	*worhte*
	brāhta	(*brōk*)	—[4]	*sōhta*	*thāhta*	*thūhta*	*warhta*
	brāhta	*brūhta*	—	*suohta*	*dāhta*	*dūhta*	*wor(a)hta.*

[1] strong.   [2] strong or weak.   [3] analogical.   [4] part. *giboht.*

This group corresponds morphologically to the type of L. *capiō—captō* (with the exception of *briggan*, *brūkan* which have 'strong' presents), but the great majority of the preterits of the first class show the connecting vowel -*i*-, a reduction of the present suffix -*eie*-. In Gothic this is preserved everywhere, but in the other dialects it is subject to syncopation. The chronology of this syncopation varies according to the dialect and the phonological type of the stem. Some of the details of the process are still obscure. The general principle, as discussed in **49,** was first stated by Sievers and is frequently referred to as 'Sievers' Law': in West Germanic the medial vowel disappeared after a long syllable, but was for the time being preserved after a short stem syllable. 'Long' stems in this sense include polysyllabic stems so that we have the three types OE *dēman* 'judge', *drencan* 'submerge', *ōrettan* 'fight'; a monosyllabic stem with short vowels whose final consonants had been doubled through the WGmc. consonant lengthening counts as 'short'. Thus, the stem of OHG *brennan* 'burn', with Gmc. *nn* < *nw*, is long, but that of *zellen* < **taljan* 'tell' is short. Paul, Btr. 7. 136 f., extends this law to Norse where, however, its consequences are quite different.

b   As explained in **49 g,** syncopation is the direct cause of 'Rückumlaut', and the general principle is this: if in a given dialect and a given type of verb umlaut preceded syncopation, the preterit is mutated; if syncopation took place sooner, rückumlaut resulted. In general, therefore, we should expect rückumlaut in long-stem verbs but not in short-stem verbs, but the actual conditions are far more complicated than that.

In literary Old Norse, all preterits of this class show syncopation. Unsyncopated forms appear in some early Run. inscriptions, e.g. *faihiðo* 'I wrote' (Einang, 4th cent.), *hlaiwiðo* 'I buried' (Kjølevig, 7th cent.). Long-stem verbs have umlaut in all forms, short-stem verbs only in the present, that is, they show rückumlaut. This apparently paradoxical condition finds its explanation in Axel Kock's umlaut-theory (**41 d** and Note in appendix): With long stems *i* disappeared during the first umlaut period (before 700); it palatalized the preceding consonant, and this caused umlaut: Go. *hausjan—hausida*, ON *heyra—heyrþa*, like Run. *ʒastiʀ* > literary *gestr*; but after short stems, *i* disappeared after this umlaut period had come to an end, and the stem vowel remained unaffected: Go. *lagjan—lagida*, ON *leggia—lagþa*, like Run. *saliʀ* > literary *salr*.

Among the WGmc. dialects, Old English seems to come closest to the original conditions.[1] The preterits without *-i-* given above, for which a Prim. Gmc. origin can justly be claimed, end in *-hte*. In addition to these, Old English has 9 more preterits in *-hte* and 5 in *-lde*: In all of these syncopation preceded mutation, so that they show rückumlaut. There is doubtless a phonetic reason for the fact that this type is restricted to stems in *k* and *l*. These consonants are particularly subject to palatalization, which was accompanied by absorption of the *i* that had caused it. Thus we must assume that *h* and *l* in these forms had palatal articulation temporarily, but soon returned to the normal OE velar position as is evidenced by the breaking of the preceding vowel. These verbs are:

cweccan 'shake'—*cweahte* *þeccan* 'cover'—*þeahte*
dreccan 'afflict'—*dreahte* *weccan* 'wake'—*weahte*
leccan 'moisten'—*leahte* *rǣcan* 'reach'—*rāhte*[1]
reccan 'narrate'—*reahte* *tǣcan* 'teach'—*tāhte*[1]
streccan 'stretch'—*streahte*

cwellan 'kill'—*cwealde*
dwellan 'hinder'—*dwealde*
sellan 'sell'—*sealde*
stellan 'place'—*stealde*
tellan 'count'—*tealde*

[1] or analogical *rǣhte, tǣhte*.

The past participles are *gecweaht, geseald* etc.; *ea* is breaking of *æ* <

Gmc. *a* (**42 e**). (This list follows J. Wright, Old English Grammar 275. A slightly longer list, which includes a few less certain forms, is given by Sievers, Angels. Gramm.³ 233).

h for *c* in the preterit and participle would indicate that these forms, too, go back to a time before the Gmc. consonant shift. But this is unlikely, since in the other dialects this type is essentially restricted to the verbs listed above as Prim. Germanic. It is more likely that we have to deal with an analogical spread of the *-ht*-type. Early syncopation resulted in forms like **cwæcte, dræcte*, and these are transformed in accordance with *þōhte, worhte*, etc. Stems ending in *c* after *n* or *s* do not show this analogical change to *h*, since their phonetic type was too different: *ācwencan* 'quench', *drencan* 'make drink', *scencan* 'pour', *screncan* 'overturn', *sencan* 'make sink', *swencan* 'vex', *tōstencan* 'scatter', *geswencan* 'injure', *gewlencan* 'make proud', *ādwæscan* 'quench', *wȳscan* 'wish'; preterit and participle are *drencte gedrenced*, etc.

These and all other OE verbs of class I have mutation in all three forms, if the vowel admits it. Long stems syncopated *-i-* soon after the mutation, and so did those in *d t*, while short stems retained the connecting vowel as *-e-*: *nerian—nerede—genered, fremman—fremede—gefremed*, but *settan—sette—geseted* or *gesett*.

d　In Old Saxon, the original conditions were greatly changed by analogy. In addition to the syncopated forms of Gmc. origin (*brāhta, sōhta, thāhta, thūhta, warhta—bohta** does not happen to occur, but we have the past part. *giboht*), it has about 10 preterits with rückumlaut; the list given in Holthausen, As. Elb. 168, resembles that of Old English: *sellian—salda, wekkian—wahta*, etc. Otherwise, short-stem verbs have unsyncopated preterits with umlaut (*fremmian—fremida, nerian—nerida*), and long-stem verbs syncopate and therefore should show rückumlaut, but there is only one that does so regularly: *sendian—sanda*. In general mutation has been carried through by analogy: *fellian* 'fell'—[*fellda*], *nemnian* 'name'—[*nemda*], *senkian* 'make sink'—[*senkta*]. Also *-i-* was frequently re-introduced by analogy: *mārian* 'praise'—*mārida, wernian* 'defend'—*wernida*.

e　Old High German presents a rather complicated picture, since the dialects do not agree entirely. Long-stem verbs consistently show syncopation and rückumlaut (as far as the stem vowel is capable of mutation): Like *suohhen* 'seek' (without umlaut on account of *hh*)—*suohta* are formed *hōren* 'hear' = [hø·ren]—*hōrta, senten* 'send'—*santa, suenen* (thus in Lorscher Beichte; usually spelled *suonen*) 'reconcile'—*suonta, wānen* 'mean' = [wæ·nen]—*wānta*, etc. See list in Braune, Ahd.

Gramm. 286. In short-stem verbs, syncopation was apt to spread as it did in Old English, but the final consonant of the stem does not seem to have had any marked influence: We have not only *decken—dahta (dacta), zellen—zalta*, but also *retten—ratta, setzen—sazta* (with the analogical affricate *z = tz* instead of the spirant) etc. Since mutation took place earlier in Franconian than in Upper German, the latter has more forms with rückumlaut: UG, especially Bav., *zalta, salta, walta* (< *wellen* 'choose') as against Franc. *zelita, selita, welita*. The mutated preterits preserve the *i* in accordance with Sievers' Law; the unmutated ones had followed the pattern of the long-stem verbs.

Class II has Gmc. -*ō*-, which goes back to IE -*ā-j-(-o/e-)*, as in Gk. **f** $\tau\iota\mu\acute{a}[j]\omega$, cf. **54 k**. This always appears as *ō* in Gothic and Old High German, and generally as *o* in Old Saxon: Go. *salbōn—salbōda*, OHG *salbōn—salbōta*, OS *salbon—salboda*. But OS also shows older forms with -*oia*-: infin. *salboian*, 3 pl. pres. *salboiad*, and forms with -*ia*-, *salbian*, as in OE. This -*ia*- differs from the suffix of the first class in that, being of secondary origin, it causes neither consonant lengthening nor mutation.

Old English has a great variety of forms. In general, it may be said that -*ōi* + consonant appears as *ō > u > o > a* (the latter especially in WS), but -*ōi* + *o*- appears as *ia*; therefore pret. *sealfode*, part. *gesealfod*, 2, 3 sg. pres. *sealfas, sealfaþ*, but infin. *sealfian* < -*ōi-onom*, 3 pl. pres. *sealfiaþ* < -*ōi-onti*; 1 sg. *sealfie* < -*ōi-ō*, with -*ō > o*; *æ, e,* like *bere* = L. *ferō*.

Old Frisian is practically identical with Old English, e.g. infin. *makia*, pres. *makie, makast, makath, makiath*; pret. *makade*, part. *makad*.

The preterit of class III (for stem formation cf. **54 g**) has -*ai*- (= [ɛˑ, **g** ɛ or ai?]) in Go., -*ē*- in OHG and no connecting vowel in the other dialects: Go. *haban* (pres. *haba, habais, habaiþ*)—*habaida*, ON *hafa—hafþa*, OE *habban—hæfde*, OS *hebbian—habda (haƀda)*, OHG *habēn—habēta*. It is hardly possible to state with any confidence which of these formations is the original one. On the one hand, the Go. and OHG forms can easily be explained as levelings from the present. The ON forms can be reconciled with either of them, since *ē* in the penult was syncopated (cf. Heusler, Aisl. Elb. 41), but may quite as well be identical with the OE OS forms. But the latter forms present problems that are as yet unsolved. Syncopation of the vowel is out of the question. The preterits and past participles of this type either must have been formed originally without the medial vowel, like the type *brāhta, skulda, þāhta*, or they must be analogical.

In the first case we should certainly expect *ft*, as in OE *þorfte*, *ht* as in OE *bohte*. To overcome this difficulty, Collitz, Sch. Prät. 109 f. and 114 ff., suggests what might be justly described as a combination of Bartholomae's Law and Grassmann's Law:

Bartholomae's Law (Ar. Forsch. 1. 1–18): IE *bh* + *t* > Sk. *bdh, gh* + *t* > Sk. *gdh*.

Grassmann's Law (KZ 12. 81–138): IE *bh* . . *dh, dh* . . *dh* > Sk. *b* . . *dh*, *d* . . *dh*, Gk. π . . θ, τ . . θ (e.g. **bheudh-*, Go. *biudan*, > Sk. *bódhati* 'he is careful', Gk. πεύθομαι 'I notice'; **dhe-dhē-* : Sk. *dadhâti* 'he puts', Gk. τίθημι 'I put').

Collitz believes that Bartholomae's Law was valid in Germanic unless the root began with a sonant aspirate.[2]

Brugmann, Btr. 39. 84 f., agrees with Collitz. Perhaps the theory is correct, although the extension of these two laws to Germanic meets with many objections which could only be overcome by the assumption of a good many analogies; e.g., Go. *mahta, ōhta* would have to be interpreted as analogical formations for **magda, *ōgda* (or **agda*).

Instead of assuming an analogical origin for these and many similar Gmc. forms, it seems equally admissible to explain the OE OS preterits of class III as analogical. Their number is limited, since this class shows a strong tendency towards transition to classes I and II. The most important verbs that are common to both dialects are these:

OE *habban—hæfde*	OS *hebbian—habda*	'have'
hycgean—hogde	*huggian—hogda*	'think'
libban—lifde	*libbian—lebda*	'live'
secgean—sægde	*seggian—sagda*	'say'.

It seems possible that these preterits are formed on the model of certain preterit-presents like OE *monde, sceolde*; *hogde*, a synonym of *monde* may have been the starting point from which the innovation spread over a few more verbs. In Old High German (chiefly Otfrid) there occur the forms *dolta* 'suffered', to *dolēn* = *dolōn* (Go. *þulan— þulaida**, ON *þola—þolþa*) and *hogta* to *huggen* (OE *hycgean*). The Monsee Fragments have the form *hapta* instead of *habēta*.

INFINITIVE AND PARTICIPLES

68. The Infinitive is a verbal noun which has retained a closer association with the verb system proper than, e.g., nouns with various types of *t*-suffixes, such as **dhē-ti-* = Go. *gadēþs*, ON *dáþ*, OE *dǣd*, OS *dād*, OHG *tāt*; **kəp-ti* = OE *hæft*, OHG *haft* 'captivity', **kəp-to-* = ON *hapt*, OE *hæft*, OHG *haft* (masc. or neut.) 'fetter'; -*n*-forms such as *bhugh-on- = OE *boga*, OHG *bogo* 'bow'; verb derivatives without a 'suffix' in the narrower sense, such as *sleb-o- = Go. *sléps*, OE *slǽp*, OS *slāp*, OHG *slāf*—and very many others.

The several IE languages differ greatly in the choice of those verbal nouns that function as infinitives. Germanic uses a neuter noun in *-no-*: Go. *bairan* < *bheronom* = Sk. *bharaṇam*:

Go.	*bairan*	*nasjan*	*salbōn*	*haban*	*fullnan*
ON	*bera*	*telia*	*kalla*	*segia*	*vakna*
OE	*beran*	*nerian*	*sealfian*	*secg(e)an*	
OS	*beran*	*nerian*	*makon*	*seggian*	
OHG	*beran*	*nerien*	*salbōn*	*sagēn.*	

In general, the infinitive is undeclined, but in WGmc. there occur gen. and dat. forms from stems in *-njo-* instead of *-no-*: OE *berennes*, *tō berenne*, OFris. *beranne*, OS *berannias*, *berann(i)a*, OHG *berannes*, *beranne*. These forms are frequently called 'Gerunds'.

NOTE: ON has also an infinitive of the preterit which is identical in form with the 3 pl. pret. ind. The auxiliaries *skyldo, mondo, vildo* are especially frequent as substitutes for the future after a preterit in the principal clause: *hann kuazk* (= *kuaþ-sik*) *koma mondo* 'he said, he intended to come, he would come'.

69. The Participles.

PRESENT: Stem + *-nt-* > Gmc. *-nd-*; for declension, cf. 88:   a

GO.	*bairands*	*nasjands*	*salbōnds*	*habands*	*fullnands*
ON	*berande*	*teliande*	*kallande*	*segiande*	*vaknande*
OE	*berende*	*neriende*	*salfiende*	*secgende*[1]	
OS	*berandi*	*neriandi*	*makondi*[2]	*seggiandi*	
OHG	*beranti*	*nerienti*	*salbōnti*	*sagēnti.*	

[1] *-ende* (*-ande, -inde*) began to be replaced by *-inge* about 1200 in Southern England. This may be a phonetic development of *-inde*, but is more probably due to the influence of the verbal noun in *-ynge, -ing* (Ger. *-ung*), which syntactically had begun to compete with it in late OE times.   [2] *mako(ge)andi, makiandi.*

PRETERIT:

Strong Verbs add *-no-* to the root, usually with the thematic vowel b *-o-*, but sometimes with *-e-*. Old English frequently uses the prefix *ge-*, Old Saxon and Old High German use it almost regularly (*gi-, ga-*), unless the verb has some other prefix.

This prefix had perfective or (in nouns) collective force and corresponds to L. *co(m)-* (possibly IE *kwom*, related to the indefinite-relative pronoun). Gmc. *ȝ-* is due to pretonic lenis articulation of *ƕ*, cf. 20 d;

the form *gi-* < *kwe-* must have lost its labial element analogically at a
time, when the *k(w)o-* and *kwe*-forms were used interchangeably. The
forms are: Go. *baúrans*, ON *borenn*, OE *boren*, OS *giboran*, OHG *giboran*
(*early* UG *ga-*).

-eno- instead of *-ono-* is sometimes assumed for ON *tekenn* < **tak-*,
dregenn < **drag-*, to explain the mutation of *a*; but more probably this
is due to the palatalizing influence of *k g*; cf. Heusler, Aisl. Elb. 23 and
121. But it does occur in Run. *haitinaʀ* 'devoted'; Go. *aigin* 'property',
by the side of the regular part. *aigans*; Go. *fulgins* 'secret', to *filhan*
'conceal'; OE *cymen* (by the side of *cumen*) to *cuman*; OFris. *ehlēpen*
(*hlāpa* 'run'), *estenden* (*stonda* 'stand').

NOTE: Kluge, Urg.[3] 175, explains the OE ON endings as Gmc. *-ēnaz*, but such
an ending is not found elsewhere. The difficulty of *-ono-* > *an, a*, in the infinitive as against *-en, enn* in the participle must be admitted. Wright, OE Gramm.
87, explains OE *boren* < **burenaz*, which is quite possible. For Old Norse, Heusler, l. c., 40, assumes 'Umfärbung' of medial *a* before *n* + consonant to *e*. Neither
of these suggestions is entirely satisfactory.

Slavic shows the ending *-eno-* (*-no-*, if the root ends in a vowel): *vedǫ* 'I lead'—
vedenъ (*znajǫ* 'I know'—*znanъ*).

Weak Verbs add *-to-* to the stem, equivalent to the suffix of Gk. λυτός,
L. *captus*; the stem appears in the same form as in the preterit:

GO.	*-þāhts*[1]	*nasiþs*	*salbōþs*	*habaiþs*	*fullnōþs*[2]	*wiss*[3]
ON	*þekþr*	*talþr*	*kallaþr*	*sagþr*	*vaknaþr*	*vīss*[4]
OE	*geþōht*	*genered*	*gesealfod*	*gesægd*		*wīs*[5]
OS	———	*ginerid*	*gimakod*	*gisagd*		*wīs*[5]
OHG	*gidāht*	*ginerit*	*gisalbot*	*gisagēt*		*wīs*[5]

[1] in *andaþāhts* 'andächtig'.   [2] stems *brāhta-, bauhta-*, but *nasida-, salbōda*,
etc.   [3] < **wid-to-*.   [4] 'certain'.   [5] 'wise'.

THE PERSONAL ENDINGS

70. Categories of the Verb. (Cf. 52).

a   ASPECTS (Actiones Verbi) were numerous and differ greatly in the
several IE languages. As conscious, standardized forms they are far
more numerous in Semitic than in Indo-European. Thus Arabic
grammar uses different stem forms at least for the following aspects:
durative-transitive, durative-intransitive, intensive-iterative, causative, conative, reflexive (medial), factitive. In Indo-European, aspects
were probably older than tenses, and the latter were originally developed
from the former. In Slavic, aspects are still a more important feature

of the verb than tenses.   In Greek and Sanskrit, they are coordinated
categories.   In Italic and Germanic, the tense system has largely superseded the aspect system, although the latter is by no means a negligible
factor.   Cf. for Germanic, Streitberg, UG 278–80 and Btr. 15. 70 ff.

TENSES.   The number of tenses differs in the several IE languages, **b**
and it is difficult to say how many can be ascribed to primitive Indo-
European, since every language made innovations, discarded some
tenses, or combined several into one.   Usually, however, IE origin is
assumed for five tenses: present, imperfect, aorist, perfect, and future.
Germanic, in the oldest form that is known to us, possessed only two
tenses: the present and the 'preterit'.   The latter, as shown in **57,** was
a Gmc. innovation, consisting for the strong verb of a combination of
perfect and aorist forms similar to the L. perfect.   The imperfect and
the future had disappeared.   For the former, English has developed a
substitute in 'progressive' forms like 'he was writing'.   The difference
between the so-called imperfect and the (compound) perfect in the
modern Gmc. languages has nothing to do with their old functions, but
rests on essentially syntactic differentiations which developed gradually
during the late Middle Ages.   For the future, several substitutes developed during the Middle Ages and later.   First of all, verbal prefixes
had in Germanic, as in Slavic, the effect of giving future meaning to the
present tense of the verb; this is particularly true of the prefix *ga-*,
which especially in Gothic has this function almost regularly; cf. Streitberg, GE 202 f.   Second, the verbs that correspond to Go. *waírþa*,
skal, man, wiljau are apt to imply future meaning and gradually one or
two of these verbs were standardized as auxiliaries of the future in the
modern Gmc. languages: In Gothic, *waírþa* alone translates the Gk.
future ἔσομαι 'I shall be'.   In Norse, (after some competition with
man) *skal* or *vil* were standardized, and similarly *shall* and *will* in
English (with a wholly artificial distinction between the two), except
that here the competition had been with *weorþan*.   In Old High German, as in Gothic, *werdan* alone could be used for 'shall be'; in New
High German grammar *werden* with the infinitive is usually designated
as future tense, but as a matter of fact the future is far more often expressed by the present (*ich komme morgen*), while the form with *werden*
expresses probability rather than futurity.   The compound perfect with
the auxiliaries *to have* or *to be* developed during the latter part of the
Middle Ages in the several Gmc. languages independently but with
similar results.

MODES.   The indicative states facts objectively, the imperative ex- **c**

presses command.   In addition to these, Indo-European had two modes
with more or less subjective function, the subjunctive and the optative.
The most frequent type of subjunctive had a long vowel, either $\bar{e}/\bar{o}$
or $\bar{a}$, between root and ending: L. *am-ē-mus am-ē-tis* ($< *am\bar{a}(j)$-*ēmus*,
-*ētis*), *leg-ā-mus leg-ā-tis*; the *ē-form* of the third conjugation, *leg-ē-mus*
leg-ē-tis, was converted to future meaning.   The optative was characterized by -ī-, in gradation with *iē*, before the ending: L. *sīmus, sītis*
(archaic sg. *siem, siēs, siet* = Sk. *syā́m, syās, syāt*), Gk. φέρ-οι-μι,
φέρ-οι-ς (*oi* < *o* + *ī*).
     The functions of the subjunctive and optative are closely related.
Generally speaking, the subjunctive expresses expectation, hope, ad-
monition, probability, and the optative wish, unreal condition, statement contrary to fact.   They were apt to be used interchangeably, and
so it happened that most IE languages merged the two modes, combining the functions of both in one form.   In this respect, Italic and
Germanic proceeded in very similar ways.   In Latin, the optative was
given up entirely with the exception of the paradigms *sim, edim*, and
velim (in early Latin also *faxim*, etc.; cf. Sommer, LLFL 585 ff.).   The
forms of the type *amem* are genuine present subjunctives, those of the
type *amārem* are subjunctives of *s*-aorists, with *s* > *r* through rhotacism; *s* is preserved in L. *es-sem* and in Osc.-Umbr. forms like Osc.
fusíd 'foret'.   Therefore, the difference between them was originally
one of aspect, not of mode.   But the function of the optative, especially
the expression of unreality, was transferred to the aorist subjunctive.
In Germanic, on the other hand, the IE subjunctive disappeared; the
so-called present subjunctive is an optative of the present stem, and the
'preterit subjunctive' is fundamentally an optative of the aorist stem:
Go. *steigai* 'er steige', *nimai* 'er nehme' < *steigh-o-ī-t, nem-o-ī-t*, as
against *stigi* 'er stiege', *nēmi* 'er nähme' < *stigh-ī-t, nēm-ī-t*.   Of course,
since the aorist had been merged in the Gmc. preterit system, equivalent
optatives were also formed from those preterit stems that had not come
from an aorist, that is of the preterits of classes VI and VII and the
weak preterits: *hōfi, haihaiti, nasidēdi*—obviously analogical forms.
The final result is that the preterit subjunctive has everywhere the
same stem as the plural of the preterit, but in function these forms
were never associated with the preterit.   Instead, the optative of the
present stem took over the functions of the extinct subjunctive, and
the optative of the preterit stem retained the function of the IE (Gk.
Sk., etc.) optative.   Thus Go. *nimai* corresponds to L. *amet, nēmi* to
amāret.

NOTE: In spite of the strong historical tradition, it would really be better, particularly in Germanic, to abandon the misleading grammatical terms for these forms; perhaps the terms 'potential' and 'optative' would be preferable; L. Bloomfield, in his German Grammar, uses 'quotative' and 'unreal'. However, in the present book the more conservative terms optative of the present stem and optative of the preterit stem are retained.

GENERA VERBI (Voices). The IE verb had an active voice and a **d** voice that combined reflexive and passive function, usually called medium or medio-passive. Of the latter, Gothic still possesses a fairly complete paradigm for the present; Old Norse and Old English have preserved a few forms, Run. *haite-ka* 'I am called' (literary Norse *heite*, 1 pers., *heiter*, 2, 3 pers.) and OE *hātte* 'I am called, he is called'. Otherwise, the IE medio-passive, as we have it in Gk. φέρεται, L. *amātur*, was replaced by compound forms consisting of the auxiliary Gmc. *wesan-* or *werþan-*, in Modern Norse *blive* 'remain', and the past participle. Besides, Norse developed reflexive forms with medio-passive function: ON, before 1200, *finnomk* 'I find myself, I am found', 2, 3 pers. *finzk*, < **finþo-mik*, **finþ-sik*, etc.; after 1200, the suffixed reflexive of the 3 pers., *-sik*, was extended to all persons, and since 1300 all forms of the reflexive-medial paradigm end in *-z*, which in Modern Norse appears as *-s*: Norw. *jeg elskes, du elskes, han elskes* 'I am, you are, he is loved' = *jeg, du, han bliver elsket*.

NUMBERS. In addition to the singular and plural, the IE verb had **e** a dual, which is preserved fairly well in Gothic.

71. Types of Endings.

Indo-European had the following groups of verb endings:

(1) The primary endings, belonging chiefly to the indicative of the present:

Sg. *-mi, -si, -ti*; Pl. *-mĕs/mŏs, -te, -nti*; Du. *-wĕs/wŏs(i), -tes/-tos*.

NOTE: *-mi* of the first singular is used only with athematic verbs (72). Thematic verbs, which form the overwhelming majority of all verbs, had no real 'ending' in the first singular, but lengthened the thematic vowel: Gk. εἰμί < **es-mi*, but φέρω. Sanskrit extends, by analogy, the ending *-mi* to thematic verbs: *bhárā-mi* 'I carry' = Gk. φέρω.

(2) The secondary endings. As far as the Gmc. verb system is concerned, these belong to the optatives and aorists. Doubtless, they represent reductions of the primary endings:

Sg. *-m, -s, -t*; Pl. *-men* or *-me/mo, -te, -nt*; Du. cannot be ascertained with certainty; probably *-we/-wo, -te/-to* (with *-s* added by analogy with the primary endings).

(3) The medial endings differ in the several IE languages. The most widespread type, and the only one of which we find a trace in Germanic, is the following:

Sg. -ai (in Greek replaced by analogical -μαι), -sai, -tai; Pl. ? -medhə, ? -dhwai, -ntai; Du. quite uncertain.

(The medio-passive, too, had primary and secondary endings. Here only the primary endings are given, since Germanic does not offer any evidence for the secondary endings.)

(4) The perfect endings are clear for the singular only, where they surely were -a, -tha (-ta), -e. Whatever the original pl. endings were, the Gmc. preterit shows merely the aoristic secondary endings. The endings of the Go. dual are evidently analogical.

NOTE: Indo-Iranian, Italic, and Celtic possess a group of endings with r whose relation to the endings given above is unknown. They appear chiefly in the 3 pl. perfect: L. fuēre, fuēr-unt 'they have been', Sk. vidur. The L. passive with r probably represents a spread of this r-type of endings. There are no Gmc. forms of this kind.

72. The present Active.
Indicative.

a

	Singular			Plural			Dual	
IE	-ō	-e-si	-e-ti	-o-mes	-e-te	-o-nti	-ŏ-wes	-o-tes
Go.	binda	-is	-iþ	-am	-iþ	-and	-ōs	-ats
ON	bind	-r	-r	-om	-eþ	-a		
OE	binde	-es(t)	-eþ			-aþ		
OS	bindu	-is	-iδ -id			-ath -ad		
OHG	bintu	-is(t)	-it	-amēs	-et	-ant.		

ACCENT. The treatment of the final spirant in the 2, 3 sg. and pl. indicates that Go. ON OHG standardized the type with root accent (Sk. bhávati), OE OS the type with suffix accent (Sk. tudáti). Therefore, the endings of the former group were subject to Verner's Law, þ > δ, s > z > NWGmc. r. In Gothic, these became again voiceless through the law of final spirants, but -and, where -δ after nasal has become -d, is evidence that there had been an intermediate voiced stage. -s in the 2 sg. of Old High German is due to the very frequent use of the enclitic pronoun -tu; -z would have disappeared in WGmc. The difference between -þ and -δ in Old English (and Old Saxon) is not one of pronunciation (both are voiceless when final), but of scribal tradition. In Old English, as in Old Norse, þ and δ were used interchangeably, without any phonetic distinction, but in OS either th or δ were used. In Old Saxon, endings in -d and even -t were also very frequent. It is not likely that this indicates different accent types within the dialect itself; they are rather due to High German influence.

LOSS OF MORAE. The last mora is lost everywhere, e.g. -ō, -esi > Go. -a, -is. In Old Norse, another mora is lost when the vowel was final and before ʀ s t þ, but not before m n r; for 2 pl. -eþ see below.

THE PERSONS.

1. *Sg.* Final ō appears as a in Gothic, as u in NWGmc. In Norse, this u (> o) is preserved in reflexive forms: *bindomk*. In such forms it also causes u-umlaut or breaking: *kǫllomk* < **kallu-mik* 'I call myself', *hiolpomk* 'I help myself'. In non-reflexive forms the stem vowel follows the 2, 3 sg.: *fell, help*.

The ending -mi appears in the following verbs:

(a) In all Gmc. languages in the verbum substantivum, IE **es-mi*, Gmc. *izmi > immi*:

Go. *im*.

ON *em* has e for i in analogy with the pl. forms *erom, eroþ, ero* whose e is due to 'sinking' before ʀ (**42 d**).

OE (WS) *eom*, unstressed form for **ēom*; *ēo* is transferred from the synonymous *bēo* < **bhw-iyō* = L. *fīo*. Anglian has a compromise form *bīom*.

OS *bium, bion*, like the Angl. form a compromise between the roots **es-* and **bh(e)w-*.

OHG *bim, bin*, compromise forms retaining the vowel of *im*.

(b) In WGmc. (partly) in the verbs 'do, go, stand':

OE (Angl.) *dōm*, OS *dōm, dōn*, OHG *tuom, tuon*.

OHG *gām, gēm (-n), stām, stēm (-n)*.

(c) In Old Saxon and Old High German in the verbs of II W: OS *makon*, OHG *machōm (-n)*.

(d) In Old High German in the verbs of III W: *habēm*.

2 sg. *-e-si*, with rhotacism in Old Norse. For s instead of z (r) in Gothic and Old High German, see above.

3 sg. *-e-ti*, replaced in Old Norse by the ending of the 2 pers., which in Modern Norse spreads to all persons.

1 pl. *-o-mes* or *-o-mos*. Old Norse transferred the ending of the preterit to the present. Old English and Old Saxon use the ending of the 3 pl. for the whole plural. OHG *-amēs* must still be considered as unexplained. Even the excellent analysis of the problem by M. H. Roberts, Lang. 11. 220–30 (with full bibliography) hardly offers a convincing result. Ordinarily OHG ē in unaccented syllables points to

Gmc. *ai*. We might think of a contracting from **bhèndhomos* + *wéis* (pronoun of the 1 pl.) > **bindama(zw)is*, originally in contrasting adhortative function (cf. Brugmann, KG 591) 'let us bind'. The ultima-accent would have prevented Verner's Law, and when later the form came to be used as an indicative, with retraction of the accent to the root, *ai* was monophthongized to *ē*.

2 pl. *-e-te*. ON *-eþ* must be transferred from the optative: *-oi-te* > *-aiþ* > *-ēþ* (loss of two morae before *-þ*; *-ete* would have lost the connecting vowel). The same explanation is possible for OHG *-et*; there, the optative ends in *-ēt*, which may have been shortened under the influence of the original indicative ending Gmc. *-þ*; the lack of umlaut (*faret* as against 2 sg. *feris*) would point to this. The pl. forms of the *jo*-verbs (*suochemes*, *suochet*, *suochent*, with *e* < *ja*) may have been a contributing factor.

3 pl. *-o-nti*. In Old Norse *nþ* had become *nn* (cf. Go. *anþar* : ON *annarr* 'other') which was at first simplified and then dropped in final position. In the Anglo-Frisian group, *n* disappeared before *þ* (**29 c**) with compensatory lengthening in stressed syllables and subsequent shortening when unstressed. In this group, the form of the 3 pl. is also used for the 1. 2 pl.

The Dual occurs only in Gothic, and there only for the 1st and 2nd pers. The ending of the 1st pers. seems to be a contraction of *-ō-wes*, like Sk. *-āvas*, > *-ōwiz*, *-ō(w)z*. The ending of the 2nd pers., *-ats*, must be identical with Sk. *-a-thas*, IE *-o-tes/-tos*, probably for earlier *-e-tes/-tos* (Sk. *th* may be an Indic innovation). This should give us Go. *-aþs*; *t* for *þ* is probably dissimilation, somewhat similar to the fact that *st* never became *sþ*.

The Weak Verbs of classes II and III add the endings to the class suffix:

II. Go. *salbō*, *salbōs*; ON *kalla*, *kallar*, pl. *kǫllom* etc.; OE *sealfie* < **salbojō*, *sealfas(t)*; OS *makon*, *makos*, OHG *machōm*, *machōs(t)*. III. Gothic has *haba*, *habais*, *habaiþ*, *habam*, *habaiþ*, *haband*, *habōs*, **habaits*. The forms with *a* are most probably transfers from thematic verbs; cf. class IV and Brugmann, Grdr. 2. 3. 203 f.; different Kieckers, HGG 246. The forms with *ai* can go back either to *-ēi-* or to its reduced grade *-ǝi-*. In Old Norse this class shows the same endings as class I: *vake*, *vaker*, *vaker*, *vǫkom*, *vakeþ*, *vaka*. This was probably due to the fact that Gmc. *ai* in unstressed syllables became ON *e*, so that four of the endings of these two classes were identical by phonetic law. The lack of *i*-umlaut still points to this origin. In Old English and Old

Saxon the verbs of this class show essentially the endings of class I, partly of class II: OE 1 sg. *hæbbe*, pl. *habbaþ*, 2, 3 sg. either *hafas(t)*, *hafaþ* < Gmc. *-ōs*, *-ōþ*, or *hæfs(t)*, *hæfþ*, compromise forms between class I and class II. OS *hebbiu*, pl. *hebbiad*; but 2, 3 sg. *habes*, *habed* correspond to the Go. forms. Old High German has *ē* < *ēi* or *əi* throughout the paradigm: *habēm*, *habēs* etc.

Class IV in Gothic forms its present like strong verbs: *fullna, -is, -iþ*, in Old Norse, the verbs of this class show the same forms as those of class II, that is, they shorten the original ō: *vakna, vaknar* etc.

Class I differs considerably in the several languages. This is due partly to a different phonological treatment of the *-jo-* and *-je-*forms of the suffix and partly to a different development according to the quantity of the stem. Umlaut and consonant gemination added to the complication. These are the paradigms:

Go.	*lagjan:*	*lagja*	*lagjis*	*lagjiþ*	*lagjam*	*lagjiþ*	*lagjand*
	hausjan:	*hausja*	*hauseis*	*hauseiþ*	*hausjam*	*hauseiþ*	*hausjand*
ON	*telia:*	*tel*	*telr*	*telr*	*teliom*	*teleþ*	*telia*
	leggia:	*legg*	*legr*	*legr*	*leggiom*	*legeþ*	*leggia*
	heyra:	*heyre*	*heyrer*	*heyrer*	*heyrom*	*heyreþ*	*heyra*
OE	*lecgan:*	*lecge*	*legst*	*legþ*		*lecgaþ*	
	hīeran:	*hīere*	*hīer(e)st*	*hīer(e)þ*		*hīeraþ*	
OS	*leggian:*	*leggiu*	*legis*	*legið*		*leggiað*	
	hōrian:	*hōriu*	*hōris*	*hōrið*		*hōriað*	
OHG	*leggen:*	*leggu*	*legis*	*legit*	*leggemēs*	*[legget]*	*leggent*
	hōren:	*hōru*	*hōris*	*hōrit*	*hōremēs*	*hōret*	*hōrent.*

A full account of the details would greatly exceed the scope of this book. These are the most important facts:

(1) Gothic shows a consistent working of 'Sievers' Law' in the sense of **49 h:** the syllabic division was *lag-jis*, but *sō-kjis*. Therefore *j* being initial was preserved after a short stem, but the syllable *-kjis*, with medial *j*, was equivalent to *-kiis* = *-keis* in Wulfila's spelling.

NOTE: From the point of view of this syllabic division, the term 'short stems' includes syllables with a short vowel followed by one consonant and those with a long vowel without consonant (open syllables). Long stems have long closed syllables, containing either a long vowel plus one consonant or a short vowel plus two consonants, or else they are polysyllabic; cf. **67 a**, end). Therefore: *stō-jis* like *nas-jis; fra-ward-eis mikil-eis* like *sōkeis*.

(2) In Old Norse, *j* was preserved before back vowels: *teliom, telia*. After a long syllable *-ji-* must originally have yielded *-ī-*, as in Gothic, and this was preserved as *e* (*heyrer*), while after a short syllable *-ji-*

became *i*, and then was dropped. Heusler, Aisl. Elb. 39 and 50. Notice that in Old Norse, in contrast to WGmc., only *g* was subject to gemination. This took place in those forms where consonantic *j* (spelled *i* in our ON orthography) had been preserved:
legg < *leggiu, leggiom, leggia.*

(3) After short vowels all WGmc. dialects have gemination of all consonants except, in general, *r* (OE *nerie, neriaþ*). As in Old Norse, *j* of -*ji*- > *ī* had been vocalized before the gemination. Therefore, we have the alternation OE *fremme*—*fremest* (*lecge*—*leg*[*e*]*st*), OS *leggiu*—*legis*, OHG *leggu*—*legis* (2 pl. *legget*, by the side of *leget*, is evidently analogical). The resulting short vowel *i e* was in Old English subject to syncopation, differing in extent according to the preceding consonant: *fremest*, but *setst, dēm*(*e*)*st*, but *hyngrest*.

b   THE STEM VOWEL is changeable according to the vowel of the ending. Gothic does not show any change at all. In the other dialects we find:

Old Norse: Norse *i*-umlaut belongs phonologically to the 2, 3 sg., but is extended analogically to the 1st pers., so that the same vowel goes through the whole singular: *falla* 'fall'—*fell, fellr, skiōta* 'shoot'— *skȳt, skȳtr*. On the other hand, the change of *e* > *i*, which appears elsewhere in Germanic in the present singular of strong verbs, does not occur in Old Norse. This is a peculiar fact for which a good explanation is lacking; perhaps we have to think of analogical influence from the plural before *e* there had been changed by breaking: *help helpr, gef gefr*.

In the plural the *l*-, *r*-verbs of class III have *u*-breaking in the 1st pers., *a*-breaking in the 3rd, and by analogy also in the 2nd pers.: *hiolpom, hialpeþ, hialpa*. But verbs of classes IV, V retain *e* throughout the whole paradigm. For a possible reason cf. Heusler, Aisl. Elb. 27 (§74, Anm. 1). -*a*- in the 1 pl. shows *u*-umlaut: *fǫllom*. This is also true for weak verbs (other than those of class I where the unmodified stem vowel -*a*- cannot occur): *kǫllom, vǫkom, sofnom*. But aside from this, weak verbs have the same stem vowel throughout the present: *kalla, kallar*—*kalleþ, kalla*.

West Germanic: The singular of strong verbs of classes III–V should show *i* for *e* in the whole singular, and this is the case in OS OHG: OS *wirðu, nimu, sihu, wirðis* etc.; OHG *nimu, nimis* etc. Likewise in class II *iu* for *eu*, OS *kiusu, kiusis*, pl. *kiosad*; OHG *kiusu, kiusis*, pl. *kiosemēs*. But in Old English, the pl. vowel has been transferred to the 1st pers.; OE *bere, biris*, (*weorþe, wierþst*), *cēose, cīest*.

NOTE: Others, however, consider the OE conditions older and interpret the 1st pers. of OS and OHG as leveling from the 2, 3 sg.

The stem vowel *a* undergoes umlaut in the 2, 3 sg.: OE *fare, fær(e)st* (for **feris, fer(e)st*) under the influence of the 1st pers.; cf. Wright, OE Gramm. 37 (§55 Note 2); *slēa, sliehst* < **slahu, slehis*; *fō, fēhst* < **fāhu, fāhis*.

OS *faru, feris*; *slahu, slehis*.

OHG (subject to the usual limitations of umlaut) *faru, feris(t)*; *slahu, slehis(t)*. (But, e.g. *wahsu, wahsis*; Bav. *haltu, haltis* as against Franc. *heltis*; UG also *slahis*, more frequently than *slehis*).

Weak verbs of class I have umlaut throughout the whole present everywhere except in Gothic, subject to the usual limitations of umlaut in Old High German; in *suohhen*, umlaut was probably prevented by *hh* < Gmc. *k*, although in the case of *a* this prevented umlaut in Upper German only. OS *hōrian*, OHG *hōren* doubtless had umlaut, although the spelling does not indicate it.

Imperative.

2 sg.:

Go.	*bind,*	*hilp;*	*lagei,*	*hausei,*	*salbō,*	*habai,*	*fulln*
ON	*bind,*	*hialp;*	*leg,*	*heyr,*	*kalla,*	*vake,*	*vakna*
OE	*bind,*	*help;*	*lege,*	*hīer,*	*sealfa,*	*hafa*	
OS	*bind,*	*help hilp;*	*legi,*	*hōri,*	*mako,*	*habe -a*	
OHG	*bint,*	*hilf;*	*legi,*	*hōri,*	*salbo,*	*habe.*	

There is no ending; the form consists of the pure stem with the thematic vowel for strong verbs and class I W, without thematic vowel for other verbs.

-e disappears completely, resulting uniformly in imperatives of strong verbs without endings. The explanation of the Go. forms of class I W is uncertain. We should expect **lagji, hausei*, but probably the former type was leveled in accordance with the latter. Differently Kieckers, HGG 232.

The other forms are self-explanatory if we allow for a certain amount of analogy. The phonological forms are found in Old English: *lege* < **laȝj = legi, hīer* < **hēarji > hīeri*; final *i* was dropped after a long syllable, but retained after a short syllable. OS OHG *hōri* can either be considered analogies after the short-stem verbs, or can be interpreted like Go. *hausei*.

The 1 and 2 pl. of the imperative are identical with the indicative: Go. *bindam, bindiþ*, OHG *bintamēs, bintet*, but the optative is often substituted especially for the 1 pl.: OHG *bintēm*. Gothic had a special form for the 3 sg. and doubtless also for the 3 pl., although it does not happen to be attested: *bindadau, *bindandau*. This probably corresponds to IE forms in *-tōd*, L. *agitō, aguntō*, with the addition of the

emphasizing particle -*u*, which is also found in the optative; cf. Sk.
bhárat-u 'he is to carry'.

Optative.

c   The mode characteristic is -*oĭ*-, i.e., *o* + *ĭ*, a diphthong with long
second element (three morae).   In Germanic, long diphthongs are
shortened in all positions, but retain the diphthongal element in spite
of the shortening by one mora.   The endings are of the secondary type.
Paradigms:

Go.	(*bindau*)	-*ais*	-*ai*	-*aima*	-*aiþ*	-*aina*	-*aiwa*	-*aits*
ON	*binda*	-*er*	-*e*	-*em*	-*eþ*	-*e*		
OE		*binde*			*binden*			
OS	*binde*	-*es*	-*e*		*binden*			
OHG	*binte*	-*ēs*	-*e*	*bintēm*	-*ēt*	-*ēn.*		

The forms of the weak verbs are nearly the same as those of the
strong verbs.   It might be mentioned that in the first class *j* is preserved in Gothic throughout: *lagjau, stōjau, hausjau—lagjais, stōjais,
hausjais*.   In Old Norse we find it preserved before the *a* of the 1 sg.:
leggia, leger etc., but *heyra, -er*.   Old English preserved it after *r* (*nerie,
nerien*), and shows gemination of other consonants in short-stem verbs
(*fremme, fremmen*).   Old Saxon carries it through the paradigm:
leggie, leggies, leggien as against the indic. *leggiu, legis, leggiað.*—Old
High German is like OE (*nerie, zelle*).

The other weak classes have secondary formations which follow
partly the indicative, partly the optative of strong verbs: Go. *salbō,
-ōs, habau, -ais, fullnau, -ais*, ON *kalla, -er, vaka, -er*, OE *sealfie, hæbbe*,
OS *mako(ie), -os, hebbie, -ies*, OHG *salbo, -ōs, habe, -ēs(t).*

Gothic.   The 1 sg. cannot be a genuine optative; probably it is merely
the indicative with the enclitic, either emphatic (adhortative) or interrogative particle -*u*, as in the 3rd pers. of the imperative: *binda* + *u*.
The 2, 3 sg., 2 pl., 2 du. are obvious: Since all strictly final consonants
except -*s* are dropped, they clearly go back to: -*oĭ-s*, -*oĭ-t*, -*oĭ-te*,
oĭ-tos.   The other three persons end in -*a*.   With the dual this may go
back to an IE long vowel: in Lith. *dìrbava* 'we (two) work', *a* is shortened
from *ō* which is preserved in the reflexive form *dìrbavos* 'the two of us
work for ourselves'.   Likewise, the Lith. reflexive form of the 1 pl.,
dìrbamės (*ė* = *ē*) points to an IE ending *mē* which would have led to Go.
-*a*; and from these two forms the -*a* would have been transferred to the
3 pl.   But it is equally possible that the -*a* of these three persons is a
Go. innovation, corresponding to the particle -*a* of certain pronominal
forms (*þata, ina*) = Sk. -*ā* (postposition and enclitic interjection;
Thumb, Hdb. Sk. 168 and 471 Footnote): -*oĭ-men-ā*, -*oĭ-we(s)-ā*, -*oĭ-*

nt-ā. Of course, the laws of final syllables would have functioned before the addition of this particle, as in the case of *þana* < **tom-ā.*

Old Norse is probably identical with Gothic. There is some doubt about the 1 sg. Phonologically this, too, could correspond to Go. -*au*, since Gmc. -*au* became -*a*, cf. Go. *ahtau* = ON *ātta* '8'. But in view of the probable origin of the Go. ending from *o* + *u*, this would be such a surprising morphological coincidence that this form must be considered problematic.

Old English has only one form for the singular and one for the plural. In the singular the three persons had become identical by phonetic law: IE -*oĭm*, -*oĭs*, -*oĭt* lost their final consonants (WGmc. -*z* disappeared regularly), and *ai* became *æ* (preserved in early documents) and then *e*. In the plural, however, the 1st and 2nd persons were replaced by the 3rd, as in the indicative.

Old Saxon shows the same development, but in the 2 sg. *s* was preserved through the support of the frequently attached personal pronoun.

Old High German preserved the long quality of the vowel except where it was final. The 2 sg. ends in -*s* for the same reason as in Old Saxon.

The stem vowel is everywhere the same in all persons. In Old Norse, the ending -*a* of the 1 sg. causes breaking in the *l*-, *r*-verbs of class III which spreads over all other persons: *hialpa, hialper, hialpe* etc.

73. The Preterit.

Indicative.

The Preterit of the *Strong Verbs* has in the singular chiefly the endings **a** of the IE perfect, -*a*, -*ta* (= -*tha*), -*e*, but in WGmc. the 2 sg. ends in -*i* (-*e*), from the ending -*es* of the IE strong (thematic) aorist. The pl. endings go back to the secondary endings of the athematic aorist, with analogical extension, as in Greek: 3 pl. -*nt* > Gk. -*αν*, Gmc. -*un*; the 1 pl. may be considered as a development from -*men* > Gk. -*μεν*, Gmc. -*um*; the 2 pl. is surely analogical—its phonological form would have been -*te* > Gmc. *þ* without connecting vowel; cf.:

Gk.	ἐλύσαμεν	ἐλύσατε	ἔλυσαν
Go.	*bundum*	*bunduþ*	*bundun.*

Thus we have the following paradigms:

Go.	*band*	*banst*	*band*	*bundum*	-*uþ*	-*un*	-*u*	-*uts*
ON	*batt*	*bazt*	*batt*	*bǫndom*	-*oþ*	-*o*		
OE	*band*	*bunde*	*band*	*bundon*				
OS	*band*	*bundi*	*band*	*bundon*				
OHG	*bant*	*bunti*	*bant*	*buntum*	-*ut*	-*un.*		

(1) For a treatment of consonant combinations resulting from the

contact of the final consonant of the root with the ending of the 2 sg., theoretical Gmc. -þ, the special grammars of the several languages must be consulted. E.g., Go. *banst*, ON *bazt* < *band-þ*, analogical **band-t*. The analogical substitution of -t for -þ started from verbs with roots ending in spirants. Phonological -t in Go. *last*, *slōht*, *gaft*, analogical -t in Go. *namt*, *stalt*. Phonologically, **band-t* would have become **bans(s)*.

(2) Old English and Old Saxon use the 3 pl. also for the 1 and 2 pl.

(3) The Go. dual also introduced the analogical connecting vowel -u-. The first person seems to go back to -u-we > -uw = -u.

b THE OPTATIVE.

The so-called optative of the preterit is genetically an optative of the aorist (cf. **57 b**). For classes I–V this means that it is based on the same root form as the pl. of the preterit. Its primary pattern is found in classes IV and V which have athematic aorists. The mode sign -ī- is added to these roots directly, e.g., 2 pl. **nēm-ī-te* > Go. *nēmeiþ*. Classes I–III have originally thematic aorists, but, as in the indicative, the type of classes IV and V is transferred to them as well as to classes VI, VII and the weak verbs. Thus, instead of **stigaiþ* < **stigh-o-ī-te* we have *stigeiþ*, and *guteiþ*, *waurþeiþ*, *fōreiþ*, *haíháiteiþ* are to be explained the same way. Paradigms:

Go.	*bundjau*	*bundeis*	-i	-eima	-eiþ	-eina	-eiwa	-eits
ON	*bynda*	-er	-e	-em	-eþ	-e		
OE		*bunde*			*bunden*			
OS	*bundi*	-is	-i		*bundin*			
OHG	*bunti*	-īs	-i	-īmēs	-īt	-īn.		

The forms are very transparent. In the Go. 1 sg. the -au of the present optative is added to the original **bundi* < -īm. Here and in the 3 sg. ī is regularly shortened to i. In the 2 sg. the quantity of -īs is preserved by analogy with other persons, especially the 2 pl. -eiþ < -īte. The Norse and OE endings are by phonetic law identical with those of the present. In Old Saxon and Old High German they are differentiated by ī (i) in the preterit as against ē (e) < -ai in the present.

The -ī- of the ending should cause umlaut where the stem vowel permits it, and in Old Norse this is the case. On the basis of the forms in the later development of the languages we must assume the same for Old Saxon and Old High German, although the spelling does not indicate it; cf. NHG *würde*, *sähe*, *führe* (with numerous later analogical substitutions such as *bände* for *bünde*, *höbe* for *hübe* etc.). But in Old English the identity of the endings with those of the present optative led to the disappearance of the umlaut. In the regular strong verbs it appears only in a few doubtful forms, such as *wyrde, hwyrfe*; cf. Sievers, Angels. Gramm. 207 (§377 Anm.).

The optative of the preterit-presents, which, of course, functions as present optative, has the same forms as the preterit optative of regular strong verbs, but in Old English it has preserved some umlaut forms: *dyge, þyrfe, dyrre, scyle, myne, mæge,* later *duge, þurfe, durre, scule, mune, mage.*

Weak verbs follow the pattern of strong verbs:
Go. *lagidēdjau, -dēdeis, -dēdi*; ON *legþa, -er, -e*; OE *legde legden*; OS *legdi, -is, -i*; OHG *legiti, -īs, -i.*

The verbs of class I have, in general, umlaut in NWGmc., with some irregularities in Old High German. In the other classes it is prevented by the intervening suffix vowel, e.g., ON *kallaþa, kallaþer,* OE *sealfode,* OS *makodi,* OHG *salbōti.*

The preterit optative of the preterit-presents is entirely regular: Go. *skuldēdjau,* ON *skylda, skylder* (< **skulðīs*; the umlaut was transferred to the indicative), OE *sceolde* (= ind.), OS *skoldi* (analogical for **skuldi*), OHG *scolti* (for **sculti*).

74. The Passive.

Aside from the few forms mentioned above, this is preserved only in Gothic, and even there only for the present:

Ind. *bindada   bindaza   bindada*;   pl. *bindanda*
Opt. *bindaidau bindaizau bindaidau*; pl. *bindaindau.*

The 2, 3 sg. and the 3 pl. have the regular medio-passive endings *-sai, -tai, -ntai*, with Verner's Law and the loss of one mora. The 3 sg. is used for the 1 sg., and the 3 pl. for the whole plural. The original thematic vowel of the singular, *-e-*, was replaced by *-o-* of the 3 pl. The optative is clearly an analogical formation: the *-au* of the 1 sg. active was extended to all persons, and the optative sign *-ai-* was substituted for the *-a-* of the indicative.

75. Anomalous Verbs.

A few verbs of especially frequent occurrence have not quite adapted themselves to the system of the 'regular' verbs. These are: in all dialects, the verbs 'to be' and 'will'; in WGmc., the verbs 'to do' and 'to go'; in Old Saxon and Old High German, the verb 'to stand'.

'BE'

All dialects show a combination of the roots **es-* (Gk. **ἐσ-μι* > a εἰμί, Sk. *ásmi*, L. *es-se*, etc.) and **wes-* (Sk. *vásati* 'dwells', Gk. ἑστία 'hearth' (dwelling place), L. *Vesta*). WGmc., especially Old English, also shows forms of the root **bheu-/bh(e)wī-* (Sk. *bhávati* 'becomes',

Gk. φύω 'beget', L. fuī 'have been'; L. fīō 'become', OSl. bimъ 'I would be'). Besides, Old English has traces of the root *er-/or- (Sk. r̥nóti 'rises', Gk. ὄρνῡμι 'arouse', L. orior 'I rise').

A. Root *es-; (a) Pres. Ind.:

Go.	im	is	ist	sijum	sijuþ	sijun	siju	sijuts
ON	em	est	es	erom	eroþ	ero		
OE	eom	(eart)	is		sind sindon			
OS	bium	bis(t)	is(t)		sind(un)			
OHG	bim	bist	ist	birum	birut	sint.		

For the general athematic character of this verb cf. **54 h, 1.** It is still preserved in most of the sg. forms: Go. im, is, ist < *es-mi, *es-si, *es-ti; *esmi > *izmi by assimilation, > *immi, im. The original pl. forms are preserved in Sk. smás, sthá, sánti < *senti. The latter form is preserved in OE OS OHG, partly with the addition of the ending of the preterit. -d- indicates Verner's Law, which is in contrast to the Sk. accent; probably we must assume IE *sentí by the side of *sénti.

The Go. plural has the ending of the strong preterit; from the ON forms we may infer that the Go. forms originally were *izum, izuþ, izun or *isum, isuþ, isun, with u from m̥ n̥ of the 1st and 3rd persons, with analogical transfer to the 2nd pers. The first syllable of these forms was replaced by sij- of the optative.

In Old Norse, the e belongs originally only to the plural where it is due to the 'sinking' before ʀ. Verner's Law is here (as in hypothetical Go. *izum) secondary, probably due to lack of sentence stress. From the plural, the e was transferred to the singular. In the 2 sg. es-t, -t is attached either from the preterit (vast) or from the suffixed pronoun þu < tu. The original 2 sg. functions as 3 sg., as everywhere in the Norse present. Since the 13th century r replaces s in the singular, either by analogy with the plural or through lack of sentence stress, as in the subordinating particle es, later er.

OE (WS) eom has its vowel from the synonym WS bīo (Angl. bīom), explained below. The initial b of the same verb is added to the 1, 2 sg. in Old Saxon, and to the 1, 2 sg. and the plural in Old High German. For OE eart see below.

(b) Pres. Opt.

Go. sijau sijai, etc.	OE sīe, sīen
ON sia ser se, etc.	OS si sis, sin
	OHG sī sīs sī, sīn sīt sīn.

The forms have zero grade of the root (cf. ind. sind); the singular was IE *s-iyē-m, siyēs, siyēt, pl. *s-ī-mé/ó; cf. Sk. syām, OL. siem, pl.

sīmus. Gothic added the usual opt. endings of the regular verbs to the **sij*-base for singular, plural, and dual, so that it really duplicated the opt. sign. Old Norse adapted the form entirely to the regular optatives. WGmc. used the *sī*-grade to which Old English added the usual opt. endings. The OS OHG forms consist of *sī*-, carried over into the singular, and the secondary endings, so that, e.g., *sīn* corresponds to L. *sīmus, sint.*

B. Root **bheu-/bh(e)wī-*:

This is preserved most completely in Old English: *bīo* (Angl. *bīom*), *bis(t), biþ*, pl. *bīoþ*; opt. *bīo, bīon*. The forms go back to the zero grade root **bhw-* with *-ī*-extension > Gmc. *bwī*-, in which *w* disappeared by assimilation; *bīo* < **biu* with the usual ending of the 1 sg., *bīoþ* has the ending *-onti* > Gmc. *-anþi* > OE *-ōþ* (reduced to *-aþ* in the regular polysyllabic verbs).

C. Root **wes-*:

This is used everywhere in the preterit indicative, optative, in the imperative, and in the verbal nouns. In Old High German it is also used in the indicative and optative of the present, usually with the concrete meaning 'exist, happen'. It is inflected as a regular strong verb of class V.

	Pret. Ind.	Opt.	Imper.	Infin.	Pres. Part.	Past Part.
Go.	was—wēsum	wēsjau	(sijais)	wisan	wisands	—
ON	vas—vǫro	vǣra	ves	vesa	vesande	veret[1]
OE	wæs—wǣron	wǣre	wes[2]	wesan[2]	wesende[2]	—
OS	was—wārun	wāri	wis	wesan	wesandi	giwesan
OHG	was—wārum	wāri	wis	wesan	wesanti	(MHG gewesen)

[1] since the 13th century, *r* for *s* is carried through in all forms.   [2] also *bīo, bīon, bīonde.*

D. Root **er-/or-*:

OE 2 sg. *eart*, Angl. *earþ, arþ* is the remnant of a preterit present, 'thou hast arisen = thou art', with regular perfect ending of the 2 sg., which appears in Anglian in the shifted form, in West Saxon as analogical *-t* as in the preterit presents (*wāst, þearft* etc.) or in Go. ON *gaft. ea* is due to breaking of *a* (*æ*) before *r* + consonant. In Anglian this form gained in influence. In the plural, *earon*, with analogical vowel from the 2 sg., appears by the side of *sind(on)*, but we also find *aron* with unbroken vowel. From *aron a* was introduced into the 2 sg., *arþ*, by the side of *earþ*, and both vowels were also introduced into the

Angl. 1 sg.: *eam, am*. The *a*-forms are the source of Modern English *am, art, are*.

'DO'

b   For this, Gothic uses *taujan* (OHG *zouwen*, MLG *touwen* 'arrange', MFr. *zauen* 'hasten'), ON *gǫrua* (OHG *garawen*, OE *gearwian* 'make ready', NHG *gerben* 'tan'). WGmc. uses the *ō*-grade of the root which in most IE languages appears with the *ē*-grade: **dhē-*, Gk. τί-θη-μι, L. *fē-cī*, Lith. *dĕti*, OSl. *dĕti*. The forms are:

Old English: Pres. Ind. *dō(m) dēst dēþ*, pl. *dōþ*
    "   Opt. *dō, dōn*; Imper. *dō*
    Pret. Ind. *dyde dydest dyde, dydon* (poet. *dǣdon*)
    "   Opt. *dyde, dyden*
    Infin. *dōn*; Participles *dōnde gedōn*.

For *dōm* as against *dēst, dēþ* cf. **54 h, 2**.

The preterit *dyde* would theoretically go back to **dudī-*, the stem vowel of the optative being transferred to the indicative. Phonologically this is possible only if Sievers' view that ǝ can appear as *u* is accepted; cf. **38 d**. But it seems more probable that *dyde* is a transformation under the influence of preterit present optatives like *dyge, þyrfe, scyle*. Otherwise, we would expect similar forms in the other WGmc. dialects too. The 2 sg. indicative adds the present ending *-st*, to distinguish it from the 1st and 3rd persons.

Old Saxon: Pres. Ind. *dōm dōs dōd*, pl. *dōd*
    "   Opt. *dōe *dōes* (*duoas* occurs), *dōen*; Imper *dō*
    Pret. Ind. *deda dādi deda, dādun* or *dedun*
    "   Opt. *dādi, dādin* or *dedi, dedin*
    Infin. *dōn*, Past Part. *gidōn* or *gidān*.

Old High German (oldest forms before the diphthongization of *ō* to *uo ua*):

    Pres. Ind. *tōm tōs tōt, tōmēs tōt tōnt*
    "   Opt. *tō tōs tō, tōm tōt tōn*
    Pret. Ind. *teta tāti teta, tātum* etc.
    "   Opt. *tāti* etc.
    Infin. *tōn*, Participles *tōnti gitān*.

The inflection is athematic, with more or less of a tendency to introduce thematic forms, e.g., OE *dēst, dēþ* < **dō-is, dō-iþ* (*-i* or *-si*, *-ti* had been dropped in Prim. Gmc., i.e., before the umlaut period), OS *dōit*, OHG (Otfrid) *duist, duit* etc. (*u* instead of *uo* as simplification of the group of three vowels.)

The OS OHG preterit forms must be transformations of a more original type. The forms with *-e-* are usually explained as reduplicated perfects: *dhe-dhō-a/e; but the contraction of the stem vowel with the ending of the 1, 3 sg. would give three morae, and we should therefore expect OHG *tetō. Perhaps Wilmanns (Deutsche Gramm. 3. 61) is right in tracing them to an imperfect of the reduplicated present system, Sk. ádadhām < *é-dhe-dhēm/dhōm. He believes that this is confirmed by OS 2 sg. dedōs (archaic for dādi); this would probably have retained the long vowel either from the 2 pl. *dedōð < *(e-)dhedhō-te, or by analogy with the present. Cf. the other e-forms in the paradigm given above. The ā-forms are undoubtedly due to analogy with the strong verbs of class V: dādi dādun, tāti tātum etc. like gābi gābun (-m) etc. But ā in the past part. gidān, gitān is not analogical, but represents the original ē-grade, as in Go. gadēþs, OE dǽd, OHG tāt (noun).

'STAND' and 'GO'; cf. **54 h.** c

Go. standan, gaggan, Crimean Go. geen; ON standa, ganga; OE stondan, gongan and gān; OS standan, gangan, rarely stān, gān; OHG stantan, gangan, rarely stān/stēn, gān/gēn.

The longer forms of the verb 'to stand' are certainly extensions of the root *stā-, but the longer and shorter forms of the verb 'to go' have no etymological connections with one another. Go. standan—stōþ corresponds to L. statuere < *stə-t-, with nasal infix in the present (and possibly the past part.); gaggan is a cognate of Gk. κοχώνη < *ghə-ghōnā 'crotch', Sk. jáṅghā 'lower leg', Lith. žengiù 'I step'. OHG gān/gēn is related to Gk. κίχημι < *ĝhi-ĝhē-mi 'I reach'.

(a) *The Long Forms:* gangan and standan are regular strong verbs as far as their endings are concerned. gangan belongs to class VII, standan to class VI, but the stem forms show slight irregularities. The forms are:

Go.   gaggan (iddja[1], once gaggida);   standan   stōþ(um)   *standans (?)
ON   ganga gekk   gengenn;   standa   stōþ(o)   staþenn
OE   gangan gēong   gangen;   standan   stōd(on)   standen
OS   gangan geng   gigangan; standan   stōd(un)   astandan
OHG   gangan giang   gigangan; stantan   stuat(um) gistantan.

The irregularities of these forms are discussed in **60.**

[1] see below, (c).

(b) *The Short Forms:*

OE	gā	gǽst[1]	gǽþ[1]		gāþ	infin. gān
OS	—	—	(be)gēd		—	gān
OHG	gām	gāst	gāt	gāmēs	gāt	gānt	gān
Opt.	gē	gēst	gē	gēn	gēt	gēn.	

[1] from *gā-is(t) gā-iþ.

For the stem vowel of OHG *gān* : *gēn* cf. **54 h 2**. The optative has only the vowel *ē*, as is the case in all present optatives (except *sī*): 1 sg. *gē* < *$ghē$-$oī$-m*.

(c) Go. *iddja*, OE *ēode* function as preterits of *gaggan, gangan/gān*. Both are inflected like weak preterits, e.g., Go. *iddjes, iddjedum* etc.

iddja is explained by Kluge, Urg.[3] 167 f., as an augment-aorist, IE *$é$-$jē$-t* (better: *$é$-$jā$-t*), Sk. *á-yāt*. IE *$jā$-* is an extension of the root *ei-*, L. *īre* (Sk. *yā-ti* 'goes', L. *iānua, Jānus*). Collitz, Sch. Prät. 142 ff., considers it an old perfect of the unextended root, L. *eō* < *ei-$ō$*, identical with L. *iī* which he analyzes as *$ī$-j-$í$* (*-j-* transitional glide, *-ī* < *-ai*, medial ending of the 1 sg. perfect). In both cases, *-ddj-* is due to 'Holtzmann's Law'.

ēode is discussed extensively by Collitz, l. c., 145–8. In spite of the copious literature listed there, the form can hardly be said to be fully explained. Its connection, or near-identity, with *iddja* seems obvious, although even that is doubted by some.[1] Without fully solving the problem the following considerations bring us perhaps a little closer to an understanding of it.

(1) The connection of the form with the root *ei-*, Gmc. *ii* = *ī* may tentatively be taken for granted.

(2) While Gothic attaches to this root the endings of the weak preterit directly, without a dental, the OE form follows the second class of weak verbs.

(3) *īo* > *ēo* (cf. Bülbring, Altenglisches Elementarbuch 1 §118) is to be compared with Go. *frijōnds* : OE *frēond*, Sk. *priyá* 'wife' : OE *frēo* 'woman' (but with Holtzmann's Law, ON *Frigg*). The phonological difficulty lies here, as in many other instances, in the fact that the exact conditions of Holtzmann's Law are not known. Cf. **33 c**.

NOTE: Middle English formed an analogical preterit of *gān* (*gōn*) : *geode*.

CLIPPED PRETERITS. In analogy with the synonymous forms *gangan—gān*, late OHG and especially MHG developed a number of shortened preterits. OHG has *gie, lie* (following the proportion *gangan* : *gān* = *gieng* : *gie*). MHG added *vie* (for *vienc*) and *hie* (for *hienc*).

Likewise, some 'contracted' presents were formed on the pattern of *gān, stān*: *hān, hāst, hāt* etc. (for *habēm, -ēs, -ēt*) and *lān, lāst, lāt* begin to appear in OHG and become frequent in MHG, where also *vān, hān* are added. It is probable that the form *gie* was the starting point of all of these analogical forms.

d 'WILL'

Go.	*wiljau*	*wileis*	*wilei*	*wileima*	*wilda*
ON	*vil*	*vill*	*vill*	*viliom*	*vilda*
OE	*wille*	*wilt*	*wil(l)e*	*willaþ*	*wolde*
OS	*williu*	*wili(s)*	*wili*	*williad*	*welda wolda*
OHG	*willu*	*wili*	*wili*	*wellemēs*	*wolta.*

The verb means originally 'choose, prefer' and belongs to L. *volō*, *velle*, OSl. *voljǫ*, *velēti*, Sk. *vṛṇītē*. Its athematic character is shown by (old) Lith. *pa-velmi*, L. *vult*. The Gmc. present is an optative with a mood sign -*ī*- (cf. L. *velīm*), as with the athematic aorists (Go. 3 sg. *nēmi*). But there is a strong tendency towards leveling with the other verb types. In Old Norse the verb follows the type *telia* (I W), except that in the 2, 3 sg. *lʀ*, due to lack of sentence stress, is assimilated to *ll* (Heusler, Aisl. Elb. §149, 2); however, in poetry the older 1 st. *vilia* is still found. *ll* in WGmc. goes back to *lj*, but the forms OHG *willu*, etc. are not identical with Go. *wiljau*. They are due to the transition to the 'regular' conjugation: OHG *willu* < *weli-ō weljō*, OE *willaþ*, OHG *wellent, -ant* < *welj-onti*.

OE *wilt* follows the pattern of the modal auxiliaries with which 'will' is related by function. Later, both Low and High German adopt the same form. In Old High German it is first found in Williram, in Middle High German it is more frequent than the older form. Gradually the 1, 3 sg., too, follow the pattern of the preterit presents: E Ger. *will*.

The stem vowel is subject to variations, but these are largely or entirely of secondary character. OS *welda* may have preserved its *e* on account of the following *a*, but OHG *wellemēs* clearly follows the analogy of strong verbs like *wellan* 'wälzen' : *willu—wellemēs*. *o* in OE *wolde*, OS *wolda*, OHG *wolta* is hardly due to old ablaut (*wl̥-*), but rather to its association with the preterit of the functionally related verb *shall* (*sceolde, skolda, scolta*).

Since the original optative character of this verb had been obliterated by these changes, a new optative was formed, OE *wil(l)e*, OS *willie*, OHG *welle* (*wellēs*, etc.).

THE NOUN
THE STEMS

76. Gradation. In the IE verb system gradation of the root vowel was of functional importance. It was the primary means of differentiating aspects or tenses. The Gmc. verb has preserved this function of gradation up to the present time almost in its original scope, while the other IE languages have greatly restricted it. In fact some of them have nearly abolished it.

The noun, too, originally had gradation of the root vowel, but it is doubtful whether it had functional importance or was merely a mechanical result of the shifting accent. In the verb, too, gradation was partly mechanical; e.g., the ablaut difference between Sk. *vavárta* (sg.) and *vavṛtimá* was clearly caused by the accent. But in the noun, as far as we can analyze its structure, we can trace only this type of gradation and at best suspect that, in an earlier period than we are able to reach, it also possessed functional gradation. Even gradation due to accent is evident only in a few languages, notably in Sanskrit, to a lesser degree in Greek and Latin. Sk. *gāus* 'Rind' has the instrumental *gávā*, cf. L. *bōs—bŏvis*; *dyāus* 'sky', gen. *divás* = Ζεύς—Δι(ϝ)όs; *pāt* 'foot', instr. *padā́* like Gk. πῶς (πούs)—ποδόs, L. *pēs—pĕdis*; Sk. *pánthās* 'path', instr. *pathā́*, corresponds to Gk. πόντοs, 'sea'—πάτοs 'path' (**pont-* : *pṇt-*), where two complete paradigms are based on different ablaut grades that originally belonged to one paradigm, as in Sanskrit.

In some cases we can infer gradation within a noun by the comparison of different languages. Thus we find the *e*-grade in Gk. γένοs as against the zero grade in Go. *kuni* 'kin'; the *o*-grade in OHG *zan(d)*, OE *tōþ* < **dont-*, the zero grade in Go. *tunþus* and probably L. *dent-* (that these may originally have been participles of the root *ed-* 'eat' does not matter; they are nouns in historical times, and **dont-/dṇt-* may be considered a genuine 'root'); **pĕd-/pŏd-* appears in L. *pēs—pĕdis*, Gk. πῶs—ποδόs, Go. *fōtus*. Cf. Kluge, Urg.³ 198–200.

a **77. Classes.** The grammatical classification of the noun is determined by the suffixes. To an extent, of course, this is also true of the verb; cf. especially the verb classes of Sk. grammar, **53**. The four classes of the Gmc. weak verb are determined entirely by their suffixes, but in the primary, not derived verbs, the 'strong verbs', the vowel grade of the root is the determining factor, and the suffix is of some slight consequence only in a small number of *-jo*-verbs, like Go. *bidjan*.

Of the numerous IE noun suffixes (listed especially by Brugmann, KG 311–54, and Hirt, Idg. Gr. 3. 183–236) the following are determining factors for the Gmc. declensional classes:

Monophthongal suffixes: *-e-/-o-* (*-je-/-jo-*, *-we-/-wo-*), *-ā-* (*-jā-/-ī-*).
Diphthongal suffixes: *-ei-/-oi-/-i-*, *-eu-/-ou-/-u-*, *-ĕn-/-ŏn-/-n-*, *-ĕr-/-ŏr-/-r-*; the suffix *-īn-* is an extension of the *-ī*-suffix.
Consonantal suffixes: *-es-/-os-*, *-ent-/-ont-/-nt-*.

Finally, there are nouns without any suffixes, comparable to the athematic verbs.

NOTE: This arrangement corresponds to an extent to the classification of the Gmc. strong verb. The monophthongal suffixes represent classes V and VI; the *-ei*-suffix class I, *-eu-* class II, *-er-* class III. But the verb classes are based on the root syllables, the noun classes on the suffixes. Since these were unaccented in Germanic, the *-i-* and *-u-*diphthongs gradually became monophthongs or even disappeared, cf. gen. sg. Go. *sunaus*, OE *suna*, OS *suno*. It is therefore entirely justified that our grammars designate the -*o*-, -*ā*-, -*i*-, and -*u*-stems as vocalic stems (or declensions) and all others as consonantic.

Accordingly, the Gmc. noun has the following classes or stems: **b**
I. **e**/**o**-stems, usually called *o*-stems, since this ablaut grade appears in the majority of case forms.

NOTE: Some Gmc. grammars unfortunately still use the misleading term *a*-stems (IE *o* > Gmc. *a*) and, inversely, speak of *ō*-stems instead of *ā*-stems. Brugmann, Hirt, Loewe avoid this confusion; Streitberg speaks of *a*- and *ō*-stems in his Gotisches Elb., of *o*- and *ā*-stems in his Urgermanische Gramm.—obviously because the former treats only one Gmc. language, while the latter compares Germanic with the other IE languages. But Boer, Oerg. Hb., turns back to the '*a* : *ō*'designations. Kluge, Urg.[3] 192, mentions the '*o*:*a*-declension'. Obviously, such uncertainty of terminology is apt to cause confusion. '*ō*-stems' and '*ā*-stems' should be the exclusive designation, both in comparative grammars and in grammars of individual Gmc. languages.

Gk. λύκ-*o*-*s*, L. *lupus* 'wolf' : Run. *stainaʀ*, Finn. *kuningas*, Go. *wulfs*
Gk. ζυγ-ό-*ν*, L. *iugum* 'yoke' : Run. *horna*, Go. *juk*.
  jo-stems:
Gk. ὑ-ιό-*s*, L. *fīlius* 'son' : Go. *harjis*
Gk. ξέν-ιο-*ν* 'guest-gift', L. *ingenium* 'mind' : Go. *kuni*.
  wo-stems:
Go. *kniu* 'knee' (*wo*-stem in Gmc. only; Gk. γόνυ, L. *genu* are *u*-stems).
II. **ā**-stems:
Gk. χώρ-ᾱ 'land', L. *mensa* 'table' : Go. *giba*.
  jā-stems:
Gk. οἰκ-ίᾱ 'house', L. *cōpia* 'supply' : Go. *bandi*.
III. **i**-stems:
Gk. πόλ-ι-*s* 'city', L. *host-i-s* 'enemy' : Go. *gasts*.
IV. **u**-stems:
Gk. πῆχ-υ-*s* 'elbow', L. *man-u-s* 'hand' : Go. *handus*.
V. **n**-stems:
Gk. ἡγεμ-ών 'leader', L. *hom-ō* 'man' : Go. *guma*
Gk. κύ-ων (masc. or fem.) 'dog', L. *nati-ō* 'nation' : Go. *tuggō*
Gk. ὄνομ-a, L. *nōm-en* 'name' : Go. *namō*.
VI. **r**-stems:
Gk. πατ-ήρ, L. *pat-er* : Go. *fadar*.
VII. **nt**-stems (participles):
Gk. φέρ-οντ-os, L. *fer-ent-is* 'carrying' (gen. sg.) : Go. *frijōnds*.
VIII. **s**-stems:

Gk. γέν-ος, L. *genus* 'kin' : Go. *agis.*

IX. root nouns (nouns without suffix):

Gk. νύξ, L. *nox* 'night' : Go. *nahts.*

78. Categories.

GENDER.

a   The literature on the origin of 'gender' is very extensive, but scholars are far from agreement on the subject. A list of the most important contributions is given by Hirt, Idg. Gr. 3, 320 f.; the appendix of this book contains a few additions. The two extremes are probably represented by Jacob Grimm, Deutsche Gramm. 3. (1831) 311–563, and Brugmann, Z. f. allg. Sprw. 4. 100, Btr. 15. 523, and KG 354–62. For Grimm's view the following paragraph (l. c., 346) is especially characteristic:

'Das grammatische genus ist demnach eine in der phantasie der menschlichen sprache entsprungene ausdehnung des natürlichen auf alle und jede gegenstände. Durch diese wunderbare operation haben eine menge von ausdrücken, die sonst todte und abgezogene begriffe enthalten, gleichsam leben und empfindung empfangen, und indem sie von dem wahren geschlecht formen, bildungen, flexionen entlehnen, wird über sie ein die ganze sprache durchziehender reiz von bewegung und zugleich bindender verknüpfung der redeglieder ausgegossen. Man kann sich, wäre das genus in der sprache aufgehoben, verschlingungen der worte, wie wir sie in der griechischen oder lateinischen syntax bewundern, nicht wohl gedenken.'

Brugmann, on the other hand, considers grammatical gender, according to Hirt (l. c., 336) 'sozusagen einen ganz mechanischen Vorgang, der im Wesentlichen durch die äussere Form hervorgerufen ist. Die Worte waren Fem., weil sie auf -ā oder -ī ausgingen, Mask., weil sie auf -*os* ausgingen.' The author has stated his conception of the problem, which is based essentially on Brugmann, in his Outline of German Historical Grammar 77 f., in the following way:

The grammatical concept of 'gender' originally had nothing to do with sex, nor are the two concepts entirely identical in our times (compare *das Männchen, das Mädchen, das Weib*). It is considered probable that the development of gender had its starting point in certain general facts of cattle raising among the early Indo-Europeans. The most numerous type of Indo-European nouns, the *o*-stems, appears in historical times generally as masculine gender. But it did not originally denote the male human being or animal exclusively, nor did it refer to inanimate objects as 'male' through a process of metaphorical sexualization. IE **ekwos* 'horse', **wḷqos* 'wolf' did not necessarily mean 'stallion', 'he-wolf', but merely signified a definite individual horse or wolf. The corresponding stems in -ā, **ekwā*, **wḷqā* had either generic or collective force, i.e., they denoted the type horse, wolf, or a group of horses or wolves ('Gestüte, Rudel'). Under agricultural conditions, the general type of domestic animal is represented by the female animal, while the male (the stallion, the bull, the rooster) appears as the exceptional individual. This is, for instance, illustrated by the fact that the Indo-European word for 'cattle', *gwōus (L. bōs), in Germanic came to mean the female animal: German *Kuh*, English *cow*. The forms in -ā, when referring to the animal type, became the starting point for feminine gender: *ekwā came to mean 'mare'. In their collective meaning these forms gave rise to the neuter plural, which has the same ending as the feminine singular (compare L. fem. sing. *mensa*—neut. plur. *verba*). Neither the generic use of the ā-stems nor the individualizing character of the o-stems was necessarily restricted to the female or male sex respectively, e.g., L. *scriba* 'scribe', *agricola* 'farmer', Slav. *sluga* 'servant' (cp. Ger. *die Bedienung, die Kundschaft*) have so-called feminine forms, but denote male (as well as female) beings of a general type.

The neuter singular was originally not distinct from the masculine, except for the lack of the nominative form, for which the accusative was substituted: L. *verbum* 'word' is both nominative and accusative. This is due to the fact that nouns of this type generally denote inanimate objects that are not very frequently used as active subjects of a sentence.

These three categories—the individual, the generic, and the objective-collective —in the course of time were generalized beyond their original scope, and the endings of pronouns and adjectives were used in agreement with their stem forms. Thus the three 'genders' became essential distinctions in the Indo-European languages, but they are by no means fundamental categories of language in general.

The three genders have been preserved in a number of IE languages, e.g. Slavic and German. In the Romance languages masculine and neuter have coalesced, and others, like English and Scandinavian, have in the noun abolished the category of gender altogether.

In other languages the number of genders varies greatly. Finno-Ugrian has no trace of gender, not even in the pronoun; Finn. *hän* corresponds to E. 'he, she, it'. Some languages of the Bantu group (southern Africa) have from 5 to 12 'genders'. The gender system of the Semitic languages is very similar to the IE conditions: there are two genders, masc. and fem. (not only of the noun, but also of the verb: *qatala* 'he kills', *qatalat* 'she kills'; *qatalta* 'you kill' (masc.), *qatalti* 'you kill' (fem.); the same endings, that denote the fem. in nouns, are also used to form collectives and abstracts, and function as pl. endings besides, similar to the several functions of IE -ā.

NUMBER.

The IE noun had three numbers, singular, plural, and dual. The **b** latter has been given up almost everywhere. In the Slavic languages it is still in frequent use, especially for those parts of the body that are pairs: Russ. *oči* 'eyes', *uši* 'ears'. In Germanic, the noun had lost the dual in prehistoric times, but the personal pronoun still shows it in Gothic and Norse: *wit*, *vit* 'both of us', *jut*, *it* 'both of you'.   Go. duals of the 2nd pers. are still preserved in the modern Bav. dialects (Ostrogoths had settled in the southern part of the Bav. territory, as e.g. the name *Gossensass* 'Gothic settlement' shows): *ös* 'you' (nom.), *enk* 'you' (acc.), *enker* 'your' are duals from a historical standpoint, but plurals in their present meaning.

c   CASES.   The number of distinct case forms varies greatly in the several IE languages, and it is hardly possible to state it with complete certainty for the period of our reconstruction of the primitive IE language.   Undoubtedly, each language had more case forms in its earlier history, and their number decreased more or less in such a way that the functions of several case forms were combined in one form.   This process is termed 'Syncretism'.   Phonetic laws are the most common cause of syncretism.   Through their action several endings were apt to become identical, and the resulting form functioned for the two or more cases from which it had developed.   Thus, the *o*-stems had in Indo-European distinct forms for the ablative and instrumental sg., *-ōd* and *-ō*, Sk. *áśvād* : *áśvā*; but in early Latin *-d* disappeared by phonetic law (about 200 B.C.; earlier inscriptions have forms in *-OD*, cf. Sommer, LLFL[2] 344), and the form *equō* was used both as ablative and as instrumental. The genitive sg. ended in *-ī*, the locative sg. in *-ei*; the latter was contracted to *-ī*, so that in classical times there is no difference between these two forms—*Corinthī* can be either gen. or loc.   In many cases it is impossible to determine the IE source of a given form.   If we did not happen to possess early L. (and other Italic) forms in *-ōd*, we could not possibly tell whether L. *equō* goes back to the IE abl. or instr., or both.   Thus, we cannot decide with certainty whether the Go. 'dat. sg.' *daga* should be traced back to the IE abl., instr. or loc. sg., for *-ōd*, *-ō*, *-oi* fall together in Gothic as *-a*.

For the following cases IE origin must be assumed, although not all of them were in use in all stem classes and numbers alike:

The *nominative* or subject case is the form used for the center of the sentence concept.

The *accusative* denotes the person, object or idea directly affected by the verb.

The *genitive* with verbs indicates a less direct and complete influence of the verb concept on the noun concept than the accusative.   With nouns it implies various types and degrees of connection between the two nouns.

The *ablative* denotes the source of action; its function is more or less closely related to the genitive on the one hand, to the instrumental on the other.

The *dative* is the case of the noun in regard to which something is done.

The *locative* designates the place of action.

The *instrumental* expresses the means by which something is done.

The *vocative* is the form of address.

This number of cases is, of course, merely a result of historical development, accidental to a certain extent. It is by no means a logical postulate. Other language groups have different numbers with different logical foundations. Thus Magyar grammar distinguishes 21 cases, Finnish 18. True, the 'endings' of many of them are clearly postpositions, but they are 'cases' just the same, quite as much so as the IE cases. Doubtless some (or all?) of the IE case endings have also come from postpositions, though we shall probably never arrive at any certainty about this. The Magyar cases (whose names indicate their functions fairly well) are: Nominative, Accusative, Dative, Inessive, Elative, Illative, Superessive, Delative, Sublative, Adessive, Ablative, Allative, Terminative, Essive, Temporal, Modal, Distributive, Comitative, Sociative, Factive, Causal. The names of the Finnish cases are similar.

79. Endings. The origin of the case endings is not known, any more **a** than that of the personal endings of the verb. Still, it is possible that a comparison with Finno-Ugrian may throw a light at least on one feature of the IE endings. Nearly every language of that group has two plural signs, a consonantic and a vocalic one. The former is mostly *-t* (*-k* in Magyar), and is used chiefly in the nom. and accus.; the latter is *-i-* (*-e-*), used in the other cases before the case ending: Finn. *kala* 'fish', nom. pl. *kalat*, gen. sg. *kalan*, gen. pl. *kalain* (both plural signs are often combined, so that there are forms of the gen. pl. in *-ten*). Aside from certain phonetic changes caused by the plural sign *-i-*, the actual case endings are the same for both numbers.

There are indications that in Indo-European, too, the actual case endings were originally the same for singular and plural. Thus *-s* was the nominative sign, and in the singular it was attached directly to the stem, but in the plural there was a connecting vowel *-e-*: Gk. (Dor.) πώς < *pōd-s*—pl. πόδ-ε-s (L. *-ēs* < *-ei-es*, ending of *i*-stems). But many nouns formed the nom. sg. without endings, e.g., πατήρ, pl. πατέρ-es; through the contrast between singular and plural forms like these, -s came to be felt as a plural sign and was attached to singular endings to pluralize them: acc. sg. λόγον < *log-o-m, pl. λόγους < *logom-s, logon-s; dat. sg. λόγῳ < *-ōi, dat. pl. λόγοις < -ōi-s. The functions of the cases were not absolutely fixed; thus the ending -ōis appears in Greek for the dat. pl., in Sanskrit and Lithuanian for the instr. pl. The accusative ending -m, mentioned above, appears in the plural with the same case function if -s is attached, but as the genitive ending, if a connecting vowel, apparently always o, but perhaps also e, is inserted: χώρᾱ 'land', acc. sg. χώρᾱν < -ā-m, gen. pl. χωρῶν < -ā-o-m (in several languages, such as Greek and Sanskrit, this ending was transferred to all stem classes). Probably this genitive had originally partitive function, similar to French 'j'ai des plumes'.

The following table lists, in general, only those IE case endings that occur in Germanic.

SINGULAR

b   **Nominative.** (1) -s with vocalic stems except ā-stems, and with stems ending in stops:

Gk. λύκ-o-s, Gmc. *wulf-a-z, Go. wulfs, ON ulfr[1]

L. host-i-s, Gmc. *ʒast-i-z, Go. gasts, ON gestr[1]

Sk. sūn-u-ṣ, Gmc. *sun-u-z, Go. sunus, ON sunr[1]

L. nox < *noct-s, Gmc. *naht-s, Go. nahts, [ON nōtt[2]]

Pres. Part., L. -n(t)s, Gmc. -ndz, Go. frijōnds (ON frǽnde, weak).

---

[1] Run. stainaʀ, gastiʀ, sunuʀ.   [2] analogical, following the ā-stems. The masc. fōtr 'foot' has -r, but this, too, is analogical, since *fōt-s would have become *fōss.

In Indo-European, some nominatives of this type had the accent on the stem and some had it on the suffix ('ending' in a wider sense); cf. Gk. λόγος, but υἱός, Sk. sūnús. Germanic standardized the type with accented stem, and therefore the ending became subject to Verner's Law. The resulting -z appears as -ʀ in Old Norse, but disappears in WGmc.:

OE wulf, giest, sunu, naht, freond, OHG wolf, gast, sun(u), naht, friunt. In Gothic, the law of the unvoicing of final spirants restores -s.

(2) **No** endings with ā-stems, ī- (-jā, -jē) stems and stems in n, r, s: Gk. θεά 'goddess', Gmc. *ʒebā, Go. giba, ON giǫf < *ʒebu.

(-ā becomes -a in Go., -u in NWGmc.).

Sk. pátnī, Gk. πότνια 'Herrin', Go. bandi 'band'; frijōndi, fem. of frijōnds

Gk. ποιμήν 'shepherd', κύων 'dog', L. homō, Go. guma 'man', ON gume

Gk. πατήρ, L. *pater*, Go. *fadar*, ON *faþer*

Gk. ἔρεβος[1] 'place of darkness', Go. *riqis* (*-z*), ON *røkkr* 'darkness'.

> [1] *-os* is not ending, but stem suffix; gen. sg. ἐρέβους < *-es-os*.

Accusative, -m:

Gk. λύκ-ο-ν, Go. *wulf*, ON *ulf* (Run. *staina*)   **c**

L. *host-i-m* > *-em*, Go. *gast*, ON *gest*

Sk. *sūn-ú-m*, Go. *sunu*, ON *mǫg* 'son' (Run. *magu*)

Gk. θεᾱ́ν, Go. *giba*, ON *giof* (analogical for **gafa*).

(*-ām* becomes *-a* in all dialects, subject, of course, to secondary changes.)

Gk. πότν-ια-ν < *-jə-m*, Go. *bandja, frijōndja* < *-jā-m*.

Gk. ἡγεμ-όν-α < *-m̥*, Go. *guman*, ON *hana*

Gk. πατ-έρ-α < *-m̥*, Go. *fadar*, ON *fǫþor* < *-r̥-m*, as L. *patrem*

L. *noct-em* < *-m̥*, Go. *naht*, ON *nōtt*

L. *-nt-em* < *-m̥*, Go. *frijōnd*.

The accusative of neuters is always identical with the nominative. It ends in *-m* in *o*-stems, but lacks an ending in all other stems: L. *iugum* = Go. *juk* < *-o-m*; Gk. ἔρεβος is nominative as well as accusative.

Genitive, -es/-os/-s with nouns, **-so** with pronouns. In Germanic, **d** and partly also elsewhere, the pronominal ending was transferred to *o*-stem nouns, possibly also to *ā-, i-, u*-stems.

(1) -es/-os/-s

Gk. κυν-ός, L. *homin-is* < *-es*, Go. *gumins*, ON *hana*

Gk. πατρ-ός, L. *patris* < *-es*, Go. *fadrs*, (ON *fǫþor*)

L. *noct-is*, Go. *nahts*, ON *nætr*, gen. of *nōtt, merkr*, gen. of *mǫrk* 'boundary', < *-iz* < *-es*.

In these classes the accent was on the stem, therefore Old Norse has *-ʀ*, but WGmc. has no ending; ON *hana* < **hananʀ* > *-nn*, Run. *-an*, with loss of *-n* in literary Norse. Gothic, of course, unvoiced final *-z*.

ON *fǫþor* may either be a transfer from the accusative, or it may correspond to Sk. *pitúr* < **pət-r-s*. OE *fōtes*, OHG *nahtes* are transfers from the *o*-class (*nahtes* in analogy with *tages*).

As far as evidence goes, we must assume *-es* rather than *-os*, since we find numerous forms with umlaut: ON *merkr* < **mark-iz, bø̄kr* < **bōk-iz* = OE *bēc*, OE *byrg*, gen. of *burg*; by the side of ON *fǫþor* we find *feþr*, and likewise *brø̄þr, mø̄þr*.

(2) -es/-os or -so

Gk. θεᾶς can be explained either as *-ā-es* (Brugmann, KG 380); or as

-ā-so (l. c., 54, Anm.). The same is true for Go. *gibōs* (ON *giafar*, OE *giefe*, OS *geƀa*, OHG *gebā*). As the long vowel shows, the ending had three morae; this can be due to the contraction of *ā + e*, or to the loss of *-o* after a long syllable, with transfer of the lost mora to the preceding syllable (Streitberg's Dehnstufengesetz, l. c., 144 f.).

Go. *anstais* (fem.), *sunaus* can likewise be interpreted either from *-oi-so*, *-ou-so* or from *-oi-es*, *-ou-es*; in both cases we have IE *-ōis*, *-ōus*, as in Lith. *naktḗs* (now spelled *naktiḗs*) *sūnaũs*. ON *āstar*, *sonar*, OE *suna*, OS *suno*, OHG *fridō* correspond to this. OE *ēste* (*-i* in the earliest documents), OS OHG *ensti* cannot be original gen. forms, but were transferred from the dative-locative.

(3) -so is the ending of the *o*-stems, as in Greek: ὁδοῦ < *sod-ó-so* or *sod-é-so*; *-sjo* appears in Sk., e.g. *vŗkásya*, and in Gk., λύκοιο (Hom.). For the Gmc. forms we have to assume that the accent was on the connecting vowel, as in the Gk. ὁδός-type, so that we have *-s* in all dialects (Go. pronominal forms like *þiz-uh*, *þiz-ei* etc. do not disprove this; the attached particle was stressed, but that has no bearing on the accent of the noun forms). Otherwise, van Helten, Btr. 36. 436, Hirt HU 2. 35. But it is difficult to decide with certainty whether the connecting vowel was *e* or *o*. Go. *wulfis* certainly had *-e-*, and frequently this is also assumed for OS OHG *-es*.[1] ON *ulfs* goes back to *-oso*, since we have Run. forms in *-as* (e.g. ʒoðagas, proper name, inscription of Valsfjord). The earliest OE manuscripts have *-æs* < *-o-so* (*dōmæs*), the later form is *-es*. For OS OHG *-es* is the regular form. OS *-as*, which is fairly frequent, is apparently a secondary development from *-es*.[2] The same is probably true for OHG *-as* which appears from the tenth century on, especially in Bavarian. The explanation of the *e* in these two dialects is hampered by the almost general belief that unaccented *e* always became *i* in Germanic. But as a matter of fact there is no evidence that it was treated differently from *e* in accented syllables (**38 a**, 2): it remained *e* before a mid or low vowel, but changed to *i* elsewhere; therefore *-eso* > *-esa* > *-es*. Thus, we must assume *-eso* for Go. OS OHG, but *-oso* for ON OE. There is nothing surprising in this; such variations may occur even within a single language, e.g., Sl. *česo/čego* 'of what' as against *kogo* 'of whom' (*kweso/kwoso*; for *g* < *z* < *s*, cf. Prokosch, AJPh 32. 434 f.).

Ablative. A genuine ablative form exists only for the *o*-stems; it ended in -ōd -ēd, Sk. *vŗkād*, OL. *Gnaivōd*, adv. *facillumēd* (classical *-ō*, *-ĕ*). The Go. dat. *wulfa* may be explained as an ablative.

e **Dative.** The ending was -ai, which became *ōi āi* (three morae) when contracted with the suffix vowel of the *o*- and *ā*-stems: Gk. θεῷ, θεᾷ. It cannot be proved that this is preserved in Gmc. True, the 'datives' of most of the *o*- and *ā*-stems can be interpreted as going back to the IE dative: ON *ulfe*, OE *wulfæ*, *wulfe*, OHG *tage* < *-o-ai* > *-ōi* > Gmc. *-ai*, NWGmc. *-e*; Go. *gibai*, OE *giefe* < *-ā-ai*; but since the datives of the other classes were clearly locatives, this would seem to be an unnecessarily complicated construction.

Locative. Of the several IE types (cf. Brugmann, KG 384 f.) of the **f** locative, the forms in -*i* explain satisfactorily all Gmc. 'dative' forms, although several of them may have other explanations too. We find it, e.g. in Gk. ποιμένι, κυνί, πατρί, νυκτί, Sk. *sūnávi* < **sūn-ou-i*. In *ā*-stems, this, of course, combines into a tri-moric diphthong (Gk. θεᾷ can be a locative quite as well as a dative), and it is generally supposed that in *o*-stems too the contraction of *o* + *i* (*e* + *i*) results in 'Schleifton' (three morae). But the only argument for this is from Gk. forms like Ἰσθμοῖ, ἐκεῖ, and Kurylowicz (Language 8. 200 ff.) has shown conclusively that the Gk. distinction between acute (two morae) and circumflex (three morae) contains a great deal of innovation. While it is an undeniable fact that contractions of *o e a* result in tri-moric syllables (cf. below, nom. pl.), it is altogether improbable that *o* + *i*, *e* + *i* would have the same result. In spite of the fact that evidence from the Greek seems to point to the contrary, it is reasonably certain that the locative of *o*-stems ended in -*ŏi*, which became -*a* in Gothic, -*e* everywhere else. It is therefore most consistent and systematic to consider Go. *wulfa* fundamentally a locative, although, of course, phonologically, ablative, instrumental and locative had fallen together in this form. Likewise, the NWGmc. forms in -*e* (early OE -*æ*) should be considered locatives.

Go. *gibai*, OE *giefe* < -*ā* + *i* are likewise locatives, and so are the datives of the other classes. As far as the scanty evidence goes, the locatives of *i*- and *u*-stems ended in -*ēi* -*ēu*, which may well have been a development from -*ei* + *i*, -*eu* + *i*; in Sk. *agnā́* (Ved.) 'in the fire' the diphthongal element is absorbed, but it appears in *Agnā́y-ī* 'the wife of Agni', similar to *sūnāu*: *Manāv-ī́* 'the wife of Manu'. For Go. *anstai*, *sunau* it is usually claimed that -*ēi* -*ēu* became -*ai* -*au* in East Germanic, but -*ei* > *i*, -*iu* > *i* in NWGmc., but there is no evidence for this, unless we consider the parallel of Go. *fadar* = Gk. πατήρ as such. It is safer to interpret Go. -*ai* -*au* as transfers from the genitive. But the -*ēi*-form appears in OS OHG *ensti*, also in OE *ēste* (in early documents the ending is -*i*), the -*ēu*-form in ON *syne* (= *syni*, with umlaut), early OHG *suniu*; OE *suna*, OS *suno* are evidently genitive forms (OE *suna*, OS *sunies* for older **suno*), or at least owe their vowel to them.

Consonantic stems, of course, drop the ending *-i*: Go. *hanin, fadr, baurg*; ON *hana, feþr*.

g **Instrumental.** Of the several IE formations, the Gmc. noun shows traces of only one: *o-* and *ā*-stems had instrumentals with a long suffix vowel, but without actual ending: Lith. *vilkù* 'by the wolf' (the long quantity is preserved in the definite form of the adjective, *gerúo-ju* 'by the good' < **gerȯ-jō*): OS *wulfu*, OHG *wolfu* < *-ō* are instrumentals both in form and function; OS *geƀu*, OHG *gebu*, ON *giof*, < *-ā*, are instrumentals in form, but function as datives.

h A **Vocative** form (IE without ending; *-e* in L. *domine* is the suffix vowel) exists only in the Go. *o-, i-, u*-stems: *wulf, gast, sunu* (*sunau*). Everywhere else the nom. functions also as a voc.

PLURAL

Nominative, -es.

In the *o-* and *ā*-stems this was contracted with the suffix vowel, re-
i sulting in *-ōs*. With the loss of one mora we find this in Go. *wulfōs*, OHG *wolfā* (length sometimes marked by Notker; probably the acc. *tagă* was frequently used instead), with the loss of two morae in ON *ulfar* (rhotacism). OE *wulfas*, OS *wulfos* are only apparently identical with the Go. form, since *-s* (*-z*) in endings disappeared in WGmc. They are usually compared with Sk. (Ved.) forms with double ending (*aśvā́sas* < *-o* + *es* + *es*), but such a remarkable coincidence is un-likely; these forms are a Vedic innovation. When we consider that in all WGmc. dialects the nom. and acc. pl. have the same form (aside from such transitional differences as OHG *tagā* : *tagă*) another explana-tion seems more probable. In the two dialects that have these forms, *n* before *s* disappeared with compensatory lengthening (29 c), *-ons* > *-ōs*; the same was the case in the corresponding L. ending: **lupons* > *lupōs*, partly also in stem syllables (reduction of *n* with nasalization of the preceding vowel): *Cēsor* by the side of *Cēnsor*. 'Bisweilen Doppel-schreibung des *s*: *mensses, messes . . .* , was dafür spricht, dass bei Re-duktion des *-n-* neben dem vorhergehenden Vokal auch das folgende *-s-* eine Quantitätssteigerung erfuhr' (Sommer, LLFL² 245). In Oscan this is even clearer than in Latin: *feíhúss* 'muros', and analogical *víass* 'vias'. It is highly probable that this was the case in Old English and Old Saxon too: *-s* < *-ns* was more strongly articulated than original *-s* and was therefore preserved; if so, *wulfas, wulfos* are accu-

sative forms. It is perhaps more than mere coincidence that Old
English and Old Saxon have the same form as Gothic: Originally, the
Goths and other East Germanic tribes were the neighbors of the (later)
Anglo-Frisian group; it may well be that of the two available forms,
nom. *wulfō and acc. *wulfans > *wulfōs(s), bilingual speakers gave the
preference to that form which their East Germanic neighbors used for
the nominative.

NOTE: But Frisian has wulfa, -ar; the former is either the old nominative or
a transfer from the n-stems, the latter is probably due to Norse influence.

ā + es gives, of course, the same result as o + es: ōs was shortened
by one mora in Gothic and Old High German, by two morae elsewhere:
Go. gibōs, OHG gebā (also gebă, probably the old accusative form),
ON giafar, OE giefæ, giefe, OS geƀa.

i- and u-stems show ĕ-grade of the suffix: -ei-es > -īs > Go. -eis
(= -īs), gasteis, ansteis, ON gester, OE ēste (analogical giestas), OS
gesti, with loss of two morae; OHG gesti must be an accusative. The
long vowel is preserved in OE þrī, OHG drī '3' < *trei-es.

-eu-es > -ius = -jus, Go. sunjus, ON syner (Run. suniʀ) and, with
regular loss of -z in WGmc., OS OHG suni (early OHG suniu). Old
English has suna (felda, handa) and sunu. The latter is doubtless the
old acc., Go. sununs; the former must go back to -ou-es which was
perhaps substituted for -eu-es under the influence of the gen. pl. and
the gen., dat. sg., possibly because the umlaut form *syne = Go.
sunjus constituted an anomaly in the OE declension, where otherwise
the stem vowel of the singular and plural are nearly everywhere the
same (for root stems like fōt—fēt see below).

Consonant stems consistently retain the -s in Gothic: gumans tuggōns, baúrgs, frijōnds; fadrjus is formed by analogy to sunjus (also, see
below, under accusative). In Old Norse, -ʀ was assimilated to preceding n r l: *hananʀ > *hanan(n) > hana, *faðriʀ > feþr (ðohtriʀ
preserved on the stone of Tune, 5th cent.), negl, but was preserved
after other consonants: fōtr, merkr, gefendr. WGmc.: OE guman, tun-
gan, fēt (analogical fæd(e)ras), OS gumon, tungun, fader, naht, OHG
gomun, zungūn, muoter (analogical faterā), naht.

NEUTER. The ending of the nom., acc. pl. is -ā, which appears as -a
in Gothic, as -u in NWGmc. (lost in Norse under all circumstances, in
WGmc. after a long syllable): Go. barna, ON bǫrn < *barnu, OE
bearn : scipu, OS barn : skipu, OHG barn; in Old High German, -u is
preserved only occasionally in -jo-stems and diminutives, through early

analogy with short-stem plurals in *-u*, which as such were no longer existent in historical OHG: *cunniu* 'families' (Tatian), for **kunni*, Al. *chindiliu* for regular *chindelī*. *-n*-stems: Go. *augōna*, ON *auga*, OE *ēagan*, OS *ōgun*, OHG *ougun*.

While the singular of *-s*-stems had virtually disappeared (cf. **86**), some plural forms were preserved in Old English: *lambru, cildru* (or *cild*; with addition of *-n* from the *n*-declension in NE *children*). In German these *-s/-r* plurals increased remarkably in number, due to the fact that the old plural of neuter *o*-stems was identical with the singular (*wort—wort*), and the *r*-ending offered a means of distinction. Old High German had about 30 *r*-plurals (e.g., *lembir, kelbir, huonir*); in Standard New High German, there are about three times as many, including some fifteen masculines, but the number varies greatly in the dialects.[3]

NOTE: The numerous *-r*-plurals of the modern Norse languages have nothing to do with the *s*-stems, but represent a spread from the vocalic stems. From *ulfar, giafar, gester, syner*, *-r* was transferred to *-n*-stems in ON (*hanar, tungor*), and in modern Norse the *-r* of consonant stems (*fōtr, næïr*) was extended to *-er*: Norw. *fǿtter, nætter*. In fact, Norwegian shows a tendency to use *-er*-plurals for all nouns, including loan words (*sofaer, studier, verber, poteter*).

k   **Accusative.** The ending is *-ns*. Very probably this is an assimilation from *-ms*, that is, the singular ending *-m* with the addition of *-s*, which had come to be felt as a characteristic of the plural (**79 a**). In Gothic, *-ns* remained intact and, moreover, prevented the loss of a mora: *wulfans, gastins, sununs, fadruns, fōtuns*; in the latter two forms, *-uns < -ns*, being identical with the ending of *u*-stems, caused partial or complete transition to that class: nom. pl. *fadrjus*; complete transition in the case of *fōtus, tunþus* (where analogy with *handus, kinnus* may have helped). With *n*-stems, *-ns* coalesced with the *n* of the suffix without the development of *u*: *hanans, tuggōns*. Some isolated consonant stems substitute the nominative for the accusative: *mans < *man-n-iz*, by the side of *mannans* (formed by analogy with *gumans*, both forms were used for both the nominative and accusative), *frijōnds, baúrgs, nahts* etc. In Norse, *-ns > -nz > -nʀ* was assimilated to *-nn, -n*, which disappeared: *ulfa, geste, vǫndo* 'rods' (*sunr* has *syne*, formed in analogy to the nom. pl. *syner*). In WGmc. nom. and acc. pl. are always identical, mostly by phonetic law. For OE OS, it is generally assumed that the nom. in *-as, -os* was substituted for the acc., but according to **79 i** the reverse is more probable; a trace of the old condition is supposed to exist in Hildebrandslied 6, *helidos ubar hringa*, but it is more likely that *helidos* is an OS, *hringa* an OHG form; cf. Braune, Ahd. Gramm. §193, Anm. 4.

After a long vowel, *-n-* of *-ns* had been absorbed in IE times, with compensatory lengthening, making the vowel tri-moric: *$*θεᾶνς$* > *$*θεᾱς$*, spelled historically θεάς. Therefore, in the *ā*-class nom. pl. and acc. pl. are identical: Go. *gibōs*, ON *giafar* etc.

Genitive. The IE ending is almost universally assumed to have 1 been *-ǒm*. We do find this in Sanskrit, Greek, Lithuanian, Germanic. But in Latin the gen. pl. ends in *-um* (*rēgum*, *host-i-um*; *hortōrum* with *z* > *r* from the pronominal declension) and in Slavic in *ъ* = *ŭ* (*vlъkъ*). These endings are the normal development of *-om*. Streitberg, IF 1. 251 ff., attempted to show that they are shortened from *-ǒm*, but at best it may be conceded that he has made it probable that such shortening may have happened, especially in Latin, but certainly not that it necessarily did happen. Osthoff, MU 1. 207 ff., assumed *-om* at least for consonant stems. Loewe, GS 2. 8, speaks of 'idg. *-ǒm*, aus stammesausl. *-o* und Endung *-om* kontrahiert', and similarly Hirt, HU 2. 31, believes 'der Stammesauslaut *o* war mit der Partikel *-om* kontrahiert worden.'

Probably we must assume the following development: in Indo-European the ending was *-om* (that is, the ending of the acc. sg. in partitive function, with insertion of the connecting vowel *-o-*). In the *o*-class and the *ā*-class contraction with the suffix vowel gave *-ǒm*, but for the other classes we must reconstruct original forms in *-om*. Every IE language generalized one or the other of these two endings: Thus, Greek transferred the ending of θεῶν = *$*θεο-ον$* and *$*θεᾱ-ον$* to all other classes (ἀνδρῶν, πατρῶν, νηῶν), and Sanskrit, Lithuanian and Germanic did the same: Sk. *nāvā́m*, *vācā́m* (with vocalic stems generally *-nām*, which had probably developed under the influence of the *n*-stems), Lith. *vilkũ*, OHG *wolfo*. But Italic and Slavic generalized *-om*, therefore not only L. *rēgum*, *hostium*, but also *deōrum* (older *deum*).

NOTE: Greek offers an apparent difficulty. According to the usual rules of contraction, *o* + *o* gives Ion.-Att. *ου* (closed *ō*), not *ω* (open *ō*). Therefore, we should expect *$*λύκουν$* (Dor. λύκων). But it is probable that we have to deal with two different periods of contraction: In the first period, *o* + *o*, without intervening consonant, was contracted to *ω*; later, *s* or *j* between vowels dropped out, and the new *o* + *o* became *ου*: gen. sg. *$*τοσο$* > τοῦ; δουλοῦμεν 'we serve' is not an old IE type, but a Gk. innovation; it was formed on the pattern of φιλοῦμεν from *$*φιλέ(j)ομεν$*; the theoretical *$*δουλό(j)ομεν$* probably never existed. However, it is also possible that *ων* represents a spread from the *ā*-class exclusively.

All NWGmc. gen. pl. go back to *-õm*, e.g., ON OE *daga* (*ulfa, wulfa*), OS *wulfo*, OHG *wolfo*; OHG *gomōno, ougōno, zungōno, fatero* etc.

In Gothic, *-ō* < *-õm* appears only in *ā*-stems and, doubtless under their influence, in feminine *n*-stems: *gibō, tuggōnō*. All other nouns have *-ē*: *wulfē, gastē, anstē, gumanē* etc. This ending has puzzled comparative grammar a good deal, but it is rather easily explained if we accept *-om* as the IE ending. This leads us to the following proportion:

NWGmc. *-as* : Go. *-is* = NWGmc. *-ō* : Go. *-ē*

IE *-o-so* : *-e-so* = *-o-om* > *-õm* : *e-om* > *-ēm*.

That is: since Gothic gave preference to the *e*-grade of the suffix vowel in the gen. sg., the same may be supposed for the gen. pl. Cf. Loewe, GS 2. 8: 'Got. *-ē* lässt sich auf idg. *-ēm* zurückführen, das aus *-e-om* entstanden sein könnte.' This also explains the ending *-ō* of the *ā*-stems: IE *-ā-om* > Gmc. *-õm* would be apt to resist the spread of the ending *-ē*; in the other classes, *-om* would have disappeared in Germanic, and the resulting forms without ending (Go. *guman-* etc.) add *-ē* in Gothic, *-ō* elsewhere. That Old High German generalized *-ō*, although the gen. sg. probably had the suffix vowel *-e-*, does not invalidate this explanation. After all, the assumption of the same suffix vowel for singular and plural that is implied for Gothic in the proportion given above, does not necessarily hold good for Old High German too.[4]

m **Ablative, Dative, Instrumental** were not as distinctly different in the plural as they were in the singular. The most widely spread type of endings was characterized by a labial element, *bh* in Sanskrit (dat.-abl. *-bhyas*, instr. *-bhiš*) and Latin (*-bus*), *m* in Balto-Slavic (dat.-abl. Lith. *-mus*, OSl. *-mъ* < *-mos*; instr. Lith. *-mis*, OSl. *-mi*). Such labial elements—perhaps rather stem suffixes than actual case endings—occur in the singular too, without the plural sign *-s*: *-bhi* in L. *tibi*, Gk. ἶφι 'with power'; *-mi* in Balto-Slavic instrumentals, like OSl. *synomъ*, Lith. *sunumi*. The Gmc. dat. pl. ends in *-m*, but it is impossible to say with certainty whether this goes back to *-mos* or *-mis*. OE *þǣm, twǣm* = Go. *þaim, twaim* point to *-mis* on account of the umlaut of OE *ā*, but it is only probable, not absolutely certain, that these pronoun or numeral forms had the same origin as the noun forms. The vowel was lost, *-mz* was assimilated to *-mm -m*. (But we have Run. *gestumʀ, borumʀ* and feminine names like *Vatvims, Aflims* in religious inscriptions.) Before this, Gothic preserves the original stem vowel: *wulfam, gibōm, gastim, sunum, gumam* < **guman-m, tuggōm* < **tuggōn-m, fadrum, fōtum* < *-m; baúrgim* follows the pattern of the *i*-stems. In the other languages there is a marked tendency to generalize -*um*, which originally belonged only to the consonant stems and the *u*-stems. We still have OHG *gebōm* (probably supported by *zungōm* < -*ōnm*), *gestim*, but ON *gestom*, OE *giestom*. ON *giofom*, OE *giefum*, OS *gebun* can be the phonological developments of -*ōm*, or transfers of -*um*.

The IE **Locative** in -*su* (-*si*) has left no trace in the Gmc. languages.

THE GERMANIC DECLENSIONS

Parallel to the distinction between 'strong' and 'weak' verbs, Jacob Grimm, Deutsche Gramm. 1. 133-7, also divided the Gmc. nouns into a 'strong' and a 'weak' type. The latter comprises the *n*-stems, the former all others. While this classification is of fundamental importance for the adjective, it is also practical for the noun during the older periods. But among the modern Gmc. languages, only German has fully preserved the distinction—in fact, it has somewhat extended its scope.

VOWEL STEMS

80. The o-Stems.   a
A. Pure *o*-Stems.

MASCULINES: Singular

	Nom.	Acc.	Gen.	Dat.	Instr.	Voc.
Go.	*wulfs*	*wulf*	*wulfis*	*wulfa*		*wulf*
ON	*ulfr*	*ulf*	*ulfs*	*ulfe*		
OE	*wulf*	*wulf*	*wulfes*	*wulfe*		
OS	*wulf*	*wulf*	*wulfes*	*wulfe*	*wulfu*	
OHG	*wolf*	*wolf*	*wolfes*	*wolfe*	*wolfu*	

Plural

wulfōs	*wulfans*	*wulfē*	*wulfam*
ulfar	*ulfa*	*ulfa*	*ulfom*
wulfas	*wulfas*	*wulfa*	*wulfum*
wulfos	*wulfos*	*wulfo*	*wulfum*
wolfā	*wolfā*	*wolfo*	*wolfum*.

NEUTERS: Nom. sg. = acc. sg. masc.

Nom. acc. pl. Go. *barna*—ON *born*—OE *bearn* : *scipu*—OS *barn* : *scipu* —OHG *barn*.

(1) The stem vowel is subject to mutation in accordance with the vowel of the ending. Thus Old Norse has *u*-umlaut of the stem vowel *a*: *armr*, dat. pl. *ormom*; *barn*, nom. pl. *born* < **barnu*, dat. pl. *bornom*.   *e* in

dat. sg. *dege*, in spite of the optional spelling *degi*, is not *i*-umlaut, but *g*-umlaut.   Old English shows the regular alternation between æ and *a*: æ in closed syllables or when followed by a front vowel, *a* before a back vowel—sg. *dæg, dæges, dæge*, pl. *dagas, daga, dagum*, sg. *fæt, fætes, fæte*, pl. *fatu, fata, fatum*.

(2) In the ON nom. sg. -ʀ is assimilated to *s* and *r* regularly, to *l* and *n* after a long or unaccented syllable: *īss* 'ice' (masc.), *akr* 'acre' (*rr* simplified), *stōll* 'stool' (but *selr* 'seal'), *steinn*.   Analogy interferes with this to a certain extent.

(3) Some ON words have in the gen. sg. -*ar*, the ending of *i*- and *u*-stems: *eiþar* (but also *eiþs*) 'of the oath'; some have no ending in the dat. sg.: *hring* (or *hringe*); these forms are probably old instrumentals in -*ō*.

B. *jo*-Stems.

b Masculines: *hairdeis* 'shepherd', *harjis* 'army'; ON *niþr* 'relative'.

	Sg. Nom.	Acc.	Gen.	Dat.	
Go.	*hairdeis*	*hairdi*	*hairdeis*	*hairdja*, pl. *hairdjōs* etc.	
	harjis	*hari**	*harjis*	*harja*	*harjōs*
ON	*hirþer*	*hirþe*	*hirþes*	*hirþe*	*hirþar, -a*
	niþr	*niþ*	*niþs*	*niþ*	*niþiar, -ia*
OE	*hierde*	*hierde*	*hierdes*	*hierde*	*hierdar*
	here	*here*	*heries*	*herie*	*heria, -ia*
OS	*hirdi*	*hirdi*	*hirdies*	*hirdie*	*hirdios*
	heri	*heri*	*heries*	*herie*	*herios*
OHG	*hirti*	*hirti*	*hirtes*	*hirte*	*hirte, -ā*.

There are no masc. short-stem nouns in OHG; *heri* and *endi* (Go. *andeis*, OS *endi*, masc.) are neuters.

Neuters: Go. *reiki* 'rule', Go. *kuni* 'kin'.

	Sg. Nom. Acc.	Gen.	Dat.	Pl. Nom. Acc.
Go.	*reiki*	*reikjis*	*reikja,*	*reikja*
	kuni	*kunjis*	*kunja*	*kunja*
ON	*rīke*	*rīkes*	*rīke*	*rīke* (gen. *rikia*)
	kyn	*kyns*	*kyne*	*kyn*
OE	*rīce*	*rīces*	*rīce*	*rīcu*
	cyn(n)	*cynnes*	*cynne*	*cyn(n)*
OS	*rīki*	*rīkies*	*rīkie*	*rīki*
	kunni	*kunnies*	*kunnie*	*kunni*
OHG	*rīchi*	*rīches*	*rīche*	*rīchi*
	kunni	*kunnes*	*kunne*	*kunni.*

The following points are to be noted:

(1) The treatment of the suffix -je/jo-, Gmc. -ja-/ji-; the difference between Go. *hairdeis* : *harjis* etc., is a consequence of the quantity of the stem syllable. According to **33 b** and **49 d, h**, this implied a difference of syllable division. The nominative Go. *harjis*, in spite of many attempts to explain it so[1] can hardly go back entirely to -jos, which would have yielded **haris*. We must assume that it introduced j from the cases with j (gen., dat. sg., all cases of the pl.); *ei* in *hairdeis*, however, is the product of contraction within the syllable, according to 'Siever's Law' (**33 b**).

Fundamentally the same holds good for the other dialects. In Old Norse, j was preserved before back vowels after a short stem and after k g, therefore gen. pl. *niþia*, *rī-kia*, but *hir-þa*. The nom., gen. sg. *hirþer hirþes* must have the same origin as Go. *hairdeis*, with the usual loss of a second mora. The acc. sg. reintroduced -e from the other cases of the singular. The forms of *niþr* correspond to those of *harjis*. -j- between consonants disappeared in *niþr* and *niþs*. The dat. sg. *niþ* is probably a dative without ending like *hring*; **niþia* should have become **niþi, niþe*.

Also the WGmc. forms correspond to the Go. ones. But it must be kept in mind that all final consonants of the stem with the exception of r were doubled before j. Therefore we have OE *cyn(n)*, *cynnes*, *secg* 'man' (for *cg* cf. **31 c**), gen. sg. *secges*; before back vowels j is often preserved and spelled e: pl. *secg(e)as*, *secg(e)a*, *secg(e)um*; OS *kunni* (for **kun*, with analogical restoration of -ni; we find *bed* and *beddi*), *kunnies*; Old High German has no difference between long stems and short stems; the analogical nom.-acc. sg. *kunni* is always used, and j is never expressed in the spelling. The fact that, strictly speaking, in historical WGmc. all jo-stems except those in r are 'long', since the double consonant implies a long syllable, has nothing to do with this; the consonant lengthening took place after these paradigms had been established, which happened essentially in Gmc. times.

C. *wo*-Stems do not differ from pure -o-stems, except that -w in final   c position becomes -u (-o-); but -wi s frequently restored analogically: masc. Go. *þius*, ON -*þēr*, OE *þeo(w)*, OS *theo-*, OHG *deo* 'servant'; neut. Go. *triu*, ON *trē*, OE *trēo(w)*, OS *treo* 'tree'—gen. *triwes*, *trēs*, *trēowes* (analogical -o-), *trewes*. The nom. sg. Go. *þius* really does not occur; it is reconstructed on the basis of *þiwōs*, *þiwē*; w after a short vowel formed a diphthong with this when final or before a consonant, cf. *naus* 'corpse', pl. *naweis* (form of the *i*-declension); it remained after a long vowel: *snaiws* 'snow'.

For the disappearance of *w* in ON *-þēr, trē*, cf. Heusler, Aisl. Elb. 39, Note 1.

81. The ā-Stems.

In Germanic all *ā*-stems are feminines, but elsewhere also masculines occur, denoting types of human beings, e.g., L. *scrība, poeta, agricola*, OSl. *sluga* 'servant', *vojevoda* 'army leader', Gk. νεανίας 'youth'.

a A. Pure *ā*-Stems.

	Singular				Plural			
	Nom.	Acc.	Gen.	Dat.	Nom.	Acc.	Gen.	Dat.
Go.	giba	giba	gibōs	gibai	gibōs	gibōs	gibō	gibōm
ON	giǫf	[giǫf]	giafar	giǫf	giafar	giafar	giafa	giǫfom
OE	giefu, ār	giefe	giefe	giefe	giefe	giefe	giefa	giefum
OS	[geba], hwīl	geba	geba	gebu	geba	geba	[gebono]	gebun
OHG	[geba], hwīl	geba	geba	gebu	gebǎ	gebǎ	[gebōno]	gebōm.

(1) In Old Norse, *u*-mutation and breaking follow the usual rules: *skǫr* 'hair' < *skaru, acc. analogical *skǫr*, dat. (instr. in *-ā* > *-u*) *skǫr*, dat. pl. *skǫrom*; *giǫf* < *ʒeƀu; *giafar* < *ʒeƀōz.

(2) In WGmc., *-u* of the nom. sg. would be preserved after short stems, dropped after long stems. But only Old English carries this out consistently: *giefu* but *ār* (*ie* in *giefu*, of course, is not a long vowel, but *i* is merely a spelling device indicating the spirantic character of *g*; cf. **24 c**, 3). In Old Saxon and Old High German short-stem nouns and long-stem nouns usually have the same ending, *-a* < *-ām*, transferred to the nom., e.g., OS OHG *ēra* 'honor', as against OE *ār*. Only a few nouns, like *hwīl* 'while' have preserved the genuine nom. form without ending. OS *thiod* 'people', as against OHG *diota*, is especially frequent.

(3) OS *geƀono*, OHG *gebōno*, instead of **geƀo, gebō*, follow the pattern of the *n*-stems.

OE *giefe*, spelled *-æ* in early documents, goes back to *-ām* in the acc. sg., to *-ās* in the gen. sg. and nom. acc. pl., to *-āi* (loc.) in the dat. sg.

b B. *jā*-Stems.

The nom. sg. shows gradation of the stem suffix, *-jā/jə/ī*: Sk. *vidyā* 'knowledge', Gk. νεᾱνίᾱ(ς); Gk. πότνια 'lady', φέρουσα 'carrying' (fem.) < *φέροντια; Sk. *patnī́* 'lady', *devī́* 'goddess'. This type was closely connected, in fact, more or less interchangeable, with *jē*-stems, cf. L. *materiēs* (with *-s* added by analogy with *diēs*) = *materia*.

In Germanic, we find the endings *-jā* and *-ī*. Gothic and Old Norse use the former with short stems, the latter with long stems: Go. *banja* 'wound', *sibja* 'relationship', *halja* 'hell', but *bandi* 'band', *þiudan-gardi* 'kingdom', *þūsundi* 'thousand'; ON **ben* 'wound', *hel* 'death' (the effect of the *-j-* is apparent in *egg* 'edge' < **akjã*, L. *aciēs*, *Frigg* < **prijã*, **30, 33 c;** with addition of *-ʀ*, following the analogy of feminine *i*-stems, *heiþr* 'heath', *ylgr* 'she-wolf' (= Sk. *vṛkîš*), *elfr* 'river'. Go. *mawi* 'girl' = ON *mǣ-r*, *þiwi* 'maid-servant' are only apparently exceptions from this rule, since they go back to **maȝwī*, *þiȝwī* and are therefore long-stem nouns.

In the WGmc. group the difference is obliterated by the doubling of the final consonant caused by *-j-*. We have therefore OE *bend* = Go. *bandi*, *hild* 'battle', *wylf* 'she-wolf', where *i* < *ī* disappeared, because the stem was long, but also *sibb* = Go. *sibja*, *benn* = Go. *banja*, *hell* = Go. *halja*: *j* of *-ju* was absorbed in the lengthened consonant, and *-u* disappeared. In Old Saxon and Old High German here, as in the pure *ā*-stems, the acc. has taken the place of the nom.: OS *sibbia*, *eggia*, *redia*, OHG *sippa*, *minna*, *redia* (*reda*). In Old Saxon only *hel* = Go. *halja* has preserved the old nom., and in Old High German the nouns in *-injā* > *-innu*, *-in(n)*, like *kuningin*, *gutin* (since the 11th cent. *-inna*).

The other cases do not differ materially from the forms of the pure *ā*-stems—Go. *bandja*, *bandjōs*, *bandjai*, pl. *bandjōs*, etc. But two effects of *j* are significant for the *ā*-stems: umlaut, where possible in Norse and WGmc., and consonant lengthening in WGmc. (*gg* also in Norse).

C. *wā*-Stems.

The inflection does not differ from that of other *ā*-stems, but the phonetic laws about the treatment of *w* are to be noted. Gothic preserves it everywhere: *bandwa* 'sign', *bandwōs*, etc. In Old Norse, *w* disappeared before Prim. Norse *o u*, but was retained elsewhere: *ǫr* 'arrow' < **aruā*, *aruu*, nom. pl. *ǫruar*; *stǫþ* 'landing', *stǫþuar*. Likewise, in WGmc. *w* disappeared before back vowels, but analogy and other secondary changes have greatly obliterated the original conditions: OE *beadu* 'battle' < **baðwā*, *-wu* (but *mǣd* 'meadow', with loss of *-u* after the long stem), dat. pl. *beadwum* with analogical *w*; Old Saxon and Old High German have retained only a few forms with *w*, thus OS *brāwon* (dat. pl.) 'eye-brows', OHG nom. sg. *brāwa*, *brāa*, *brā*.

82. The i-Stems.

MASCULINES: Singular   Plural

	Nom.	Acc.	Gen.	Dat.	Nom.	Acc.	Gen.	Dat.
Go.	*gasts*	*gast*	*gastis*	*gasta*	*gasteis*	*gastins*	*gastē*	*gastim*
ON	*gestr*	*gest*	*gests*	*geste*	*gester*	*geste*	*gesta*	*gestom*
OE	*giest*	*giest*	*giestes*	*gieste*	*gieste, -as*		*giesta*	*giestom*
OS	*gast*	*gast*	*gastes*	*gaste*	*gesti*		*gestio*	*gestiun*
OHG	*gast*	*gast*	*gastes*	*gaste*	*gesti*		*gest(e)o*	*gestim*

NEUTERS:

OE	spere[1]	spere	speres	spere	speru	spera	sperum
OS	ur-lagi[2]	-lagi	-lag(i)es	-lag(i)e	-lagu	-lag(i)o	-lagiun

[1] 'spear'. [2] 'war'.

FEMININES:

Go.	-dēþs	dēþ	dēþais	dēþai	dēþeis	dēþins	dēþē	dēbim
ON	(Forms of the ā-class,			see below, 3)				
OE	dǣd	dǣd	dǣde	dǣde	dǣde	dǣda	dǣdum
OS	dād	dād	dādi	dādi	dādi	dādio	dādiun
OHG	tāt	tāt	tāti	tāti	tāti	tāt(e)o	tātim.

(1) The endings of the singular of the masculine are everywhere the same as those of the ŏ-stems, certainly due more to analogy than to phonetic law. Gothic has the vocative *gast*, Old Saxon and Old High German show the instrumental in *-u*. The plural preserves far more of the characteristics of the *i*-class; but the analogical character of some forms, like gen. *gastē*, *gesta*, dat. *gestom* etc. is obvious. In Old English the old ending of the nom. pl., *-e*, occurs with common nouns only in very early documents, but is regularly preserved with names of peoples, such as *Dene*, *Engle*, *Seaxe*.

(2) According to **49 c**, WGmc. preserves *-i* after short stems, but drops it after long stems. Therefore we have OE *giest* but *wine*, OS OHG *gast*, *wini*; feminines: OE *dǣd* (no short-stem feminine exists), OS *dād*, *stedi*, OHG *tāt*, *turi*. But analogy has greatly interfered with this, especially in Old High German where we have, e.g. the masculines *slag*, *biz* (OS *slegi*, *biti*), the feminines *stat* (OS *stedi*), *snur* 'daughter-in-law'. It should be noted that *-i* < *-ins* or < *-īz* is not subject to this rule, therefore *gieste*, *gesti*. For OHG n. pl. *gesti*, etc. it is probable that we really have to deal with an accusative form, since otherwise the length of *-ī* would be likely to be indicated at least occasionally. The OE and OS forms can be equally well nom. or acc.

(3) The feminines, on the whole, preserve the original forms rather well. The OS OHG gen., dat. sg. in *-i* must go back to *-ei-so* (*-ei-es*), instead of *-oi-so* as in Gothic.

The Norse feminines, with few exceptions, have gone over to the ā-declension: *dǭþ*, gen. *dāþar*; the nom., acc. pl., *dāþer*, has the ending of the *i*-stems (nom. ending for both cases), but no umlaut.

(4) Umlaut. The theoretical postulate, that there should be *i*-umlaut in NWGmc. wherever the ending has *i* at the time of mutation is carried out only to a certain extent. In Old Norse, the feminines do not show it at all, on account of their transition to the *ā*-class. The masculines have *i*-umlaut for long stems, no umlaut for short stems, according to **49 d,** therefore *gestr*, but *staþr*, and they carry this through in the whole paradigm, singular and plural (dat. pl. *stǫþom*). In Old English, umlaut took place before the disappearance of *-i*, and therefore the stem vowels of the singular and plural do not differ: *giest—gieste, dǣd—dǣde, cwēn* 'queen'—*cwēne* (< WGmc. **kwānīz*; *ā > ō* before nasals, *ō > ē* by *i*-umlaut).

Old Saxon and Old High German, where the mutation took place later, doubtless had regular umlaut quite in keeping with modern conditions, although it is indicated by the spelling only in the case of *ă*. Since the nom. sg. of long-stem masculines like *gast* had lost the *i* of the ending before the period of mutation, singular and plural are differentiated by umlaut: *gast—gesti*; short-stem nouns like OS *seli* 'hall' (masc.), *stedi* 'stead' (fem.) had kept it; and therefore have umlaut both in the singular and the plural. Long-stem feminines have umlaut not only in the plural, but also in the gen., dat. sg.: OS *fard*, OHG *fart* 'journey': gen., dat. sg. *ferdi, ferti*, pl. *ferdi, ferdio, ferdiun—ferti, fertea, fertim*. Words with vowels other than *ă*, like OS *dād*, OHG *tāt*, OS OHG *kuri* 'choice', OFris. *kere* < **kyri*, surely had umlaut within the scope of the phonetic laws (unless prevented or extended by analogy), even though the spelling fails to indicate it.

The great morphological importance of *i*-umlaut in the modern German declension (still growing by analogical spread) is due to this factor of chronology. Its relatively late appearance preserved the contrast between singular and plural.

83. The u-Stems

MASCULINES:

	Singular				Plural			
	Nom.	Acc.	Gen.	Dat.	Nom.	Acc.	Gen.	Dat.
Go.	*sunus*	*sunu*[1]	*sunaus*	*sunau*	*sunjus**	*sununs*	*suniwē*	*sunum*
ON	*sunr*	*sun*	*sonar*	*syni*	*synir*	*sunu*	*sona*	*sunum*
OE	*sunu*	*sunu*	*suna*	*suna*	*suna, -u*		*suna*	*sunum*
OS	*sunu*	*sunu*	*suno*	*suno, -i*	*suni*		*sunio*	*sunun*
OHG	*fridu*	*fridu*	*frides*[2]	*fride, -iu*[3]	*fridi*		*frid(e)o*	*fridim.*

[1] vocative also *sunu*.   [2] also *frido*.   [3] instr. *fridu* or *fridiu*.

NEUTERS:

Go.	*faihu*	*faihaus**	*faihau*	'cattle'
OE Angl.	*feolu*	*feolu*	*feolu*	'much'
OS	*widu-*	*widu-*	*widu-*	'wood' (?)
OHG	*fihu*	*fehes*	*fehe*	'cattle'

FEMININES:

Go.	*handus*	*handu*	*handaus*	*handau*	*handjus*	*handuns*	*handiwē* *handum*
ON	(No feminine *u*-stems)						
OE	*hand*	*handa*	*handa*		*handa*	*handa*	*handum*
OS	*hand*	*hando**?	*hendi*		*hendi*	*hando*	*handum*
OHG	*hant*	*henti*	*henti*		*henti*	*hent(e)o*	*hantum.*

(1) The *u*-class, which was never very numerous, is rather disintegrated even at the beginning of our tradition of the Gmc. languages. The masculines tend to go over to the *o*- or *i*-class, the feminines to the *ā*-class. The latter is entirely the case in Old Norse where the transition was favored by the near-identity of the nom. sg.: *hǫnd < *hǫndr < *handus = skǫr < *skaru*. There are very few neuters, hardly more than Go. *faihu* and *filu* and their cognates; of *filu* we have scarcely more than the nom., acc. sg.; ON *fē* belongs to the *o*-declension with the exception of the gen. sg. *fiár*; the nom., acc. sg. is rarely *fø̄ < *fehu*. OS *widu-* occurs only as the first member of compounds; Holthausen, As. Elb. §309, considers it a neuter, but ON *viþr*, OE *wudu* are always masculines, and OHG *witu* occurs as a neuter only once, in Otfrid, otherwise it is masculine; also MHG *der wite*.

(2) Nom., acc. sg. are subject to apocope of *-u* after long stems, cf. OE *sunu : feld, hand : duru*, OHG *hant : fridu*. Old High German has no long-stem masculines, Old Saxon no short-stem feminines; *u* in Go. *handu(s)* is almost certainly analogical, **49 c.** OHG *sunu* preserves the *-u* only in the oldest Franconian sources, otherwise the form is *sun*, which has gone entirely over to the *i*-declension. Also *hant*, the only OHG feminine of the *u*-class, has gone over to the *i*-class, with the exception of the dat. pl. *hantum* (later *hentin*), from which New High German has the adverbial phrase **abhanden** (cf. the dat. sg. in *behende < bi-henti*).

(3) The forms of the gen. sg., as far as not replaced by forms of the *o*-class, are the regular development of *-ou + so* (*-ou + es*) except the OHG *henti* (perhaps also OS *hendi*? the form is not preserved) which is really a dat. form. The dat. sg. of Gothic and Old English, and the form *suno* in Old Saxon go back to *ou-i*, under the influence of the gen. sg. with the ablaut grade *ou*. But the *i*-forms of Old Norse and

Old Saxon go back to $eu + i = \bar{e}i$ (Gk. πήχει). OHG *fride* is a transfer from the *o*-stems, but early *fridiu*, *suniu* comes from *-eu + i*, unless we prefer to consider it an instrumental, formed under the influence of the *o*-stems and *i*-stems (*gastiu*, itself an analogical form).

In the OE nom., acc. pl. the *u*-forms are obviously accusatives, = Go. *sununs*, while the ON OS OHG forms with *i* come from the nom. of *i*-stems in *-ei-es*, *-īz*; in Old High German there also occurs (once, in Otfrid) a genuine acc. pl. *situ*. The OE forms in *-a* must be innovations under the influence of the gen., dat. sg., gen. pl.

(4) Umlaut occurs everywhere (except in Gothic) where the ending contains *i*, as the paradigm of *hand, hant* shows. In Old Norse it is combined with *u*-umlaut and *a*- and *u*-breaking, so that we find considerable variety of the stem vowel, e.g.:

Umlaut: *vǫndr* 'rod' (Go. *wandus*), *vǫnd, vandar, vende; vender, vǫndo, vanda, vǫndom.*

Breaking: *skiǫldr* 'shield', Go. *skildus* (root IE **kel-* 'split'), *skiǫld, skialdar, skilde; skilder, skioldo, skialda, skioldom.*

CONSONANT STEMS

In accordance with **77,** these are primarily nouns with the suffix *-es-/-os-* or *-ent-/-ont-/-nt-*, and nouns without any suffixes (athematic nouns). The *-n-* and *-r*-suffixes are l. c. properly listed as 'diphthongal', but, as pointed out in the note to that section, for valid systematic reasons our grammars class nouns with these suffixes as 'consonant stems', and it seems expedient to follow this practice.

84. The n-Stems.

MASCULINES:

	Nom.	Acc.	Gen.	Dat.	Nom.	Acc.	Gen.	Dat.
		Singular				Plural		
Go.	*guma*	*guman*	*gumins*	*gumin*	*gumans*	*gumans*	*gumanē*	*gumam*
ON	*gume*	*guma*	*guma*	*guma*	*gumar*	*guma*	*gum(n)a*	*gumom*
OE	*guma*	*guman*	*guman*	*guman*		*guman*	*gumena*	*gumum*
OS	*gumo*	*gumon*	*gumen*	*gumen*		*gumon*	*gumono*	*gumun, -on*
OHG	*gomo*	*gomon,-un*	*gomen,-in*	*gomen,-in*		*gomon,-un*	*gomōno*	*gomōm*

NEUTERS:

	Go.	ON	OE	OS	OHG
Nom.-Acc. Sg.	*augō*	*auga*	*ēage*	*ōga*	*ouga*
Nom.-Acc. Pl.	*augōna*	*augo*	*ēagan*	*ōgun*	*ougun, -on.*

All other cases like the masculine.

FEMININES:

Go.	*tuggō*	*tuggōn*	*tuggōns*	*tuggōn*	*tuggōns*	*tuggōnō*	*tungōm*
ON	*tunga*	*tungo*	*tungo*	*tungo*	*tungor*	*tungna*	*tungom*
OE	*tunge*	*tungan*	*tungan*	*tungan*	*tungan*	*tung(e)na*	*tungum*
OS	*tunga*	*tungun*	*tungun*	*tungun*	*tungun*	*tungono*	*tungun*
OHG	*zunga*	*zungūn*	*zungūn*	*zungūn*	*zungūn*	*zungōno*	*zungōm.*

a (1) A mere glance at these paradigms makes it clearly apparent that the variety of case forms of the *n*-stems, that is, of the 'weak declension' is much less than that of the vowel stems. Grimm says, Deutsche Gramm. 1. 135 f., 'Die schwache Declination kann nicht so viel Casus an einem Worte ausdrücken wie die starke. . . . Die Unterarten der schwachen Decl. sind sich sehr ähnlich und gleichsam nach einem Fusse geschnitten. . . . Die schwache Declination verdirbt schneller als die starke. Zum Beispiel die erste starke zählt im Gotischen acht Endungen für acht Casus, die erste schwache nur sieben. Im Alt-Nordischen ist dieses Verhältnis von acht : sieben bereits gesunken auf sieben : vier und im Alt-Hochdeutschen auf vier : zwei. Im heutigen Englischen haben sich zwar noch einige Trümmer der starken Decl. erhalten, aber die schwache ist völlig erloschen.' (Footnote: 'Diese Beispiele können einiges Licht auf die Frage werfen: ob nicht die schwache Decl. überhaupt als eine Verschlimmerung der uranfänglichen starken betrachtet werden müsse?).' The reason for this relative uniformity of the *n*-declension lies, of course, in the fact that the vowels of the endings coalesce more or less with the suffix vowel of the vocalic stems, giving a multitude of different results, while they largely disappear after consonants.

b (2) The *Suffix Vowel* appears in every possible grade: *-en-/-on-* in Gk. ποιμένος, ἡγεμόνος; *-ēn-/-ōn-* in ποιμήν, ἡγεμών; *ṇ* in Gk. ὄνομα, Sk. *nāma*, L. *nōmen*; and finally *-ō*, without *-n*, in Lith. *akmuõ* 'stone' (as against Gk. ἄκμων), L. *homō*, Sk. *áśmā*.

The explanation of the suffix vowel in the Gmc. languages offers several difficulties, although the majority of the forms are quite clear.

c (a) *-ō* as against *-ōn/-ēn* in the nom. sg. is probably a result of sandhi (sentence connection); cf. Thumb, Hdb. Sk. 211: 'die *n*-losen Formen wechselten wohl in uridg. Zeit mit den Formen auf *-ēn -ōn* . . . unter bestimmten satzphonetischen Bedingungen.' It is not unlikely that the necessary 'satzphonetischen Bedingungen' were similar to the loss of *n* in the acc. pl. ending *-āns* : θεάνς > θεᾶς (cf. **49 n**), but we cannot know whether this loss occurred only before *-s* or also before other consonants—possibly before *bh dh gh* in case these were voiceless aspirates.

In the selection between these two forms the Gmc. dialects go different ways. The ending with two morae (-*ēn*/-*ōn*) is used in Gothic and Old Norse with masculines, but in WGmc. with feminines and neuters. On the other hand, the tri-moric ending -*õ* is used in Gothic and Old Norse with feminines and neuters, in WGmc. with masculines (in Old Saxon there is a good deal of variation between the MSS).

ON *gume* must surely go back to -*ēn*; IE *ē* > NWGmc. *æ* became *ā* in accented syllables, but *e* in endings. In Gothic, *ē* in endings became *a*, cf. *fadar* : Gk. πατήρ, but so did *ō*. Therefore Go. *guma* can go back to -*ēn* as well as -*ōn*, but the former is more probable since Gothic and Norse otherwise agree so well in the *n*-declension. The WGmc. masculine forms represent the same reduction of the -*õ* that we see in the gen. pl.

In the feminine and neuter Gothic reduces -*õ* by one mora, Old Norse by two. The WGmc. forms show the same treatment of -*ōn* as of -*ām* in the acc. sg. of the *ā*-stems: *tunge, tunga, zunga* like *giefe, geƀa, geba*.

(b) The Oblique Cases. Masculines and Neuters: Probably Gothic **d** comes closest to the original condition, especially since it is in a measure confirmed by Old Saxon and Old High German. In the masculine and neuter the acc. sg. and all cases of the plural have -*an*- < -*on*-, the gen. and dat. sg. -*in*- < -*en*-. Even in Gothic there are almost certainly some innovations. In particular, it is likely that the gen. pl. has introduced -*a*- from the other cases. We have zero grade of the suffix surely in Go. *abnē* 'of the men', *áuhsnē* 'of the oxen', *mannē* 'of the men', and probably in ON *gumna, augna, (hiartna), tungna, yxna*, OE *oxna, ēagna*; in the Run. gen. pl. *arƀijanō* (standard Norse nom. sg. *arfe* 'inheritance'), *a* may have been introduced from the rest of the paradigm, and the same is true for OE *gumena, tungena* (medial *a* > *æ* > *e*). This is supported by the fact that the regular masculine gen. pl. in Old Norse has the ending -*a* instead of -*na*; this started probably with nouns in *n*, perhaps also *m*, like *hane* 'rooster', *granne* 'neighbor', *māne* 'moon', *gume* 'man' (gen. pl. *gumna* and *guma*), where *n* was assimilated to the preceding nasal: **hanna* > *hana*, identical with the gen. pl. of the *o*-stems (but fem. *kuenna, kuinna* 'of the women', nom. sg. *kona*).

Aside from this and the normal generalization of -*om* in the dat. pl., Old Norse has carried through the suffix vowel *a*. The fact that the final *n* (including -*nn* < -*nz*) disappeared doubtless facilitated the spread of a masculine gen. pl. without *n*. With the exception of the

gen. pl. feminine and neuter (*tungna, hiartna*), the ON 'weak declension' has entirely lost the former characteristic *n*.

In Old English likewise, the *a* of the gen., dat. sg. represents leveling
from the acc. sg., *-an* < *-anu* < *-on* + *m*.

Old Saxon and Old High German present considerable difficulties and
the author is far from claiming that his explanations are entirely adequate. The OHG conditions seem to be the original ones. The parallelism with Gothic, back vowel in the acc. sg. and nom., acc. pl., front
vowel in the gen., dat. sg., can hardly be accidental; in Old Saxon *-on*
is carried through the whole paradigm, displacing *-en* entirely, but that
is doubtless a secondary change, like *-an* in Old English. As in Gothic,
the different suffix vowels must go back to different ablaut grades;
but *-on-*, as in ἡγεμόνα and Go. *guman*, does not exist in these dialects.
Efforts have been made to explain *-un*, *-on* as a phonetic development
from *-an-*, but they are not convincing.[1] *-un* and *-in* (the high vowels)
occur essentially in Upper German (later weakened to *-on*, *-en*), *-on*, *-en*
(the mid vowels) in Middle German. *-un/-on* must go back to the zero
grade of the suffix, which appears not only in the above mentioned
gen. pl. forms, but also, e.g., in dat. pl. *abnam, watnam*, nom., acc. pl.
namna; outside of Germanic we find it, e.g., in gen. sg. L. *carnis*, Gk.
ἀρνός, instr. sg. Sk. *rājñā, nāmnā*. In Franconian, where the vowel
development is in general earlier than in Upper German, *-un* was
weakened to *-on* in our earliest sources (following the normal trend of *u*,
cf. **38 a,** 2), while the more conservative Upper German preserved *-un*
throughout the 8th and 9th centuries. (The same holds good for the
dat. pl. in all classes where it ends in older *-um*: *-un* in early Upper
German, *-on* is Franconian: *tagun, tagon*. This fact alone should be
sufficient to disprove the assumption of labialization from *-anu*, or of
compromise between *a* and *u*, referred to in the appendix. We find
the same weakening in the ending of the 3 pl. pret. of the verb—*-un*
> *-on* (although, for some reason, slightly later, cf. Braune, Ahd.
Gramm. §320, Anm. 2; Schatz, Ahd. Gramm. §521.)—OS *-on* is, of
course, likewise weakening of *-un*.

Probably Franc. *-en* as against early UG *-in* must also be explained as
weakening; like *-un* > *-on* it also occurs in the dat. pl.; *gastim, gastin*
are 'die formen des 8. und 9. jh's, die abschwächung *-em*, *-en* tritt
jedoch schon in älterer zeit vereinzelt auf.' (Braune, l. c., §215, Anm.
6). It should be admitted, however, that another factor may have
contributed: The genitive ended in IE *-en-os*, the dative (locative) in
-en-i; the former should have given *-en*, the latter *-in*. It is not quite

impossible that Franconian leveled in favor of the former, Upper German in favor of the latter, but there is no clear evidence for that. In early documents we occasionally find umlaut of the stem vowel, caused by -in: nemin, henin, scedin. But this is leveled to -a- from about 800 on.

The Feminine has primarily the suffix vowel -ō-, as in L. ratiōnis, ratiōnem. In Gothic this is carried through entirely, and probably the NWGmc. forms go back essentially to the same vowel. The Norse gen. pl. has zero grade, as in the masculine and neuter. The OE forms are identical with those of the masculine and are probably analogical transfers. But in ON OS OHG, most cases show a change ō > ū. This ū is kept intact in OHG (zungūn), and in most OS documents (tungun; -on is partly analogical transfer from the masculine, partly later weakening of -ūn/-un; Holthausen, As. Elb. §314, 2). In Old Norse, -o is the (classical) Icelandic spelling for u < ū; its u-color is definitely proven by u-mutation: saga has the stem vowel ǫ (sǫgo) in the oblique cases of the singular, and in the plural with the exception of the gen. (sagna). Very probably unstressed ō before n in a closed syllable became ū, which would be in keeping with the preservation of ŭ before nasal combinations 38 a). According to Heusler's very plausible view (Aisl. Elb. §233 and 112) this started before nn < nz, that is, in the gen. sg. (-ōn-es or -ōn-os), nom. pl. (-on-es), acc. pl. (-ōn-ns) and was transferred from these cases to the others, where ō stood in a (Gmc.) closed syllable: dat. sg. ON sǫgo < *saȝūn < *saȝōn[-i, OS tungun, OHG zungūn. In the gen. pl. ō stood in an open syllable and was therefore preserved: OS tungono, OHG zungōno. The OHG dat. pl. followed the analogy of the gen. pl.: zungōm. (For the standard ON nom., acc. pl. in -or, see below).[2]

(3) The endings of the dat., acc. pl., Go. -am, -ōm, -ans, -ōns are obviously shortened from -on-mis, -ōn-mis, -on-ns, -ōn-ns (-nm- assimilated to mm).

The ON nom., acc. pl. in -or for original -o (*tungōnn < -nz) add -r in imitation of the plurals of the ā- and i-stems.

(4) The neuter nom., acc. pl. adds the usual ending -ā (as in Go. **e** waúrda) to the suffix with ō-grade. The forms in the several dialects are regular phonetic developments of -ōnā.

NOTE: Stems in -jen-/-jŏn- or -wen-/-wŏn- do not differ in any material way from the 'pure' n-stems and therefore do not require special treatment here. Instances are Go. gudja 'priest', sparwa 'sparrow'; raþjō 'account' (= L. ratio, possibly borrowed from this), gatwō 'street'.

f   Go. *manna* 'man' with its Gmc. cognates is originally an *n*-stem with zero grade of the suffix (like L. *caro—carnis*), but lost almost completely the characteristics of this class and is therefore treated below, with the root nouns, although it does not form a completely consistent member of that group either.

    Go. *watō* 'water', dat. pl. *watnam* (no other forms preserved) is an interesting survival of very early conditions. Originally it belonged to a type of nouns in which *n*-suffix and *r*-suffix alternated (called *r/n*-stems in Sturtevant's Hittite Grammar), like L. *femur—feminis* 'thigh', Gk. ὕδωρ—ὕδατος < -*ntos* 'water', Gk. ἦπαρ—ἥπατος < -*ntos* 'liver' (cf. L. *iecur—iecineris*), Sk. *ūdhar—ūdhnas* 'udder'. In Hittite, *n* and *r* alternate in the declension: nom. sg. *watar*, gen. sg. *wetenas*. In Gothic, we have a pure *n*-stem. The WGmc. languages have standardized the *r*-stem: OE *wæter*, OFris. *weter*, OS *water*, OHG *wazzar*. Old Norse has regularly the *n*-stem *vatn*, but also, though rarely and only in early documents, *vatr*. With the exception of Gothic, these words follow the *o*-declension. Also the word for 'fire' shows alternation between *n* and *r*: Go. *fōn*, gen. *funins*, ON *funi* or *fūrr*, OE *fȳr*, OHG *fiur*, *fuir*. It is doubtless related to Gk. πῦρ 'fire', Hitt. *pahur* 'fire' (abl. sg. *pahunaz*, nom., acc. pl. *pahwaz*, gen. pl. *pahwenas*) and probably comes from a root **peu-* 'purify' (L. *pūrus*, Sk. *punāti* 'he purifies', *pāvakás* 'fire').

g   **The -īn-Stems.**

    In addition to the regular *n*-stems with *e/o*-gradation, the Gmc. languages developed a type with the suffix -*īn*-. All of them are feminines, chiefly abstract nouns (for the feminine of the pres. part., Go. *nimandei*, cf. **90**). In Gothic, their declension does not differ from that of the feminine *ō*-stems, except that we have -*ei*- instead of -*ō*-. The numerous ON nouns of this type show only singular forms, with -*e* from -*ī*, -*īns*, -*īn*. In Old English, these nouns were absorbed in the *ā*-class, in Old Saxon in the *i*-class. In Old High German, the type as such persisted (pl. forms are very rare), but in a standardized form, since in most documents the nom. form in -*ī* is used for the whole singular, while in a few others the form of the oblique cases in -*īn* has been transferred to the nominative. Paradigms:

	Singular			Plural		
	Nom.	Acc., Dat.	Gen.	Nom., Acc.	Gen.	Dat.
Go.	*managei*[1]	*managein*	*manageins*	*manageins*	*manageinō*	*manageim*
ON	*elle*[2]	*elle*	*elle*	—	—	—
OHG	*menigī(n)*	*menigī(n)*	*menigī(n)*	*menigī(n)*	*menigīno*	*menigīm*

    [1] 'multitude'.   [2] 'old age', < **alþīn-*, cf. Go. adj. *alþeis* 'old'.

    The origin of this group is not entirely clear, but probably it is chiefly an extension of adjective stems in -*jā/-ī* (Gk. πότνια, Sk. *patnī*, cf. **81 b**).

    Gothic developed a subtype of this class. Abstract nouns derived

from weak verbs of class I had the suffix -*īn*-, but the endings of the
i-feminines, except the nom., gen. pl., which followed the *ā*-class.
E.g. (from *laisjan* 'teach'):
laiseins 'teaching'—*laiseinais*, pl. *laiseinōs, -ō, -im, -ins.*

85. The r-Stems.

	Singular				Plural			
	Nom.	Acc.	Gen.	Dat.	Nom.	Acc.	Gen.	Dat.
Go.	brōþar	brōþar	brōþrs	brōþr	brōþrjus	brōþruns	brōþrē	brōþrum
ON	brōþer	brōþor	brōþor	brōþor	brø̄þr		brø̄þra	brø̄þrom
OE	brōþor	brōþor	brōþor	brēþer	brōþor		brōþra	brōþrum
OS	brōðer	brōðer	brōðer	brōðer	brōðer		brōð(e)ro*	brōðrun
OHG	bruoder	bruoder	bruoder	bruoder	bruoder		bruodero	bruoderum.

All Gmc. *r*-stems are terms of relationship, such as Go. *fadar, dauhtar,
swistar*; *fadar* occurs in our Go. texts only once, in the voc. (Gal. 4, 6),
but its declension can be ascertained from the forms of *brōþar*, which
occurs in all cases of the singular and plural.   The general Gmc. word
for 'mother' (ON *mōþer*, OE *mōdōr*, OS *mōdar*, OHG *muoter*) does not
occur at all; it must have been **mōdar*, with *d* instead of *þ* through
analogy with *fadar* (the IE forms are **pǝtér* and **mātér*, requiring
Verner's Law for the former, but not for the latter).   Wulfila's regular
words for 'father' and 'mother are *atta* (diminutive *Attila*) and *aiþei*.

(1) The lost endings were partly replaced analogically.   Thus Old
English has *fæderas* (nom. pl.), OHG gen., dat. sg. *fateres, fatere* by the
side of *fater*, and the nom., acc. pl. is always *faterǎ*, in late Old High
German also *bruodera, muotera, tohtera, swestera*.   In Old English, the
plural forms *brōþru, mōdru, dohtru* occur, with *-u* from the neuters.

(2) The suffix vowel of the nom. sg. was IE *ē* or *ō* (πατήρ : φράτωρ).
ON OS OHG *-er* must go back to *ē*, and for Go. *-ar* we should assume
the same, although theoretically it could come from *-ōr* as well as
from *-ēr*.   The word for 'sister', however, was IE **swesōr*; we have Run.
swestar, but *faþir*.   (For the inserted *t* cf. **29,** 1 b.)   In Old English,
the suffix vowel was determined by the quality of the stem vowel:
fæder, but *brōþor, mōdor, dohtor*; dat. sg. *brēþer, mēder, dehter*.   Probably
this started in the gen., dat. sg. that had IE *-tr-* (πατρός, πατρί); a
vowel developed regularly in such consonant groups, as in *æcer* <
*akr, Go. *akrs*, but *fugul, -ol* < **fugl*, Go. *fugls*.   Otherwise, the treatment of the suffix vowel is self-explanatory.   The *o* in the NWGmc.
words for 'daughter' is due to the following *ē* > *æ* > *e*; *ō* in Old Norse
is due to the disappearance of *h*, but the change of *u* > *o* is not '*h*-
sinking' (**42 d**), which occurs much later than the Gmc. umlaut *u* > *o*.
(*aú* in Go. *daúhtar*, of course, is due to the *h*.)

(3) Old Norse shows both *u*- and *i*-umlaut, with some analogical innovations: gen., acc. sg. *fǫþor* < **pǝtrs* (Sk. *pitúr*), **pǝtrm*; dat. sg. *feþr* < **pǝtri*; gen. sg. (late) also *feþr*, either transferred from the dat. sg., or from **pǝtres*. The plural carries *i*-umlaut through all cases: *feþr* < **pǝtres*, analogical acc. *feþr*, gen. *feþra*, dat. *feþrom*; likewise *mø̄þr, brø̄þr, dǿtr, syster*.

Old English has *i*-umlaut of *ō* in the dat. sg.: *brēþer, mēder, dehter*, but pl. *fæderas, brōþor, mōdor, dohtor*.

In Old Saxon and Old High German umlaut does not occur in this class. (The umlaut in Ger. *Väter, Mütter, Brüder, Töchter* developed by analogy in MHG times; Paul, Deutsche Gramm. 2. §17.)

86. The s-Stems. In Indo-European these constituted an important class of neuter nouns, like L. *genus, generis*, Gk. γένος, gen. γένους < **ĝen-es-os*. Also in Germanic they must have been fairly numerous in prehistoric times. The material is collected by Kluge, Anz. z. Anglia 5. 85 and Nominale Stammbildungslehre §85. Finnish has loan words like *kinnas, lammas, lannas* = ON *skinn*, OHG *lamb, lant*. But in historical times the transition to the *o*-class is nearly completed. Go. *riqis* 'darkness', ON *rǿkkr* = Gk. ἔρεβος, *agis* 'fear' = Gk. ἄχος, *sigis* 'victory' = Sk. *sáhas* are inflected like *waúrd*, and so are most of the sparse remainders in the other dialects: OE *dōgor* 'day', *hālor* 'health', *sigor* 'victory' (= *sige*, an *i*-stem). In the word for 'ear of corn' the *s* (or *r*, through rhotacism) of the stem is preserved everywhere: Go. *ahs* (gen. *ahsis*), ON *ax*, OE *ēar* < **eahor*, OHG *ahir*, but its declension does not differ from that of neuter *o*-stems; the NHG fem. *Aehre* comes from the MHG pl. *ehere* (with analogical *-e*).

For the survival or even extension of *r* in the plural cf. **79 j.**

87. The Root Stems.

a   Most nouns of this class, which was fairly numerous in Indo-European, have been shifted to other declensions, especially to the *o*-, *i*-, and *u*-declensions, and even in those that can still be designated as 'root nouns' the influence of the other classes is considerable. The following typical examples are selected more or less at random; individual grammars should be consulted for details:

Go., masc. *reiks* 'ruler', *mēnōþs* 'month', *weitwōþs* 'witness'; *fōtus* 'foot' < **pōd-s* (phonologically it would have given **fōss*) was transferred to the *u*-class on account of the dat., acc. pl. *fōtum, fōtuns* < *-miz, -ns* (but also cf. **79 k,** under acc. pl.); fem. *baúrgs* 'city', *alhs* 'temple', *nahts* 'night' (dat. pl. *-am*, after *dagam*).

ON, masc. *fōtr, mōnoþr* (pl. also *i*-stem); fem. *nōtt* 'night', *mǫrk* (1) 'mark' (money or weight), (2) 'forest', *gōs* 'goose'; *sȳr* 'sow', *kȳr* 'cow' (decl.: *kȳr, kū, kȳr, kū, kȳr, kȳr, kūa, kūm*). IE **sū-s*, *gwōu-s* are not really 'consonant stems', but, being root stems, follow their type (the vowel in *kȳr* is due to analogy with *sȳr*).

OE, masc. *fōt, tōþ* 'tooth'; fem. *neaht, burg, bōc, gōs, mūs, lūs, cū* (nom., acc. pl. *cȳ*).

OS, masc. *fōt* (nom., acc. pl. *fōti*, after the *i*-stems, but gen., dat. pl. *fōto, fōtun*); *tand* 'tooth' has dat. pl. *tandon*; fem. *naht, burg* (nom., acc. pl. *burgi*), *kō, bōk*.

OHG, masc. *fuoz* (nom., acc. pl. *fuozi*, dat. pl. *-um* and *-im*); fem. *naht, buoh; burg* has become an *i*-stem, but still has the gen., dat. sg. *burg*.

An original neuter root stem is Go. *fōn*, OHG *fiur*, discussed in **84** Note, end; but, as far as evidence goes, it has gone over to the *n*-stems in Gothic, to the *o*-stems elsewhere.

Paradigms of comprehensive scope cannot be given, because the individual words differ considerably. The following table merely intends to show a few of the most important characteristics. Obvious analogical forms are in brackets.

MASCULINES:

	Singular				Plural			
	Nom.	Acc.	Gen.	Dat.	Nom.	Acc.	Gen.	Dat.
Go.	*reiks*	*reik**	[*reikis*]	*reik*	*reiks*	[*reiks*]	*reikē*	[*reikam*]
ON	*fōtr*	*fōt*	[*fōtar*]	[*fōte*]	*fø̨tr*	[*fø̨tr*]	*fōta*	*fōtum*
OE	*fōt*	*fōt*	[*fōtes*]	[*fōte*]	*fēt*	[*fēt*]	*fōta*	*fōtum*
OS	*fōt* (other cases not attested)				[*fōti*]	[*fōti*]	*fōto*	*fōtun*
OHG	*fuoz*	*fuoz*	[*fuozes*]	[*fuoze*]	[*fuozi*]	[*fuozi*]	*fuozo*	*fuozum*

FEMININES:

	Nom.	Acc.	Gen.	Dat.	Nom.	Acc.	Gen.	Dat.
Go.	*baúrgs*	*baúrg*	*baúrgs*	*baúrg*	*baúrgs*	[*baúrgs*]	*baúrgē*	[*baúrgim*]
ON	[*mø̨rk*]	*mø̨rk*	*merkr*	[*mø̨rk*]	*merkr*	[*merkr*]	*marka*	*mø̨rkom*
OE	*gōs*	*gōs*	*gēs*	*gēs*	*gēs*	[*gēs*]	*gōsa*	*gōsum*
OS	*naht*	*naht*	[*nahtes*]	*naht*	*naht*	*naht*	*nahto*	*nahtun*
OHG	*naht*	*naht*	*naht*[*es*]	*naht*	*naht*	*naht*	*nahto*	*nahtum.*

The numerous analogical forms are to be expected in such a small class as this. The nom. sg. can be reconciled everywhere with the root-stem type, with the exception of ON *mø̨rk* which is either a transfer from the *ā*-stems, or formed under the influence of the acc. *mø̨rk* < **marku* < *-m̨*. The gen. sg. ending *-es* is phonologically *-s* in Gothic, *-ʀ* with umlaut in Old Norse (*merkr*) and disappears in WGmc., with umlaut in Old English. ON *fōtar* = Go. *fōtaus* is transferred from the *u*-stems, OHG *fuozes*, OS *nahtes*, OHG *nahtes* (only in adverbial use, otherwise *naht*) from the *o*-stems, the latter under the influence of *tages*; cf. NHG *nachts*. ON dat. sg. *mǫrk* has its *ǫ* from the nom., acc. sg.

In the plural, the nom. sg. ending *-es* should have the same effect as that of the gen. sg. The analogical deviations are obvious. It is the cause of the few plurals with umlaut in Modern English: *geese, lice, mice, teeth, ki(ne), men* (for this, see below). The acc. sg., which ended in *-ns* > *un, -u*, should always occur without ending and without *i*-umlaut, but it takes the form of the nominative (in OS OHG *naht* the form was phonologically the same for both cases; ON *merkr* stands for phonological **mǫrk*).

b

MAN:	Singular				Plural			
	Nom.	Acc.	Gen.	Dat.	Nom.	Acc.	Gen.	Dat.
Go.	*manna*	*mannan*	*mans*	*man*	*mans*	*mannans*	*mannē*	*mannam*
ON	*maþr*	*mann*	*man(n)z*	[*manne*]	*menn*	*manna*	*mǫnnom*
OE	*man(n)*	*man*	[*mannes*]	[*manne*]	*menn*	*manna*	*mannom*
OS	*man*	*man*	[*mannes*]	*man*[*ne*]	*man*	*manno*	*mannum*
OHG	*man*	*man*	*man*[*nes*]	*man*[*ne*]	*man*	*manno*	*mannum.*

Originally, this is not a root noun, but an *n*-stem of the type of L. *caro—carnis*, that is, with zero grade of the suffix in all cases. But being isolated, it was exposed to the influence both of the *o*-stems and of the root stems; on the whole it resembles the latter most and is therefore treated here rather than with the *n*-stems; cf. **84 d**. The *nn*, which originally belonged only to the gen., dat. sg., and to the plural with the exception of the nom., was transferred to the nom. sg. in Gothic, Old Norse and Old English, and to the nom. pl. everywhere (*n* in Old Saxon and Old High German must be a simplification from *nn*, since the ending *iz* would have caused umlaut after the short stem *man-*; in Old Saxon *men* occurs occasionally). Go. *manna, mannan* stands for **mana, manan* < **mon-ōn, mon-on-m*, cf. *guma, guman*. For ON *maþr* cf. **29 c**, end and Heusler, Aisl. Elb. §156.

88. The -nt-Stems.

	Singular				Plural		
	Nom.	Acc.	Gen.	Dat.	Nom. Acc.	Gen.	Dat.
Go.	*frijōnds*	*frijōnd*	[*frijōndis*]	*frijōnd*	*frijōnds*	*frijōndē*	*frijōndam*
ON	(*frǽnde*	*frǽnde*	*frǽnda*	*frǽnda*)[1]	*frǽndr*	*frǽnda*	*frǽndom*
OE	*frēond*	*frēond*	[*frēondes*]	*friend*[2]	*friend*[3]	*frēonda*	*frēondum*
OS	*friund*	*friund*	[*friundes*]	[*friunde*]	*friund*[4]	*friundo*	*friundun*
OHG	*friunt*	*friunt*	[*friuntes*]	*friunt*[*e*]	*friunt*[*a*]	*friunto*	*friuntum.*

[1] the singular is declined like a weak adjective, but the *i*-umlaut, which phonologically belongs only to the nom., acc. pl. (prim. Norse **frīandiʀ* > *frjǽndr* > *frǽndr* 'relatives') is carried through the whole paradigm. On the other hand, *fiánde* 'enemy' has generalized the forms without umlaut. [2] or analogical *frēonde, frēond*. [3] or *frēond, frēondas*. [4] or *friundos, friunda*.

These stems are present participles that are used as nouns (masculines). While the participles in their function as verbal adjectives go over into other declensions (-*n*- or -*jo*-, **90**), these noun-participles retain essentially the original declension of the IE participles in -*nt*-, as consonant stems: Gk. gen. sg. φέρ-οντ-ος, dat. φέρ-οντ-ι, nom. pl. φέρ-οντ-ες. There is, of course, some analogical influence from larger classes, so from the *o*-class in the Go. and WGmc. gen. sg., from the *n*-class in the whole ON singular. The number of these nouns varies in the several dialects. Gothic has 12, Old Norse 4, Old English about 20, Old Saxon 11, and Old High German only 2. Instances: Go. *fijands* 'enemy', *gibands* 'giver', *nasjands* 'saviour', *bisilands* 'neighbor'; ON *fiande*, *gefende*, *būande* 'dweller, peasant'; OE *fēond*, *tēond* 'accuser', *wīgend* 'warrior', *wealdend* 'ruler', *hǣlend* 'saviour' (the last three with -*ra* in the gen. pl.); OS *fīond*, *wīgand*, *waldand*, *hēliand*, *neriand* (the last two with gen. pl. in -*ero*); OHG *fīant* (*wīgant*, *heilant* etc. have become *o*-stems).

NOTE: An additional, very similar class of the consonantic declension is represented by the -*t*-stems, of which WGmc. alone has retained a few fragments. They are to be compared to nouns like L. *nepōt-* 'nephew'. The nom. sg. apparently lost its early ending, like *naht*, etc., and the final -*t* (WGmc. -*þ*) after a vowel disappeared subsequently, but in the masculines and feminines it was reintroduced by analogy. Old English has four such nouns: the masc. *hæle*(*þ*) 'hero', *mōnaþ* 'month', the fem. *mæg*(*e*)*þ* 'maiden', and the neut. *ealu* 'beer'; *hæleþ* and *mōnaþ* follow the *o*-declension with the exception of the nom., acc. pl. *hæleþ*, *mōnaþ*; *mæg*(*e*)*þ* has no endings except -*a*, -*um* in the gen., dat. pl.; *ealu* has *ealoþ* in the gen., dat. sg., *ealeþa* in the gen. pl.; the other cases are not preserved. In Old Saxon and Old High German the type as such still exists, but the transition to the *o*-stems is complete (OS *heliδ*, -*es*; dat. sg. *mānutha*; OHG *helid*, -*es*, *mānod*, -*es*).

The Adjective

Systematically, the declension of the adjectives should be treated after that of the pronouns, since they have incorporated a large number of pronominal endings. But the earlier, more fundamental structure of the adjective connects it with the noun, so that it seems, on the whole, more expedient to place it between the noun and the pronoun, although this requires frequent references to the chapter on the pronouns.

89. Stems and Declensions. Morphologically, adjectives are nouns, a and in Indo-European their declension does not differ from that of the corresponding noun stems: L. *bonus* like *hortus*, *bona* like *mensa*, *fortis* like *cīvis* (masc. and fem.). But they denoted quality and therefore their most frequent syntactic function was that of an attribute connected with a noun: *hortus magnus*, *mensa parva*. In this respect they formed a separate type in speech consciousness and were apt to develop new declensional groups.

This development was especially marked in Balto-Slavic and Germanic. The methods differed, but there is considerable similarity in the underlying principle. In Balto-Slavic there is an 'indefinite' and a 'definite' declension of the adjective. Roughly speaking, the two types can be likened to the use of the indefinite or definite article in the Gmc. and Romance languages (however, the 'indefinite' adjective is also used predicatively). The indefinite forms are identical with the corresponding noun declension: Lith. *gĕras žmõgus* 'a good husband', *gerà žmonà* 'a good wife', but *geràsis žmõgus*, *geróji žmonà* 'the good husband, the good wife'; OSl. *dobrъ rabъ* 'a good servant', *dobra žena* 'a good woman', but *dobrъjь rabъ*, *dobraja žena* 'the good servant, the good woman'. The suffixed element of the definite form is certainly a pronoun, probably a contamination of the stems *i-* (L. *is*) and *jo-* (the relative pronoun, Sk. *yas*). In both branches the compound character of these forms is still quite distinct, especially so in Old Slavic. The adjective preserves its noun declension, and the attached pronoun is, with very few contractions, declined exactly like the pronoun of the third person (except the nominative, which in the pronoun is replaced by *n*-forms, like *onъ* 'he', *ona* 'she'): gen. sg. *dobra-jego raba*, dat. sg. *dobru-jemu rabu* etc.

b   The Gmc. adjective likewise has a nominal and a pronominal type of declension. But their syntactic functions are virtually the reverse of those of Balto-Slavic. The strictly nominal forms are, in a sense, 'definite', the pronominal type is relatively indefinite. The contrast, however, is intrinsically not as great as it seems at first glance. For the nominal declension is used chiefly when a pronoun (pronominal adjective) precedes: Ger. *der gute Mann, des guten Mannes*; the pronominal type occurs mainly when that is not the case: *guter Mann, gute Männer*.

In accordance with his classification of the Gmc. nouns, Jacob Grimm termed the two adjective declensions as strong (= pronominal) and weak (= nominal).

THE WEAK DECLENSION consists in the change of all adjective stems to *n*-stems—that is, essentially in the addition of an *n*-determinant.[1] This formation has a close counterpart in Latin. The masc. adjectives could be changed to *n*-stems to denote permanent quality, and these new stems formed proper names: *catus* 'sly', *Catō, -ōnis* 'the sly one'; *rufus* 'red', *Rufō, -ōnis* 'Red-head'. The 'indefinite' function of the 'strong' and the 'definite' function of the 'weak' declension is closely related to the individualizing sense of the former and the generalizing sense of the latter, which is still fairly clearly apparent in Modern Standard German: *gute Menschen* (*viele, manche, einige gute Menschen*) designates a limited number of individuals, *die guten Menschen* (*alle guten Menschen, diese guten Menschen*) refers to the totality of a type or at least a definite group.

THE STRONG DECLENSION adds pronominal elements to the stems, substituting them for the usual endings of the *o*- and *ā*-stems. These elements are identical with the endings of the pronominal adjectives, but the resulting forms are not compounds as in Balto-Slavic. The process may rather be likened to the substitution of pronominal for nominal endings in the nom. pl. masc. and fem. of Gk. and L. nouns and adjectives with *o*- and *ā*-stems: οἶκοι, χῶραι, *hortī* < *-oi, mensae*; ἀγαθοί, *-ai, bonī, -ae*. It is not impossible that this transfer of pronominal endings to the 'strong' adjective declension was at least in part due to the fact that 'weak' adjectives are usually preceded by pronominal forms: on the pattern of *þana blindan guman* there may have been formed *blindana guman*; *þata blindō barn* may have been the starting point for *blindata barn*.

DISTRIBUTION OF THE DECLENSIONS. The use of either the strong or the weak forms is approximately the same in all Gmc. languages. Details should be ascertained from the special grammars of the individual languages, but the following general principles hold more or less good everywhere:

(1) Primarily, the weak form is used when a pronominal adjective, especially the definite article, precedes, the strong form when this is not the case; see above.

(2) The comparative always has the weak endings, and the superlative nearly always. Ordinal numbers are always weak. The present participle is in general weak, but in Old Saxon and Old High German it can also follow the strong declension. The past participle is declined strong or weak, under exactly the same circumstances as a common adjective.

90. Paradigms.

The great majority of all Gmc. adjectives are *o/ā*-stems. But there are also stems in *wo/wā, jo/jā, i*-stems and *u*-stems. But the distinctions are disappearing. In Gothic, the *jo/jā*-stems have nearly absorbed the *i*-stems and *u*-stems, and in the other dialects this simplification has gone still further than in Gothic, as will be shown below.

The Strong Declension

Following a convenient practice that was first suggested by Hirt and adopted by Streitberg, GE, Hirt, HU, Wright, G. G. L., Kieckers, HGG in the following paradigms the pronominal and nominal forms are differentiated by the type. The details of this differentiation vary somewhat in the several grammars. In these tables the clearly pronominal endings are printed in bold-face, e.g. Go. blind**amma**. There are, indeed, forms that can be either nominal or pronominal (printed in plain italics by Streitberg, in spaced italics by Hirt), such as gen. sg. masc. *blindis* (*dagis*—*þis*); no effort is made here to characterize them by type. Masculine and neuter are given in one column; where the ending of the neuter differs from that of the masculine, it is given in a half-bracket: nom. sg. *blinds* [-, -**ata** means that *blinds* is the masculine, and that the neuter is either *blind* or *blind***ata**.

Singular

		Masculine, Neuter				Feminine			
	Nom.	Acc.	Gen.	Dat.	Nom.	Acc.	Gen.	Dat.
Go.	*blinds* [-, ata	-**ana** [-, ata	-*is*	-**amma**	-*a*	-*a*	-**aizōs**	-*ai*
ON	*blindr* [-t[1]	-**an** [-t	-*s*	-**om**	—	-*a*	-**rar**	-**re**
OE	*blind*	-**ne** [-	-*es*	-**um**	-*u*	-*e*	-**re**	-**re**
OS	*blind*	-**an** [-	-*es*	-**um**	—	-*a*	-**era**	-**eru**
OHG	*blint*(-**ēr**) [-, -**az**	-**an** [-, -**az**	-*es*	-**emu**	-(-*iu*)	-*a*	-**era**	-**eru**

Plural

Go.	*blindai* [-*a*	-*ans* [-*a*	-**aizē**	-**aim**	-*ōs*		-**aizō**	-**aim**
ON	*blinder* [-	-*a* [-	-**ra**	-*om*	-*ar*		-**ra**	-*om*
OE	*blinde* [-		-**ra**	-*um*	-**a**		-**ra**	-*um*
OS	*blinde* [-		-**aro**	-*um*	-*a*		-**aro**	-*um*
OHG	*blinte* (-) [-**iu** (-)		-**ero**	-**ēm**	-**o** (-)		-**ero**	-**ēm.**

[1] *dt, ðt* simplified to *t*: *blint, hart* from *harþr* 'hard', *kallat* from *kallaþr* 'called'; but *spakt, siūkt* 'sick'.

The endings in bold-face are explained after the chapter on pronominal adjectives, **95**. The nominal endings have been explained in the sections pertaining to the noun declension. Very few additional remarks are necessary.

(1) In Gothic, the *jo/jā*-stems, the *i*-stems, and the *u*-stems are standardized in favor of the former in the oblique cases of the singular and in the whole plural, but the nom. sg. still preserves the difference: **wilþeis** 'wild', like *hairdeis* (long stem), *midjis* 'middle', like *harjis*

(short stem), fem. *wilþi* like *bandi*, *midja* like *sibja* (**81 b**); acc. sg. masc. *wilþjana*, *midjana*; *hrains* 'clean' (masc. and fem., like *gasts*, *ansts*), acc. sg. masc. *hrainjana*; *hardus* 'hard' (masc. and fem., like *sunus*, *handus*), acc. sg. masc. *hardjana*. The transition of *u*-stems to the *jo/jā*-declension probably started in the feminine, where we find a similar trend in other IE languages: Gk. βαρύς 'heavy', fem. βαρεῖα < *βαρεϝja, Sk. *svādúṣ* 'sweet', fem. *svādvī́*, Lith. *saldùs* 'sweet', fem. *saldì* < *saldvī̄*. The *wo*-stems retain their -*w*- throughout the paradigm: *triggws* 'true', nom. pl. *triggwai*.

In the other Gmc. languages the standardization goes still further. The *u*-stems have gone over to the *o*-declension, with the exception of a very few nom. sg. forms: OE *feolu*, OS OHG *filu* (in Old Norse the stem form *fiǫl-* occurs in compounds), OE *cwic(u)* 'alive'. In Old Norse, the short *jo/jā*-stems retain *j* (*i*) under the same circumstances as the corresponding nouns (80 B 1): *miþr* 'middle' like *niþr*, dat. sg. masc. and pl. *miþiom* like *niþiom*; with umlaut, *sekr* 'guilty', dat. *sekiom*; long-stem adjectives follow the analogy of *o*-stems entirely, except for the umlaut: *villr* 'wild' for *viller* (cf. *hirþer*), *fleygr* 'flying', *lægr* 'lying'.

(2) The effect of the vowel of the ending on the stem vowel is largely leveled out. However, in Old Norse we find *u*-umlaut wherever the ending contained *u(o)*: *spakr* 'wise' has the dat. sg. masc. and dat. pl. *spokǫm* < -*um* (cf. *ǫrmom*), nom. sg. fem., nom., acc. pl. neut. *spǫk* <. -*u* (cf. *skǫr*), dat. sg. neut. *spǫko*; the latter form seems to be an instrumental, like OHG *tagu* < -*ō*, but it has not been satisfactorily explained (Heusler, Aisl. Elb. §112, Anm. 2: 'fraglich'); perhaps it is a compromise between the pronominal form in -*om* and the nominal instrumental in -*ō* > -*u*, where the ending would have disappeared. It should be noticed that in the noun the form of the nom. sg. fem., *skǫr*, was transferred to the accusative, while the adjective preserves its original form: *blinda*, *spaka*.

In Old English, there is the regular interchange between *a* and *æ* according to the following vowel: *glæd* 'glad' but *gladu*.

(3) In WGmc., the *jo/jā*-stems show lengthening of the final consonant after a short syllable: OE *wilde*, but *midd* 'middle' (*dd* is phonologically required where *j* was preserved in Germanic, e.g. gen. sg. masc. *middes*; for the nom. sg. masc. and nom., acc. sg. neut. which, phonologically, would have been *mide* like *here*, *ende*, cf. Wright, OE Gramm. §274), OS *thikki* 'thick', *middi*; OHG *dicki*, *mitti* (*dickēr*, *mittēr*).

(4) Instrumentals are not included in the above paradigms. They occur where the noun has them: OE *blinde*, OS *blindu*, OHG *blintu.*

The Weak Declension

b   The declension resulting from the transfer to *n*-stems agrees almost completely with the nominal *n*-declension (**84**), therefore in the following table some of the most self-evident forms are omitted.   In Old Norse, the plural is simplified; for all three genders the nom., acc., gen. pl. end in *-o*, the dat. in *-om*; the OE gen. pl. has usually *-ra* instead of *-ena*.   The great majority of adjectives are *e/o*-stems (*ā*-stems for the feminine), and these have, e.g. in Gothic, the forms of *guma* for the masculine, of *augō*, *tuggō* for the neuter and feminine:

		Masculine			Neuter		Feminine	
Go.	*blinda*	*-an*	*-ins*	*-in*;	*-ō*, pl. *-ōna*;		*-ō*, pl. *-ōns*	
ON	*blinde*		*-a*		*-a*	*-o*	*-a*	*-o*
OE	*blinda*		*-an*		*-e*	*-an*	*-e*	*-an*
OS	*blindo*	*-on*	*-en*	*-en*	*-a*	*-un*	*-a*	*-un*
OHG	*blinto*	*-on*	*-en*	*-en*	*-a*	*-on*	*-a*	*-ūn*.

(1) In Old Norse, *u*-umlaut appears wherever the ending has *o*: *spake* 'the wise one', acc., gen., dat. sg. and pl. *spǫko*.

(2) For the *jo/jā*-stems, *i*-stems, *u*-stems, *wo/wā*-stems the conditions are the same as in the strong declension, e.g., Go. *niuja* 'the new one', *hrainja* 'the clean one', *hardja* 'the hard one', *triggwa* 'the true one'; ON *seke* 'the guilty one' (fem. and neut. *sekia*), *fǫlue* 'the pale one'; OE *midda*, *gearwa*; OS *mārio*, *rīkio*, *garwo*; in Old High German, there is usually a loss of *j*, *mitto*, *dicko*, but in old sources we also find *-eo* (*māreo* for regular *māro* 'the famous one'); *w* remains: *gar(a)wo*.

(3) The present participle shows some variations in the several dialects.   In Gothic and Old Norse it follows the weak declension, but in Gothic the nom. sg. can also be strong: masc. *bindands bindanda*, neut. *bindandō*; in Gothic, the feminine is declined as an *-īn*-stem (*bindandei* like *managei*, **84** End), and in Old Norse this is true not only for the feminine, but also for the plural (fem. sg. *bindande* like *elle*, l. c., pl. of all genders nom., acc., gen. *-e*, dat. pl. *berǫndom*).   In WGmc., where it can be strong or weak, it is treated as a *jo/jā*-stem: OE *bindende*, *-a*, like *wilde*, *-a*, OS *bindandi*, *-io*, like *māri*, *mārio*, OHG *bintanti* (or pronominal form *bintantēr*), *bintanti*.   For the past participle, the comparative and superlative cf. **89** end; the feminine of the comparative follows in Gothic and Norse the *-īn*-declension, like the present participle.

c   ADVERBS that were formed from adjectives are really case forms.   The most frequent type goes back to IE ablatives in *-ōd*, *-ēd* (cf. L. *certō*, *certē*): Go.

galeikō 'like', ON *illa* 'ill', *vīþa* 'widely', OS *gilīco*, OHG *gilīcho*, *ubilo*. In Old English, the -ōd-type is rare, e.g. *fela* 'much', *gēara* 'formerly', *geostra* 'yesterday' (the last two not derived from adjectives). The -ēd- form is found in Go. *sware* 'in vain', OE *wīde*, *hearde*.

Besides, Gothic has adverbs in -*ba*, like *ubilaba*, *harduba*; this ending is also clearly a case form related to Gk. -φι (Hom. ῑφι 'with power'), but its exact character is uncertain; cf. Kieckers, HGG 166, Hirt, HU 2. 105.

Also other cases were used, so the nom., acc. neut. sg., Go. *filu*, *leitil*, OHG *luzzil*, OE *lӯtel*; cf. Gk. πολύ, L. *multum*. Occasionally the gen. sg. occurs, especially in Old English (*ealles* 'by all means', *nealles* 'by no means'). In the WGmc. dialects the adverb -*līkō* (-ē) is often used as a suffix to form adjectival adverbs, and in English this has become the standard type: OE *heardlīce* (NE -ly), OS *gāhlīko* 'quick', OHG *gitriulīcho* 'truly'.

Adverbs that are not derived from adjectives, but represent independent formations, like Go. *þan* 'then', *han* 'when', *har* 'where', *haþrō* 'whence', *hadre* 'whither' are not a problem of grammar in the strict sense, but belong to lexicography.

91. Comparison.

A. THE COMPARATIVE had in Indo-European the suffix -*jos*/ **a** -*jōs*/-*is*: L. *mel-iōr* (r analogical, from the forms with case endings, like *meliōrem*), *mel-ius* < -*ios*, Gk. ἡδίων < *swād-is-ōn*, with transition to the *n*-stems, as in Gmc.

In Germanic, -*jos*- was both medially and finally weakened to -*is*- and this was subject to Verner's Law: Go. *alþiza* 'older', ON *ellre*, OE *ieldra*, OS *aldiro*, OHG *altiro*.

In addition to this, Germanic has comparatives in -*ōz*-, which have no parallel in other IE languages. Probably the starting point for these were adverbs in -*ō*(+ -*iz*, -*z*) cf. Brugmann, Grdr. 2. 1². 560 f. While in Gothic both types are frequent, in the other dialects the -*ōz*-type, which does not cause umlaut, has largely superseded the umlaut-causing -*iz*-type:

Go. *swinþs* 'strong'—*swinþōza*, *garaihts* 'just'—*garaihtoza*; ON *spakr* 'wise'—*spakare*, *rīkr* 'powerful'—*rīkare*; OE *glæd* 'glad'—*glædra*, *lēof* 'dear'—*lēofra*; OS *liof*—*liobora* (-*ara*, -*era*, also, with syncopation, *leoδra*), *naro* 'narrow'—*narowora*; OHG *liob*—*liobōro*, *lioht*—*liohtōro*.

B. THE SUPERLATIVE.

The ending was -*isto*-: Gk. κρατύς 'strong'—κράτιστος, μέγας 'great' **b** —μέγιστος, Sk. *priya*- 'dear'—*prēṣṭha*, *balin*- 'strong'—*baliṣṭha*. Probably this is merely an extension of the comparative ending, -*to*- having intensive force, as frequently in verbs (cf. L. *captō*).[1] In Germanic, we find -*ōsta*- by the side of -*ista*-, and in general the superlative agrees with the comparative in the use of *i* or *ō*: Go. *reikista* 'the might-iest', *háuhista* 'the highest'; ON *lengstr* 'the longest', *fegrstr* (from *fagr* 'beautiful'); OE *lengsta, hiehsta*; OS *eldist* 'the oldest', *nāhist* 'the near-est'; OHG *lengisto, hōhisto*.　Go. *armōsta* 'the poorest'; ON *rīkastr, spak-astr*; OE *lēofosta, earmosta*; OS *rīk(i)ost, kraftigōst*; OHG *liobōst, liohtōst*.

NOTE: In Gothic, and to a lesser extent also in Old English, there occur a few superlative forms with *-m*-suffixes (*-mo-, -ʋmo-*), corresponding to L. *prīmus, optimus, minimus, intimus* (*-tʋmo-*) Sk. *madhyama* 'middle'.　In Gothic, they express either the comparative or the superlative: *fruma* 'the former or first', *aftuma* 'the following, next'; to restrict them to superlative meaning, the usual ending *-ist-* could be added: *frumists* 'first', *aftumists* 'last'.　In Old English conditions are similar, except that forms without *-st-* are very rare, and that there is little or no difference in meaning between the two forms: *forma = fyr-mesta, meduma = midmesta* 'middle' (in size), *æftemesta* 'hindmost' (*-umist-* > *-ymist-* > *-imest-, -emest-*).　Forms corresponding to Go. *fruma* are also found elsewhere, but in general not as real superlatives: ON *frum-burþr* 'firstborn', OS *formo* 'first', OS OHG *fruma* 'use', etc.

For irregular comparatives and superlatives the special grammars of the several languages should be consulted.

The Pronoun

92. Characteristics.

(1) Both the stem formation and the declension of the pronoun differ from that of the noun in several respects.　In a sense, the adjective may be said to occupy an intermediate place between the two categories, being, however, much closer to the noun.　Like the adjective, most pronouns have three (or two) genders and are declined in a similar way: L. *is, ea, id—quis, quid*, like *bonus, bona, bonum—dulcis, dulce*.　Syn-tactically, this type of pronouns is akin to the adjectives, although nominal function is extremely frequent, and therefore the term 'pro-nominal adjectives', common in English grammar, has certain advan-tages, although its exact scope can hardly be defined (e.g. is 'what' a 'pronoun' or a 'pronominal adjective'?).　Another type, the 'personal pronoun', has no gender and the term 'declension' can hardly be applied to its variety of forms (the non-reflexive pronoun of the third person belongs originally to the former type).

(2) Analogy is a powerful factor in all types of inflection, but it has had greater influence on pronouns than on any other part of speech. Much of it goes back to IE times, and this is one of the reasons why for many forms a reliable reconstruction is apparently impossible.

(3) Pronouns have a strong tendency to add or insert various consonantic or vocalic elements. Some of them are clearly particles of syntactic or semantic function, as in L. *quis-que*, *qui-cum-que*, Go. *sah* 'and he', *hvazuh* 'each', *hvaparuh* 'each of two'. Others are pronominal stems: *-c* in L. *hic* is identical with the *ce-* of *ce-do* 'give here' and related to Gk. κεῖνος 'that'; *t* in *iste* belongs to the pronominal stem *to-*; *s* in *ipse* is undoubtedly a pronominal element, although its exact origin is not certain (cf. Sommer, LLFL 431 f.). In many cases a reliable interpretation can hardly be given. Thus, *s* in OHG *dese* 'this' belongs without any doubt to the stem *so-*; but should we assume the same for *s* in Sk. gen. sg. masc. *tásya*, fem. *tasyās*, gen. pl. masc. *tēṣām*, fem. *tāsām*? Is *sm* in Sk. loc. sg. masc. *tásmin*, abl. *tasmāt* a 'particle' (Thumb, Hdb. Sk. 244, 249) or does it belong to the pronominal stem meaning 'the same', Sk. *samás*, Go. *sama*, Gk. ὁμός?

An especially frequent extension is *-i-*: *y* in the Sk. forms given above; *i* (*j*) in ON *siā* 'this' (cf. the Vedic stem *sya-*/*tya-*); the ending of the nom. pl. masc.: Gk. τοί (οἱ), Go. *þai*. It is possible, but hardly likely, that this element is connected with the pronominal stem *i* (*ei*).

93. The Demonstrative Pronoun.

The most widely used stem is *to-*; its paradigm is more or less ᵃ typical for all declined pronouns. It had the relatively weak demonstrative meaning that is termed 'der-Deixis' by Brugmann (Die Demonstrativ-Pronomina der indogermanischen Sprachen, Leipzig 1904). It was therefore well adapted to be used as definite article, and it has that function in Greek and in the WGmc. languages; in Gothic, this development is not quite completed, but the trend is the same as in WGmc.

In IE times, the stem *to-* had no forms for the nom. sg. masc. and fem. For this, a stem of stronger deictic force was used, *so-*: Sk. *sa(s)* (with analogical *-s*), *sā*, Gk. ὁ, ἡ (Dor. ἁ), Go. *sa*, *sō*. This was doubtless due to the fact that the subject case was expressed by the ending of the verb, and a pronominal form was needed in emphatic use only. In Greek, the *s*-form was also transferred to the nom. pl. masc. and fem. (οἱ, αἱ), while, inversely, in WGmc. the *s*-forms were gradually replaced by *t*-forms: E. *the* (but OE *sĕ*, *sēo*), Ger. *der*.

Paradigm:

As in the adjective paradigms in **90,** masculine and neuter are given in one column; where the ending of the latter differs from that of the masculine it is given with half-bracket.

1. The Stem *so-/to-*.

Singular

| | Masculine, Neuter | | | | Feminine | | | |
	Nom.	Acc.	Gen.	Dat.	Nom.	Acc.	Gen.	Dat.
Go.	*sa* [*þata*	*þana*	*þis*	*þamma*	*sō*	*þō*	*þizōs*	*þizai*
ON	*sā* [*þat*	*þann*	*þess*	*þeim* [*þuī*	*sū*	*þā*	*þeirar*	*þeire*
OE	*sĕ* [*þæt*	*þone*	*þæs*	*þæm*	*sēo*	*þā*	*þære*	*þære*
OS	*thĕ* [*that*	*thena*	*thes*	*themu*	*thiu*	*thia*	*thera*	*theru*
OHG	*der* [*daz*	*den*	*des*	*demu*	*diu*	*dea*	*dera*	*deru*

Plural

Go.	*þai* [*þō*	*þans*	*þizē*	*þaim*	*þōs*	*þōs*	*þizō*	*þaim*
ON	*þeir* [*þau*	*þā*	*þeira*	*þeim*	*þær*	*þær*	*þeira*	*þeim*
OE	*þā*		*þā*	*þāra*	*þæm*	like masc., neut.			
OS	*thea* [*thiu*	*thea*	*thero*	*thĕm*	like masc.			
OHG	*dē* [*diu*	*dē*	*dero*	*dēm*	*deo*	*deo*	*dero*	*dēm.*

The WGmc. dialects have instrumentals for the sg. neut. (in Old Saxon and Old High German also sometimes used for the masc.): OE *þȳ* or *þon*, OS *thiu*, OHG *diu*. In Gothic, an instrumental *þē* occurs in the idiom *ni þē haldis* 'none the more' and in several conjunctions, e.g. *bi-þē* 'while'.

Singular

(1) NOMINATIVE. *Masculine*. The stem without ending, *so-*, appears in Gothic, Old Norse and Old English. The lengthening of the vowel in Norse is regular for monosyllables, with open syllables, (cf. *suā* 'so', *þū* 'thou'); in Old English and Old Saxon the quantity depends on sentence stress. Old Saxon and Old High German substitute the *to-/te*-stem, and Old High German adds *-r*, an analogical transfer from other pronouns (*er, hwer*). In old sources forms without *r* are found occasionally: *dhe, ðe, the, dee*. Old Saxon has also the form *thie*; its diphthong is probably due to the influence of the nom. pl. masc., which has the forms *thea, thia, thie, thĕ*.

Feminine. IE **sā* in Gothic and Old Norse, **sjā* in WGmc.; in Gothic the accented form is used, in Old Norse the unaccented in which *ā* became *u* (**49 j**); this, however, was later lengthened because it was final in a monosyllable (see above). In WGmc., the diphthong *iu* < *jā* is treated exactly like *iu* < *eu*, therefore OE *ēo*.

Neuter. IE **tod* (cf. L. *id, is-tud*). Gothic adds a particle of undetermined origin; it is usually likened to the Sk. postposition $\bar{a}$ (with acc., 'towards') or to the second element of Gk. ἐγώ, ἐγών.

(2) ACCUSATIVE. *Masculine.* IE **tom* > Gmc. *þan*, with final *m* > *n*. Gothic, Old English, and Old Saxon add the particle *-a*. *-nn* in Old Norse is due to the influence of the anaphorical pronoun *hann* < **han-m*. Old Saxon and Old High German show the *e*-grade, which is taken over from the gen. and dat.

Feminine. IE **tām* in Gothic, Old Norse, Old English, **tjām* in Old Saxon and Old High German. After the long vowel *-m* was lost (cf. nom. sg. of *n*-stems like L. *homō*, or acc. pl. fem. *-āns* > *-ãs*). ON OE *þā* have not originally long vowels, as Gothic has, but represent shortened forms in unstressed position (*þā* > **þa*), with secondary lengthening, as in ON *sā*, OE *sē*. In OS OHG *jām* > *ja* = *ia, ea*.

(3) GENITIVE. *Masculine.* IE **te-so* in Gothic, Old Norse, Old Saxon, Old High German, **to-so* in Old English (cf. the noun ending *-æs* in early documents, **79 d, 3**). *ss* in Old Norse is not explained, cf. Noreen, Aisl. Gramm. §270, Anm. 4. Perhaps it originated under the influence of *nn* in *þann* and was then transferred to other gen. forms (*huess* by the side of *hues*, occasional writing *hirþess*).

Feminine. IE **tesãs*, probably an extension of **teso*, which originally served for all genders (Brugmann, KG §501, 2), formed by adding the fem. noun ending *-ãs*. Old Norse and Old English substitute the diphthong *ai* for the single stem vowel, a transfer from the gen., dat. pl. For Old English a form Gmc. **þaizjōz* must theoretically be reconstructed (corresponding to Sk. *tasyās*), to account for the umlaut.

(4) DATIVE. *Masculine.* Indo-European had stem forms with *-sm-* (> Gmc. *zm mm*), such as Sk. abl. *tasmāt*, dat. *tasmai*, but also forms with *m*, like Lith. dat. *tamui*, OSl. *tomu*, OSl. instr. *těmь*. Gothic shows the former stem form, the other dialects apparently the latter; it is, however, possible that their *m* represents simplification of *mm* due to lack of stress. The endings point to different case forms. Go. *þamma* is probably an instrumental in *-ē*, since *ē* is preserved in *hvammēh* (indefinite pronoun); the contradicting form *þammuh* can more easily be explained as analogical than this *ē*. Old Norse and Old English have transferred the diphthong *ai* from the plural; in Old English, the umlaut points to an ending *-i*, so that the form corresponds exactly to the OSl. instr. *těmь*; probably the ON form has the same origin. The OS OHG forms show *-u* < *-o* and must be instrumentals.

The ON dat. sg. neut. *þ(u)ī* is a locative, **te-i* > **þī* = Go. *þei*, with optional insertion of *u* from the interrogative *huī*, where it belongs to the stem.

Feminine. The Sk. dat. *tásyāi* points to IE **tesjāi*, by the side of which there may have existed **tesāi* = Go. *þizai*. The ON and OE endings also go back to -*āi*; in Old English the umlaut seems to require -*jāi*, but since there also occurs *þāre* < **t[o]isāi*, it is more likely that it was caused by analogy with the genitive; as in the genitive, these two dialects introduce *ai* into the stem from the plural. The OS OHG forms must be instrumentals in IE -*ā* and are probably due to analogy with the *ā*-stem nouns.

INSTRUMENTAL. The OS OHG forms are clearly old instrumentals, **tjō*, and probably OE *þȳ* has the same origin, but the exact phonological development has never been explained satisfactorily. The alternative form *þon* (used chiefly with comparatives and in adverbial phrases, like *þon mā* 'more than that', *bi þon* 'therefore') probably corresponds to the OSl. dat. *tomu*, aside from the vowel of the ending. (Slavic *u* < *ou* is a transfer from the *u*-stem nouns; the original vowel of the OE form cannot be determined.)

Plural

NOMINATIVE. *Masculine.* IE **toi* is clearly preserved in Go. *þai*, OE *þā* and, with addition of -*r* from the noun plurals, in ON *þeir*. In Old Saxon we should have *thē* (unstressed *thĕ*), which as a matter of fact does occur; *thea, thia* is probably the feminine form **tjās*. In Old High German we should expect *dei* when stressed, *dē* when unstressed; *dei* occurs in Upper German, but for the neuter; *dē* is diphthongized to *dea, dia* since the ninth century, that is, it had the closed quality of *ē²*. Probably this was due to the influence of the stressed form *dei* with which it must have competed for some time.

In Old English and Old Saxon the same form is used for all three genders.

Neuter. IE **tā*- appears in Gothic, **tjā* in Old Saxon and Old High German. Old Norse adds to this the ending of neuter nouns, *þo-u* > *þau*.

Feminine. IE **tās* in Gothic and Old Norse, **tjās* in Old High German. *æ* in Old Norse is due to R-umlaut (**42 d**). In Old High German we should expect **dea, dia*, like *suntea, suntia*; *o* may either be due to the frequent stressed use of this monosyllabic form, or it may have been preserved through the influence of the genitive.

ACCUSATIVE. *Masculine.* IE **tons* clearly appears in Go. *þans*; in Old Norse, *ns* > *nz* > *nn* disappeared, and *a* was lengthened because it stood in final position in a monosyllable. In WGmc., here as everywhere the acc. pl. is like the nominative.

Feminine. Accusative = nominative.

GENITIVE. Sanskrit uses a diphthongal stem for the masculine and neuter, a monophthongal stem for the feminine: **toisōm* > *tēṣām*, **tāsōm* > *tāsām*. Probably this was the IE condition. In Germanic there is, in general, no difference between the genders, but the dialects vary: Gothic, Old Saxon, and Old High German have the monophthongal stem **tes-*, Old Norse and Old English the diphthongal stem **tois-*. The ending is everywhere the same as that of the nouns, so that only Gothic shows a difference between the masc.-neut. and the fem. (*þizē* : *þizō*).

DATIVE. All forms, without difference between genders, go back to IE **toimis* (OSl. *tēmi*, with *i* instead of *ъ* probably under the influence of the nom. pl. masc.). Old English shows umlaut *ā* > *ǣ*, Old Saxon and Old High German monophthongization, which in the former is the general phonetic law, and in the latter is due to unstressed function.

2. Compounds of so-/to- are formed in all Gmc. languages. In general, their function is stronger deixis—approximately the force of E. *this* compared with *the*. The following are the most important: b

GOTHIC.

Masc. **sah,** *fem.* **sōh,** *neut.* **þatuh.**

This is a compound of *sa/þa-*, in its regular declension, and the two particles *u* and *h*. The latter is without doubt the equivalent of L. *que*, which is also used as an extension of pronouns (*quisque, quicumque*). *-u-* may either be the enclitic interrogative particle (cf. *wileiz-u* 'do you want?', *sa-u ist* 'who is it?'), or it may really be *ū* (probably shortened in the unstressed syllable) < *n̥*; *unh* > *ǔh*; the indefinite function of the negative particle (*n̥* being the zero grade of *ne*) is frequent, cf. E. *and what not.*—The case ending *-a* is elided before *-uh*, but after long vowels we have *-h* instead of *-uh*: *þatuh*, but *sōh*.

The meaning of this compound pronoun is not intensified deixis, but closer reference to a preceding noun. It means approximately 'and he', but implies greater importance of the following sentence. It is very similar to the use of Ger. *der* in phrases like 'es war einmal ein König, der hatte drei Söhne'.[1]

OLD NORSE has a demonstrative with intensified deixis that came from three sources. The majority of the forms are compounds of the stems *to-* and *so-* in which, through a network of analogy, the inflection of either the first or the second element prevails: gen. sg. masc. *þessa*, fem. *þessar*; dat. sg. masc. *þessom*, etc. Other forms might be likened to the Go. compounds with *-uh* (see above; so Noreen, Aisl. Gramm. §460, Anm. 1), but might also have as their second element the particle

-*a* seen in Go. *þata*, etc., preserved, contrary to phonetic law, by the emphatic character of this pronoun: acc. sg. masc. *þenna*, nom., acc. sg. neut. *þetta*. The final consonant is doubled in all of these forms which is at least in part due to the emphatic meaning. Until 1250 (in Old Icelandic), the nom. sg. masc. and fem. is *siā* (Run. masc. *sa-si*) with the insertion of -*j*- which is so frequent in pronominal forms. The anomalous *ā* of the fem. (as against *sū*) is probably due to the prevalence of -*a* in the general paradigm. These two nominatives are later replaced by *þesse* and similar forms.

WEST GERMANIC. Everywhere in WGmc. we find a compound pronoun with strong deictic force consisting of the stems *to-* and *so-*. Apparently, the first part was originally inflected and -*se* treated as an uninflected suffix, but more and more the inflection was transferred to the end of the word. The process is very similar to the development of L. *ipse* < **is-se*; in the older language there occur forms like *eum se, eumpse* (-*p*- developed as a transitional sound between *m* and *s*, cf. *sumo—sumpsi*), *eampse, eāpse* etc.;[2] in classical Latin, only the second part is inflected: *ipsa, ipsum* etc.

The earlier condition is seen most clearly in OE nom. sg. masc. *þĕs* < **te-se*, nom. sg. fem. *þīos* < **tjā-se*, acc. sg. fem. *þās* < **tām-se*, **þa-se*, with secondary lengthening, nom. pl. (all genders) *þās* < **toi-se*, instr. sg. neut. *þȳs*; the other cases carried through the stem form *þis(s)*, with end-inflection: acc. sg. masc. *þisne*, gen. sg. *þis(s)es* etc.

Old Saxon has very similar forms: nom. sg. masc. **these* (inferred from MLG *dese*), fem. *thius*, pl. *thius*, but acc. sg. masc. *thesan*, gen. sg. *theses*. Old High German has nom. sg. masc. *dese*, but also *desēr*, but otherwise end-inflected forms, with the exception of the nom., acc. sg. neut. This shows in OE *þis* the same formation as the other cases, but OS *thit*, occasionally spelled *thitt*, OHG *diz* (*z* is the affricate), MHG *ditz(e)*. These forms must go back either to **þet-jo*, with WGmc. *j*-gemination, that is, to a *j*-extension of the mere *to*-stem, or to a combination of the *to*-stem with the *i*-stem.

Aside from this form, the alternation between the stem vowel *e* and *i* in the paradigm (cf. OE *þĕs—þisne*, OHG nom. sg. fem. *desiu* and *disiu*) was originally due, partly to accent conditions, partly to the vowel of the ending, but was largely leveled out. Thus in Old High German *e* prevails in the older sources, but towards the end of the OHG period (e.g., in Notker) *i* is carried through.

c   3. **The Stem *kio-/ko-.** This corresponds to L. *ci-s, ci-ter* 'on this side', Lith. *šis*, OSl. *sь* 'this'; Gk. ἐ-κεῖ (loc.) 'there', (ἐ)-κεῖ-νος 'that' (= Ger. *jener*).

The pure stem in the function of a demonstrative pronoun is preserved in Germanic only in a fragmentary way, namely in a few adverbial phrases: Go. *himma daga* 'on this day', *und hina dag* 'to this day', *fram himma* 'from now on', *und hita* 'until now'; ON nom. sg. neut. *hit* 'this', *hineg, hinnveg* 'this way, hither'; OE *hēodæg* 'to day'; OS *hindag* 'to-day' (acc.), *hiudag* 'to-day' (instr.); OHG *hiutu* < **hiu tagu* 'to-day, heute', *hiuru* = *hiu jāru* 'this year, heuer'. It is also the basis of the adverb Go. ON OE OS *hēr*, OHG *hier* (lengthened grade **kēi-* > Gmc. *hē-*, with *ē²*).

For its use as anaphorical pronoun, cf. **94**.

4. The Stem eno-/ono-: Sk. *aná-*, Lith. *anàs*, OSl. *onъ* 'this, that, he'; it is also the second element of Gk. *κεῖνος* < **κει-ενος* (or *κε-ενος*).

Whether the pure stem occurs at all in Germanic is uncertain. Notker's spelling **enēr* for '*jener*' may go back to uncompounded **enos*, but more probably we have to assume with Braune, Ahd. Gramm. §289 'Im Oberdeutschen ist das anlautende *j* abgefallen.' The ON postpositive article *enn* also *may* go back to the simple stem; see below.

Go. **jains** '*jener*' and its WGmc. cognates is as yet an unsolved riddle, in spite of the extensive and excellent treatment by Hoffmann-Krayer, KZ 34. 144 ff. We have the following forms: Go. *jains* (adv. *jainar* 'there', *jaind* 'thither', *jaindrē* 'thither', *jainþrō* 'from there'); OE *geon* (occurs only once as a pronominal adjective; *bē-gen* 'both'; adv. *geond* 'through', *begeonda* 'on the other side'); OS *gendra* (once; glossed 'citerior', which probably stands for 'ulterior'); OHG *genēr* (Otfrid), *enēr* (Notker).

The difficulty is chiefly the explanation of the stem vowel; cf. Hoffmann-Krayer, l. c., and Brugmann, Dem.-Pr. 91 ff. and 113. Out of the numerous possibilities the following seems most likely: the word is a combination of the pronominal stems *jo-/i-* (**94**) and *eno-/ono-*. But in Gothic, the first element is the locative **joi-*, in WGmc. it is the stem in the zero grade, **i-* (*j-*). Thus the reconstruction would be **joi-eno-* > **jai-ina-, jaina-* for Gothic, **j-ono-* and **j-eno-* for Old English, **j-eno-* for Old Saxon and Old High German. (*g* for *j* before front vowels is normal in Old High German, cf. Braune, Ahd. Gramm. §116, Anm. 1.) Brugmann, l. c., whose view is accepted by Kieckers, HGG 145, reconstructs Go. *jains* as a compound of the *i*-stem and the numeral **oinos* 'one': *j-ains*; this separates it, needlessly, from the WGmc. forms.

ON **hinn** '*jener*' is a compound of **ki-* and **(e)nos*: **hinʀ* > *hinn*.

NOTE: *The Norse Postpositive Article.* While in Gothic and WGmc. (and to an extent in modern Norse: Norw. *den gode konge* 'the good king') the definite article developed from the stem *to-*, the Norse languages used the stem *-eno-*, which originally (this is especially clear in Old Swedish) belonged to the adjective, but gradually came to be suffixed to the noun: *enn gamle maþr* 'the old man' was equivalent to *maþr enn gamle*, and from this developed *maþrenn*. This article *-enn, -en, -et* (< *-ent, -ett*) was for some time in competition with *hinn* (fem. *hin*, neut. *hitt*), and it is possible but not certain that it is merely the weakened form of this pronoun. For its declension and the changes of the noun endings caused by it, consult the special grammars, e.g., Noreen, Aisl. Gramm. §462.

94. The Anaphorical Pronoun, commonly termed the personal pronoun of the third person, is really a demonstrative pronoun with lessened deictic force, but its formation differs so greatly in the several Gmc. (in fact, IE) languages, that a separate treatment seems expedient. The following stems are represented:

(1) **i-*, in various ablaut grades: *ei-, ejo- (ejā-), i-, jo-*. Cf. L. *is*, *id—eius—e(j)a*; Lith. gen. (abl.) sg. masc. *jō*, nom. sg. *jìs* for **is*, with analogical *j-*. This seems to be identical with, or an extension of, the stem *e-/o-* which we find, e.g., in Sk. *a-syá* 'of him', and in certain prefixes such as Gk. ἐ- in ἐ-κεῖ 'there', ἔ-φερον 'then I carried' (augment). In Germanic, as in Latin, it is not always possible to determine whether we have to deal with the *e*-type or the *i*-type.

(2) *sjo-/sjā-/sī-*.

(3) *ke-/ko-*, alone or in combination with *eno-/ono-*.

(4) *to-*.

Paradigms:

Singular

	Nom.	Acc.	Gen.	Dat.	Nom.	Acc.	Gen.	Dat.
	Masculine, Neuter				Feminine			
Go.	*is* [*ita*	*ina* [*ita*	*is*	*imma*	*si*	*ija*	*izōs*	*izai*
ON	*hann* [-	*hann* [-	*hans*	*honom*	*hon*	*hana*	*hennar*	*henne*
OE	*hĕ* [*hit*	*hine* [*hit*	*his*	*him*	*hīo*	*hīe*	*hiere*	*hiere*
OS	*hĕ* [*it*	*ina* [*it*	*is*	*imu*	*siu*	*sia*	*ira*	*iru*
OHG	*er* [*iz*	*in(an)* [*iz*	(*sīn*) [*es*	*imu*	*siu sĭ*	*sia*	*ira*	*iru*

Plural

	Nom.	Acc.	Gen.	Dat.	Nom.	Acc.	Gen.	Dat.
Go.	*eis* [*ija*	*ins* [*ija*	*izē*	*im*	**ijōs*	*ijōs*	*izō*	*im*
ON	—	—	—	—	—	—	—	—
OE	*hīe hĭ*	*hīe hĭ*	*hiera*	*him*	like masc., neut.			
OS	*sia* [*siu*	*sia* [*siu*	*iro*	*im*	like masc.			
OHG	*sie* [*siu*	*sie* [*siu*	*iro*	*im*	*sio*	*sio*	*iro*	*im.*

The endings hardly need any comment, since, with a few obvious exceptions, such as the -*s* -*r* (< -*z*) of the nom. sg. masc. of Go. *is*, OHG *er*, the explanations given for the paradigm of *so-/to-* apply to these forms too.   Stems:

Gothic: There is no reason to assume a combination of the *i*-type and the *e*-type; the former fills all requirements.   The nom. pl. masc., *eis*, was probably formed under the influence of *gasteis*, otherwise we would rather expect the same form as in the feminine, **ijōs*.   Nom. sg. fem. *si* stands in the same relation to **sjā* (OS OHG *siu*) as *bandi* to *sibja*, that is, it is one of the two IE nom. forms of *jā*-stems.

Old Norse: The stem of all cases of both genders is *hān-* < **k̑ēn-*, probably **k̑e-eno-*.   The shortening of the vowel is phonologically necessary before *nn*, but would also be apt to happen in unstressed position.   Forms with long vowels, such as *hōnom*, *hōn*, *hāna* occur. *o* in *honom*, *hon* (< **hanu*) is *u*-umlaut, with further backing from *ǫ* to *o* by the influence of *n*.   *hennar*, *henne* has *i*-umlaut due to a suffix *-izōs*, *-izai*, instead of the usual *-aiz-*; Heusler, Aisl. Elb. §250 Anm., §272 Anm. 1.

For the neuter singular and for the plural of all three genders the corresponding forms of the *to*-stem are used (*þat*, *þeir*, etc.).

Old English: The neut. *hit* possibly stands for *it*, due to analogy with the masculine and feminine; at least, the OS forms would point to that.   Modern E. *it* may equally well be a weakening of *hit*, or a survival of the old form.   The gen. pl. *hiora*, *heora*, *hiera* shows *o*-umlaut from *hira* (which also occurs), and from this form the vowel was transferred to the gen., dat. sg. fem.; cf. Wright, OE Gramm. §102.

NOTE: Since late OE times, at first in the north, and gradually spreading south, Scandinavian *þ*-forms (*they*, *their*, *them*) supplanted the old forms, which, through the operation of phonetic laws, were on the way to lose the distinction between singular and plural.

Old Saxon: No comment needed.

Old High German: The alternation between *e*-forms and *i*-forms cannot be explained with certainty.   *ir* instead of *er* is always used in the Isidor translation.   Perhaps it is safest to assume that *e* originated in the gen. sg. neut., *es* < **i-so* and was from there transferred to the nom. masc., later also to the nom. neut., but there have been analogical cross currents.   For *siu/sī* cf. the remark on Go. *si*.

95. The Strong Adjective.   On the basis of this analysis the explanation of the pronominal endings of the strong adjective, printed in bold-face in the paradigm in **90,** is obvious:

Singular, Nom. Masc.: OHG -*ēr* as against *der* must be due to the use of **dēr* in stressed function as against unstressed *der*, cf. OE *sě*, OS *thě*. Probably **dēr* is only accidentally not attested in MSS.

Neut. -*ata*, etc. like *þata*.

Acc. Masc. -*ana* like *þana*.

Gen. Fem. -*zōs*, etc. like *þizōs*, in Gothic with -*ai* from the plural.

Dat. Masc., Go. -*amma* like *þamma*, OHG -*emu* like *demu*; the endings of Old Norse, Old English, and Old Saxon are modified under the influence of the dat. pl.

Fem., noun-ending in Gothic, pronoun-ending elsewhere.

Plural, Nom. Masc. -*ai* like *þai*, etc., with secondary weakening except in Gothic.

Gen. -*zē*, -*zō*, like *þizē*, *þizō*, with the analogical diphthong (from the dative) in Gothic, syncopation of the connecting vowel in Old Norse and Old English. (Old Saxon has -*ero* as well as -*aro*; interchange between *e* and *a* is common before *r*.)

Dat., pronominal in Gothic and Old High German, nominal elsewhere.

96. The Relative Pronoun. Indo-European had a relative pronoun **jo-/je-*: Sk. *yas*, Gk. ὅς, OSl. *i-že* (neut. *je-že*, fem. *ja-že*). It seems certain that this stem is a thematic variety of the athematic *i*-stem treated in **94** 1. As a matter of fact, in Balto-Slavic it is used as an anaphoric pronoun (in Slavic with the exception of the nominatives for which the stem *on-* is substituted): OSl. gen. sg. masc., neut. *jego*, dat. *jemu* etc.; Lith. sg. masc. *jìs*, gen. *jõ* etc.[1] In Slavic, relative function is imparted to it by the particle -*že*.

jo-/je- was a slightly strengthened anaphoric pronoun, somewhat similar in function to Go. *sah* (**93**, **2**), which very often is best translated into English by a relative pronoun. Just like **i-*, it was in competition, and to an extent synonymous, with the stem **e-* (**94** 1); and in two Gmc. languages, Gothic and Old Norse, forms of this pronoun are used as relative particles. Gothic uses the locative *ei* (**e + i* = Gk. εἰ 'if'), ON *es* (since about 1250 *er*, through lack of sentence stress); the latter is considered by Heusler (Aisl. Elb. §453) a loc. pl., **esi*, **ezi*. This is quite probable, since unstressed *i* appears normally as *e* in Old Norse (cf. Go. *bundeis*, ON *bynde*; Go. *ik*, *is(t)*, ON *ek*, *es*), but it can also be a gen. sg. masc., neut., **e-so*.

In Gothic, *ei* is as a rule suffixed to a pronoun. For the third person, the forms of *so-/to-* are used most frequently, but often we find combinations with the anaphoric pronoun, *i-/si-*, especially for the feminine: *saei*, *þatei*, *sōei*, acc. *þanei/þōei* (with the exception of the nom. *saei*, -*a* is omitted in these compounds); *izei*, *sei* < *is* + *ei*, *si* + *ei²*; the last two forms are undeclined, that is, they have assumed the character of relative particles, like *ei* itself; *izei* is used also for the plural. *ei* is also combined with the personal pronouns: *ikei*, *þuei*. It is also used as a general subordinating conjunction, 'that, where, when'. Another relative particle is *þei*, which may either be the stem *þa-* + particle *ei*, or an old locative of the *to*-stem, IE **tei*.

ON es is generally not enclitic: *sā maþr, es* (er) *þorsteinn hēt* 'the (a) man whose name was Th.'. In early literature the particle *at* is frequently used instead, but since about 1350 *sem* (East Norse *sum*), more rarely *þær*, replaced both of them. More and more, forms of the interrogative stem came into use (Norw. *hvad, hvem, hvilken*), although even in modern Norse *som* is the most frequent relative; as in English and German, but much less frequently, *to*-forms are used (*der, den, det, de*).

WGmc., too, has relative particles, but they belong mostly to the *to*-stem: OE *þĕ*, OS *thĕ*, OHG *de, the, thi, thie*. These particles are probably the generalized nom. sg. masc., like Go. *izei*. In Old Saxon and Old High German the particle *sō* is also very frequent.

But in addition to the relative particles, Old Saxon and especially Old High German also use the fully inflected forms of the *þa*-pronoun, and in Old English they very commonly precede the relative particle (*se, þe*, etc.).

Jacob Grimm, Deutsche Gramm.², 3. 15 f., assumed an OHG relative particle -*ī* (*derī, ihhī, wirī, duī, irī*). He may have been right, but there is no real evidence.

NOTE 1: The development of the *to*-stem to a relative pronoun is usually explained as a change from coordination to subordination of sentences. *Der Mann, den ich meine* is supposed to have developed from *der Mann; den meine ich*. But this is entirely improbable since it would presuppose a rather late period of Germanic without any relative clauses, although we know that they existed even in primitive Indo-European. The development was almost certainly this: Go. *sa manna, ei qaþ þata* 'the man who said that', *sa manna, ei* [ik] *gasah* 'the man I saw' required syntactic extension; the former phrase was clear enough; the latter was not; therefore, first in the oblique cases and gradually also in the nom., the demonstrative (correlative) pronoun was repeated in the case that was required by the relative clause: *sa manna, sa, ei gasah* became by 'attraction' *sa manna, þan(a)-ei gasah*. Following the Gmc. tendency, first, to use relative particles instead of relative pronouns, second to omit even the particles, -*ei* was dropped and the *þa*-stem alone assumed the function of a relative pronoun.[3]

NOTE 2: To a much greater extent than in Norse, the relative-indefinite stem *kwo-* (see next section) assumed relative function in WGmc., most of all in German: the starting point for this was undoubtedly relative clauses without antecedents, which can very often be interpreted equally well as indirect questions or as relative clauses, e.g., 'I do not know who told you that', 'tell me what you did'. In addition to this use of the pronouns 'who' and 'what', WGmc., especially German, also attached relative function to the pronominal adjective corresponding to Go. *ƕileiks* 'what sort of' (see below): OE *hwilc* (*hwelc*) = modern E. *which*, OS *hwilik* = Dutch *welk*, OHG *hwalīh* (different ablaut) > (*h*)*welīh* = Modern Ger. *welcher*. The development of the relative function of this *what* is treated by Behaghel, Z. f. d. Wortf. 13. 157 ff.

The substitution of the interrogative-indefinite for the relative pronoun occurred in other languages too, e.g., in Hittite (*kwis*), in Latin (*qui, quae, quod*), in Balto-Slavic, in late Greek; while classical Greek has the relative pronoun ὅς, ἥ, ὅ, the *kwo*-stem superseded it more and more, and modern colloquial Greek uses chiefly the relative particle (adverb) ποῦ 'where' for all genders, numbers, and cases. In the oblique cases it is usually followed by the syntactically required form of *to-*, e.g., ὁ γιατρός ποῦ τὸν ἔστειλα 'the physician whom I sent'. This is an almost exact parallel to modern Bavarian *der Mann, wo i ksēn hān* or *der Mann, den wo i ksēn hān* 'the man I saw', which offers a good illustration of the probable Go. development indicated above.

a   **97. The Interrogative and Indefinite Pronoun.** The stem **kwo-/kwi-* combines in all IE languages, including Hittite, interrogative and relative function. It is probably impossible to determine historically which of these functions was the original one—quite possibly there never was any priority, since the two meanings are very closely related to one another; cf. Ger. *wer hat das zerbrochen?* and *das hat wer zerbrochen*, or *was brennt da?* and *da brennt was*. It should be noted, however, that in most languages the indefinite function of this stem is preferably indicated by some prefix or suffix, cf. L. *aliquis, quisque, quicumque*, Gk. ὅστις 'somebody', Ger. *etwas* (see below). This might seem to point to a secondary development of the indefinite function, especially when we consider that it is easier to conceive of a language without indefinite than without interrogative pronouns; the indefinite function is easily and often taken over by other parts of speech, especially nouns: E. *somebody, something, one, they*, Ger. *man, (irgend) einer, jemand*. The analysis of those numerous substitutes in the Gmc. languages belongs rather to vocabulary than to grammar; in the following only the all-important stem *kwo-* and its derivatives will be taken up. The basic forms are the following:

Masculine, Neuter

	Nom.	Acc.	Gen.	Dat.	Instr.
Go.	*ƕas* [*ƕa*	*ƕana* [*ƕa*	*ƕis*	*ƕamma*	—
ON	— [*huat*	— [*huat*	*hues*(s)	*hueim* [*huī*	—
OE	*hwā* [*hwæt*	*hwone* [*hwæt*	*hwæs*	*hwǣm*	— [*hwȳ*
OS	*hwē* [*hwat*	*hwena* [*hwat*	*hwes*	*hwem*	— [*hwī*
OHG	(*h*)*wer* [(*h*)*waz*	(*h*)*wen*(*an*) [(*h*)*waz*	(*h*)*wes*	(*h*)*wemu*	— [(*h*)*wiu*.

Gothic has feminine forms, probably a secondary development on the pattern of *sō*: *hƀō, hƀō, *hƀizōs, hƀizái*. The original distribution of the ablaut was probably *o* in the nom., acc., dat., *e* or *o* in the gen.

OE *hwă* must have developed in unaccented position, which implies that the indefinite function prevailed over the interrogative. Likewise Go. *hƀa* as against ON *huat* etc. must go back to the unaccented form. The IE forms are, of course, **kwos, kwod*; we should expect loss of *w* before *o*, but it was retained (or reintroduced) by analogy in the forms with the stem vowel *e* (*i*); OSw. has (rarely) nom. *har(r)*, acc. *han*. OE *hwā* shows secondary lengthening. Old Saxon and Old High German transferred *ĕ* to the nom. and acc. masc., under the influence of the gen. and the pronouns *he, the* and *er, der*.

DERIVATIVES. The most important forms are:

(1) Go. *hƀarjis*, ON *huerr* 'which?'; the latter is also used as a substi- **b** tute for the nom. and acc. sg. masc. of the simple interrogative pronoun (neut. *huat*); the acc. has in prose the syncopated form *huern*, but in poetry also the regular form of *jo*-adjectives, *huerian*.

(2) Go. *hƀaþar*, ON *huārr* (< **huaþr*; *þ* = *ð* generally disappears before *r* and *n* with compensatory lengthening, cf. *norrǫn* = *norþr* 'northern', *Skān-ey* 'southern Sweden', Swed. *Skåne*, Ger. *Schonen* < **Skaðin-auju*, L. *Scandinavia*, cf. **3 a**), OE *hwæþer, hweþer*, OS *hweðar*, OHG (*h*)*wedar* 'which of two?' = Gk. πότερος, OSl. *kotoryi* 'which'.

(3) Go. *hƀileiks*, OE *hwelc* (*hwilc*, NE *which*), OS *hwilīk*, OHG (*h*)*welīh*, NHG *welch*, with *e*-umlaut (which corresponds to a Go. **hƀaleiks*) 'what sort of, which'; it obtained relative function in English and German.

The number of derivatives with indefinite function is very large; some of them are:

Go. *hƀazuh* 'each'; ON *ein huerr* 'each'; OE *ǣghwā* < **ā* ('ever' = Go. *aiw*-) + prefix *ge-* + *hwā* 'each', *ǣ-g-hwæþer* 'each of two, both' (NE *either*), *nāhwæþer* 'neither'; OS *endihweðar* 'one of two'; OHG *ette-, ete-wer* 'somebody', *etewaz* 'something', *etelih* 'some, a few' (*ette-, ete-, edde-* = Go. *aíþþau* 'perhaps, about'.

98. The Personal Pronoun does not possess 'declension' in the usual **a** sense, but is primarily a grouping together of several stem forms, although actual 'endings' also appear. The forms are:

Singular

	First Person				Second Person			
	Nom.	Acc.	Dat.	Gen.	Nom.	Acc.	Dat.	Gen.
Go.	*ik*	*mik*	*mis*	*meina*	*þu*	*þuk*	*þus*	*þeina*
ON	*ek*	*mik*	*mēr*	*mīn*	*þū*	*þik*	*þēr*	*þīn*

Singular

	Nom.	Acc.	Dat.	Gen.	Nom.	Acc.	Dat.	Gen.
		First Person				Second Person		
OE	*ic*	*mec mĕ*	*mĕ*	*mīn*	*þŭ*	*þec þĕ*	*þĕ*	*þīn*
OS	*ik*	*mi(k) me*	*mĭ me*	*mīn*	*thŭ*	*thi(k)*	*thĭ*	*thīn*
OHG	*ih*	*mih*	*mir*	*mīn*	*dŭ*	*dih*	*dir*	*dīn*

Reflexive

	Acc.	Dat.	Gen.
Go.	*sik*	*sis*	*seina**
ON	*sik*	*sēr*	*sīn*
OE		(pers. pron.)	
OS		(pers. pron.)	
OHG	*sih*	—	*sīn*
		(for all numbers)	

Plural

Go.	*weis*	*uns(is)*	*uns(is)*	*unsara*	*jus*	*izwis*	*izwis*	*izwara*
ON	*vēr*	*ōs øss*	*ōs øss*	*vār*	*ēr*	*yþr*	*yþr*	*yþvar*
OE	*wĕ*	*ūs(ic)*	*ūs*	*ūser ūre*	*gĕ*	*ēow(ic)*	*ēow*	*ēower*
OS	*wĭ we*	*ūs*	*ūs*	*ūser*	*gĭ ge*	*eu*	*eu*	*euwar*
OHG	*wir*	*unsih*	*uns*	*unsēr*	*ir*	*iuwih*	*iu*	*iuwēr*

Dual

Go.	*wit*	*ugkis*	*ugkis*	*ugkara**	*jut**	*igqis*	*igqis*	*igqara*
ON	*vit*	*okkr*	*okkr*	*okkar*	*it*	*ykkr*	*ykkr*	*ykkar*
OE	*wit*	*unc(it)*	*unc*	*uncer*	*git*	*inc(it)*	*inc*	*incer*
OS	*wit*	*unk*	*unk*	*unkero*	*git*	*ink*	*ink*	*inkero**.

Singular

FIRST PERSON.

b   *Nominative.* The IE forms are **eĝō(m)* in L. *egō*, Gk. ἐγώ(ν); **eĝhom* in Sk. *ahám*, Av. *azəm*, OSl. (*j*)*azъ*. Gmc. *ek/ik* cannot be directly reconciled with any of these forms, but may go back to **eĝom* or **eĝ*, representing variants under different sentence stress. Run. *-ka*, *-ʒa* (*haitika, hateka, haiteʒa* 'I am called') requires **eĝom*, but that need not have been the only form. (*-ʒa* is either a 'Restwort' (**17 d**), or it may go back to the variant **eĝhom*). The stem vowel *i*, which appears consistently in all dialects except Old Norse (where *e* is probably due to the *a* of the following syllable), would rather seem to point to **eĝ*,

corresponding to Lith. *àš* (Pruss. *es*, Lett. *es*; *e* for *a*, dialect variation, cf. *ašvà* = L. *equa*; **eš* < **eĝ* with sandhi-variant *k̂* for *ĝ* before
voiceless consonants).

The Oblique Cases have the stem *me-*, corresponding to L. *mē*, Gk.
(ἐ)μέ etc. The vowel shows stress variants and also the alternation
between *e* and *i* for which an entirely acceptable formula has not yet
been found: OE *mec*, *mĕ*, OS *mik*, *mĭ*, *me*. ON *mēr* is not a stress
variant, but shows the regular lowering and occasional lengthening of
i to *ē* (**42 d**; Heusler, Aisl. Elb. §78 and §83, 2).

-k in the accusative forms is usually explained as identical with -γε
in Gk. ἐμέ-γε. That this emphasizing particle should have been generalized to such an extent is not very likely; more probably *-k* is a
transfer from the nominative.

-s of the dative is explained in various ways: as an original gen. ending (**me-so* like Umbr. *se-so* 'sibi'), with change to dat. function;[1] as
transfer from the pl. form *uns*;[2] but by far the most plausible explanation
is the one offered by Sturtevant:[3] *mis*, etc. are old ablative forms in
-ts, zero grade of *-tos* (L. *funditus* 'from the bottom', Gk. ἐκτός 'outside'), which under sandhi conditions became either *-t* (Sk. abl. *-āt*) or
-s. The OE OS dat. *mĕ* (OS also *mĭ*) may be identical with *mis*; the
varying sentence stress would be apt to produce doublets, with *-z* >
-r (OHG *mir*), in relatively accented position, and with WGmc. loss
of *-z* in enclitic use. But it is just as possible that these forms are the
pure stem, without any ending, like L. *mē*.

The genitive is an adjective in *-īna-* (cf. Go. *gulþ-eins* 'golden') which
had the function of a possessive pronoun: Go. *meins*, etc.[4]

SECOND PERSON.

Apparently there are two stems, **tŭ* and **tĕ*: L. *tū*, OSl. *ty*, Gk.
(Dor.) τύ: L. *tē(d)*, OSl. *tebe* (abl.). But it is nearly certain that they
are merely variations of one stem, for which the formula **twe* may be
used: Sk. nom. *tvám*, abl. *tvád*, loc. *tvé*; Gk. acc. σέ < **twe*.

The Gmc. nominative has *ū* or *u* according to sentence stress. The
oblique cases probably lost their *w* through lack of sentence stress:
*þwĕ > *þĕ*. For the Go. forms *þuk*, *þus* it is generally assumed that
they took over their *u* from the nom., and probably that is true; but
they may also be alternative forms of the stem **þwe*.

THIRD PERSON (Reflexive).

The stem is **swĕ*, **sĕ*; as in the 2nd pers., the two forms may be variations of one stem: Gk. ϝέ, ἕ < **swe*, L. *sē*, OSl. abl. *sebe*.

Plural

c There seems to be a connection between the plural (and dual) forms of the 1st and the 2nd pers. In the historical periods of each IE language they differ. We find the following stems: 1st pers., nom. *we-* (Sk. *vayám*, OSl. *vē*, Lith. du. *vè-du*); oblique cases, *ne-* in various ablaut grades: acc. Sk. *nas* < **nes* or **nos*, L. *nōs*, OSl. *ny* < **nōs*, instr. *nami* < **nōmis* (cf. L. *nōbis*), Go. *uns* < *n̥s*, Gk. (Lesb.) ἄμμε, Sk. *asmā́n* (acc.) < *n̥s-m-* (or *n̥s-sm-*?). But we also find *m-*, as in the singular: nom. Sl. *my*, Lith. *mēs*, and the second element of the Sk. and Gk. forms just given (if it was *-m-*, not *-sm-*).

The 2nd pers. has primarily the stem **ju̯*: nom. Sk. *yūyám*, Gk. ὑμμε < **us-me* or **jus-me*, Lith. *jūs*, but also **we-* (with gradation), as the 1st pers.: L. *vōs*, Sl. *vy*, Sk. acc. *vas-*, Go. *iz-wis*.

This occurrence of labial stems in both the 1st and 2nd persons can hardly be a coincidence. Perhaps the explanation is this: Many languages have two types of the plural (dual, trial) of the 1st pers., the inclusive and the exclusive forms (e.g., most Australian languages, nearly all of the Austronesian and most of the Dravidian group, many North American Indian languages, some Caucasian languages). The inclusive plural includes the person(s) addressed; the exclusive plural excludes them. Therefore 'we' of the first type means 'I (and he or they) and you'; of the second type, 'I and he or they'. Thus, logically, the inclusive plural combines the 1st and 2nd persons (possibly also the 3rd pers.), the exclusive plural, the 1st and 3rd persons. A real plural of 'I' cannot exist, of course—there is no 'I plus I plus I'; but psychologically, by force of contrast, the exclusive plural is apt to be felt as a 1st pers., the inclusive plural as a 2nd pers. It is not unlikely that the difference between the two types existed in primitive Indo-European, and that the development of the contrast between the 1st and 2nd persons differed somewhat in the various languages; in Germanic and Sanskrit, the *we*-stem was used as an exclusive plural, coming to be felt as 'first person'; in Latin, Slavic and some of the oblique cases of Greek (also in Sk. *vas*, 2 pl. acc.), it was used in the inclusive sense, = 'second person'.

The **ju̯*-stem may well be connected with the **we*-stem: When used as a genuine 2nd pers. pl. the pronominal (demonstrative) element *i-* was prefixed.

But what about the **ne*-stem? It should not be overlooked that it competes with the **me*-stem: L. *nōs*, Go. *uns*, Sl. *ny* as against Balto-Slavic *mēs*, *my*. Perhaps it is a reasonable guess to suppose that they are really the same. *ṃs would obviously be assimilated to *ṇs, and from this ablaut grade the dental might have been transferred to m-forms: Sk. nas, L. nōs for earlier *mos, *mōs. Of course, this process could not be 'einzelsprachlich', but at least in its beginnings would have to go back to IE times.

FIRST PERSON.

Nominative. To the stem *we- is added the pronominal pl. sign -i. In Sanskrit, there is further affixed the emphasizing particle -am (vayám), while in Germanic a second nominal pl. sign, -s is added: Go. weis < Gmc. wīs, wīz. OHG wir, ON vēr are obviously weakened forms in unstressed position (the latter with lowering of i to e and secondary lengthening). The OE and OS forms are probably further weakenings in enclitic position (cf. mě); i and e alternated as is so frequently the case in unstressed syllables (cf. OE wine, OS wini). Old Saxon has wĭ by the side of wě.

The Oblique Cases have the stem Gmc. uns < *ṇs, which, as remarked above, probably goes back to -ṃs. To this is added optionally -is in Gothic (from the dat. sg. mis), -ic, -ih in Old English and Old High German (from the acc. sg. mec, mih); for the distribution over the cases cf. the paradigms. n before s disappears with compensatory lengthening (**29 c**) in Old Norse, Old English, and Old Saxon, in Old Norse with lowering of u to o; the form ōs, however, is rare; usually -is (-iz) is attached as in Gothic, causing umlaut, and the vowel is shortened before ss: øss; the most frequent form is a contamination of ōs and øss: oss.

The genitive is, as in the singular, a case form of an adjective, but with an r-suffix (like L. alter, Go. anþar). The Go. and WGmc. forms are self-explanatory. ON vār can only be understood (at least partly) from the paradigm of the possessive adjective vārr; there, the stems vār-, ōr-, oss- alternate in a very irregular way, the details of which go beyond the limits of this book (cf. Heusler, Aisl. Elb. 86); we have to start out from the form ōr (nom. sg. fem.) < Gmc. *unsarō (rather than *unzarō); in spite of Heusler, l. c. §255 and §149 Anm. 2, we can hardly derive it from primitive Norse *unʀarō, since nʀ would give nn (in fact, Heusler says 'in ōra 'nostram' . . . hat sich wohl das ʀ schon urn. dem n angeglichen'—apparently the opposite of what he means); *unsarō would first have been *ōs(a)ru, and sr would then be assimilated to r (ʀ). To this ōr- was prefixed v- under the influence of the nom., but later this had to disappear again before an old back vowel (**33 a**) (not before the new back vowel ǫ, cf. dat. sg. masc. vǫrom).

On the pattern of such pairs of words as *varþ—orþenn*, the new form *vār* was created, as a contrast to *(v)ōr*.

SECOND PERSON.

Nominative. Go. *jŭs* (**jŭ-* + plural sign *s* = Gmc. *jŭz) appears in Old Norse and Old High German in the weakened form *iz > *iʀ; in Norse, there is lowering and lengthening to *ē*.[5] The OE OS forms are remade on the pattern of the 1st pers. (*g-*, of course, is the palatal spirant, cf. E. *ye*).

The Oblique Cases. The stem is the same as in the nom., *ju-*. The WGmc. forms are clear. OS OHG *iu* (*eu*) represent the pure stem, *ju-* being treated exactly as the diphthong *eu*. Where another syllable follows, Holtzmann's Law operates (**33 c**) so that the semi-vowel (diphthongal glide) is doubled: OHG *iuwih*, OE *ēowic* (with analogical *ēo* instead of the umlaut form *īe*), OS gen. *euwar* (and analogical *iuwar*). OE *ēow* (= NE *you*) is an analogical transfer from the forms with suffixes.

But the Go. and ON forms present difficulties. What is perhaps the leading view connects them with Cymric *chwi* 'you', in which the *we*-stem has a prefix *s-*; to this stem, it is supposed, was added another prefix, *e-*, as in Gk. ἐ-κεῖνος. It is far better to connect the Go. and ON forms with the WGmc. ones. Gmc. *iwiz (**ju-*, + *is* as in *unsis*) would develop *ggw* through Holtzmann's Law in those two dialects; but before its operation, *s* (*z* through Verner's Law) was inserted by analogy with *unsis*. This accounts fully for the Go. form. In Old Norse, *iʀwiʀ shows dissimilation of ʀ . . ʀ to ð . . ʀ (Heusler, Aisl. Elb. §151). It is possible to consider *iz-* as a weakening from *jus*, as in OHG *ir*, with extension by *-wis* corresponding to Sk. *vas*, but the explanation just given seems simpler and has the advantage of explaining the forms of all Gmc. dialects in a uniform way. *y* in *yþr* is *u*-umlaut of *i*, because of the following *w*. The other forms are obvious.

Dual

d FIRST PERSON.

Nominative. Go. *wit* etc. is clearly identical with Lith. *vè-du* 'we two', reduced in unstressed position from *we-dwŏ (Gk. δύω, δύο, L. *duo*). After the loss of *-o*, *we-tu became *witu > *wit*.

The Oblique Cases have the stem *ņ* which, as in the plural, may go back to *ṃ*, assimilated to [ŋ] before *k*. This *k* had been transferred from the sg. *mik*, so that intrinsically Gmc. *uŋk has no dual meaning at all. It merely obtained it by force of the contrast to *uns*. (Whether this was partly due to the fact that Go. *weis* and *uns* both end in spirants, *wit* and *ugk* both in stops, is immaterial.)   In Gothic and Old Norse *-is* (*-iz*) was added, as in the plural; for its probable origin cf. *mis*.   ON *okkr* shows assimilation of *ŋk* and lowering of *u* to *o* (**42 a**). The suffix *-iz* (Go. *-is*) > ʀ, *r* should cause *i*-umlaut (*ø*), but that was prevented, or *o* was restored by analogy with *okkar*.

The genitive shows the same *r*-suffix as in the plural.

SECOND PERSON.

The forms are equivalent to Lith. *jù-du*.   Go. *jut* does not happen to occur in Wulfila's text, but it can be safely inferred from the proportion *weis* : *wit* = *jus* : **jūt*.   The other three dialects that have dual forms show the same weakening as the plural OHG *ir*.

The Oblique Cases are entirely analogical in character.   The proportion *unsis* : *ugkis* = *izwis* : *x* led unavoidably to the formation of *igqis*. *y* in *ykr* (for **ykkr*), *ykkar* follows the analogy of the pl. *yþr*; *i* (cf. Go. *igqis*) undergoes *u*-umlaut to *y*, but this would phonologically show lowering to *ø*, so that the forms for the 1st and 2nd persons would be the same: **økr* (for the 2nd pers. also gen. **økkar*).

NOTE: It is generally assumed that old High German had lost the dual in prehistoric times and that the Bav. dual forms (in pl. function) *ös, enk, enker* (see above) are of Go. origin.   Probably that is so, but the dual form *unkēr zweio* occurs once in Otfrid.   Middle Franconian and Low German have *jit, ink*, used as plurals; also in modern Icelandic the old dual forms have plural meaning. Cf. Kluge, Urg. 3. §254; Baesecke, Einführung in das Althochdeutsche §97, 9.

THE POSSESSIVES are adjectives derived from the personal pronoun stems with the suffix *-īno-* for the singular, *-oro-* for the plural and dual; they follow, in general, the strong declension:

Go.	*meins*	*þeins*	*seins*	*unsar*	*izwar*	**ugkar*	*igqar**
ON	*minn*	*þinn*	*sinn*	*várr*	*yþuarr*	*okkarr*	*ykkarr*
OE	*mīn*	*þīn*	*sīn*	*ūser (ūre)*	*ēower*	*uncer*	*incer*
OS	*mīn*	*thīn*	*sīn*	*ūsa*	*euwa*	*unka*	*inka*
OHG	*mīn*	*dīn*	*sīn*	*unsēr*	*iuwēr*.		

The phonology of these forms is discussed above, under the genitive forms.   For details of declension and use consult the individual grammars of the several languages.

THE NUMERALS

99. The Cardinals.
A. FORMS.

	Go.	ON	OE	OS	OHG
1.	*ains*	*einn*	*ān*	*ēn*	*ein*.

IE **oinos*, Gk. *οἰνή* 'one-spot on a die', L. *ūnus* < *oinos*. Sk. *ē-ka*

< *oi- seems to indicate that -no- is a suffix, probably belonging to the demonstrative eno-/ono-; perhaps the first part of the stem is the o-grade of the pronoun *i-.

2. a. Masc. twai tveir twēgen twēne zwēne
   Fem. twōs tvǣr twā twā twō zwā zwō
   Neut. twa tvau tū twā twē zwei.

The IE stem was in the uninflected form *dwo = Gk. δύο, L. duo, Go. neut. twa. This was treated like a noun dual; the IE dual forms are imperfectly known, but -ōu/-ō was the characteristic nom.-acc. of masc. o-stems, -ai of ā-stems and -oi of neut. o-stems: Sk. dvāu '2', aśvāu (masc.) (from áśva- 'horse', masc.), Gk. ἀμφώ, L. ambō; áśvē (< -ai, from áśvā 'mare'), Sk. dvē (fem., neut.), OSl. rǫcě 'two hands'.

Go. masc. twai corresponds to the fem., neut. forms of the dual, but the form may at least partly be due to the pronominal pl. þai; the masc. forms of the other dialects also have diphthongal stems. OE -gen, OS OHG -ne belong to the pronoun *(j)en- (93); in Old English, -j- caused umlaut of ā < ai. OS ē was monophthongized from ai at a time, when the word was still felt as a compound, and ai therefore was in final position; cf. wēnec (by the side of weinec), from *wai- 'woe'.

The fem. Go. twōs follows þōs and gibōs, and the forms of all other dialects can be reconciled with it; Old Norse shows ʀ-umlaut ā > ǣ, like the pronoun þǣr; OE twā can be explained as *twai, but can just as well correspond to the ending -ōs with partial weakening to ā (cf. pronoun þā); in nouns the ending is further weakened to -e (giefe). Old Saxon and Old High German have either the same partial weakening, or the unweakened vowel ō.

The neut. Go. twa is either the uninflected IE form *dwo (see above), or it followed waúrda. Old Norse can be the original du. masc., IE *dwōu, but more likely it followed the pronoun þau (þa + u, from the plural of neut. nouns). OE tū is weakened twa (*tŭ), with secondary lengthening. The other WGmc. forms are genuine neut. duals in -ai or -oi (see above).

b. bai bāþer bā(-þa), bēgen bē-thie bē-de, bei-de.

Stem IE *bhō, Gk. (ἀμ)φώ, L. (am)bō. In accordance with its meaning 'the two, both', it is generally connected with a pronominal element, in general the þa-stem, but Old English has also the jen-stem, as in twegen; for ē/ei in Old High German cf. zwēne. ā in Old Norse comes from the acc. masc., bāþa < *bansþans; there is also a rare form beiþer.

3. Masc. *þreis þrīr   þrī(e) thria, -e drī
   Fem.   *þreis þriār ·þrīo threa   drīo
   Neut. þrija þriū   þrīo   thriu   driu.

IE *trei-es (an i-stem), Gk. τρεῖς, L. trēs, Sk. tráyas. The masc. and fem. forms follow, in general, the nominal i-stems, without their vowel shortening and with analogical influence from the ā-stems in the feminine. The neut. þrija follows the normal jo-stems.

4. fidwōr fiōrer fēower fiuwar fior fior.

Old Norse has the fem. fiōrar and the neut. fiǫgor, which are discussed under B (declension). In the other dialects the same form is used for all three genders.

IE *kwetwōr-, Sk. catvấras, Gk. τέτταρες, L. quattuor. In Gothic t > ð through Verner's Law. The forms of the WGmc. dialects go back to a parallel form IE *kwekwōr-, with assimilation of the second consonant to the first (or by analogy with *penkwe). kw > ʒw under Verner's Law; ʒw became either ʒ or w, cf. 23 b, c.

The initial f of the Gmc. forms is probably due to analogy with fimf; cf. 23 end.

5. fimf fimm fīf fīf fimf.

IE *penkwe, Sk. pañca, Gk. πέντε, L. quinque (with qu- from quattuor or by assimilation to the medial qu). For -kw > -f cf. 23 end. (Upper German has ch in fuchtsēn '15'.) ON mm < mf is probably due to the ordinal fimte where f had been lost between consonants; regularly, a nasal before f disappears with compensatory lengthening, as in Old English and Old Saxon; 29 c.

6. saíhs sex siex sehs sehs.

IE *s(w)eks, Gk. ἕξ, L. sex. Old English shows breaking before hs; the older form is seohs, but in the group eohs (like eoht), eo became ie, later i, at an early period in West Saxon and Kentish.

7. sibun siau seofon sibun sibun.

IE *septm̥, Gk. ἑπτά, L. septem. p > ƀ through Verner's Law. The loss of -t- is due to the influence of the ordinal (*septm̥tó), where it was omitted in the heavy consonant group. Also the preservation of the final nasal is due to the ordinal. ON siau may possibly be explained this way: ƀ before u disappeared by assimilation, as in *habuk- > hauk- 'hawk', *Geƀukā > Giūke;[1] u caused breaking, e > io; the frequent diphthong au was substituted for the abnormal diphthong ou. Old English shows u-umlaut of e.

8. ahtáu átta eahta ahto ahto.

IE *oḱtō(u), an old dual form, Sk. aṣṭau, Gk. ὀκτώ, L. octō. In Old

Norse *ht* > *tt* with lengthening of both vowel and consonant. Old English shows breaking.

9. *niun   nīo   nigon   nigun   niun.*

IE **neun, newn*, L. *novem* with -*m* for -*n* after *decem*. Gmc. -*n* is due to the ordinal, as in *sibun*. ON *nīo* is irregular; front vowel plus back vowel otherwise formed a diphthong with long second element, cf. **sehan* > **sēa* > *siā*. Probably the different treatment in the words for 'nine' and 'ten' is due to their rhythmical, contrasting pronunciation in counting. *ī* for *ĭ* must have come from *tīo*. *g* (*ʒ*) in Old English, and in Old Saxon is apparently a transitional glide between *i* and *u*.

10. *taíhun   tīo   tīen   tehan   zehan.*

IE **dékm̥*, Gk. δέκα, L. *decem*, Lith. *dešim̃tis*. OS OHG (and probably OE) -*an* point to a parallel form **dekom* for which there is no other evidence. -*n* preserved as in *sibun*. ON: **tehun* > **tihun, tīun, tīu* = *tīo*; see above. In Old English we should expect **tēon* < **tehan*; cf. ordinal *tēoþe*. There must have existed an inflected form **tēoni-* (*ēo* > *īe* through *i*-umlaut), but there is no direct evidence for this.

11. *áinlif   ellefo   endleofan   ellevan   einlif*
12. *twalif   tolf   twelf   twelif   zwelif.*

The formation is exactly as in Lithuanian: *venúo-lika, dvýlika.* -*lika* is the reduced ablaut grade of *liẽkas* 'left over', Gk. λοιπός, root **leikw-* (L. *linquo*). For Gmc. *f* < *kw*, cf. **23** end. The meaning was '(ten and) one left over, two left over'.

In Old Norse and Old Saxon, *nl* was assimilated to *ll*, and the diphthong was shortened before the double consonant. In Old English, on the other hand, *d* developed as a transitional sound between *n* and *l*; *en-* is weakening from *ain-* > *ān-*, probably by way of some ending with -*i*-, perhaps **ainina-* (acc. sg. masc. of the *n*-declension) > **æn-*. But that is entirely hypothetical; -*eo*- is also uncertain; it may go back to a form in -*un* (taken over from **tehun*), with breaking of *e* before *u*, so that the form would represent a contamination of two different forms. -*an* in Norse and WGmc. was most probably taken over from the number 'ten'; if the attempt at an explanation for *eo* in the OE word for 'eleven' is at all correct, we have to assume for that dialect parallel forms with -*un* (-*on*) and -*an*. Also for ON *tolf* the phonological conditions are uncertain. Heusler, Aisl. Elb. §82, 2: 'Postkonsonantisches *wa* und *we* sind oft zu *o* geworden; die genaueren Bedingungen sind fraglich.'

13–19. These are simply combinations of the words for 3–9 and the word 'ten': *fidwōr-taíhun, fimf-taíhun*, etc. In Old Norse, the numbers 13–16 (*þrettān, fiōrtān*, etc.) have *-tān*, corresponding to Go. *tēhund* (see below), 17–19 have *-tiān* (*āttiān*) = OHG *zehan*.

The Decades.

In principle, these are combinations of the numerals 2–10 and forms of Gmc. **teʒund-* 'decade', a derivative of **dek̑m̥t*, nearly identical with Gk. δεκάς, -άδος. In the dat. and acc. pl. this was apt to lose the *d* in the heavy consonant groups that resulted: **teʒun[d]mis, *teʒun[d]ns* > **tiʒum, *tiʒuns*; since these forms are identical with *u*-stems, the analogical nom. Go. *tigjus*, gen. *tigiwē* were added to the paradigm. The numeral 'twenty' originally had the dual of this noun, and this is still preserved in ON *tottogo* probably from the acc. form, Go. *twans tiguns*, with *wa* > *o* as in *tolf* and assimilation of *nt* to *tt*; *o* of the middle syllable must be ascribed to the influence of the *o(u)* of the surrounding syllables. Not all of the forms given below actually occur in our documents; e.g., we have Go. *þrins tiguns, þrijē tigiwē*, but not *þreis tigjus*; but since the reconstruction is entirely certain, no asterisks have been added.

20.	*twai tigjus*	*tottogo*	*twĕntig*	*twēntig*	*zweinzug*
30.	*þreis tigjus*	*þrīr tiger*	*þrītig*	*thrītig*	*drīz(z)ug*
40.	*fidwōr tigjus*	*fiōrer tiger*	*fēowertig*	*fiuwartig*	*fiorzug*
50.	*fimf tigjus*	*fimm tiger*	*fīftig*	*fīftig*	*finfzug*
60.	*saíhs tigjus*	*sex tiger*	*siextig*	*sextig*	*sehzug.*

ON *tiger* like *syner*. In WGmc. *-tig* (NE *-ty*) has become a mere suffix, with loss of the ending through lack of stress. Note that *z* in Old High German denotes the affricate (*ts*) after consonants, but the spirant (*z* = *ss*) after the vowel in *drīz(z)ug*, NHG *dreissig*. The *u* in the OHG forms as against *i* everywhere else is unexplained.[2]

The formation of the numbers from 70 to 100 was different. Only Old Norse carries the multiples of *tiger* through. In the other languages we have formations that indicate that Gmc. *hund* did not necessarily mean '100', but could be applied to any of the decades from 70 to 100 (or, in fact, 120). We have in this a remnant of a conflict between the Decimal and the Duodecimal (Sexagesimal) systems of counting. The former is commonly ascribed to the Indo-Europeans, the latter was apparently introduced through contact with Babylonian institutions.[3] In the modern Gmc. dialects this difference has been leveled out; but traces have persisted for a long time, partly into modern times. Thus Ger. *Schock* = 60 implies the end of a scale of counting. The difference between the everyday 'hundred' = 10 x 10, and the 'great hundred'

= 10 x 12 is observed through centuries in legal tradition, especially in the Norse countries. We have in the earlier periods the following forms:

70. *sibuntēhund*	*siau tiger*	*hund seofontig*	(*ant*)*sibunta*[3]	*sibunzo*
80. *ahtáutēhund*	*átta tiger*	*hund eahtig*	(*ant*)*ahtoda*	*ahtoza*
90. *niuntēhund*	*nīo tiger*	*hund nigontig*	*nichonta*	*niunzo*
100. *taíhuntēhund*	*tīo tiger*	*hund tēontig*[2]	*hund*(*erod*)	*zehanzo*[4]
110.		*ellefo tiger hund endleofantig*		
120.		*hundraþ*[1] *hund twelftig.*		

[1] 'the great hundred'; *tuau hundroþ* = 240.   [2] or *hund hundred* (*-red* corresponds approximately to L. *ratiō*, cf. Go. *raþjan* 'count').   [3] OS *ant-*, which may be omitted, is weakening from *hunt*; in *nichonta*, it is used as a suffix instead of a prefix.   [4] *hunt* is used for '100' since the 11th century, *hundert* since the 12th century.

The explanation of these forms is a moot question, at least for Gothic. The conflict is due to a doubt as to the correct division of the words. Joh. Schmidt, Die Urheimat der Indogermanen und das europäische Zahlensystem 26 ff., divided *sibun-tēhund* = 7 decades; Brugmann, Grdr. 2. 2. 35 ff., *sibuntē-hund*.[4] The decision should not be very difficult, if we venture the intrinsically very probable assumption that Gothic and WGmc. have the same formations. OHG *sibunzo*, OS *antsibunta* are certainly gen. pl. of a noun Gmc. **sibunt-*, a formation similar to Gmc. **tihund-* < **dekṃt-*, and identical with Gk. δεκάς < **dekṃd-*. OHG *sibunzo* is abbreviation for *hunt sibunzo* or *sibunzo hunt* 'ein hundert von Siebenern'. Thereby, Brugmann's analysis is as good as proven: *sibuntēhund* = *sibuntē-hund* 'a hundred consisting of groups of seven, ein Siebener-Hundert', while *taíhuntē-hund* meant 'a hundred consisting of decades, ein Zehner-Hundert'. (That the spelling *taíhuntaíhund* also occurs, Luc. 16, 6.7 and Luc. 8, 8, does not disprove this; *ai* for *e* in the second element is easily understood as analogical spelling.)[5]

200–900 *twa hunda   tuau hundroþ* '240' *tū hund*(*red*)   *twā hund*
        þrija hunda þriū hundroþ '360' *þrēo hund*(*red*)   *thriu hund*
                                                              zwei hunt
                                                              driu hunt.

(Only Old Norse has preserved the meaning '120' in the multiples.)
1000 *þūsundi   þūsund* '1200' *þūsend   thūsundig   dūsunt.*

IE **tūs-kṃtī* 'power hundred', **tū-*, **tewe-* 'be strong, swell' (Sk. *tavas* 'strength', L. *tū-meō* 'swell'). Gmc. *þūs-hundī* lost the *h* in the unstressed part of the word. Being a *jā*-stem, it is originally a feminine but in OE it appears as a neut., and in Old High German both as fem. and neut. The anomalous change $d > t$ in New High German (but beginning to occur in late Old High German, cf. Braune, Ahd. Gramm. §168, Anm. 8—a third consonant shift, it might be called) is probably due to its emphatic meaning, rather than to sandhi, in forms like 'sechs tausend, acht tausend'. This is made virtually certain by the fact that the change took place in High German, where the d was voiceless (lenis) anyway and therefore could not be made voiceless by a preceding voiceless sound.

B. DECLENSION.

1. Go. *ains* etc. is declined as a strong adjective. b

2. The nom. forms have been given in the tables above; the dat. and gen. forms are:

Go. *twaim, twaddjē*; ON *tueim, tueggia*;

OE *twǣm, twēg(e)a*; OS *twēm, tweio*; OHG *zweim, zweio*.

Go. *ddj*, ON *ggi* is due to Holtzmann's Law; so is OE *ge* = *jj*. Old High German has occasionally the corresponding spelling *zweiio* (Isidor), Old Saxon has simplified.

3. Dat. and gen. forms: Go. *þrim, þrijē* (irregular for *þriddjē*); ON *þrim, þriggia*; OE *þrim, þrīora* (following the strong adjective); OS *thrim, *thrīo*; OHG *drim, drīo*.

4–12. These numbers are usually uninflected, but follow the *i*-declension when they are used as nouns or follow the noun, e.g., Go. *twalibim, twalibē*, OE *fīfe, -um, -a*, OS *fīvi, -iun, -io*, OHG *finfi, -im, -eo*. In Old Norse the numeral '4' is always inflected; the forms are:

	Masc.	Neut.	Fem.
nom.	*fiōrer*		
acc.	*fiōra*	*fiǫgor*	*fiōrar*
dat.		*fiōrom*	
gen.		*fiǫgorra.*	

The stem is *feður-, fiðr- (weakened form like Go. *fidur-* in compounds). *ðr > r* with compensatory lengthening; breaking *e > iǫ* before *u*; for *g* cf. Heusler, Aisl. Elb. §173, Anm. 2: 'Ein Uebergang *ð > g* zeigt sich in *fiǫgor* '4' Ntr.: got. *fidur-*; wohl partielle Angleichung an die umgebenden velaren Vokale.'

20–60 (in Old Norse,—110): Go. *tigjus*, ON *tigur* are inflected as *u*-stems (*tiger* without breaking). The corresponding elements in WGmc. are uninflected.

70–90 are uninflected everywhere except in Old Norse, where *tiger* has taken the place of the Go. formation.

100: *hund* is a regular *o*-stem neuter.

1000: Go. *þūsundi* is inflected as a *jā*-stem, Old Norse *þūsund* as a fem. *i*-stem; OE *þūsend* had become a neut. noun and is often declined like a neut. *o*-stem; OS *thūsundig* (with *-ig* from *twēntig* etc.) is uninflected; OHG *dūsunt* is inflected either as an *ā*-stem or as a neut. *o*-stem: Tatian, *zwā thūsuntā*, Notker, *driu tūsent*; the dat..ends in *-un* or *-in*.

100. The Ordinals follow the weak declension, only Go. *anþar* (with its cognates) is strong.

With the exception of the first two numbers, the ordinals are derived from the corresponding cardinals.

'The first' is a superlative of the preposition IE **pr-*, Go. *faúra*, OE *fore*, OS *fore*: with the suffix *-mo-* in Go. *fruma*, OE *forma*, OS *formo*; with *-to-* in ON *fyrstr*, OE *fyrest*, OS OHG *furisto*; another form, with *-sto*-suffix, belongs to Go. *air*, ON *ār*, OE *ǣr*, OS OHG *ēr* 'early, before': OE *ǣresta*, OS OHG *ēristo*.

'The second' is a comparative in *-tero-* (cf. Gk. δεύ-τερος) of the demonstrative stem *ono-*: Go. *anþar*, ON *annarr*, OE *ōþer*, OS *ōthar*, OHG *ander*. (NHG 'der zweite' was formed shortly before 1500).

All other ordinals are superlatives in *-tjo-/-to-*, with some variations between the dialects. For the numbers 3–12 the dialects agree. 'The third' was formed with the suffix *-tjo-*, the others with *-to-*:

3.	*þridja*	*þriþe*	*þridda*	*thriddio*	*dritto*
4.	—	*fiorþe*	*feorþa*	*fiorðo*	*feordo*
5.	*fimfta*	*fimte*	*fīfta*	*fīfto*	*fimfto*
6.	*saíhsta*	*sētte*	*siexta*	*sehsto*	*sehsto*
7.	—	*siaunde*	*seofoþa*	*siƀunda*	*sibunto*
8.	*ahtuda*	*ātte*	*eahtoþa*	*ahtodo*	*ahtodo*
9.	*niunda*	*nīonde*	*nigoþa*	*nigundo*	*niunto*
10.	*taíhunda*	*tīonde*	*tēoþa*	*tehando*	*zehanto*
11.	—	*ellepte*	*enlefta*	*ellifto*	*einlifto*
12.	—	*tolfte*	*twelfta*	—	*zwelifto*.

Originally, all of these forms were doubtless accented on the suffix, cf. Go. *þridja*, OE *þriddo* (WGmc. gemination before *j*), ON *siaunde*, OS *siƀunda*, OHG *sibunto*, but the rhythm of counting led to anomalous accent changes, so that we have, e.g., OE *seofoþa*, OHG *feordo*, *ahtodo*. —After voiceless spirants, of course, *t* had to remain: Go. *fimfta*. Some of the OHG forms may be ascribed to analogy with this: *sibunto* after *sehsto*.

The ordinals 13th–19th originally had the same formation as L. *tertius decimus*, but such forms are preserved only in Gothic and Old High German: Gothic *in jēra fimftataíhundin* 'in the fifteenth year'

(Luc. 3, 1); in Old High German this is in the earlier period the regular formation: *drittozehanto, fiordozehanto*; only with Notker a new form with the cardinal number as first element began to spread: *fierzēndo*. In the other dialects this is the case throughout: ON *þrēttande*, OE *þrēotēoþa*, Old Saxon not preserved, but probably like Old English (**thriutehando*).

Beginning with 20, Old Norse and Old English use the -*to*-suffix throughout, Old High German the -*ōsto*-suffix, as with most superlatives; there are no Go. or OS forms extant: ON *tottogonde, þrītogonde*, OE *twēntigoþa, þrītigoþa*, OHG *zweinzugōsto, drīzugōsto*.

SPECIMEN TEXTS

GOTHIC (Matth. 6. 9–13)

Atta unsar þu in himinam, weihnai namo þein. Qimai þiudinassus þeins. Wairþai wilja þeins, swe in himina jah ana airþai. Hlaif unsarana þana sinteinan gif uns himma daga. Jah aflet uns þatei skulans sijaima, swaswe jah weis afletam þam skulam unsaraim. Jah ni briggais uns in fraistubnjai, ak lausei uns af þamma ubilin.

OLD NORSE

Faþer várr, sā þū ert ī(ā) hifne (himnum), helgesk nafn þitt. Til kome þitt rīke. Verþe þinn vile, suā ā iǫrþ sem ā hifne. Gef oss ī dag vārt dagligt brauþ. Ok fyrerlāt oss ossar skulder, suā sem vēr fyrerlātom ossom skuldo-nautom. Ok inn leiþ oss eige ī freistne. Heldr frels þū oss af illo.

WEST SAXON

Fæder ūre þū þe eart on heofonum, sī þīn nama gehālgōd. Tōbecume þīn rīce. Geweorþe þīn willa on eorþan swā swā on heofonum. Ūrne gedæghwāmlīcan hlāf syle ūs tō dæg. And forgyf ūs ūre gyltas, swā swā wē forgyfaþ ūrum gyltendum. And ne gelǣd þū ūs on costnunge, ac ālȳs ūs of yfele.

HELIAND

Fadar ūsa, thu bist an them himila rīkea. Geuuīhid sī thīn namo. Cuma thīn rīki. Uuertha thīn uuilleo, sō sama an ertho, sō an them himilo rīkea. Gef ūs dago gehuuilikes rād, endi ālāt ūs managoro mēnsculdio, al sō uuē ōthrum mannum dōan. Ne lāt ūs farlēdean lētha uuihti, ac help ūs uuithar allun ubilon dādiun.

WEISSENBURGER KATECHISMUS

Fater unsēr, thu in himilon bist, giuuīhit sī namo thīn, quaeme rīchi thīn. Uuerdhe uuilleo thīn, sama sō in himile endi in erdhu. Broot unseraz emezzīgaz gib uns hiutu. Endi farlāz uns sculdhi unsero, sama sō uuir farlāzzēm scolōm unserēm. Endi ni gileidi unsih in costunga, auh arlōsi unsih fona ubile.

TATIAN

Fater unser, thū thār bist in himile, sī giheilagōt thīn namo, queme thīn rīhhi, sī thīn uuillo, sō her in himile ist, sō sī her in erdu. Unsar brōt tagalihhaz gib uns hiutu, inti furlāz uns unsara sculdi, sō uuir furlāzemēs unsarēn sculdīgōn, inti ni gileitēst unsih in costunga, ūzouh arlōsi unsih fon ubile.

SANKT GALLER PATERNOSTER

Fater unseer, thū pist in himile, uuīhi namun dīnan, qhueme rīhhi dīn, uuerde uuillo dīn, sō in himile, sōsa in erdu. Prooth unseer emez-zihic kip uns hiutu, oblāz uns sculdi unseero, sō uuir oblāzēm uns sculdīkēm, enti ni unsih firleiti in khorunka, ūzzer lōsi unsih fona ubile.

FREISINGER PATERNOSTER

Fater unsēr, dū pist in himilum, kauuīhit sī namo dīn. Piqhueme rīhhi dīn. Uuesa dīn uuillo, sama sō in himile ist, sama in erdu. Pilipi unsraz emizzīgaz kip uns eogauuanna. Enti flāz uns unsro sculdi, sama sō uuir flāzzamēs unsrēm scolōm. Enti ni princ unsih in cho-runka, ūzzan kaneri unsih fora allēm suntōn.

GOTHIC (Matth. 9, 1–8)

Jah atsteigands in skip ufar-laiþ jah qam in seinai baurg. þa-nuh atberun du imma usliþan ana ligra ligandan. Jah gasai ƕands Jesus galaubein ize qaþ du þamma usliþin: þrafstei þuk, barnilo, afle-tanda þus frawaurhteis þeinos. þaruh sumai þize bokarje qeþun in sis silbam: sa wajamereiþ. Jah witands Jesus þos mitonins ize qaþ: Duƕe jus mitoþ ubila in hair-tam izwaraim? ƕaþar ist raih-tis azetizo qiþan: afletanda þus frawaurhteis, þau qiþan: urreis jah gagg? Aþþan ei witeiþ þatei waldufni habaiþ sa sunus mans ana airþai afletan frawaurhtins, þanuh qaþ du þamma usliþin: Ur-reisands nim þana ligr þeinana jah gagg in gard þeinana. Jah urrei-

OLD NORSE

Ok er Jesus stē ā skip, fōr hann yfer um aptr, ok kom ī sīna borg. Ok siā, at þeir fǿrþo til hans ikt-siūkan mann, sā er ī sæng lā. En sem Jesus leit þeira trū, sagþe hann til hins iktsiūkan: þīnar synder ero þēr fyrergefnar. Ok siā, at nok-korer af skriptlærþom sǫgþo meþ siǫlfom sēr, siā guþlestar. Ok sem Jesus sā þeira hugsaner, sagþe hann: huar fyrer hugseþ ēr suā vǫndt ī yþrom hiǫrtom? Huārt er auþveldara at segia: þēr ero þīnar synder fyrergefnar eþa at segia: statt upp ok gakk? En suā at ēr viteþ, þat manzens son hefer makt ā iǫrþ synder at fyrergefnar, þā sagþe hann til hins iktsiūka: statt upp, tak īlegu þīna, ok gakk ī þitt hūs. Ok hann stōþ upp ok fōr ī

sands galaiþ in gard seinana. Ga-
saiƕandeins þan manageins ohte-
dun sildaleikjandans jah mikili-
dedun guþ.

sitt hūs. En þā folkit sā undra-
þesk þat ok prīsaþe Guþ.

WEST SAXON

þā āstāh hē on scyp, and ofer-
seglode and cōm on his ceastre.
þā brōhton hig hym ǣnne laman
on bedde licgende; þā geseah sē
Hǣlend hyra gelēafan and cwæþ
tō þām laman, Lā, bearn, gelȳfe;
þē bēoþ þīne synna forgyfene. þā
cwǣden hig sume þā bōceras him
betwȳnan, þes spycþ bysmor-
sprǣce. þā sē Hǣlend geseah hyra
geþanc, þā cwæþ hē, Tō hwī þence
gē yfel on ēowrum heortum?
Hwæt is ēaþlīcere tō cweþenna, þē
bēoþ forgyfene þīne synna, oþþe tō
cweþanne, Ārīs and gā? þæt gē
sōþlīce witon þæt mannes sunu
hæfþ anweald on eorþan synna tō
forgyfanne, þā cwæþ hē tō þam laman, Ārīs and nym þīn bedd and
gang on þīn hūs. And hē ārās and
fērde tō hys hūse. Sōþlīce þā þā
sēo mænigeo þis gesāwon, þā on-
drēdon hig hym and wuldrodon
God.

OLD SAXON

Thō he im giuuēt eft an Galileo
land. Thar drōgun ēnna seocan
man erlos an iro armun, bārun mid
is beddiu. Hē thō farstōd, that sie
mikilana te imu gelōbon habdun.
Quath that hē thene siakon man
sundeono tōmean lātan uueldi.
Thō sprākun im eft thea liudi an-
gegin, quāthun that that ni mahti
giuuerthen sō. "Ik gidōn that"
quath he, "an thesumu manne
skīn, that ik geuuald hebbiu sun-
dea te fargeƀanne endi ōc seocan
man te gehēleanne." Hēt ina far
them liudiun astandan endi an is
ahslun niman is bedgiuuādi. Hē
geng imu eft gesund thanan, hēl
fan themu hūse. Uueros uund-
radun, quāthun that imu uual-
dand self fargeƀan habdi mēron
mahti than elcor ēnigumu mannes
sunnie.

EAST FRANCONIAN

Steig tho in skifilin inti ferita
inti qam in sina burg. Senu tho
fior gomman tragenti in bette man
thie thar uuas lam, suohtun inan
in zi sezzenne furi then heilant.
Thero giloubon soso her gisah,
quad: giloubi, kind, thanne uuer-
dent thir furlazano thino sunta.
Bigundon tho thenken thie buoh-

BAVARIAN (Copy from Rhen. Franconian)

Enti genc her in sceffilin, ubar-
ferita dhen geozun enti quam in
sina burc. Enti see saar butun
imo bifora laman licchentan in
baru. Enti gasah Jesus iro ga-
laupin, quhad dhemo lamin: Ga-
true, sunu, forlaazsenu dhir uuerdant dhino suntea. Enti see saar
ein huuelihhe scrībera quhātun

hara sus quedante: uuer ist these thie thar sprihhit bismarunga? Tho ther heilant furstuont iro githanka, antvvurtenti quad zi in: zi hiu thenkent ir ubil in iuuaren herzon? Uuedar ist odira, zi quedanne: sint thir furlazano sunta, edo zi quedanne: arstant inti gang? Zi thiu thaz ir uuizit thaz mannes sun habet giuualt in erdu zi furlazenne sunta, quad themo lamen: thir quidu: arstant, nim thin betti inti far in thin hus. Her tho arstantenti sliumo fora in nam thaz thar her analag inti gieng in sin hus. Inti forhta bifieng sie alle, inti mihhilosotun got.

untar im: Dhese lastrot. Enti so Jesus gasah iro gadancha, quhat: Zahuuiu dencet ir ubil in iuueremo muote? Huuedar ist gazelira za quhedanne, forlaazseno dhir uuerdant dhīno suntea, odo za quhedanne, arstant enti ganc? Daz ir auh uuizit dhaz mannes sunu habet gauualt in erdhu za forlaazsanne suntea, duo quhat dhemo lamin: Arstant, nim dīn betti enti ganc za dhīnemo hūs. Enti er genc za sīnemo hus. Gasāhhun iz diu folc, gaforahtun im enti ærlihho lobotun got.

GOTHIC (Luc. 1, 5–10)

Was in dagam Herodes þiudanis Judaias gudja namin Zakarias, us afar Abijins, jah qeins is us dauhtrum Aharons, jah namo izos Aileisabaiþ. Wesunuh þan garaihta ba in andwairþja gudis, gaggandona in allaim anabusnim jah garaihteim fraujins unwaha. Jah ni was im barnē, unte was Aileisabeiþ stairo, jah ba framaldra dage seinaize wesun. Warþ þan, miþþanei gudjinoda is in wikon kunjis seinis in andwairþja gudis, bi biuhta gudjinassaus, hlauts imma urrann du saljan, atgaggands in alh fraujins, jah alls hiuhma was manageins beidandans uta ƕeilai þymiamins.

OLD NORSE

Suā seger lukas euangelista, at ā dǫgom Herodis konungs vas biskop, sā er Zakarias hēt; en kona hans hēt Elisabēþ, hon vas komen frā Āron brōþōr Moises. þau vǫro rētlǫt bǣþe fyr guþe, ok gerþo epter hans boþorþom, suāt enge fann at þeim. Ekke ǫtto þau barna, þuī at Elisabēþ vas obyria. En þā er kom at hleyte Zakarias at fremia biskops embǣtte, þā ferr hann til templum domini at bera þar reykleset. Enn aþrer menn stōþo ā bønom ūte meþan hann bar reykleset

WEST SAXON

On Herodes dagum Judea cyninges, wæs sum sācerd, on naman

OLD SAXON

Than uuas thar ēn gigamalod mann, that uuas fruod gumo, uuas

Zacharias, of Abian gewrixle, and his wīf wæs of Aarones dohtrum, and hyre nama wæs Elisabeþ. Sōþlīce hig wǣron būtū rihtwīse beforan Gode, gangende on eallum his bebodum and rihtwīsnessum būtan wrōhte. And hig næfdon nān bearn, for þām þe Elisabeþ wæs unberende, and hȳ on heora dagum būtū forþ ēodon. Sōþlīce wæs gewordon þā Zacharias his sācerdhādes brēac on hys gewrixles endebyrdnesse beforan Gode, æfter gewunan þæs sācerdhādes hlōtes, þā hē ēode þæt hē hys offrunga sette, hē on Godes tempel ēode; eall werod þæs folces wæs ūte gebiddende on þære offrunga tīman.

fan them liudeon Levias cunnes, Zacharias uuas hie hētan. Hie simblon gerne gode theonoda; deda is uuīf sō self, uuas iro gialdrod idis. Uuas im thoh an sorgun hugi, that sie erbiuuard ēgan ni mōstun, ac uuārun im barno lōs. Than scolda he gibod godes thar an Hierusalem sō oft sō is gigengi gistōd, hēlag bihuuerban hebancuninges. Thō uuarth thiu tīd cuman, that thar gitald habdun uuīsa man mid uuordun, that scolda thana uuīh Godes Zacharias bisehan. Thea liudi stōdun umbi that hēlaga hūs.

TATIAN

Uuas in tagun Herodes thes cuninges Judeno sumēr biscof namen Zacharias fon themo uuehsale Abiases inti quena imo fon Aarones tohterun inti ira namo uuas Elisabeth. Siu uuārun rehtiu beidiu fora gote, gangenti in allēm bibotun inti in gotes rehtfestīn ūzzan lastar, inti ni uuard in sun, bithiu uuanta Elisabeth uuas unberenti inti beidiu framgigiengun in iro tagun. Uuard thō, mit thiu her in biscofheite giordinōt uuas in antreitu sīnes uuehsales fora gote, after giuuonu thes biscofheites, in lōzze framgieng, thaz her uuīhrouh branti ingangenti in gotes tempal, inti al thiu menigī uuas thes folkes ūzze, betōnti in thero zīti thes rouhennes.

OTFRID

In dagon eines kuninges uuas ein ēuuarto; ze hīun er mo quenun las. Uuārun siu bēthiu gote filu drūdiu ioh iogiuuar sīnaz gibot fullentaz. Unbera uuas thiu quena kindo zeizero; so uuārun se unzan eltī thaz līb leitendi. Zīt uuard thō gireisōt, thaz er giangi furi got: opphorōn er scolta bi die sīno sunta; zi gote ouh thanne thigiti, thaz er giscouuōti then liut, ther gināda tharūze beitōta. Ingiang er thō skioro thaz hūs rouhenti.

BIBLIOGRAPHICAL NOTES

To give a complete bibliography of comparative Germanic grammar would be a futile undertaking. Many of the works and articles are obsolete, and besides, a complete list would fill several volumes. A selection from the abundance of material must necessarily be subjective and arbitrary. An attempt is made, first, to quote those works that are indispensable to the student and, second, to give fairly adequate references on moot questions. Such restriction is especially justified since bibliographical data are conveniently available in F. Löwenthal, Bibliographisches Handbuch zur deutschen Philologie (Halle 1932).

1. [1] Hermann Hirt, Die Indogermanen, ihre Verbreitung, ihre Urheimat und ihre Kultur, 1905-7; Matthäus Much, Die Heimat der Indogermanen im Lichte der urgeschichtlichen Forschung, [2]1904; an abundance of material is offered in 'Germanen und Indogermanen' (2 vols., dedicated to Hermann Hirt on his seventieth birthday, December 19, 1935; edited by Helmuth Arntz), Heidelberg 1936.

[2] Otto Schrader, Sprachvergleichung und Urgeschichte, [3]2. 506, 514 (1907); Die Indogermanen 160 ff.

[3] Otto Bremer, Ethnographie der germanischen Stämme, PG[2] 3. 757; Siegmund Feist, Kultur, Ausbreitung und Herkunft der Indogermanen (1913), chapter XX, Die Lage der Ursitze, 486-528, offer a good survey of the whole problem; so does T. E. Karsten, Die Germanen PG[3] 35-48 (1928). Hermann Güntert, Zur Frage nach der Urheimat der Indogermanen (in Deutschkundliches, Friedrich Panzer zum 60. Geburtstag 1-133 [1930]) favors central Asia.

[4] 'Das eurasische Gleis'; Gunther Ipsen, Der alte Orient und die Indogermanen, in Stand und Aufgaben der Sprachwissenschaft (Festschrift für Wilhelm Streitberg [1924]).

[5] Friedrich Ratzel, Der Ursprung und das Werden der Völker geographisch betrachtet, Ber. d. kgl. sächs. Ges. d. Wissensch., Phil.-hist. Klasse 1888. 146: 'in einem zusammenhängenden Länderraum, der sich vom 35. Grad n. Br. südostnordwestlich gegen den Polarkreis hinzieht, von der Abdachung zum persischen Golf bis zur Ostsee.'

[6] Paul Kretschmer, Einleitung in die Geschichte der griechischen Sprache 60 (1896): 'einen ziemlich schmalen und langgestreckten Landstreifen, welcher von Frankreich durch ganz Mittel-Europa und die Kirgisensteppe Asiens bis nach Iran reicht.'
A very important recent contribution to the problem of the origin of the Indo-Europeans is given by Alfons Nehring, Studien zur indogermanischen Kultur und Urheimat (Wiener Beiträge zur Kulturgeschichte und Linguistik, 4, 1936); in agreement with Frh. v. Eickstedt, Rassenkunde und Rassengeschichte der Menschheit (1934) he offers strong arguments for southern Siberia.

[7] Compendium d. vgl. Gramm.[4] 9 (1876); similarly Die deutsche Sprache 81 (1860).

[8] Die Verwandtschaftsverhältnisse der indogermanischen Sprachen 27 (1872):

299

'Wenn wir nun die Verwandtschaftsverhältnisse der indogermanischen Sprachen in einem Bilde darstellen, welches die Entstehung ihrer Verschiedenheit veranschaulicht, so werden wir die Idee des Stammbaums gänzlich aufgeben. Ich möchte an seine Stelle die Welle setzen, welche sich in konzentrischen, mit der Entfernung vom Mittelpunkt immer schwächer werdenden Ringen ausbreitet.'

[9] Les dialectes indo-européens 134 (1908).

[10] F. Kauffmann, Deutsche Altertumskunde (1913); Meillet, Caractères généraux des langues germaniques (1916); Feist, Indogermanen und Germanen (1914); H. Hirt, Etymologie der deutschen Sprache 58 (1909); E. Prokosch, The Hypothesis of a Pre-Germanic Substratum (Germanic Review 1.47 ff.); W. Streitberg, Geschichte der indogermanischen Sprachwissenschaft, 2². 50 ff.; A. Nordling, De Första Germanerna (1929); E. Lewy, Die Heimatfrage, KZ 58. 1–15; J. Pokorny, Substrattheorie und Urheimat der Indogermanen, Mitt. der Anthrop. Ges. in Wien 66. 69–91 (with very full bibliography).

2. Some of the most important general reference works on the Indo-European languages are:

K. Brugmann, Grundriss der vergleichenden Grammatik der indogermanischen Sprachen, ²1897–1916.

H. Hirt, Indogermanische Grammatik, 1921–29.

K. Brugmann, Kurze vergleichende Grammatik der indogermanischen Sprachen, 1904.

A. Meillet, Introduction à l'étude comparative des langues indo-européennes, ⁶1924.

Grundriss der indogermanischen Sprachwissenschaft (K. Brugmann, A. Thumb, et al.), 1916–1931.

J. Schrijnen, Einführung in das Studium der indogermanischen Sprachwissenschaft, 1921.

[1] F. Hrozný, Die Sprache der Hethiter, 1916–17; E. H. Sturtevant, Transactions of the American Philological Association, 50. 25 ff. (1929), and Language, 25 ff. (1926); J. Friedrich, Stand und Aufgaben der Sprachwissenschaft 304 ff. (1924), and Geschichte der idg. Sprachwissenschaft (1931); L. Delaporte, Éléments de la grammaire hittite, 1929; E. H. Sturtevant, A Comparative Grammar of the Hittite Language, 1933.

[2] A. Meillet, Idg. Jahrbuch, 1913; Sieg-Siegling, Tocharische Sprachreste, I (1921); E. Sieg, Gesch. d. idg. Sprwsch. 2⁵; Sieg-Siegling-Schulze, Tocharische Grammatik, 1932.

[3] Against the close connection between Italic and Celtic, C. I. S. Marstrander, De l'unité italo-celtique, Norsk Tidsskrift for Sprogvidenskap, 3. 241 ff. Cf. also G. S. Lane, Germanic-Celtic Vocabulary, Lang. 9. 244 ff.

3. ETHNOGRAPHY: Of the extensive literature on the origin and spread of the Germanic (Teutonic, Gothonic) group, the following works are of special importance.

K. Zeuss, Die Deutschen und die Nachbarstämme, 1837; Manul reproduction, 1925.

O. Bremer, Germanische Ethnographie, in PG².

R. Much, Deutsche Stammeskunde³.

R. Loewe, Die ethnische und sprachliche Gliederung der Germanen, 1899.

O. Montelius, Germanernas hem. Nordisk tidskrift för vetenskap, kunst och industri 1917. 401–16; Kulturgeschichte Schwedens von den ältesten Zeiten bis zum 11. Jahrhundert, 1906.
S. Feist, article 'Germanen' in Ebert's Reallexikon der Vorgeschichte; Germanen und Kelten in antiker Ueberlieferung (1927), and other works.
R. Braungart, Die Südgermanen, 1914.
J. Hoops, Waldbäume und Kulturpflanzen im germanischen Altertum, 1905.
F. Kluge, Die Entstehung des Germanentums. Westermanns Monatshefte 121. 418–21.
A. Nordling, De första Germanerna, 1929.
G. Kossinna, Die Herkunft der Germanen, ²1920.
T. E. Karsten, Die Germanen, PG³, 1928.
H. Arntz, Urgermanisch, Gotisch und Nordisch, in Germanische Philologie (Festschrift für Otto Behaghel) 1934. 29–74.
　GRAMMAR:
J. Grimm, Deutsche Grammatik, 1819–37 and 1870 ff.
A. Noreen, Abriss der urgermanischen Lautlehre, 1894.
W. Streitberg, Urgermanische Grammatik, 1896.
F. Dieter (and others), Laut- und Formenlehre der altgermanischen Dialekte, 1900.
F. Kluge, Urgermanisch, PG³, 1913.
R. O. Boer, Oergermaansch Handboek, ²1924.
R. Loewe, Germanische Sprachwissenschaft, ³1922.
A. Meillet, Caractères généraux des langues germaniques, 1917.
H. Hirt, Handbuch des Urgermanischen, 1931–34.
　'GERMANI': The origin and meaning of the name is unknown. Cf. especially:
G. Kossinna, Der Ursprung des Germanennamens, Btr. 20. 258–301.
F. Kluge, Der Name der Germanen, Germania 3. 1–3.
Fr. Panzer, Der Name Germanen, ZfdU. 33. 189–97.
Th. Birt, Die Germanen, 1917.
R. Much, Der Name Germanen, Akad. d. Wiss. in Wien 1920.
E. Norden, Die germanische Urgeschichte in Tacitus' Germania, 1920.
H. Neckel, Kelten und Germanen, 1929.
H. Neckel, Die Verwandtschaften der germanischen Sprachen untereinander, Btr. 51. 1–17.
　4. General Works on Norse:
A. Noreen, Geschichte der nordischen Sprachen, PG³, 1913.
A. Noreen, Altisländische und altnorwegische Grammatik, ³1913.
A. Noreen, Altschwedische Grammatik, 1894.
A. Noreen, Vårt språk, 1916 ff.
A. Heusler, Altisländisches Elementarbuch, ²1921.
R. C. Boer, Oudnoorsch handboek, 1920.
Falk-Torp, Norwegisch-Dänisches etymologisches Wörterbuch, 1911.
A. Helmquist, Svensk etymologisk ordbok, 1922.
E. Haugen, The Linguistic Development of Ivar Aasen's New Norse, PMLA 48. 558 ff.

5. [1] T. E. Karsten, Die Germanen 73.

[2] Cf. E. Norden, Altgermanien (1934) 191–213.

[3] 'Gutland was discovered by a man by the name of Þieluar. At that time Gutland was bewitched so that it sank by day and rose (above the water) at night. But after it was settled it did not sink any more. This Þieluar had a son by the name of HafÞi, and HafÞi's wife was called Hwitstierna. These two founded the first settlement in Gutland... (Of their sons,) Graipr, the eldest, received the northern third, Guti the middle, and Gunnfiaur, the youngest, the southern third.'

[4] Reallexikon der Vorgeschichte 8 (1927), article 'Niveau', esp. 532 f.

General Works on East Germanic:

W. Braune, Gotische Grammatik, [10]1928.

W. Streitberg, Gotisches Elementarbuch, [5,6]1920.

J. Wright, Grammar of the Gothic Language, 1910 (last reprint 1930).

M. H. Jellinek, Geschichte der gotischen Sprache, PG[3], 1926.

E. Kieckers, Handbuch der vergleichenden gotischen Grammatik, 1928.

C. C. Uhlenbeck, Kurzgefasstes etymologisches Wörterbuch der gotischen Sprache, 1900.

S. Feist, Etymologisches Wörterbuch der gotischen Sprache, [2]1923 (3rd edition appearing).

F. Holthausen, Gotisches Etymologisches Wörterbuch, 1934.

F. Wrede, Die Sprache der Ostgoten in Italien, 1891.

R. Loewe, Die Reste der Germanen am Schwarzen Meer, 1896.

A. Erdmann, Om folknamnen Götar och Goter (Antiqvarisk Tidskrift för Sverige 11. No. 4 (1891).

F. Wrede, Ueber die Sprache der Wandalen, 1886.

R. Kögel, Ueber die Stellung des Burgundischen innerhalb der germanischen Sprachen, ZfdA 37. 223 ff.

6. General Works on West Germanic:

English:

E. Sievers, Angelsächsische Grammatik, [3]1898 (1921).

H. Sweet, A History of English Sounds, 1888.

K. D. Bülbring, Altenglisches Elementarbuch, 1, 1902.

F. Kluge, Geschichte der englischen Sprache, PG[2], 1901.

J. Wright, Old English Grammar, [3]1925.

L. Morsbach, Mittelenglische Grammatik, 1, 1896.

R. Jordan, Handbuch der mitteleng. Gram., 1925.

O. Jespersen, A Modern English Grammar, 1910 ff.

W. Luick, Historische Grammatik der englischen Sprache, 1914–29.

F. Holthausen, Altenglisches etymologisches Wörterbuch, 1934.

Frisian:

Th. Siebs, Geschichte der friesischen Sprache, PG[2], 1901.

W. Heuser, Altfriesisches Lesebuch, 1903.

W. Steller, Abriss der altfriesischen Grammatik, 1928.

Dutch:

Jan Te Winkel, Geschichte der niederländischen Sprache, PG[2], 1901.

J. Franck, Mittelniederländische Grammatik, [2]1910.

J. Franck—N. van Wijk, Etymologisch Woordenboek der Nederlandsche Taal, 1929.

Low German:

F. Holthausen, Altsächsisches Elementarbuch, ²1921.

E. Sehrt, Vollständiges Wörterbuch zum Heliand und zur altsächsischen Genesis, 1925.

A. Lasch, Mittelniederdeutsche Grammatik, 1914.

High German:

W. Braune, Althochdeutsche Grammatik, ⁴1911.

J. Schatz, Althochdeutsche Grammatik, 1927.

G. Baesecke, Einführung in das Althochdeutsche, 1918.

H. Naumann, Althochdeutsche Grammatik, ²1922.

E. G. Graff, Althochdeutscher Sprachschatz, 1834 ff.

H. Paul, Mittelhochdeutsche Grammatik, ⁹1913.

V. Michels, Mittelhochdeutsches Elementarbuch, ²1912.

W. Wilmanns, Deutsche Grammatik, 1896 ff.

O. Behaghel, Geschichte der deutschen Sprache, ⁵1928.

H. Paul, Deutsche Grammatik, 1916 ff.

E. Prokosch, Sounds and History of the German Language, 1916.

E. Prokosch, Outline of German Historical Grammar, 1933.

H. Hirt, Geschichte der deutschen Sprache, ²1925.

G. O. Curme, A Grammar of the German Language, ²1922.

O. Behaghel, Deutsche Syntax, 1923 ff.

J. Grimm (and others), Deutsches Wörterbuch (still unfinished; 1st volume published in 1854).

K. Weigand, Deutsches Wörterbuch, ⁵1909 ff. (by K. v. Bader, H. Hirt, K. Kant).

Trübner's Deutsches Wörterbuch, ed. by A. Götze, 1936–.

F. Kluge, Deutsches etymologisches Wörterbuch, ¹¹1934.

H. Hirt, Handbuch der deutschen Etymologie, ²1921.

H. Arntz, Deutsche Grammatik (in Germ. Phil., Festschrift für O. Behaghel, 1934, 75-109).

W. Bruckner, Die Sprache der Langobarden, 1895.

10. [1] Walde, KZ 34. 461 ff.; E. Hermann, KZ 41. 27 ff.; H. Hirt, Idg. Gr. 219 and HU 80 ('Auch mir ist es durchaus wahrscheinlich, dass der Ansatz von Mediä Aspiratä nicht richtig ist. Aber was wir als ursprachlich anzunehmen haben, weiss ich nicht, und daher behalte ich das Alte bei.')

[2] Prokosch, Mod. Phil. 16. 105 f.

[3] E. H. Tuttle, Mod. Phil. 18. 52: 'Dravidian possessed voiceless and voiced aspirates some two or three thousand years ago.'

[4] Tuttle, l. c.: 'Admitting that the reverted linguals came from Dravidian, we can safely say that the voiced aspirates have the same origin.'

[5] Sommer, Krit. Erl. 65; Prokosch, Mod. Phil. 16. 550 ff.; H. Hirt, Idg. Gr. 1. 246: 'Auch Prokosch, Modern Phil. 16, 159 hält die Tenuesaspiratä für jung und aus den Tenues durch Nachdruckverstärkung der Konsonanten entstanden, so dass in ihnen eine Art Lautverschiebung vorläge. An und für sich ist der Gedanke glücklich, und vielleicht gelingt es noch, ihn lautgesetzlich zu begründen. Es läge dann so, dass diese Laute erst später entstanden wären und nicht zu dem ursprünglichen Lautstand des Idg. gehört hätten.'

[6] Prokosch, Mod. Phil. 16. 551.

[7] H. Collitz, Language 2. 179: 'Prokosch . . . is too much inclined to make con-

cessions to current views in Greek and Sanskrit grammar that run contrary to his theory. I can see no necessity, e.g., for conceding that the so-called Greek aspirates were actually at the earliest Greek period voiceless aspirates . . . Ascoli's theory, ascribing to the Graeco-Italic period the existence of surd spirants, instead of the so-called Greek and Latin aspirates, is no doubt preferable to the doctrine obtaining at present in most Greek grammars.'

[8] Collitz, l. c., 178: 'I share the view set forth by Prof. Prokosch in a series of articles in the XV and XVI volumes of Modern Philology that instead of the alleged voiced aspirates primitive IE actually possessed surd spirants. I was able to extend to this view a word of welcome and approval (AJPh 39, 415, note 4) before the last of Prof. Prokosch's articles had appeared, and I now wish to state that I regard Professor Prokosch's theory as one of the most helpful and important among recent contributions toward solving the problems connected with "Grimm's Law".'

H. Hirt, Idg. Gr. 1. 219 (referring to Prokosch, l. c.): 'Was er gegen die Ansetzung von Mediä Aspiratä anführt, ist durchaus beachtenswert und dürfte ihnen endgültig den Garaus machen. Ob wir mit idg. stimmlosen Spiranten auskommen, lässt sich vorläufig noch nicht sagen. Jedenfalls wird man sich sagen müssen, es waren Laute, die den meisten Sprachen fremd waren, und bei denen man mit Lautsubstitution rechnen muss.' Similarly HU 1. 80.

Also H. v. Velten, Germanic Review 7. 77 (1932) accepts my theory.

15. H. Paul, Zur Lautverschiebung, Btr. 1. 147–68; J. M. N. Kapteyn, De germaansche en de hoogduitsche klankverschuiving, 1924; H. Güntert, Ueber die Ursache der germanischen Lautverschiebung, Wörter und Sachen 10. 1–22 (1927); J. Pokorny, Keltische Lehnwörter und die germanische Lautverschiebung, W. S. 12. 303–15 (1929); W. S. Russer, De germaansche klankverschuiving, 1931; A. Nordmeyer, Lautverschiebungserklärungen, JEGPh 35. 482–95 (1936). High German only: W. Braune, Zur Kenntnis des Fränkischen und zur hochdeutschen Lautverschiebung, Btr. 1. 1–56; N. O. Heinertz, Eine Lautverschiebungstheorie, 1925.

In an abstract of a paper which he probably intended to read before the Linguistic Society of America (put at my disposal by his widow), Collitz restates his view in the following words:

Rasmus Rask's Share in "Grimm's Law"

The term "Grimm's Law" has become the current designation in English of the rules governing the Germanic consonant shifting, so much so that we are in danger of overlooking or at least of underrating Grimm's obligations in this connection to the great Danish scholar Rasmus Rask. Not only was the latter Grimm's chief predecessor, but he left comparatively little of importance for Grimm to add concerning the rules of the first or general Germanic shifting. Nevertheless Grimm's Law in its entirety remains something rather different from Rask's rules. In considering the mutual claims reference will be made to Prof. Holger Pedersen's Introduction to the new edition of Rask's Udvalgte Afhandlinger published on the occasion of the one hundredth anniversary of Rask's death by Det danske Sprog- og Litteraturselskab in two volumes. Copenhagen, 1932–33.

The arguments that Pedersen brings forth against Collitz are, to the author, far from convincing. His tone probably amazed those who know Collitz's personality and scholarship. Some specimens are these: 'Die [Collitz's] Äusserung in ihrer ganzen Bösartigkeit . . . dass Collitz niemals Rasks Buch in der Hand gehabt hat . . . einfach haarsträubend . . . Durch Vorführung derartiger törichten Sachen versündigt er sich auch an Grimm . . . hat von Grimms Grösse absolut nichts begriffen.' (Pages 53, 54 of the Introduction).—Death prevented Collitz from reading his paper.

Streitberg, Geschichte der indogermanischen Sprachwissenschaft, 2. 2. 260 ff. [1936], offers a comprehensive, thoroughly objective survey of the controversy.

20. [1] Hirt (Idg. Gr. 5. 96 and HU 1. 90) and de Saussure (Cours de linguistique 201) formulate V. L. differently: Gmc. *f þ ħ s* normally become voiced; exceptions: (1) in initial position, (2) before voiceless sounds, (3) medially between voiced sounds when the IE accent was on the preceding syllable.

22. H. Osthoff, Btr. 8. 297 ff.; H. Kluge, Btr. 9. 149 ff.; the law is not accepted by M. Trautmann, Germ. Lautgesetze 62, nor by A. Meillet (in his review of Hirt's HU 1), Bulletin de la société linguistique 33. 3. 107–9.

24. W. Braune, Zur Kenntnis des Fränkischen und zur hochdeutschen Lautverschiebung, Btr. 1. 1–56.

25. E. Prokosch, Die deutsche Lautverschiebung und die Völkerwanderung, JEGPh 16. 1–11.

34. [1] BB 2. 291–305 (1878), and BB 3. 177–234 (1879).

[2] Cf. especially H. Hirt, Idg. Gr. 2. 76–100, and H. Güntert, Idg. Ablautsprobleme, 1916.

35. [1] It used to be assumed that *oi* could also become $\bar{\imath}$ in Latin ($\varphi o\bar{\imath}\delta a = v\bar{\imath}d\bar{\imath}$). Sturtevant, Lang. 10. 6–16, has refuted this.

36. [1] Prokosch, Studies in Honor of Hermann Collitz 70–82 (1933).

An excellent survey of the main problems of Gmc. vocalism is offered by L. E. van Wijk, De Klinkers der oergermaanse stamsyllaben in hun onderling verband, Utrecht 1936.

41. [1] M. Diez, Analogical Tendencies in the German Noun Declension (1919).

[2] Berga (Sweden), 6th cent.: *SaligastiR*; Bratsberg (Norway), 6th cent.: þaliR; Tomstad (Norway), 6th cent.: *warur*, etc.

42. [1] Hirt, HU 1. 48–50.

46. [1] Hirt, Idg. Gr. 2. 95, where bibliography is given.

[2] IF 3. 305 ff. and Hirt, Idg. Gr. 2. 37 ff.

49. [1] Hirt, IF 1. 216 ff.; van Helten, Btr. 15. 455 ff.

[2] Prokosch, PMLA 42. 331 ff.

51. [1] Hirt, Idg. Gr. 3. 82: 'Wir unterscheiden also zwischen Suffixen mit und ohne Bedeutung, oder Suffixen und Determinativen.' The standard work on determinants is P. Persson, Beiträge zur indogermanischen Wortforschung, 1912; p. 589: 'Die Determinative sind im allgemeinen als Formantien zu betrachten, deren Bedeutung verblasst ist, und die demgemäss mit der Wurzel mehr oder weniger fest verwachsen sind.'

53. [1] Cf. especially A. Thumb, Handbuch des Sanskrit 305 ff.

54. [1] H. Osthoff, Btr. 8. 287 ff.

[2] W. Streitberg, UG 292.

[3] K. Brugmann, IF 6. 89 ff.; F. A. Wood, Germanic Studies of the University of Chicago; both 1895.

[4] Hirt, HU 2. 173, under 'Herkunft'.

[5] Ibid., 166: 'Der Ton lag auf der Wurzelsilbe, obgleich diese meist Schwundstufe ist' (?).

[6] Cf. especially T. E. Karsten, Beiträge zur Geschichte der $\bar{e}$-Verba im Altgermanischen, 1897; W. Wilmanns, Deutsche Grammatik 2. 87 ff.

[7] Esp. Streitberg, UG 307; Hirt, HU 171.

67. [1] Cf. Paul, Btr. 7. 143: 'Das angelsächsische repräsentiert für uns im grossen und ganzen noch die eigentümlichste stufe, und zwar liegt das offenbar daran, dass hier im gegensatz zum althochdeutschen und altsächsischen der umlaut der synkopierung vorausgegangen ist.' Prokosch, The Old English Preterit Without Medial Vowel, PMLA 42. 331 ff.

[2] L. c., 110: 'Indog. Wurzeln mit anlautender und auslautender Aspirata (also die sog. Grassmann'schen Wurzeln) geben im Germanischen beim Antreten eines t-Suffixes die Aspiration im Auslaute ganz auf, während sonst (also bei Wurzeln, die nicht mit Aspirata anlauten) die Aspiration von der auslautenden Aspirata auf das t des antretenden Suffixes übergeht.'

75. [1] Feist, GEW 216: 'Ae. $\bar{e}ode$ "ich ging" ist fernzuhalten.' Holthausen, IF 14. 342 explains $\bar{e}ode$ as an augment aorist of $*w\bar{a}dh$- : $*e$-udh- (but Ae. Etym. Wb. 91, 'unbek. Herk.'); this is justly rejected by Collitz, l. c.

77 Royen, De jongere Veranderingen van het indogermaanse nominale Drieklassensystemen, 1926.

79. [1] Streitberg, UG 227: 'Auffällig ist das e der nichthaupttonigen Silbe im As., Ahd.' Bethge in Dieter, Laut- und Formenlehre 140, assumes '$es < eso$ mit Ablaut des Themavokals,' but does not comment on it. Naumann, Ahd. Gramm. 28, believes that 'Idg. $\breve{e}$ in Nebensilben wird natürlich durchaus zu $\breve{\imath}$' and considers WGmc. $dages$ 'eine Kompromissform aus germ. $dagas < $ idg. $*dhoghoso$ und germ. $dagis < $ idg. $*dhogheso$.' Similarly, Loewe, GS 2. 7.

[2] Holthausen, As. Elb. 45, 'wegen seiner breiten Aussprache in a übergegangen.'

[3] Cf. H. Gürtler, Zur Geschichte der deutschen $-er$-Plurale, besonders im Frühneuhochdeutschen, Btr. 37. 492; H. Paul, Deutsche Gramm. 2. 22–33; M. Diez, Analogical Tendencies in the German Noun Declension (1919).

[4] Brugmann, IF 33. 272 ff., considers Go. $-\bar{e}$ a form of an adjective in $-\bar{e}jo$-; Sehrt, Studies in Honor of Hermann Collitz 95 ff., explains it as an instr. sg. (Eduard Hermann, reviewing it, Göttinger Gelehrte Anzeigen 1932. 40, remarks: 'Dabei übersieht er, dass der Instrumentalis sein $-\bar{e}$ nur in den einsilbigen bewahrt, sonst aber in $-a$ verwandelt hat.' This does not necessarily refute Sehrt's view.)

80. [1] E.g. Streitberg, UG 234; Boer, Oerg. Hb. 178 f.; Hirt, HU 2. 40.

84. [1] Van Helten, Btr. 15. 40 ff.: 'Leveling of $-an$- through the former $-u$ of the acc. sg. ($anu < -on$-m)'. Loewe, GS 29: 'Mischung von a und i im Gen.-Dat. Sg. [muss] das mittlere e, von a und u im Akk. Sg. und Nom. Pl. das mittlere o erzeugt haben.' Similarly Naumann, Ahd. Gramm. 74: 'Akk. 1. $hanan$ . . . 2. $hanun$, $hanon$ aus derselben Form, mit dunkler Form des Suffixvokals unter dem Einfluss des nachfolgenden u . . . $hanon$ ist möglicherweise eine Ausgleich- (Kompromiss-) form aus 1 und $hanun$.'

[2] Cf. Baesecke, Einführung in das Althochdeutsche 153: '$\bar{u}$, das sich vor dem schliessenden n aus dem durchstehenden $\bar{o}$ des Suffixes entwickelt hat. . . . Nur im Gen. und Dat. Pl., wo es nicht vor schliessendem n steht, hat sich $\bar{o}$ erhalten.' —Streitberg, UG 258, assumes for $-\bar{u}n$ 'dass . . . eine Beziehung zu den slav. Femininis auf $-ynji$ wie $bogynji$ 'Göttin' bestehe.'

89. [1] Hirt, HU 2. 98 f., considers this n 'das postponierte Pronomen en (slaw.

onū), das im Sinne des Artikels steht, genau wie im Lit. Slaw. *-is, -jo* postponiert ist, lit. *geràs-is,* abg. *dobrŭjĭ.*' Considering the fact that Norse did form its definite, postpositive article from this pronominal stem, almost certainly at first between article and noun (*Eiríkr enn rauþe* 'Eric the Red', cf. **93**), this seems quite plausible, but it is hardly possible to prove it.

91. [1] Hirt, HU 2. 90, assumes a suffix *-stho,* which is related to *sthā* 'stand', since '*-tho* als Suffix ist kaum vorhanden.' But Sanskrit has so frequently *th* after *s* where the other IE languages have *t* that a phonetic law *st > sth* seems probable, although the exact conditions under which it operated are not known. Cf. Prokosch, Mod. Phil. 16. 551.

96. [1] Wiedemann, Lit. H. 76, differs with this: '*ja-* 'er'; *es* ist der stamm idg. *i-* (lat. *is*); mit dem relativstamm idg. *jo-* fällt *ja-,* ausser im nom. sg. masc. und fem., zusammen, hat aber mit ihm nichts zu schaffen.'

[2] A different view is held by Streitberg, GE 228 f.

[3] For the coordination theory: Erdmann, Syntax Otfrid, V ff.; Paul, Prinzipien der Sprachgeschichte[5] 277 ff.; Tomanetz, Die Relativsätze bei den hochdeutschen Uebersetzern des 8. und 9. Jahrhundert, Wien (1879); Tobler, Ueber Auslassung und Vertretung des Relativpronomen, Germ. 17 (N. F. 5). 257 ff.; Neckel, Ueber den germanischen Relativsatz, Palaestra 5 (1900); Wundt, Völkerpsychologie 2. 29;—against it: Delbrück, Vgl. Synt. 3. 347 ff.; Prokosch, Germ. Dem.-Pr. 7 f. (1905).

98. [1] Hermann, Die Silbenbildung im Griechischen und in den anderen idg. Sprachen 33.

[2] Brugmann, Grdr. 2. 818: (Einwirkung des **nes, *ẏes* des Plurals) 'die aussergermanisch durch ai. *nas, vas,* av. *nō, vō* . . . vertreten waren, und von denen das letztere im Germanischen selbst in got. *izwis,* ahd. *iu,* ags. *ēow* steckt. Vielleicht entstand zunächst *sis* (plur. und sg.), dem dann *mis, *þis* folgten.'

[3] Lang. 8. 1–10; cf. also Hitt. Gramm. 173.

[4] Kieckers, Vgl. G. G. 135: 'Urgerm. wurde eine Verbindung wie **ẏurðō *mīnō* 'verba mea, meine Worte' dann umgedeutet in 'verba mei, Worte von mir'.

[5] Slightly different Kieckers, Vgl. G. G. 137 and Heusler, Aisl. Elb. §248.

99. [1] Heusler, Aisl. Elb. §90; Anm.: 'Ein angrenzender Fall ist *siau* '7': got. *sibun*'; Noreen, Aisl. Gramm. §208 Anm.: 'Etwas unklar ist die Entwicklung des alleinstehenden Triphthongs *iau* in *siau.*'

[2] Streitberg, UG §167: 'Der Wurzelvokal von *tigjus* usw. verhält sich zu dem von *-togo, -zug* wie idg. *e : ə.*' (But for *-togo,* see above).—56: 'Idg. *ə* wird in nicht-haupttonigen Silben zu germ. *u.*' Cf. **38 d.**

[3] Joh. Schmidt, Die Urheimat der Indogermanen und das europäische Zahlensystem, 1890; Kluge, Urg. 255 f. Cf. Fr. *soixante,* but *soixante-dix* (Walloon *septante*).

[4] For detailed analysis and bibliography, cf. Jellinek, Geschichte der gotischen Sprache 139 f.

[5] Kieckers, Vgl. G. G. 178, presents Schmidt's explanation, remarking about Brugmann's view: 'Das Missliche an dieser Deutung ist, dass got. *-hund* die Bedeutung 'Dekade' haben soll, während doch schon idg. **k̂mtom* die . . . Bedeutung '100' besass, die ihm auch einzelsprachlich allein nachzuweisen ist.' But the interpretation given in the text does not impute the meaning 'decade' to *hund*; it merely assumes that its meaning was elastic. That it meant '100' as well as '120' cannot be denied. A spread of its meaning over 70, 80, 90, 110 is probable enough. For another theory cf. Hirt, Idg. Gr. 3. 312; HU 2. 113 f.

INDEX OF WORDS

GERMANIC LANGUAGES

GOTHIC

-wardjan 45
wasjan 14
watō 84 f
waurd 49 c, j, 84 e, 86, 99 a
waurk 51 c
waurkjan 67 a
waurms 51 c
waurstw 49 d
weihan 20 d, 54 c, i, j, 58 a, 59 b
weihnan 54 i
weihs 33 a, 47 b
-weis 65 b
-weitan 65 a
weitwōþs 65 b, 87 a, d
-widan 58 b
widuwō 33 a
-wigan 18
wiljau 70 b, 75 d
wilþeis 90 a
windan 53 b, 54 j, 58 a, c
winds 39 b, 46 c
wisan 20 d, 59 b, 75 a
-wiss 65 b, 69 b
wit 78 b, 98 a, d
witan 65 a
wrikan 33 a
wulfs 13 c, 19, 23 c, 47 b, 77 b, 79 b, 80 a

CRIMEAN GOTHIC

ada 33 c
broe(t) 40 a
bruder 31 a, 37
geen 40 a, 75 c
oeghene 40 a
plut 31 a
tag 31 a

VANDALIC

armes 40 a
froja 40 a

OLD NORSE
(Old Icelandic)

ā 20 d, 27 d, 42 j, 65 b
aka 45
akr 30, 38 c, 80 a
aldenn 20 c, d

andlit 33 a
ann 65 d
annarr 29 c, 31 b, 100
ār 33 a
ār 42 j, 100
armr 80 a
at 38 c
ātta 38 c, 72 c, 99 a
ātte 100
āttiān 99 a
auga 40 a, 84
auka 21, 62 g
ausa 63
ax 86
barn 49 j, 80 a
bāþer, beiþer 99 a
-bærr 47 b
beiþa 54 f
bekkr 30
belgr 47 b
bera 18, 24 b, 38 c, 59 a, 68
biarga 41 e
bifa 53 b
binda 24 b, 39 a, 42 a, 47 b, 58 c
biōþa 39 a, 42 j, 47 b, 58 b
bīta 58 a
bitr 30
bīþa 58 a
biþia 30, 38 d, 54 c, e, 59 b
blāsa 62 g, 63
blindr 90 a
blōme 37
blōta 62 g
borg 47 b
boþe 47 b
bregþa 58 c
bresta 58 c
brōþer 18, 19, 20 a, 27 b, 37, 85
brȳtr 18, 24 b
būa 62 g
būande 88
byggia 58 b, 65 c, 67 a
dagr 18, 49 o
dapr 30
dāþ 18, 68
dauþr 20 d, 47 b, 49 c
deyia 54 e
deypa 47 b

hatr 49 c
hauk- 99 a
hefia 20 d, 47 b, 54 c, f, 60
heita 47 b, 54 c, 62 g
heiþr 81 b
hel 81 b
hēr 39 b, 93 c
here 20 d
heyra 28, 49 g, 67 b, 72 a
hialmr 47 b
hialpa 47 b, 58 c
hiarta 41 e, 49 n
himinn 27 d
hineg, hinnveg 93 c
hinn, hin, hitt 93 d
hiǫrr 41 e
hirþer 42 d, 80 b, 90 a
hiǫrþ 47 b
hlaupa 47 b, 54 c, 62 g
hlǣia 27 d, 54 c, e
hlø̄gia 54 f
hnīga 23 c, 27 d
holmr 5 b
hǫndugr 49 e
hoppa 22, 54 i
hōr 19
hreinn 27 d
huārr 97 b
huat 19, 27 d, 97 a
huel 23 c
huerr 97 b
hund(raþ) 19, 20 c, 99 a
hyggia 30
hǫfoþ 20 c
hǫggua 33 c
hǫnd 83
ı̃ 47 b
illa 90 c
īss 80 a
it 78 b, 98 a
iǫr 23 c, 41 e
iǫrþ 41 e
Iǫtar 5 b
kalla 54 k, 68, 72 b
kalþr 21
kann 65 d
ker 28
kiōsa 20 d, 21, 28, 58 b, 63

klīfa 51 d
kliūfa 42 j
knē 21, 49 d
knosa 29 b
knylla 29 b
koma 21, 23 c, 47 b, 54 c, 59 a
kona 21, 23 c, 84 d
kuæn 23 c, 47 b
kueþa 20 d, 23 c, 59 b
kuikna 54 i
kuikr 21, 54 i
kūþr 29 c, 65 d
kyn 21, 49 d, 80 b
kȳr 42 d, 87 a
lamb 24 b
langr 24 b
lāta 41 d, 46 d, 47 b, 62 g
latr 38 c, 46 d, 47 b
laþa 54 k
lǣgr 90 a
leggia 31 b, 54 f, 67 b, 72 a
leika 62 g
leiþa 30
lesa 58 a, 59 b
lætr 23 c, 42 d
liā 19
liggia 30, 54 e
lītell 30
līþa 20 d, 58 a
liūga 58 b
lokka 22
lokkr 22
lūka 54 c, 58 b
lūta 58 b
lykna 22
mā 65 g
māl 29 b
mala 60
man 65 e, 70 b
māne 84 d
maþr 87 b
maþrenn 93 d
mǣr 23 c, 81 b
meire 20 c, 28
merkr 79 i, 87 a
meta 54 k
minn 98 e
miþr 18, 90 a

sund 29 c
sunr 49 c, 79 b, k, 83
sūpa 22, 54 c, 58 b
sūrr 37
symia 29 c
sȳn 23 c
syngua 23 c
sȳr 87 a
søg 49 j
søkia 67 a
søkkua 42 a, 58 c
taka 46 d, e, 54 b, c, 60, 61, 65 g
telia 49 g, 68, 72 a, 75 d
tiā 19, 27 d, 58 a
tiger 20 c, 99 a, b
timbra 21
tiō 19, 21, 38 c, 99 a
tiōa 20 d, 58 b
tīonde 100
titra 53 b
tōft 29 c
tolf 99 a
tolfte 100
tottogo 99 a
tottogonde 100
trē 47 b, 80 c
troþa 54 c
tryggr 14, 33 c, 41 d
tueggia 14, 32, 33 c
tueir, tuǣr, tuau 21, 39 b, 99 a
tunga 49 n, 84
Tȳr 33 a, 39 b, 41 d
tǫ 42 j
þann 93 a
þarf 20 d, 65 d
þarfa 65 d
þat 19
þeir 47 b
þekkia 67 a
þēr 80 c
þiggia 54 e
þing 27 b
þiūfr 40 a
þiwi 81 b
þola 38 d, 67 g
þorp 21
þōrr 42 a
þrettān 99 a

þrēttande 100
þrīr, þriār, þriū 19, 99a
þrītogonde 100
þriþe 100
þryngua 20 d, 58 c
þū 19, 75 a, 93, 98 a
þunnr 29 b
þurfa 20 c, d, 42 d
þūsund 99 a, b
þykkia 31 b, 41 d, 67 a
ulfr 23 c, 47 b, 79 b, 80 a
ūr 49 m
vā 54 c
vaka 30, 54 i
vakna 22, 54 i, 68
valda 54 c
vārr 98 c
vatn, vatr 84 f
vaþa 46 d, 54 b, c, 60
vē 47 b
vega 18, 20 d, 54 c, 58 a, 59 b
veit 40 a, 56 b, 65 b
vekia 30
vēr 42 d, 98 a, c
verþa 20 a, d, 39 a, 47 b, 58 c
vesa (vera) 20 d, 59 b, 63, 75 a
vil 70 b, 75 d
vinda 58 a
vīss 29 a, 65 b, 69 b
vissa 29 a
vit 78 b, 98 a
vīþa 90 c
viþr 83
vǫndr 83
ylgr 23 c, 81 b
ȳmiss 29 a
yrkia 67 a
ø̄skia 29 c

RUNIC

Aflims 79 m
aӡar 18
arbijanō 84 d
barutr 18, 24 b
borumʀ 79 m
dohtrir 24 b, 41 d
faihiðo 67 b
faþiʀ 85

OLD FRISIAN

BAVARIAN

NON-GERMANIC LANGUAGES

SANSKRIT

(including Vedic)

GREEK

vadum 46 d
vehō 10 e, 45
Venedi 38 e
veniō 10 c, 11 c, d, 21, 23 a, c, 45, 46 b,
    54 c, 57 a, b
ventus 39 b, 46 c
verbum 11 b, 78 a
vergō 51 c
vermis 51 c
vertō 39 a, 51 c
vesper 5 c
Vesta 75 a
vestīgium 10 e, 11 d, 35
vestis 14
vetō 23 c
via 49 j
vīcus 33 a
videō 33 a, 54 d, 65 a
vidua 33 a
vincō 20 d, 54 c
vir 13 b, 51 b
vītis 58 a, c
vīvus 21, 23 a
volō 46 f, 70 c, 75 d
vorsus 13 b
vōs 98 c
vōx 45

OSCAN

aa-manaffed 66 c
feihúss 79 i
fusíd 70 c
mais 20 e
mefiaí 10 e, 20 a
víass 79 i

UMBRIAN

rufru 10 e, 20 a
se-so 98 b
tefe 20 a

FRENCH

cas 16 c
cent 11 d
devoir 17 c, 24 a
gonfalon 23 c
garder 32
guerre 32

isle 23 c
pas 16 c
percevoir 54 d
recevoir 54 d
tasse 16 c

SPANISH

deber 16 c, 17 c, 24 a

CELTIC

(Old Irish, unless otherwise indicated)

chwi (Cymric) 98 c
brāthir 34 c
dā 34 c
gort 34 c
-leldar 56 b
macc 23 c
map (OCymr.) 23 c
māthir 34 c
-rīx (Gallic) 34 b, 36 a
sīl 34 b
Vercingetorīx (Gallic) 36 a

SLAVIC

('Old Slavic'—Old Church Slavonic,
    unless otherwise indicated)

-achъ 66 c
bǫdǫ, byti 54 j
berǫ 34 c
bimь 75 a
bljudǫ 35
bolšiy (Russ.) 10 c
bratъ 34 b
česo, čego 79 d
čtvrtku (Czech) 13 a
dal(ъ) (Russ.) 52 a
danъ 8, 41 a
darъ 34 b, 41 a
dat' (Russ.) 52 a
davat' (Russ.) 52 a
delēachъ 66 c
desętь 34 c
dēti 34 b, 75 b
dobrъ 30
drъžati 61
dъva 34 b

BALTIC

(Lithuanian unless otherwise indicated)

TOCHARIAN

HITTITE

FINNISH

ansas 38 e
haka 49 j
hän 78 a
huva 41 a
kala 79 a
kinnas 86
kuningas 28, 49 b, **77 b**
lammas 86
lannas 86
mort- 44
pähä 41 a
pala- 44
panku 49 j
poltta- 44
ringas 28, 49 b

ARABIC

'aqtala 44, 52 a
hasuna 44
qatala 44, 52 a, 78 a
sakira 44
yabisa 44

IE RECONSTRUCTIONS

ad 38 c
aĝō 34 c
agros 38 c
akjá 81 b
akmen- 11 c
ákwā 23 c
akwjá 23 c
altós 20 d
arō 34 c
ausro/usro 29 a
aweg-/aug- 21, 46 f, 51 f
bel-/bol- 10 c
bheidh- 34 c, 35, 38 d
bhér- 8, 10 e, h, 18, 34 c, 38 c, 58 c
bheudh- 35, 38 d, 39 a, 67 g
bhéug- 20 d
bhéuk- 20 d
bhewe- 51 b, 62 g, 66 c, 72 a, 75 a
bhlā- 62 g
bhleu- 33 c, 58 b
bhendh- 39 a, 42 a
bhō 99 a
bhrátēr 10 e, h, 18, 34 b, 37

bhəgnó 22
deik- 19, 35, 52 b
dek̂m̥(t) 10 c, 17 d, 19, 21, 34 c, 38 c, 99 a
dhē-/dhō- 10 e, h, 18, 34 b, 37, 46 e, 51 b, 66 c, 67 g, 75 b
dheigh- 54 c
dheub-/dheup- 21
dhōm- 37
dhregh- 58 c
djēws 33 a, 35
dō 34 b
dom- 10 c, 21
dont-/dn̥t- 76
dou- 66 c
dreu- 58 b
drewā 33 c
dwo, dwō (i, -u) 10 c, 17 d, 21, 32, 34 b, 99a
də- 34 c
ĕd- 34 c, 37, 38 c, 76
eĝō(m), eĝhom, eĝ 98 b
ei- 75 c
ek̂wā 78 a
ek̂wo- 11 c, 23 c, 78 a
enos 93 d
er-/or- 75 a
es- 29 b, 34 c, 54 h, 72 a, 75 a
ĝel- 21
ĝen-/ĝnō-/ĝen(ē) 11 d, 21, 34 b, 65 a
ĝene-u/ĝen-u 46 f, 65 d
ĝenos- 10 c, 11 c, 19
ĝeus- 21, 35
ghē- 54 h
ghebh- 11 a
ĝheim 10 e, h, 11 c, d
ĝhengh- 10 e, h, 18
gheu-/gheud-/gheus 10 e, h, 18, 51 b, 54 b
ĝhi-ĝhē-mi 75 c
ghləwo- 33 c
ĝhonghti 19
ghorto- 10 e, h, 19, 34 c, 38 c
ghosti 10 c, h, 11 c, 19, 34 c, 38 c, 49 c
ghwen-/ghwn̥- 10 e, h, 23 c
ghwermos/ghwormos 10 e, h, 23 c
ghwn̥tyá 18
ghwren- 23 c
ĝhəghōnā 75 c

CPSIA information can be obtained at www.ICGtesting.com
Printed in the USA
LVOW010536301111

257107LV00002B/18/P